CORPORATE RESILIENCE

DEVELOPMENTS IN CORPORATE GOVERNANCE AND RESPONSIBILITY

Series Editor: David Crowther

Recent Volumes:

DEVELOPMENTS IN CORPORATE GOVERNANCE AND
RESPONSIBILITY   VOLUME 21

CORPORATE RESILIENCE: RISK, SUSTAINABILITY AND FUTURE CRISES

EDITED BY

SHAHLA SEIFI

Social Responsibility Research Network, UK

And

DAVID CROWTHER

Social Responsibility Research Network, UK

United Kingdom – North America – Japan
India – Malaysia – China

Emerald Publishing Limited
Howard House, Wagon Lane, Bingley BD16 1WA, UK

First edition 2023

Reprints and permissions service
Contact: permissions@emeraldinsight.com

British Library Cataloguing in Publication Data
A catalogue record for this book is available from the British Library

ISBN: 978-1-83753-783-9 (Print)
ISBN: 978-1-83753-782-2 (Online)
ISBN: 978-1-83753-784-6 (Epub)

ISSN: 2043-0523 (Series)

Printed and bound by CPI Group (UK) Ltd, Croydon, CR0 4YY

INVESTOR IN PEOPLE

CONTENTS

LIST OF CONTRIBUTORS

Ajmal Bakerally	University of Mauritius, Mauritius
Ambareen Beebeejaun	University of Mauritius, Mauritius
Dianne Bolton	Western Sydney University, Australia
Elaine Conway	Loughborough University, UK
David Crowther	Social Responsibility Research Network, UK
Shailja Dixit	Amity University, India
Elda du Toit	University of Pretoria, South Africa
Victor Ediagbonya	University of Brighton, UK
Leana Esterhuyse	University of South Africa, South Africa
Ana Maria Davila Gomez	University of Quebec, Canada
Rajendra Parsad Gunputh	University of Mauritius, Mauritius
Mohshin Habib	Laurentian University, Canada
Parminder Johal	University of Derby, UK
Md. Humayun Kabir	Sol Plaatje University, South Africa
Terry Landells	Bolton Landells Consulting, Australia
Fatima Mayowa Lukman	Universiti Brunei Darussalam, Brunei
Oren Mooneeapen	University of Mauritius, Mauritius
Carlos Noronha	University of Macau, China
Lukman Raimi	Universiti Brunei Darussalam, Brunei
Dineshwar Ramdhony	University of Mauritius, Mauritius
Sabelo G. Sifundza	Ministry of Public Service, Eswatini
AkanshaAbhi Srivastava	Institute of Hotel Management, India
Amit Kumar Srivastava	Invertis University, India
Comfort Tioluwani	University of Essex, UK
Ruopiao Zhang	Macau University of Science and Technology, China

PART 1
BUILDING GLOBAL RESILIENCE

RESILIENCE, DYNAMISM AND SUSTAINABLE DEVELOPMENT: ADAPTIVE ORGANISATIONAL CAPABILITY THROUGH LEARNING IN RECURRENT CRISES

Dianne Bolton, Mohshin Habib and Terry Landells

ABSTRACT

Being resilient is often equated with the capability to return to a state of normalcy after individuals and organisations face unprecedented challenges. This chapter questions the notion of 'normalcy' in complex and ongoing turbulence as experienced variously in diverse cultural and sectoral contexts. In theorising organisational resilience and associated transformation, it draws on insights provided by a microfinance institution (MFI) operating in the Philippines. The chapter details its efforts to transform business in light of experience gained in frequent and overlapping emergency conditions (including COVID-19) to create a new level of resilience in its clients and itself. For clients, the goal is often to self-manage loss associated with socio-economic development and for the organisation, to stabilise and cordon the investment needed to support clients survive and move on from the relatively constant adverse impacts of disasters. Published accounts of such experience and insights provided by board members and the President illustrate the nature of transformational resiliency strategies planned, including changes to the business model around provision of micro-insurance services and strategic adaptation of digital services aligned with the organisation's mission. A model of 'practical resiliency in emergency conditions' details the culture of resiliency adopted, demonstrating how stakeholders gain confidence and opportunity to practice resilient behaviours in emergency contexts. It highlights the significance of cultural consistency across purpose, values and

Corporate Resilience
Developments in Corporate Governance and Responsibility, Volume 21, 3–32
ISSN: 2043-0523/doi:10.1108/S2043-052320230000021001

capability to create an adequate level of trust and certainty across stake-holders to support transformational resiliency behaviours in shifting and dynamic ecosystems.

Keywords: Transformational resilience; emergency management; Philippine microfinance; business model adaptation; micro-insurance; stakeholder culture

1. REFLECTIONS OF RESILIENCE AND DEVELOPMENT IN TURBULENCE

Traditionally the notion of resilience reflected its Latin root, i.e. 'resilire' suggesting the capacity to spring back as in a coil. Essentially this definition suggests a return to a state of normalcy. In relation to development trends and goals, the notion of 'normalcy' might be questioned in the context of the complex turbulence that is radically challenging any formulaic representation of economic growth patterns. This is particularly the case concerning 'normalcy' underpinning the development trajectory of the Global North, described by Ziai (2017) as ' ... a failed project of universalising the way of life of the "developed" countries on a global scale which has for the overwhelming majority of affected people led to the progressive modernisation of poverty'.

The conceptualisation of resilience in the face of change dynamics has been increasingly critiqued in environments characterised by turbulence and unpredictability and has been perceived and experienced variously in different stages of organisational growth and in diverse cultural and sectoral contexts by individuals and organisations. This chapter theorises organisational resilience and associated transformation in contemporary complex environments experienced in a developing nation and exemplified by a microfinance institution (MFI) operating in the Philippines. It emphasises the impact of dynamic change on the culture, structure and behaviour of an organisation for which 'normalcy' constitutes the delivery of microfinance services and continual review of the organisations' services to align with increased client well-being and sustaining development gains. The focus here is on its efforts to transform its business in light of experience gained in emergency conditions (including unique lessons of COVID-19) to create a new level of resilience in its clients and itself. For clients, the goal is to self-manage development loss and for the organisation, to stabilise and cordon the investment needed to support clients survive and move on from the relatively constant adverse impacts of disasters. It could be argued that for many organisations operating in developing countries, this form of organisational resilience requires transformative capacity particularly in the context of climate change, natural disasters and geo-political turbulence that impact economic and social development. COP27 (the 27th Conference of the Parties to the United Nations Framework Convention on Climate Change) has highlighted such vulnerabilities that require new perspectives on the financing of resilience strategies.

Jones and d'Errico (2019, p. 1) note that ' ... [a]s resilience continues to rise to top of the international policy agenda, development funders and practitioners are under mounting pressures to ensure that investments in resilience building are effective and targeted at those most in need'. This has implications for definitions and measurement of individual and organisational resilience, yet resiliency characteristics have often been sectoral and disciplinary specific. In social work, the notion of resilience usually refers to the resilience of clients and their capability to continue to lead functional lives whilst withstanding various forms of hardship. The goal appears to be holding out against or coming back from adversity to pre-existing states of coping and well-being. Psychological resilience also has a focus on the ability of individuals to cope mentally or emotionally with a crisis, to stabilise or enhance pre-crisis coping capability as quickly as possible, i.e. restoring equilibrium or regaining a pre-adversity position strengthened by coping with adversity. The importance of coping models is revisited later in the chapter. In healthcare, resilience is often conceptualised as creating adaptive capacity to respond to systemic challenges and changes, managing such tensions whilst maintaining high quality care. In engineering and ecology, the objective appears to '... the ability of a system to return to a normalised state after disturbance or change' (Jones & d'Errico, 2019, p. 2).

Although there has been a tendency to normalise the notion of resilience around that adopted by the disciplines of engineering and ecology, social scientists have emphasised that it is important to acknowledge how societies adapt and transform, particularly to contemporary pressures such as climate change, environmental degradation and pandemics (Pelling, 2010). Organisations comprise complex multifunctional and multidisciplinary entities and as such organisational resilience would reflect all of these characteristics to some extent, i.e. forms of social, structural, systemic and psychological resilience in perceiving challenge and adversity and responding to it holistically. This supports the argument that a subjective understanding of resilience relying on self-evaluation is a critical complement to widely used objectively oriented approaches leveraging external definitions of resilience (Jones & d'Errico, 2019, p. 1).

This tension constitutes a useful lens in critiquing institutional approaches and interventions to assist resiliency-building. From a business perspective, governments have recognised the need for resiliency awareness in increasingly turbulent global environments, and many have attempted to help organisations prepare for such conditions by developing organisational cultures and behaviours that embed support for organisational resiliency. For example, the Australian Government's Department of Home Affairs defines organisational resilience as '... a business's ability to adapt and evolve as the global market is evolving, to respond to short term shocks – be they natural disasters or significant changes in market dynamics – and to shape itself to respond to long term challenges' (Department of Home Affairs, 2020). It advises businesses to reflect on the sustainability of their organisation given that: organisational viability and sustainability is continually threatened under conditions of volatility and constant change; risk cannot be contained by traditional reliance on corporate strategies; and an organisation essentially needs to absorb the impact of unseen events, adapt and develop capability to continually sustain business, including growth and profitability dimensions.

The Australian Government's organisational resilience website suggests that organisations will tend to approach adverse events in four ways. First, they might accept that current adversity may result in the decline and even cessation of business. Second, resilient behaviour is employed to survive adversity, albeit in a reduced form of activity. Third, the resilience goal is to bounce back and regain a pre-adversity position as quickly as possible. Fourth, the resilience objective is not only to bounce back but to 'bounce-forward', i.e. to improve aspects of its functioning so that it not only survives but gains from the adverse situation. This latter approach is essentially adaptive, transformative and reflects a resilience to cope with and build from involvement in unpredictable dynamism characteristic of complex adaptive systems. Later, these manifestations of resilience goals and behaviours are captured in Fig. 1.

Folke et al. (2010) emphasise the importance of resilience thinking in addressing both the dynamics and development of complex social-ecological systems. Their focus on the adaptability and transformability features of resilience is seen as highly relevant to better understanding organisational responses in achieving integrated sustainability-related development goals covering economic, social and environmental domains. A key tenet of their argument is that resilience implies the capacity for organisations '... to continually change and adapt yet remain within critical thresholds'. Drawing from complexity theory, they suggest that a perturbation can bring a system over a perceived threshold because the stimulus to which it is responding shifts as a result of dynamism in the ecosystem, an increasingly common contemporary phenomenon. By responding innovatively to new stimuli, an organisation can achieve a new sense of stability

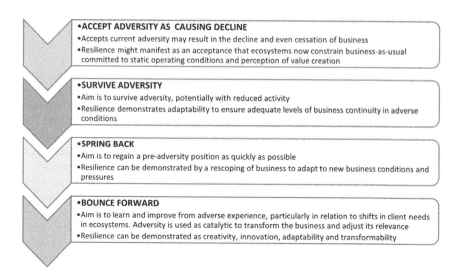

Fig. 1. Manifestations of Organisational Resilience Behaviours in Turbulent Environments (Informed by the Department of Home Affairs' (2022) Organisational Resilience Website and Resilience Literature Discussed Above).

and thus does not return to a previous state. These critical transitions are part of transformative process that can better align organisations with ecosystems. The case study below explores how an institution attempts to meet client survival needs as part of a more sustainable ecosystem, aligned with sustainable development goals, through transformative process.

Of key significance here is the manner in which adaptability and transformability represent different forms of resilience. Adaptability requires experience and knowledge that allows organisations to '... continue developing within the current stability domain' (Folke et al. citing Berkes et al., 2003) by maintaining certain approaches, despite changing internal conditions and external pressures. A contrasting form of resilience associated with transformability requires '... the capacity to create a fundamentally new system when ecological, economic or social structures make the existing system untenable' (Folke et al. citing Walker, Holling, Carpenter, & Kinzig, 2004, p. 5).

Thus, from a complexity perspective, Folke et al. (2010) ask how resilience behaviours can provide insights into system renewal, reorganisation and innovation and how these behaviours might be measured and assessed in relation to outcomes. Particularly, they suggest that variables such as organisational identity, core values and world views might constrain adaptability. In the case below, we suggest the organisation's culture supported broad-based adaptive behaviours rather than constrained them. We discuss the impact of stakeholder perceptions of organisational culture as supporting adaptive, transformative behaviour and suggest these perceptions play a significant role in shaping coping and resilience behaviours. Folke et al. exploring social-ecological resilience to better understand how ecosystems and social systems that use and depend on them are inextricably linked, ask '... what are the features of agency, actor groups, social learning, networks, organizations, institutions, governance structures, incentives, political and power relations or ethics that enhance or undermine social-ecological resilience' (2010, p. 4). They infer the relationship between adaptability and transformation implies recognition of thresholds crossed, which we consider in terms of organisational purpose, goals, strategy and capability.

The notion of organisational 'adaptability' appears to align with the definitions of organisational resilience concerned with 'survival' and 'bounce-back', and that of 'transformation' with the notion of 'bounce-forward'. Fig. 1 above summarises the specific organisational resilience categories discussed here, seen as relevant to analysis of the ASA Philippines case study, but also warranting critique of their capacity to represent the essentially dynamic nature of resilience thinking, potentially challenging a more discrete understanding of resilience behaviours associated with declining, surviving, adapting and transforming organisations in turbulence.

2. THE GLOBAL NORTH AND GLOBAL SOUTH EXPERIENCE OF UNPRECEDENTED EMERGENCIES

The discipline of political economy has traditionally questioned notions of linear thinking as embedded in the politics of modernisation that largely ignore the legacy of colonialism and structural inequality as a significant determinant of a country's capacity to respond to contemporary unprecedented global crises.

Sachs (2017) describes the concept of development or 'expansive modernity' as being in its death throes given that the world is in crisis as manifest in the destruction of the biosphere and the widening gap between the rich and poor.

More recently, the COVID-19 pandemic constituted an emergency situation with unknown parameters, impacts and time frames. It affected all sectors of organisational activity and coincided with heightened tensions in Cold War politics that introduced new dimensions in already ailing economic systems in both the Global North and South. In both regions, new forms of organisational resilience have been demonstrated in response to COVID, some organisations going further than merely handling unanticipated shocks by evolving and reconfiguring their businesses (BCG, 2021). This is not to underplay or ignore the unequal impact that pandemic and geo-political tensions have on organisations in the North and South in maintaining resilient responses to adversity. COP27 has highlighted inequalities in climate finance as one significant example that impacts on resiliency options for the Global South.

A key differentiator emphasised in this chapter is the influence of organisational goals, culture and strategic drivers on a 'bounce-forward' approach to resiliency. The Australian Government has highlighted benefits of a 'bounce-forward' approach to resilience to the private sector including significant growth potential and profit, despite unprecedented disruption to existing business models. The case study here has a more social-ecological focus on transformation as resilience strategy, highlighting synergies between organisational and client resilience in achieving development gains framed within the Sustainable Development Goals (SDGs). We suggest that this case exemplifies a more Southern mindset highlighting resiliency as an interdependent and core capability amongst and between stakeholders. Our focus on this treatment of resiliency resurfaces Jones and d'Errico's (2019) argument around the importance of ensuring that subjective insights are included in identifying and evaluating resiliency behaviours, whether defined in the SDGs or in instruments such as RIMA (Resilience Index Measurement Analysis) developed by the UN's Food and Agriculture Association.

3. SDGS AND RESILIENCY

Sachs (2017) links the development of the SDGs and associated Agenda 2030 with the transformation of the concept of development. On the premise that 'development as growth' is leading to a planet that is 'inhospitable to human growth' (Rockström et al., 2009), Sachs suggests that SDGs have narrowed down 'development' to conditions of survival, characterising the SDGs as embedding goals indicative of human and ecological vulnerability. He further identifies shifts in the discourse away from the classical development narrative towards equating the urgency of development with security interests of and crisis prevention within developed nations. In this context, resiliency of nations, organisations, the community and individuals has been essentially redefined.

Ziai (2017) however warns against 'throwing out the baby with the bathwater' by suggesting although SDGs have been accused of fostering Western concepts of development, post-development mindsets must not ignore the development goals of the South which often embrace positive consequences of development and modern science as public goods, and as elements of globally defined living standards. This is not to deny that in reality the vision of global social equality has receded consistent with '... the abandonment of the "development" promise in the neoliberal discourse of "globalisation"' (2017, p. 2550).

Sachs (2017) draws attention to the contribution of SDGs in burying the politics of modernisation by introducing an agenda that is global and universal. SDGs perceptibly disposed of the myth of the South catching up with the North. The South was given no continuing exemption from responsibility concerning biospheric damage, recognising the impact of the burgeoning middle classes with Western tastes and indicators of success and well-being. The North could no longer deny the negative externalities that their economic systems posed for less-developed countries. Indeed, SDGs themselves embed the tensions between growth and social policy. 'On the one hand, the Agenda 2030 recognises the decline of ocean-ecosystems and the increasing social inequality, but on the other hand it calls for economic growth and affirms the WTO trade regimes' (p. 2577).

A key precursor to the SDGs was the 1992 Earth Summit and Agenda 21 which acknowledged its development agenda '... was a dynamic program, with complex policy interlinkages to be interpreted and adapted across countries and regions at different stages of development, with different agendas and capabilities ... that member responses would evolve over time in light of changing needs and circumstances and that new forms of global partnership could potentially provide collaborative and targeted support to this end' (Bolton & Landells, 2021, p. 160). Consequently, perceptions of resilience in achieving sustainable outcomes would be broad-based and historically, regionally and organisationally specific to context. So, do SDGs accommodate a more holistic and subjective understanding of resiliency as suggested as necessary by Jones and d'Errico (2017)?

Bahadur, Lovell, Wilkinson, and Tanner (2015) recognise that although strengthening resilience is vital to achieving SDGs, a measure of resilience is of limited value if it cannot relate sustainability outcomes to the scope of shocks and stresses experienced during their achievement. They see SDG1 as the core resilience target, aiming to increase resilience of the poor and vulnerable to climate-related extreme events and other economic, social and environmental shocks and disasters. It relates to other resiliency targets including: 'strengthen resilience and adaptive capacity to climate-related hazards and natural disasters ...' (target 13.1); 'develop quality reliable sustainable and resilient infrastructure ...' (target 9.1); 'ensure sustainable food production systems and implement resilient agricultural practices ...' (target 2.4); 'significantly reduce the number of deaths and the number of people affected and decrease by [x percent] the economic losses relative to gross domestic product caused by disasters, including water-related disasters, with a focus on protecting the poor and people in vulnerable situations ...' (target 11.5); and, 'substantially increase the number of cities and human settlements adopting and implementing integrated policies and plans towards inclusion, resource efficiency, mitigation and adaptation to climate change, resilience to disasters, develop and implement, in line with the Sendai

Framework for Disaster Risk Reduction, holistic disaster risk management at all levels' (target 11b).

They acknowledge that measurement of resilience is complex and that international standards are lacking as people's resilience needs to be considered '... in terms of a set of interrelated capacities to absorb, anticipate and adapt to different kinds of shocks and stresses' (p. 3). These capacities include adaptive capacity whereby social systems can adapt to multiple, long-term and future risks, learning to adjust after disasters; anticipatory capacity whereby social systems can anticipate and prepare for shocks and reduce their impacts; and, absorptive capacity which they describe as coping capacity of social systems, applying relevant skills and resources to recover from adverse conditions. They suggest that SDGs target development outcomes rather than considering inputs/ outputs, and that targets measuring resilience capacities should also measure the impact of shocks and stresses as a dimension of resilience. In other words, Bahadur et al. (2015) suggest that a comprehensive analysis would require the measurement of both disaster resilience and systemic preparedness to deal with adverse events. Although SDGs claim to recognise and accommodate detail and complexity associated with local interpretation and implementation of activities to achieve SDGs, there is still a heavy reliance on standardised, objective, quantitative measures to track progress or achievement. As noted by Jones and d'Errico (2017), there is little evidence being provided of more subjective, perceptive, contextual and qualitative insight into resiliency of institutions, communities and the poor and vulnerable individuals for whom resiliency efforts are primarily directed.

Sachs (2017) accepts that the data revolution has brought benefit, for instance, in education, health, oceanology and food security sectors, helping the formulation of growth targets as a basis for understanding trends and comparative indicators. However, he also notes the tendency in these targets and measurements towards a homogenising effect that reduces diversity and difference, reinforcing the 'development creed' and its associated 'dictatorship of comparison'.

> The Human Development Index, like the GDP is a deficit index; it categorises countries according to a hierarchy, thereby presupposing that there is only one kind of social evolution. The SDGs with the scales and indices of the 17 goals and 169 sub-goals follow in this legacy (2017, p. 2578).

The need for subjective insight into the challenges faced by the Global South in achieving development goals is underrated. COP27 appears to be a forum in which this reality has been brought to the table, challenging expectations of the Global North that the Global South can demonstrate resiliency in the face of social, economic, political and ecological turbulence, without consideration of funding in the context of historical liabilities of the North.

Sachs (2017) suggests that another tension between the Global North and South in interpreting the role of resilience-building in SDGs is an apparent disregard of exceeding ecological limits. Only conditions of risk and scarcity frame the North's neoliberal interpretation of requisite resilient behaviours. Yet, social inequality is exacerbated by increasing numbers of people on a finite planet in which unequal levels of consumption continue to cause ecological destruction, adding an additional dimension to the nature of resilience required for survival. Sachs notes that Pope Francis, in the 2015 encyclical *Laudato Si'*, argues for '...a strategy of sufficiency embedded in cultural change: it is indeed the rich who have to change, not the poor; it is wealth that needs to be alleviated, not poverty. By requiring the rich to refrain from appropriating the surroundings of the poor, the powerless are accorded more freedom' (2017, p. 2581).

Assarkhaniki, Rajabifard, and Sabri (2020) also critique the lack of definitional complexity around the notion of resilience when attempting to measure it as a subjective and multidimensional concept in SDGs. They acknowledge that '... four resilience indicators in SDGs measure disaster resilience, while resilience refers to the ability of a system to prepare for, absorb, recover from, and adapt to *any shocks and adverse events*' (2020, p. 2 citing Siebeneck & Cova, 2012, emphasis added). However, rather than acknowledge the localised, contextual nature of subjective experience of resilience and associated capacities needed, they consider the fundamental impediment to effective resilience being the lack of '...global agreement on the concept and its dimensions' (p. 1). Consequently, they developed a common framework of five key dimensions of resilience (social, economic, institutional, infrastructural and environmental) and an associated 318 resilience indicators (compared to the 231 indicators comprising the complete SDG framework) suggesting future research is needed to consider how these resilience indicators might be included in SDGs. They also suggest that this more comprehensive list of resilience indicators should be tested through case studies to study the impact of inclusion on SDG measurement.

By contrast, it is suggested here that resiliency behaviours emerge in ongoing emergency environments experienced by many organisations in the Global South. Although their capture in inventories is useful, it lacks meaning without contextualisation. The case study below illustrates the dynamic, complex and subjective nature of resilience through the lens of an organisation and its stakeholders seeking to address its own development goals and those of its clients through microfinance and associated services. The case suggests that institutional and stakeholder resilience can be explored through an SDG lens, including a local stakeholder perception of the impact of dynamic challenges on pathways to greater sustainability and enhancement of resiliency capability on this journey. Thus, an understanding of resiliency within an SDG framework is essentially contextual and requires resilient behaviours to be understood in context. Insight into resiliency challenges and coping strategies can be ascertained more comprehensively by reference to contextual and subjective appraisal of risk and adversity that will in turn influence both institutional and stakeholder responses.

At a high level, the notion of resilience embedded in SDGs could be better conceptualised as continuous development in the face of dynamic challenge, particularly experienced in the Global South. Achieving SDGs requires local interpretation of unique and complex political, economic, social, environmental and institutional challenges and responses, and reflective and collaborative stakeholder practice in achieving sufficient stability to allow action to be taken.

We suggest resilience can accrue through survival, adaptation and transformation strategies relevant to the achievement of integrated SDGs, contextually relevant to the challenges faced.

This conceptualisation of resiliency is explored through ASA Philippines Foundation (ASA), a microfinance institution, adapting its services and transforming its operations in accordance with its mission towards the goals of institutional and client development and sustainability of their development achievements.

4. THE CASE OF ASA PHILIPPINES: DEVELOPING RESILIENCY STRATEGIES

ASA is a non-profit MFI extending microfinancial services to around 2 million clients through 1,683 branches all over the Philippines. Its strategic focus has been significantly shaped by its ongoing responses to emergencies that have stimulated reflection on its mission in the context of more broadly supporting the 'development' needs of its clients and helping them cope more resiliently with ongoing extreme environments. The vision of this social enterprise includes 'helping an increasing number of poor Filipino families rise out of poverty by providing microfinancing to help them establish or otherwise improve their own microenterprises' as well as improving the well-being of the poor more holistically by 'giving them greater access to life support goods and services in the most cost-effective and sustainable manner' (ASA Philippines Foundation, 2021).

The continuing onset of natural disasters, social upheavals and more recently, the COVID-19 pandemic has deepened the focus of ASA on providing assistance to promote a smoother trajectory of well-being for its clients. The pursuit of well-being in turbulence provides fertile ground for considering how to sustain both resilient organisations and resilient clients in periods of unforeseen turmoil. As noted above, although the notion of resilience is embedded within SDGs, concern has been expressed about a reliance on standardised outcomes and measurements, including indicators of levels of resource loss during emergencies as a basis for assessing trends and comparison of resiliency levels. This approach does not reflect the complexity of achieving resiliency levels needed in diverse, unique and evolving emergencies. In the case of ASA, various interventions have been introduced in different emergency settings, accruing experience of effectively helping clients cope and building organisational resilience under emergency conditions. A means of understanding ASA's strategy for adaptation is to trace its development and adaptation of client community services (CCS) that help sustain clients in emergencies and enhance the positive impact of microfinance initiatives.

Since its inception in 2004, ASA has provided CCS to its clients and non-client community members, additional to microfinance, i.e. disaster relief, healthcare, child-feeding, education through scholarships, environmental programmes. Providing supplementary support through CCS has become an integral part of ASA's organisational values and mission, increasing and tailoring services relevant to client needs in emergency and non-emergency environments. Not only have CCS become core to ASA's mission, their provision has also elicited appreciation by clients that has resulted in expansion of business (Tarafder & Custodio, 2017). Also, these services have helped clients' capacity for resilience during ongoing emergencies. Resiliency-building in clients can be perceived as fostering both ASA's organisational survival and adaptation and that of the businesses of ASA clients. The extent to which these developments have been transformational, or could be in the future, is also discussed below.

Consideration of CCS in the context of resiliency generation requires a more dynamic appraisal of the iterative, interactive and emergent nature of resilience than is perhaps evident in Fig. 1. For instance, the pursuit of organisational resilience in complex and volatile decision-making processes creates the potential for opposing views, tensions and synergy embedded in stakeholder perspectives, which will manifest in organisational culture as supporting resiliency generation. Thus, organisational services provided to clients might be perceived as:

- having ongoing benefit in promoting business *survival* in adverse conditions
- helping the organisation *spring back* to regain a pre-adversity position, possibly by adapting and rescoping the business
- remodelling business mindset, strategy and operations to gain *transformative capability* from adversity and turbulent ecosystems, requiring creativity and innovation

We now examine more closely these different resiliency goals in relation to ASA's experience.

4.1 Services Seen as Core to Promoting Ongoing Business Resilience and Survival

Table 1 identifies the total amount of expenditure on CCS assistance over the period 2005–2022. Tarafder and Custodio (2017) describe how ASA anticipated the impact on its clients of limited resources for social infrastructure such as health, education, sanitation and family bereavement that could impact business continuity and growth, client well-being and ultimately timely payment of loans. Whilst pursuing the goal of profitability, the organisation also recognised the need for flexibility in its business planning to include provision for enhanced assistance as relief in frequent emergency conditions that have potentially devastating effects on microfinanced projects. The significance of the item 'Relief Activities and Grants' demonstrates the importance of this contingency. Thus, attempts to foster and support resilience in clients has been a primary concern and driver of the organisation, evidence increasingly indicating that client resilience fostered organisational resilience of ASA and its growth through tailoring its business services to perceived and often emergent client needs.

Burial assistance was the initial client service introduced in ASA's first year of operation as one of a series of services that recognised the significance of family responsibilities and potential impact on the development of microfinanced business as a means of escaping poverty traps. By 2007, ASA had introduced

Table 1. Client Community Services Expenditure 2005–2022.

CCS Categories	Total Amount of CCS Expenditure (2005–2022) US$m
Burial assistance	14.250
Hospitalisation assistance	8.788
Relief activities and grants	33.735
Scholarship	8.881
Business development programme	3.427
Medical mission and healthcare	1.126
Environmental programme	0.042
Child-feeding	0.217
Total	**US$ million 70.466**

Source: ASA Philippines Foundation (2022a); Conv. Rate 50 Pesos = 1 USD.

educational support to the children of clients and non-clients with above-average grades in high school. It recognised education was a complementary 'development strategy' for many families and introduced a scholarship programme to fund university tuition fees and education expenses. ASA scholarships support students for up to a four-year course. Scholarship recipients also benefit from a guaranteed job in ASA after graduating. As of March 2022, 1,012 scholarship recipients have graduated, and 8,529 are currently undertaking undergraduate studies in universities across the Philippines.

ASA also recognised the importance of business education as a resiliency tool for its clients. In collaboration with institutions such as University of Asia and the Pacific and the Quezon City Local Government, ASA provides business development, training, mentoring and marketing support including marketing initiatives to promote client products. Until March 2022, it supported more than 277,000 individual businesses with grants of US$3.427 million. With ASA's focus on client development, there is also the intention to enhance business training from basic planning and accounts to include capability to transform business assets to achieve growth through more effective management of risks and opportunities. It is central to the development of such client capability for ASA to 'know' its client. Experience has taught ASA that this knowledge deepens by 'being with' its clients in emergency environments and shaping business and individual resilience in partnership with them (Tarafder & Custodio, 2018).

As in all stages of economic development and particularly the early stages, medical services play a significant role in promoting resilience capability, and ASA introduced these services over 2013–2014. Volunteer medical professionals provide health and dental check-ups; hospitalisation benefits are provided free of premium to clients and beneficiaries, covering expenses associated with hospital stay, including doctors and medications. Clients can receive cataract/pterygium and cleft lip/palate operations for themselves and their children free of charge and have access to one-time operations for goitre, cyst, hernia, Pierre Robin syndrome, cancer and bone fracture/deformity.

The importance of sanitary conditions in facilitating development goals is also recognised by ASA. It launched a programme, in collaboration with water.org, to educate clients and provide loans tailored to construct clean water access and sewage disposal facilities.

In 2015, a fifty-per cent interest rate rebate was given to clients with, or whose family member had, a disability, including blindness, hearing loss, muteness, Down syndrome, autism, physical deformity or psychiatric disorder. This initiative recognised the burden of associated medical expenses on client capacity to leave poverty through successful business development.

As of June 2022, ASA had spent US$70.466 million through its CCS programme over the last 18 years and directly assisted 5,776,483 individuals (member and non-member). Thus, ASA recognises that building resiliency in its clients (as a basis for exiting poverty) is dependent on helping them maintain a sense of purpose, sustain and develop their businesses through better health, education and infrastructure and have access to resources needed in adverse circumstances.

This approach to resiliency-building supports ongoing and simultaneous organisational and client survival and growth. It could be argued that this approach is coterminous with the resiliency scenario described as 'springing back' from disaster, in that both scenarios share many aspects of a common culture. Hamel and Välikangas (2003, p. 53) discussed resilience as an organisational capacity '... to dynamically reinvent business models and strategies as circumstances change'. They further noted that organisational resilience is more than responding to individual crises, rather '... its about having capacity to change before the case for change becomes desperately obvious' (pp. 53–54). It could be argued that ASA, from its early days anticipated the need for its business model to adapt in constant emergency scenarios to meet client needs and to limit the trauma inflicted by these emergencies.

A 'springing back' resiliency approach is discussed next and demonstrates ASA's continuing service ethos, particularly how it tailors its services and client commitment in periods of emergency. It is also consistent with its contingency planning and provisioning for emergency conditions that characterise the circumstances faced by the poor in their efforts to leave poverty through microfinance services.

4.2 Service Adaptation and Business Planning that Help Spring Back *from Disasters to Regain a Pre-adversity Position*

ASA's approach to dealing with clients in emergencies fostered a shift in mission towards 'being with your client' rather than merely 'knowing your client'. Nevertheless, prior efforts to better know client needs facilitated urgent and targeted assistance through CCS in emergency conditions. It also provided insight into effective ways of helping clients become more resilient in turbulent conditions that threatened business as usual. Fostering client resiliency also required post-emergency support for clients who appreciated ASA's design and delivery of appropriate services at the local level. As Hamel and Välikangas (2003) noted, the resilient organisation morphs its strategy to align with emerging opportunities and developing trends and in this way is 'constantly making its future rather than defending its past' (p. 54). Being with clients helped ASA refine its strategic approach in emergencies to mitigate incipient threats to the evolving improvement in the economic status of its clients, contingent upon the development of their individual businesses. This had implications for ASA's business model and its support of clients to cope.

Bolton (2004, p. 61) noted that

> ...the resilience literature not only identifies the personal characteristics that aid successful coping or stabilisation in change, it also identifies the significance of event characteristics and coping resources that mediate the impact between the person and the change event, and influence the re-stabilisation process.

Drawing from Lazarus and Folkman (1984), she elaborated on the coping process in heavy change environments from the perspective of organisations supporting the resilience of employees. It is argued here that some features of this model have relevance to a discussion of ASA's experience of, and relationship with, its stakeholders, particularly its employees and clients in emergency environments. Lazarus and Folkman perceive individual coping as involving two stages. Initially a stakeholder's stress in heavy change environments is shaped by an appraisal of the event as positive, neutral or negative. However, a secondary appraisal of potentially stressful events can be significant in terms of response to crisis and related behaviour, and this involves an individual's assessment of their coping abilities and resources available to meet the threat. Bolton (2004) identifies that organisations committed to facilitating effective coping by salient stakeholders might usefully develop cultures that facilitate change with limited trauma. Aspects of culture will include: the organisation's commitment to empowering others to respond innovatively; helping others set meaningful and realistic goals in the crisis; developing, adapting and supporting increased flexibility in systems as appropriate; facilitating and adapting networks and alliances appropriate to context; and maintaining effective monitoring of all these accumulated change impacts on decisions around strategic, operational and flexible resourcing matters. This conceptual approach is a useful lens for understanding ASA's support of client and staff resilience in emergencies towards the goal of not only springing back from disaster to regain a pre-adversity position, but as Hamel and Välikangas (2003) also point out, achieving resiliency in emergencies less traumatically by prior consideration and planning where possible. This includes developing staff resources to support clients in adverse conditions.

ASA has broad experience of emergencies that reduce clients' capacities to maintain their businesses. For example, the Super Typhoon Haiyan (known as Yolanda) hit 16 provinces in November 2013 affecting 72 branches and approximately 105,000 active borrowers. Riecke (2016) recorded the following details of ASA's response to Typhoon Haiyan. The first action was to visit clients, the President travelling to Tacloban, largely destroyed by the typhoon, to determine together with staff members the immediate relief work needed. Staff visited members' homes and spoke with clients about conditions and immediate family needs. Where a family member had died, ASA Philippines provided the necessary burial assistance, trusting the clients' word rather than insisting on standard claims documentation. Other immediate assistance included the distribution of solar lamps, mosquito nets and fishing boots. ASA also collaborated with other MFIs and institutions to deliver medical services.

ASA had pre-existing policy that allowed borrowers a rehabilitation advance loan if required. In recognition of the impact of the event, half of the loan was gifted, the other half was interest-free to be repaid within one year. Borrowers were also given a moratorium of two months on repayments, extendable by negotiation. All relief was to be administered within 24 hours after reporting. Clients affected had outstanding loans of approximately US$7.3 million (PHP365 million). Of the 104,708 affected, there were only 848 write-offs valued at approx. US$50,000 and borrowers could re-join ASA later, as could members whose repayments were disrupted by relocation. These relief operations were possible due to ASA's fund created specifically for such calamities. After interest-free loans were returned, Typhoon Haiyan cost ASA about PHP75 million (US$1.5 million) in relief activities (Riecke, 2016). ASA increased its CCS expenditure from 2012 to 2013 by 50% to provide urgent cash and relief assistance of over US$2 million to 180,000 families. All but a 1000 families resumed their business within a year (Tarafder, Habib, & Bolton, 2022) suggesting a strong capacity to come back from adversity by leveraging perceived support structures adapted to meet their needs in context.

The ongoing impact of typhoons continued between September and October 2022. On 24th September Typhoon Noru, known as Super Typhoon Karding in the Philippines, affected 3 provinces, 34 ASA branches and 4,483 clients. Again, ASA Philippines' staff immediately visited the affected clients providing cash relief assistance of PHP1,793,200 and 'washed-out' assistance of PHP502,800 (totalling approx. US$46,000), the increased amount of PHP400 per family reflecting an inflation rate rise affecting basic commodity prices. On October 13th–16th Tropical Storm Nesat, locally called Neneng, affected one province, 11 branches and 1,224 clients requiring PHP489,600 cash relief (approx. US$10,000). A tropical cyclone experienced later in the month on October 28th affected 21 provinces, 145 branches, 39,296 clients and 6,256 non-clients who were assisted, cash and relief goods assistance amounting to PHP12,838,803 (approx. US$257,000) (ASA Philippines Foundation, 2022b). Internal reports include images of staff delivering relief assistance at considerable risk to personal well-being, reflecting their personal commitment to the values of ASA Philippines consistent with its adaptive mission and vision (ASA Philippines Foundation, 2022b).

Coutu (2002, p. 52) defined resilience as '... the skill and the capacity to be robust under conditions of enormous stress and change'. She notes three overarching qualities which might be indicative of ASA's response to what has been called the Battle of Marawi in the Southern Philippines. These three qualities are a sober and almost pessimistic sense of reality about the challenges faced; a propensity to make meaning in such terrible times; and a capacity to improvise and invent as long as the culture of improvisation has clear boundaries. Tarafder and Custodio (2018) detail this event. The 5-month armed battle between government troops and Islamic State supporters started on 24 May 2017 and killed 1,200 people, injured more than 1,400 government forces and displaced an estimated 350,000 people.

ASA's resiliency culture and value set demonstrated the resiliency qualities identified by Coutu (2002), enabling an immediate response in the difficult Marawi environment. It delivered relief goods to clients and community members during and after the Battle of Marawi. The next day after the battle commenced, staff repacked relief goods into individual packages of rice, coffee, sugar, creamer, sardines and noodles, and by May 27th were loading 150 sacks at a time onto the Deputy Director's truck and their own motorcycles before seeking out their clients and distributing relief. Some clients asked for help and gave locations, but the staff also searched for clients at the various evacuation centres. By the end of May 27th, 2,500 people had received food relief from ASA. In contrast to many other microfinance organisations, ASA responded immediately to the crisis, it being the first NGO to distribute relief goods to the people of Marawi displaced in the battle. Consistent with its motto of 'being with your client' during times of disaster, its staff stayed with clients in the conflict zone and helped rebuild social and human capital and critical infrastructure. In addition, on 25 September 2017, it distributed relief to 1,000 non-client beneficiaries affected by the battle who were isolated in Lumba-Bayabao. In December 2017, further calamity compounded the situation in Mindanao when Typhoon Vinta hit Lanao del Norte and Lanao del Sur, requiring further relief support from ASA Philippines.

The COVID pandemic also demanded a robust sense of reality, capacity to meaning-make and to improvise in unique circumstances. As elsewhere, it affected the whole nation-state and created new and emergent forms of crisis in economic, political, social and environmental systems requiring resiliency qualities and behaviour in unprecedented times. Initially, it appeared to require efforts to sustain the business during the short to medium term. It soon became clear that the impact of lockdown required significant forms of adaptation. In the longer term, responding to these conditions suggested the potential for more positive transformative approaches with implications for ASA's strategic direction, business model and culture.

COVID-19 severely affected the Philippines; by 28 November 2022, 4,034,658 cases were recorded and 64,608 deaths (Worldometer, 2022). When COVID-19 struck, microfinance programmes served almost 140 million clients globally of which 81% were women (Convergences, 2021). Lockdown measures thus affected women and poor households disproportionally. As with previous emergencies, during COVID-19 ASA delivered food, medicine and other support, recognising that often one day of isolation for the poor meant going hungry for the day. It also recognised the impossibility for many clients of continuing repayments. Interest-free loans were offered during lockdown and the post-lockdown recovery period. Applying the lens of resilience offered by Coutu's (2002) model demonstrated a sober sense of reality about the challenges faced, its business model catering for extensive relief operations due to its special fund for calamities. In addition, the culture of decentralised decision-making supported ASA's propensity to make meaning of appropriate responses in this unique disaster as well as improvise and innovate in a manner that assured key stakeholders of the need to maintain businesses and loan commitments whilst providing significant loan relief.

Murshid and Murshid (2022), in discussing the impact of COVID on MFIs operating in Bangladesh, indicated that according to the claims of NGO management they interviewed '[w]hile debt cancellation might be the relief most clients need ... NGOs will rely on their clients' neoliberal sensibilities to recognise that debt cancelation is [an] impossibility ...' (p. 243). By contrast, among MFIs in the Philippines ASA provided the highest amount of reserves for probable loan losses in 2020 of US$52 million, which accounted for 10.94% of the portfolio in that year. It also wrote off the highest percentage of loans in 2021 (4.54%). Also, disaster recovery loans to bankrupted businesses reached US$49 million in 2021 and another US$122 million in 2022. Thus, its business model accommodated a significant shift to loans required to maintain existing business and provide recovery finances without any interest. These were called MalASAkit (a local term of compassion) loans, allowing restructuring of debt and an associated repayment schedule. Further, COVID required increased CCS outlays, as 2.25 million clients and community members were assisted to the amount of US$17.1 million in 2020 and an additional US$13 million in 2021, representing a 59% increase from 2019 CCS outlays. This resulted in a significant turnaround through an increased repayment rate and profitability in the following year, ASA reporting a net profit of 4.2 billion Pesos (approx. US$83.7 million) in 2021 (ASA Philippines Foundation, 2021), also reported by ASA as greater than the aggregated income of all MFIs supervised by the MNRC (Microfinance NGO Regulatory Council) in the Philippines.

Client feedback suggested that ASA was resilient in itself and that its business model had facilitated the resilience of its clients. For the vast majority of clients ASA's approach allowed them to achieve business continuity and to experience and communicate a sense of limited risk in microfinance borrowing even in the direst of pandemics. Interviews with executive staff suggested that many of ASA's clients paid back loans that had been forgiven as they so appreciated ASA's capacity to assure and support them during COVID and wanted to play their part in ensuring that ASA could continue this role into the future. The write-off recovery increased dramatically in 2021 to 10.02% and in 2022 to 30.39% against the written-off loans on an annual basis. This outcome signifies the mutual trust and strong resiliency of ASA and its clients.

ASA's inclusive and decentralised decision-making during the crisis illustrated its capacity to sense-make and innovate to achieve client outcomes that strengthened resiliency. This was demonstrated in its growth and financial results; its capable and committed workforce; and in the trust reflected across stakeholders engendered by adherence to its values even in the direst conditions. As noted earlier, this established and evolving culture helped ASA staff take action quickly in providing relief and support to its members and local communities, despite the pandemic taking its toll on staff. Nine hundred staff were infected and six staff died despite receiving urgent hospital treatment. A senior ASA staff member suggested that during COVID field officers demonstrated continuity of care and support to clients fostering some level of certainty that they could recover. The staff member described them as 'towers giving light to all areas', by demonstrating that strategies were available to support and enhance client efforts in maintaining and adapting their goals in unprecedented volatility.

The impact of COVID on client health was significant. ASA's President indicated that by March 2022, approximately 4,000 borrowers had been confirmed with COVID-19 and 309 had succumbed, ASA extending financial assistance to defray burial expenses and writing off their loan balances. Many families not infected by the virus were also significantly affected through the impact of lockdown on their access to income generation. All families had to manage the health hazard, maintain isolation and social distancing while finding new ways or work harder to provide food for the family (personal communication with ASA Philippines President, April 2022).

As noted earlier, one of the key resiliency qualities identified by Coutu (2002) was the capacity to improvise and invent as long as the culture of improvisation set clear boundaries. This is difficult to put in place in emergencies. ASA facilitated effective information flows, allowing a real-time understanding of the concerns of salient stakeholders about the multiple dimensions of the emergency and the effectiveness of responses to it, using Viber groups and social media. Resources were made available urgently, e.g. phone allowance was increased for staff to talk to clients, including advising about accessing government support. ASA quickly entered into collaborative arrangements, including with local government units, enhancing many networks from previous emergencies. Deputy directors in the field extended operational assistance and mobilised support staff to promote physical and mental health in the community. Health codes were formalised; medical support was provided 24/7 for staff; medical missions were sent out to Luzon, Visayas and Mindanao regions; and a PCR lab was hired to perform and record COVID testing. Thus, ASA was able to restrain the infection rate to 8% of 11,000 staff. Vaccinations were provided for ASA staff at branches or at urban immunisation centres.

4.3 Resilience Through Transformative Capability, Creativity and Innovation in Remodelling Business Planning

Many commentators on life after the COVID experience have emphasised that it has in common with other disasters (such as wars) the capacity to generate creativity and innovation under pressure that can transform organisational mindsets and practices. Brooks, Curnin, Owen, and Boldeman (2019) identified how post-event analyses of the handling of emergencies have identified the importance of imagination, policy, capabilities and management in responding to emergencies. They purport that '...imagination, is – or at least should be, an important component of emergency and crisis response and recovery regardless of the industry or the origin of the event itself' (p. 24). They also note the importance of building agility into their core capabilities, suggesting that '[t]he future will demand that leaders ... use higher cognitive skills such as creativity and divergent thinking to address failures of imagination. Processes in creativity include thinking skills that are conducive to taking new perspectives on problems, pivoting among different ideas, thinking broadly and making unusual associations' (p. 24.). Such creativity can be essential when developing joint capability across public, private and not-for-profit sectors to reduce community vulnerability to hazards and assist it cope with disasters.

Brooks et al. (2019) also discuss team creativity as a dimension of capability needed in emergency management, which aggregates individual and team creativity to generate creative responses (Taggar, 2002). Three complementary components important for creativity combine individual capability with cultural support. These include: skills in the task; a culture that supports creativity-relevant processes and an intrinsic motivation to do the task (Amabile, 1988; Amabile & Pratt 2016; van Knippenberg & Hirst, 2015). It is argued here that leaders and managers create the conditions for these capabilities, embedding them in culture to foster both individual and organisational resiliency. A focus in the ASA case has been on the organisation's willingness to provide sufficient infrastructure within and external to the organisation to access and consolidate necessary information as a basis for decision-making in emergencies. When time is limited for exploring solutions, sense-making processes need to facilitate creative solutions. In this context, a sense of trust between stakeholders is important as is the perceived availability of a physical, financial and cultural resource base from which to generate creative solutions. Boundaries also need to be set for creativity in emergency situations and in transformative thinking that follows. We indicate below the process of boundary setting that is influencing ASA's conceptualisation of its future value contribution to its clients as a result of its ongoing experience in helping clients remain resilient in achieving their goals, despite the impact of ongoing environmental exigencies. Brooks et al. (2019) argued that an increase in creative output will occur when emergency and crisis management personnel faced constraints around resources and context in which to think divergently. A study by Medeiros, Partlow, and Mumford (2014) also found this to be the case; however, imposition of multiple constraints led to poorer creative problem-solving. The ASA case suggests that in emergencies management made efforts to make constraints transparent, whilst demonstrating flexibility to apply resources in a targeted and problem-focussed manner, consistent with values, key systems and established culture in emergency response.

Owen, Hayes, Brooks, Scott, and Conway (2018) suggest core management capabilities relevant to operating in these emergency and crisis environments include: the capacity to model integrity, influence and governance; facilitating sense-making of scenarios and consequences for stakeholders; and practising self-awareness that supports adaptation and perseverance by displaying and fostering resilience and agility whilst recognising personal and organisational limitations. We argue these are critical in the process of 'bouncing forward' and leverage accrued experience of managing emergencies. In relation to the ASA case study, we ask to what extent could the learning around resiliency lead to creative and transformative thinking around business opportunities, tempered by holistic appraisal of business continuity and organisational development. The

ASA case examines this potentially transformative stage through the lens of two areas of creativity. One is the transformative nature of introducing insurance in multiple and unprecedented crises to limit risk to the organisation and improve outcomes for clients. The second is a critical appraisal of the role of digitalisation. Its introduction needs to balance the tension between preserving organisational values of knowing and being with clients, thus maintaining client loyalty, whilst also recreating business process that leverages new technologies to add value to clients.

4.3.1 Insurance

As noted previously, ASA provides cash 'burial assistance' to current members and a member's nominated beneficiary. An ASA member, their family or nominee receive varying amounts of financial assistance in accordance with the length of membership and in the case of the member's death, ASA writes off the outstanding loan amount. ASA does not charge fees or premiums to its members for this service. If a member or nominated beneficiary (i.e. husband, son or daughter) passes away or, should both pass away, family members receive burial assistance for both the member and the nominated beneficiary. Table 2 below details the amount of assistance by membership duration. The rationale behind offering burial assistance to current clients is that when the borrower or the principal earner dies, so does the breadwinner and the family's livelihood is at risk.

Table 2. Amount of Burial Assistance by Membership Duration.

Membership Category	Membership Duration	Burial Assistance
Mabuhay	Day 1–24 Months	10,000 pesos
Silver	25–48 Months	15,000 pesos
Gold	49–119 Months	20,000 pesos
Diamond	120 Months onwards	25,000 pesos

Thus, ASA already offers its clients a form of assistance to deal with the consequences of the death of members and their family members. However, ASA recognises that the frequency of disasters is exposing it and its clients to increasing risks concerning the scope of and certainty of assistance available. ASA is now planning to gain an insurance 'licence' so that it can offer its clients life insurance of up to US$2,000, which is twice as large an insured sum than other micro-insurance offerings in the Philippines. This appears consistent with strategies raised in global forums such as COP27 suggesting an enhanced role for insurance services to respond to the constancy and unpredictability of emergency conditions. ASA is also intending to provide business and credit insurance. It claims that rather than perceiving insurance as a significant revenue generator, it constitutes a mechanism to recover defaulting loans. Treating insurance as a separate business is intended to help set boundaries around the size of its contingency funding for the ever-increasing emergency events experienced in the Philippines. The insurance offerings will meet the needs of clients through providing new and extended forms of certainty and resilience in emergencies and as such can also be seen as important for relief of poverty through sustaining assets. Again, this suggests that building resilience is complex and contextual in its relationship to SDGs, particularly SDG1.

ASA's insurance service to clients is intended to break even. The feedback from clients is that they would appreciate this service and that ASA would be more attractive to them and their neighbours if they had an insurance programme. ASA estimates that by offering clients this form of added security, their client base could double in 3–4 years and their net income could increase PHP12-16 billion in 4–5 years ($US240-320 million) on an investment of around $US30m. ASA has a business plan approved and staff training has commenced. However, it will have to resolve client expectations concerning new forms of bureaucracy and verification that characterise the processes associated with accountability and governance around management of claims.

In relation to poverty alleviation goals, clients would be able to exceed the current loan limit of PHP6,000. Five percent of borrowers have graduated to be able to borrow up to 1 million pesos, 30–40 times ASA's limit. Thus, there appears to be a basis for significant expansion of lending which in turn incurs increased risk, so that the insurance business becomes more critical both to ASA's sustainable growth and capacity to fulfil its development brief.

4.3.2 Implications for SDGs

ASA's approach to extending services to support the achievement of SDGs (by enhancing local client capacity to develop assets and maintain them during emergencies) reflects debates in the industry but also demonstrates innovation in its approach to the tailoring of these services. The Impact Finance Barometer 2021 (Convergences, 2021, p. 8) noted problems in the MFI sector between 2000 and 2010 around over-indebtedness, market saturation and aggressive practices. This caused a review of risk and the limitations on investment and client base in an otherwise profitable industry. These problems generated discussion around achieving a more client-oriented attitude in the sector, through offering more holistic financial solutions including '... other types of financial products, such as access to renewable energy, water and sanitation, education, health or sustainable agriculture'. This inclusion of a broader dimension of social performance became indicative of new forms of impact measurement consistent with the integrated nature of SDGs. ASA's approach to working with clients and better understanding needs, particularly in emergencies, reflects its philosophical perspective that microfinance promotes the 'development' aspirations of the poor, its solutions also reflecting an understanding as to how these achievements were difficult to sustain in emergency environments.

By offering insurance of lives and loans it is intended that clients have more protection in managing development gains in the face of ongoing and unprecedented emergencies. ASA, through this insurance development, is consolidating its learning accrued by dealing with multiple emergencies and critiquing its value generation in contemporary environments. Insights from multiple stakeholders are enabling it to innovate, create and transform its business to both sustain its microfinance mission and to meet the emergent, transformative challenges of the sustainable development agenda, facilitated by various UN agencies since, at least, the 1987 Brundtland Commission. Thirty-five years later, COP27 has continued to focus on the need for innovation in its broadest sense to address global issues in various forms of urgent change and transformation. It has also highlighted the crucial nature of reflection on historical patterns of development, both legacies and emergent challenges, as a basis for transformative action, particularly in relation to agricultural challenges, adaptation and climate change (United Nations, 2022a). However, COP27 has also highlighted significant tensions around policies to use insurance as a means of risk management. Currently ASA has protected its clients through direct support and loan forgiveness. The goal is to assist clients who survive resume business practice by minimising a legacy of debt. Given the frequency of natural disasters ASA is aiming to spread the risk, standardise benefits and increase the capacity of self-reliance for clients who choose more comprehensive insurance against loss (particularly in the context of increased loan limits).

In discussing various perspectives raised at COP 27 concerning insurance for loss caused by climate-related natural disasters, Bernards (2022a) highlights two related and key issues, i.e. by introducing an insurance solution, how does the business model determine who pays and how are trigger events to be identified in the process of insurance coverage. These issues have been identified to some extent by ASA's proposing an up-front investment of $US30m for an initial fund. The embedding of appropriate ethics in insurance business administration and culture will no doubt benefit from ASA's traditional mission and experiences but requires significant transformation of these principles into a viable insurance model.

In this chapter we have considered the extent to which an organisation is attempting to reflect on its historical pattern of development, legacies and emergent challenges and manage its transformative thinking and strategy to redefine characteristics of its clients' development challenges and the nature of resilience required by its clients, whilst maintaining essential services in their current form.

Creating new forms of value is multi-faceted. As was the case with many other companies, COVID-19 presented ASA with urgent challenges and opportunities to reconsider the value of digitalisation strategies. The next section describes ASA's attempts to think both creatively and sustainably in its approach to digitalisation, assessing the notion of organisational and client resilience in the transformation process.

4.3.3 Digitalisation

ASA's President recognises the comprehensive influence of the digital revolution on business, governance and society, as well as the opportunities over the last few years to experience its benefits, often in emergency conditions. He is also cognisant that embracing digitalisation requires a holistic appreciation of organisational transformative capacity and the need for inclusive change at a pace that supports the resilience of all target groups, especially clients. He reflects that ASA used to be known as a 'paper and pencil' company but digitalisation has been a strategic concern since 2016 when all of its 1,150 branches at the time were interconnected using a cloud-based system (ADB, 2018). Information supporting strategic and operational planning was greatly facilitated. As the President noted, 'previously I had to wait almost until the end of the month to understand the performance, audited status of the institution, profitability, portfolio quality, etc.' It also enabled growth of its loan portfolio from two products (business loans and water and sanitation loans) to nine products, including the financing of education, housing and agriculture, also facilitating expansion into remote areas, e.g. to Itbayat in the northern province of Batanes and to Sitangkai in the southern-most municipality.

ASA's schedule of digitalisation acknowledged its importance to critical stakeholders significant to its future development strategy, including the government, the Asian Development Bank (ADB) and the Rural Bankers Association of the Philippines (RBAP), the latter representing 454 member banks. These banks all accept digitalisation as a critical facilitator of business efficiency, financial inclusivity and sustainable development impact. The Philippines' government have highlighted the centrality of digitalisation to economic development by introducing key national initiatives to facilitate regulation and security in the digital revolution. These include a national identity system and the mandatory registration of SIM cards to prevent spam text messages and scams. These digitalisation initiatives could give banks greater access to clients of microfinance services and therefore MFIs need to understand advantages and limitations created by the process of digitalisation for their current and potential customer bases.

In September 2022, ASA established a technical office with a dedicated head whose brief is to manage the development of a comprehensive digital system, including internal training and associated change agendas. The President recognises that, in some areas of the business, this can necessitate a paradigmatic shift in thinking, requiring reflection and monitoring from a holistic risk perspective. Digitalisation is seen as part of the 'bounce-forward' paradigm but brings with it certain risks, including how ASA clients will be embraced in a digitalised world without losing benefits that have been highly valued, particularly during emergencies.

The 2021 edition of the Microfinance Trends Barometer (MFC, 2021), focussing on the microfinance sector in Europe, concludes that the digitalisation processes of MFIs were not only sped up to meet urgent need but also the emergency response to COVID highlighted '... the challenges of low outreach, poor targeting and ineffectiveness of legacy information systems' (p. 3).

Nevertheless, the digitalisation process can be a double-edged sword. Whilst it supports innovation in products, services and opportunities for improved financial inclusion, it also introduces the risk of digital exclusion, breaches of privacy and client distancing. The MFC highlighted that new streamlined processes and use of social media helped more targeted marketing campaigns so that an '… MFI was able to reach out to a smaller number of well-profiled customers, which resulted in good quality loan applications with a high conversion rate' (2021, p. 3). In contrast, ASA's strategy and intent described earlier is based more on financial inclusion than selective targeting, supporting client resilience (including that of the very poor) through absorbing losses to ensure clients are able to sustain and bounce back in relation to their established businesses, or if not possible due to reduction in trade, to sustain themselves and their families until trade resumes. This strategic approach to improved financial inclusion is aligned with its approach to keeping clients central to its digitalisation strategy.

Murshid and Murshid (2022) described how COVID's lockdown and social physical distancing measures in Bangladesh allowed initiatives such as Brac's door-to-door campaign to sign up households to the 'bKash mobile wallet', a phone application linked to a Brac bank account that supports instant transfer of money between users. They expressed concern however that clients, previously reluctant to adopt digital payment services due to the potential loss of flexibility and privacy, the relatively high transaction costs, and the significant reliance on technology, could be pressured to adopt a fin-tech solution against their wishes. ASA Philippines' President emphasises that ASA clients will not be forced into a digital system until they understand and appreciate its benefits and become comfortable users. Manual and digital systems will run in parallel for at least 2–3 years, perhaps longer.

It is projected that only 30–35% of clients will embrace digitalisation, the remaining 70–65% will continue as before. Therefore 'conversion clients' as pilot groups will test the extent and characteristics of infrastructure required to transact digitally, whilst maintaining cash-based systems as appropriate.

Consistent with its 'development' ethos, ASA has a strategic focus broader than an increase in productivity through digital efficiencies. In fact, it sees significant risk to its mission by adopting a narrow efficiency perspective. It is aware that others intend to target a narrow, well-profiled clientele that do not need a single meeting to initiate and transact business. This is in line with the philosophy of the European microfinance sector identified above. However, ASA interprets its mission through the lens of development processes and particularly SDG1 concerning poverty alleviation. Its experience suggests that 50–60% of its clients require access to both microfinance and related services as assistance to meet their development goals. To achieve this, the President anticipates staff will continue to meet clients once a week to maintain their goal of being with their clients and understanding their needs. This is critical in an environment facing multiple and continuous emergencies.

Many MFIs have emphasised the need to support client digital business skills, requiring education of clients to assist their access to a range of financial services and to use social media, e-commerce etc., in their own businesses. ASA would potentially seek partnerships with banks with similar development ethoses to achieve these ends and optimise client development opportunities. It cannot afford however that technological shifts contravene the essence of its mission and culture.

Although ASA's staff will require tailored skills to manage this staged transformation and bring clients along appropriately, published accounts of their experiences suggest that they have evolved capability to adapt and extend services as appropriate in dynamic, complex and demanding emergency environments (Tarafder & Custodio, 2017, 2018). In such environments, ASA's culture has encouraged employees to view changes in ASA's service to clients, including nuanced CCS activities, as a normal adaptation of its development mission and their own roles. Bolton and Landells (2017) have noted that sensitivity to change challenges in dynamic and turbulent environments requires leadership and cultural characteristics that can harness emergent opportunities, identify and manage risk more holistically (particularly important in this instance is that risk is shared between stakeholders), synergise and critique dynamic information sources and, most importantly, leverage knowledge generated through dynamic interactions with salient internal and external stakeholders (pp. 76–77).

An additional issue for ASA is to ensure that leadership and culture reflect support for the development of resilience qualities and resiliency processes for itself and its clients. Evidence suggests that ASA is well down this path, reflected in its pursuit of a transformational approach which remains consistent with its mission and values, and thus potentially in 'bounce-forward' mode. In relation to digitalisation, the President emphasises that ASA's approach will continue to demonstrate to clients that organisational efficiency is being pursued to support client benefit. Being with your clients in COVID had the effect of increasing client trust and expanding business. This increase in business continued in 2022, to an extent that business targets had been met in the 10th month. Consistent with this approach, a debate arose around what percentage of loan disbursements might be allocated in the form of zero interest loans, thus optimising the level of support to clients whilst maintaining ASA's commercial sustainability. As the President stated, the intention is that 'as we do better, we give more subsidy to clients', reflecting the 'development' goals of the organisation. This is also consistent with his concern that the strategic focus on digitalisation be in the context of creating efficiencies and effective services that transparently benefit clients.

5. PRACTICING RESILIENCY IN EMERGENCY CONDITIONS

The scenarios described above suggest that in addressing emergency conditions the design and structure of organisational culture has been critical in developing coping capability for both individuals and the organisation. The model below (Fig. 2) captures the importance of organisational culture in providing support for resilient behaviour in emergencies. The culture manifests consistency across purpose, values and capability in emergency environments to create an adequate

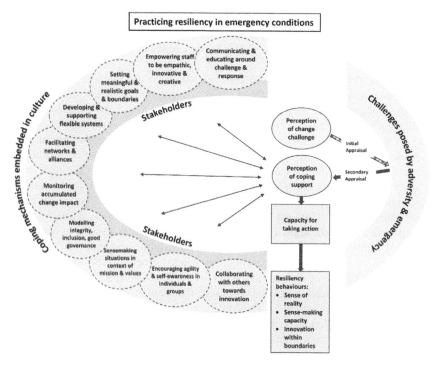

Fig. 2.   Practising Resiliency in Emergency Conditions.

level of trust and certainty that the organisation is ready and resourced to survive, bounce back or transform its business model and bounce forward, when and as appropriate to meet client needs and expectations in shifting and dynamic ecosystems.

The resiliency model above not only details a culture of resiliency as exemplified here, but it also demonstrates how clients dynamically perceive and access support (in this case from ASA services) to give them confidence and opportunity to practice resilient behaviours in emergency contexts. This is in line with Panter-Brick and Leckman's (2013) conclusion that resilience can also be seen as process by which individuals sustain a state of well-being through harnessing resources. To demonstrate this dynamism, the model leverages coping and resiliency literature relevant to emergency management to explain how stakeholders (in this case mainly ASA's clients and staff) initially perceive change challenges confronting them as employees or entrepreneurs and how their secondary or subsequent appraisal and coping behaviour is shaped by their perceptions of support available from ASA (as a microfinance provider and deliverer of social services relevant to social and economic development). It is seen as providing insights into all four types of resiliency scenarios described in Fig. 1, i.e. decline, survive, spring back and bounce forward when facing adversity, albeit that these scenarios will be contextually different. The model might also stimulate identification of additional factors relevant to client and staff well-being demonstrated in different contexts requiring resilient behaviour.

6. CONCLUSION

This chapter has noted that turbulence faced by many organisations has regenerated debates around organisational resilience and even warranted government promotion of organisational education around different manifestations of resiliency as responses to turbulence and uncertainty. Fig. 1 identifies different forms of acceptance, survival, spring back and bounce forward behaviours commonly identified in the literature, as a basis for better understanding the case of a microfinance company in the Philippines. Specifically, we apply this framework to explore its journey in the broader context of its reflection on its mission in dealing with the stark reality of constant emergency environments, this experience having shaped its interpretation of its mission of helping the poor use microfinance services to develop and preserve assets in such environments. A core focus of ASA has been to develop appropriate and aligned forms of resiliency across its stakeholders through a culture that supports various forms of accommodation, adaptation, survival, regeneration and transformation as appropriate to fulfilling its mission.

In addition to considering ASA's experience against these various resiliency scenarios, we also review it through the lens of coping and resiliency thinking to better understand how it has identified its client needs and supported clients operate more resiliently. Fig. 2 suggests that the unprecedented nature of emergencies will be complex and dynamic and that clients will be better prepared for resilient responses to adversity if they have confidence that their microfinance agent prioritises and understands their needs by 'being with them' in emergencies and demonstrates pre-planning for emergencies and agile and flexible responses in the situation itself. Fig. 2 suggests features of culture that enable such a response.

It has been demonstrated that ASA has developed this culture of client support by closely observing its clients' needs to withstand ongoing emergencies over many different types of adversity, causing it to reflect on its purpose and redefine its business as more than a microfinance business, rather one that needs to help its clients sustain development outcomes in adverse environments. To understand the dynamics of resiliency in achieving SDGs in local contexts requires appraisal of client needs and the strategy and culture underpinning agential interventions. This case illustrates the complex nature of local responses to achieving resiliency targets mentioned or implied in SDGs.

Finally, the chapter has described how ASA's response to resiliency creation has evolved towards a transformational model, this stage of development re-evaluating the nature of risk demonstrated over time in differing emergency situations, all of which have required ASA to intervene by providing services to contain the loss suffered by its clients. Provision of insurance services might cordon risk for both ASA and its clients. ASA would limit its exposure through its relief-activity/contingency fund and clients would be covered more comprehensively against business loss. Recognising the challenge for the vulnerable in managing the risks associated with the climate change emergency, UNICEF announced its 'Today and Tomorrow' initiative on 15 November 2022 which '... for the first time combines funding for immediate resilience and risk prevention programs for children today with risk transfer finance provided by the insurance market to help cope with future cyclones' (United Nations, 2022b). UNICEF's Children's Climate Risk Index estimated that 400 million children are currently at high exposure to cyclones. This focus on insurance as a feature of resilience-building appears consistent with ASA's thinking, innovation and creativity in addressing shared risks to itself and its clients through re-conceptualising its business in the broader context of development needs of its clients. This thinking seems to exemplify the willingness needed by organisations to review their businesses in the context of contribution to the achievement of SDGs at a local level in the face of ongoing and unpredictable adversity associated with climate change and currently by economic disruption caused by geo-political tensions, the combination of which has led the UN to predict deleterious impacts, especially for the poor and vulnerable such as food affordability and dire global food shortages in 2023 (United Nations, 2022c).

The ASA case study also identifies how the organisation is attempting to deal with tensions outlined by Bernards (2022b, p. 5) who describes lending to the poor as '...prepar[ing] the ground for the profitable deployment of finance capital, but ... typically driven not so much by the dictates of finance itself, but by fraught efforts to coax it into serving developmental ends. Unambiguous success stories are exceedingly rare'. In contrast, ASA appears to be undertaking transformative action to achieve its goals.

Given the huge risks to nations of the Global South, facing continuing and increasingly severe emergency situations, organisational transformation towards business models that reflect diverse forms of resilience-building seem to be worth consideration. Such an approach exemplifies the Brundtland report's message that we can no longer think in terms of predictable patterns of development and that we need new forms of conceptualising responses to sustainability challenges at global, national and local levels. We have focussed on ways of conceptualising and facilitating resilience behaviours at a local level as a means of achieving sustainable development nationally and globally, and highlighted associated complexity. Stakeholder collaboration based on common experience in emergencies has been identified as essential for transformational thinking, resilience building and increased organisational responsiveness to emergent stakeholder challenges in the pursuit of a sustainable development trajectory.

REFERENCES

ADB (Asian Development Bank). (2018). More Philippine rural banks, microfinance firms embrace digital technology for expansion. Retrieved from https://www.adb.org/news/features/philippine-rural-banks-microfinance-firms-digital-technology

Amabile, T. M. (1988). A model of creativity and innovation in organizations. *Research in Organizational Behavior, 10*(1), 123–167.

Amabile, T. M., & Pratt, M. G. (2016). The dynamic componential model of creativity and innovation in organizations: Making progress, making meaning. *Research in Organizational Behavior, 36*, 157–183. doi:10.1016/j.riob.2016.10.001

ASA Philippines Foundation. (2021). *ASA Annual Report 2021*. Retrieved from https://asaphil.org/reports/annual-reports/

ASA Philippines Foundation. (2022a). Client Community Services. Retrieved from https://asaphil.org/corporate-social-responsibility.aspx

ASA Philippines Foundation. (2022b). ACCS Reports 001-22 (Oct 3) and 003-22 (Nov 7).

Assarkhaniki, Z., Rajabifard, A., & Sabri, S. (2020). The conceptualisation of resilience dimensions and comprehensive quantification of the associated indicators: A systematic approach. *International Journal of Disaster Risk Reduction, 50*, 101840.

Bahadur, A., Lovell, E., Wilkinson, E., & Tanner, T. (2015). *Resilience in the SDGs: Developing an indicator for Target 1.5 that is fit for purpose*. ODI Briefing, August, 1–7.

BCG (Boston Consulting Group). (2021, May 18). Perspectives on building a resilient company. Retrieved from https://www.bcg.com/publications/2021/perspectives-on-resilience-in-business

Berkes, F., Colding, J., & Folke, C. (Eds.). (2003). *Navigating social–ecological systems: Building resilience for complexity and change*. Cambridge: Cambridge University Press.

Bernards, N. (2022a, November 17). COP27: Why a new insurance scheme for climate-vulnerable countries is a bad idea. *The Conversation*. Retrieved from https://theconversation.com/cop27-why-a-new-insurance-scheme-for-climate-vulnerable-countries-is-a-bad-idea-194704

Bernards, N. (2022b). *A critical history of poverty finance: Colonial roots and neo-liberal failures*. London: Pluto Press.

Bolton, D. (2004). Change, coping and context in the resilient organisation. *Mt Eliza Business Review, 7*(1), 56–66.

Bolton, D., & Landells, T. (2017). Decision-making as sustainable leadership: The Garbage Can revisited. In G. Eweje & R. Bathurst (Eds.), *CSR, sustainability, and leadership*. New York, NY: Routledge. doi:10.4324/9781315525976

Bolton, D., & Landells, T. (2021). Bruntland and after: Through commitment to capability. In D. Crowther & S. Seifi (Eds.), *The Palgrave handbook of corporate social responsibility*. London: Palgrave Macmillan Cham. doi:10.1007/978-3-030-42465-7

Brooks, B., Curnin, S., Owen, C., & Boldeman, J. (2019). New human capabilities in emergency and crisis management; from non-technical skills to creativity. *Australian Journal of Creativity Management, 34*(4), 23–30.

Convergences. (2021). *Impact finance Barometer 2021*. Paris: Convergences. Retrieved from https://www.convergences.org/en/impact-finance-barometer/

Coutu, D. L. (2002). How resilience works. *Harvard Business Review, 80*(5), 46–50.

Department of Home Affairs. (2020). Organisational resilience. Retrieved from https://www.organisationalresilience.gov.au

Folke, C., Carpenter, S. R., Walker, B., Scheffer, M., Chapin, T., & Rockström, T. (2010). Resilience thinking: Integrating resilience, adaptability and transformability. *Ecology and Society, 15*(4), 20. doi:10.5751/ES-03610-150420

Hamel, G., & Välikangas, L. (2003). The quest for resilience. *Harvard Business Review, 81*(9), 52–63.

Jones, L., & d'Errico, M. (2019). Whose resilience matters? Like-for-like comparison of objective and subjective evaluations of resilience. *World Development, 124*, 104632. doi:10.1016/j.worlddev.2019.104632

Lazarus, R., & Folkman, S. (1984). *Stress, appraisal and coping*. New York, NY: Springer Publishing.

Medeiros, K., Partlow, P., & Mumford, M. (2014). Not too much, not too little: The influence of constraints on creative problem solving. *Psychology of Aesthetics, Creativity, and the Arts, 2*(8), 198–210.

MFC (Micro Finance Centre). (2021). The MFC Microfinance Trends Barometer. Retrieved from https://mfc.org.pl/mfc-barometer-of-trends-in-microfinance-2021-edition/

Murshid, N. S., & Murshid, N. (2022). "Innovations" during COVID-19: Microfinance in Bangladesh. *Affilia: Feminist Inquiry in Social Work, 37*(2), 232–249. doi:10.1177/08861099211054024

Owen, C., Hayes, P., Brooks, B., Scott, C., & Conway, G. (2018). Evidence to support incident management team capability. *Australian Journal of Emergency Management*, *33*(3), 44–49.

Panter-Brick, C., & Leckman, J. F. (2013). Editorial Commentary: Resilience in child development-Inter-connected pathways to well-being. *Journal of Child Psychology and Psychiatry*, *54*, 333–336. doi:10.1111/jcpp.12057

Pelling, M. (2010). *Adaptation to climate change: From resilience to transformation*. London and New York, NY: Routledge.

Riecke, J. (2016). Responding to tragedy: ASA Philippines and Typhoon Haiyan. Retrieved from https://www.centerforfinancialinclusion.org/responding-to-tragedy-asa-philippines-and-typhoon-haiyan

Rockström, J., Steffen, W., Noone, K., Persson, Å., Chapin III, F. S., Lambin, E. F., ... Foley, J. A. (2009). A safe operating space for humanity. *Nature*, *461*, 472–475. doi:10.1038/461472a

Sachs, W. (2017). The sustainable development goals and *Laudato si'*: Varieties of post-development. *Third World Quarterly*, *38*(12), 2573–2587. doi:10.1080/01436597.2017.1350822

Siebeneck, L. K., & Cova, T. J. (2012). Spatial and temporal variation in evacuee risk perception throughout the evacuation and return-entry process. *Risk Analysis*, *32*(9), 1468–1480.

Taggar, S. (2002), Individual creativity and group ability to utilize individual creative resources: A multilevel model. *Academy of Management Journal*, *45*(2), 315–330. doi:10.2307/3069349

Tarafder, K. H., & Custodio, B. (2017). Built-in sustainable CSR program in a microfinance institution: Experience of ASA Philippines Foundation. OIDA international. *Journal of Sustainable Development*, *10*(3), 23–34. Retrieved from https://ssrn.com/abstract=3046532

Tarafder, K. H., & Custodio, B. B. (2018). Microfinance in a conflict zone: The Battle of Marawi. *OIDA International Journal of Sustainable Development*, *11*(9), 11–24. Retrieved from https://ssrn.com/abstract=3286480

Tarafder, K. H., Habib, M., & Bolton, D. (2022). Maintaining Growth and Community Service during COVID-19 at ASA Philippines Foundation. *7th European Conference on Microfinance* (20–22 June). Yunus Centre for Social Business and Health, Glasgow Caledonian University, UK.

United Nations. (2022a, November 12). Adapt or starve: COP27 spotlights agriculture challenges and solutions in the face of climate change. *UN News*. Retrieved from https://news.un.org/en/story/2022/11/1130517

United Nations. (2022b, November 16). UNICEF launches new child-focused climate initiative to head off disasters. *UN News*. Retrieved from https://news.un.org/en/story/2022/11/1130652?utm_source=UN+News+-+Newsletter&utm_campaign=10d5ad7deb-EMAIL_CAMPAIGN_2022_11_16_12_23&utm_medium=email&utm_term=0_fdbf1af606-10d5ad7deb-107858253

United Nations. (2022c, November 16). Act together now, to prevent 'raging food catastrophe' next year: Guterres. *UN News*. Retrieved from https://news.un.org/en/story/2022/11/1130607?utm_source=UN+News+-+Newsletter&utm_campaign=b09ffc071f-EMAIL_CAMPAIGN_2022_11_15_04_53&utm_medium=email&utm_term=0_fdbf1af606-b09ffc071f-107858253

van Knippenberg, D., & Hirst, G. (2015). A cross-level perspective on creativity at work: Person-in-situation interactions. In J. Zhou, M. A. Hitt, & C. Shalley (Eds.), *The Oxford handbook of creativity, innovation and entrepreneurship* (pp. 225–244). Oxford: Oxford Library of Psychology.

Walker, B. H., Holling, C. S., Carpenter, S. R., & Kinzig, A. (2004). Resilience, adaptability and transformability in social–ecological systems. *Ecology and Society*, *9*(2), 5. Retrieved from http://www.ecologyandsociety.org/vol9/iss2/art5

Worldometer. (2022). Philippines. Retrieved from https://www.worldometers.info/coronavirus/country/philippines

Ziai, A. (2017). Post-development 25 years after *The Development Dictionary*. *Third World Quarterly*, *38*(12), 2547–2558. doi:10.1080/01436597.2017.1350822

SOCIAL ASPECTS OF TELEWORK AND ORGANISATIONS DURING AN UNFORESEEN CRISIS

Ana Maria Davila Gomez and David Crowther

ABSTRACT

The recent pandemic has seen a considerable shift in patterns of work, some of which may well be permanent. One of these changes is the increase in teleworking, which has risen considerably in use. Some of this change has been at the insistence of employers while some have been desired by employees. This has had many implications and possible consequences for the future, and even for the mental health of those involved or affected by this change to home working. In this chapter, these changes and their implications are explored in detail, with a prognosis being considered.

Keywords: Home working; transparency; domestic conflict; mental health; learning; work-life balance

1. INTRODUCTION

Many of us who, before the pandemic, belonged to the culture of on-site work favouring human interaction, have had to accommodate to a telework model. This has come during the past two-and-a-half years, mostly as a societal necessity aimed at taking care of the health of individuals, either to answer to a governmental mandate or as an organisational choice. For some of us, as academics who work bound by a social contract with an educational institution, this has come with consequences for our family life and, in some cases affecting, not only our mental health but also our family members. Before the pandemic there was the possibility for distance learning, but it was not the norm. Some universities have used that modality in the past offering some courses or programmes. Before the pandemic, distance learning programmes were rather rare in primary or

Corporate Resilience

Developments in Corporate Governance and Responsibility, Volume 21, 33–52

Copyright © 2023 by Emerald Publishing Limited

All rights of reproduction in any form reserved

ISSN: 2043-0523/doi:10.1108/S2043-052320230000021002

secondary education. That was also the case for many office workers worldwide in other kinds of organisations who worked mostly on-site. With this reality, the aim of our chapter is to explore how this transformation at work affects employees' mental and social health, and in consequence, identify some challenges for managers of these transformed organisations, in order to take into account their responsibility towards the social component of their employees' health.

As such, we reflect about the consequences for individuals that a transformation of their work modality and alternate work arrangements bring to their personal life, and consequently, the challenges for the maintaining of the well-being of employees. Many of these challenges arise for decision-makers (managers, owners) of transformed organisations, but also, for determination and self-evaluation of employees in terms of what is worth or not to accept from those in power inside these transformed organisations.

We develop our reflection as follows: (1) We contextualise the work modality transformation inside a societal, worldwide, pandemic situation, which was not predicted, nor foreseen. (2) We explore how the telework modality became mandatory in many societies for many organisations, and how, even after various governmental measures were lifted (by February to April 2022), this alternate work arrangement ended up being favoured, despite evidence of the need for socialising at work, or even taking into account the increase of domestic violence during long periods of time isolated at home while teleworking. (3) We analyse how inside these reshaped work modalities, abuse and harassment arrive when coalitions in control of information and power behave inhumanly. (4) We discuss about how power, fear and unfairness are present in telework modality. (5) As telework became more and more popular, we explore how, theoretically, the discipline of management could offer some aid for managers, in terms of human values, identifying the suffering of employees, adapting working chores to favour alternative arrangements, and not exclusively telework, and offering alternatives to employees. Finally, we conclude by claiming the need for human values in managers in order to take into account the well-being of employees (socially and psychologically) as a component of the social pillar of sustainability.

Methodologically, we follow a qualitative exploratory approach (Maxwell, 2013) in which we value an ethnography based on observations (Rouleau, 2013) method and a critical humanistic view (Aktouf, 1987) for analysing organisational phenomena. As we develop our discussion, some time we take evidence from what we have lived as professors during these past two-and-a-half years, comparing the way of living before the pandemic, as well as evidence from what we have lived as citizens of societies that have reshaped (temporarily or not) aspects of its societal life such as children education and business permits to allow or not operations. All along the way, we serve ourselves of public information of some governmental websites or scientific documentation.

2. A TRANSFORMING SOCIETY – A RESHAPING OF ORGANISATIONS

It has been already 2 years and some months since many organisations had to adjust their everyday life due to the magnitude of the pandemic. Some organisations have changed internally, others externally, some have closed their doors during long periods of time, and others have gone bankrupt as a consequence of the pandemic, as it has been the case for several small and medium-sized enterprises that lack the financial leverage to sustain themselves (the financial position specially salaries and inventory). In other areas, hospitals, for instance, had to operate well above their capacity and often collapsing due to and overcrowding of patients, which indicated a need for additional funding as well as medical equipment, coming mostly from additional funding from government sources (taxpayers' money or even national debt increase). It ended up in a health system crisis.

Some of the organisational changes came as a vital necessity for the survival of human beings, as it is the case for hospitals, while others came as a consequence of governmental mandates trying to protect lives as a result of the pandemic. Some organisations were forced to expand while others needed to constrain or to reorganise, and other organisations were compelled to shut down operations. With this wide variety of consequences for organisations, also came other problems such as employment retention, loss of jobs and consequently a decrease in family income, and as such, it is detrimental to the quality of life of numerous people; increasing cases of burnout on nurses and doctors; increasing cases of domestic violence and abuse, as people were isolated by governmental policies orders of mandatory lockouts and curfews, demanding to work from home whenever the information technology (IT) allows it, as well as for children to study from home for several months. Some events and documentation of these consequences can be traced – some history – and consulted on the public websites of various governmental institutions (i.e. Gouvernement du Québec, 2021, 2022; Government of Canada, 2022a; INSPQ – Québec, 2020; Ontario, 2022a; Public Health Ontario, 2022), or even in academic research (i.e. Université de Sherbrooke, 2022 – conducted by Généreux et al.) and denounces made by media (i.e. Le Journal du Québec, 2022).

For instance, the Government of Quebec imposed two curfews (see MSSS – Québec, 2022). Contrary to that situation, Quebec's neighbour, Ontario (see Ontario, 2022a), decided not to impose a curfew, but to implement instead other educational measures for law-abiding citizens. Nevertheless, comparing the dates in which both provinces declared distance learning as mandatory for primary and secondary students, Quebec relied less in that measure than Ontario (see some history of events and mandates at Ontario, 2022a; Public Health Ontario, 2022). In that part, various allocutions of the Quebec Government explained that counting less and less on distance learning for children will improve social and psychological health in both children and parents (see Gouvernement du Québec, 2022b).

Many societies, countries or even states or provinces (depending on particular political structures) had tried to address the need for 'continuity' of organisations, private and public, in order to procure a stable or decent quality of living of their citizens. Every society act, of course, depending on their wealth, but also, depending on the way that they consider as fair and honourable for their people. In Canada, for instance, not only the federal government offered financial help to private businesses touched with less revenues or even zero revenues (e.g. gyms, bars during, either lockdowns, or while compelled to close, whereas businesses of other kinds were able to stay open). It is also true that many business financial losses are also the consequence of the accommodation of societies, as lockouts were temporary; therefore, individuals had the choice to isolate (including entire families) hitting hard on businesses that operate in a one-on-one approach, or even, many shop magazines had to compete with big corporations dealing with online shopping, as many clients did not want to enter in contact directly with people.

The first 2 years of pandemic showed us two phases of living with the crisis, as a society, which entails two different approaches on governmental mandates and individuals' choices. The first one occurred while scientists worldwide were trying to create a vaccine, and the second one emerged while a certain percentage of a society's population received their second vaccine. The first phase, with no vaccine protection, lasted from March 2020 to almost August 2021, when, for some societies, a big part of the population had already received a second vaccine (i.e. in case of Quebec, where a 70–80% of 12-year-olds and above had two doses of vaccine).[1] The second phase, to us, is still ongoing in various parts of the world since kids of 5 years old and above were able to get a second vaccine since December 2021. An interim period within the two phases took place between August 2021 and December 2021. A relatively short period of time, where supposedly, having more than 70% of the population of 18 years old and above vaccinated, would allow to 'reclaim' a normal life. That was the spirit; that was the hope. In general, the majority of businesses re-opened, public services were again offering a one-on-one approach, hospitals would see a decrease on patients suffering from COVID-19, and primary, secondary and post-secondary educational institutes would function 100% in-person again, among other society measures procuring social and psychological well-being.

However, as history showed, a new COVID-19 variant emerged making it difficult to control, jeopardising, not only unvaccinated people but also vaccinated people with other health issues, as well as COVID-19 side effects, and children (who waited until the end of December to get their first shoot of the vaccine). Again, health policies call for new mandatory governmental measures, and as such, in various societies, by the end of October or mid-November 2021 where certain business were closed temporarily, distance learning was reinstated at various levels of education, new rules of social distancing and isolation

---

[1]See some history of events and mandates at Gouvenerment du Québec (2022a) and MSSS – Québec (2022).

reappeared, as well as a new short curfew period. During this transitional time, from phase one to phase two, in various countries, kids from 5 to 12 years old were vaccinated and generated protests regarding these measures, worldwide. Finally, by February, and up to May 2022, governments started to drop some measures showing a plan of lifting restrictions to the population.[2] Nevertheless, governments are now shifting their norms and shifting to the population responsibility of their own well-being to individuals by taking care of their own safety, by applying social distancing measures, personal hygiene and total isolation (in the case of testing positive or presenting symptoms of the illness), as well as asking businesses and public institutions to do their part in cleaning and sanitising, as their own choice.

During the first phase, there was fear about health issues, even arising questions about the survival of humanity. During the second phase, there is hope and decision for living a fulfilled life. Sometimes, we do not appreciate a good quality of life that includes liberty, until we lose the things that we have taken for granted. This comes in all spheres of our life: being able to be outside, sharing with family and friends, being served as costumers in businesses on a person-to-person basis, going to parks, travelling, taking a plane, going to the beach, dining at a restaurant, seeing our children happy as they play with their classmates, free to interact in a playground, allowing our children to visit the grandparents and having fun with them, among others. Many of these real-life situations were restricted, or even banned at different times through this period of more than 2 years.

At the same time, these families' social life was affected not only because of governmental mandates seeking to protect human lives, but also due to the way in which organisations were transformed as a consequence of the pandemic (either by owners' choice or by government mandatory norms and regulations). New working methods arose, bringing about significant changes. Among some of the work-related changes, telework had the biggest impact. In order to comply with the government's social distance policy, many organisations worldwide had to transform their ways of work, their work spaces and, consequently, transforming indirectly the daily life of households. Workers had to accommodate, at the same time, two desks (in the case of two working parents) as well as, at least, one or two desks for children in which distance learning was required. Overcrowded spaces at home and parents forced to multi-tasking, as workers, tutors as well as caring and supervising for their children, this situation generated a new dynamic of the traditional way of living for families.

Were the new work spaces and family transformations swiftly accepted? How difficult was to adapt to these transformations? Were there some unwanted experiences? How did the role of managers helped to improve or to worsen these social experiences? How managerial responsibility is at stake here?

---

[2] See *Gouvernement du Québec* (2022a, 2022b).

3. LACK OF TRANSPARENCY, CONTROL AND HARASSMENT

When the time comes to reflect about the appropriateness of the practice of management during these times of unforeseen crisis, as academics in the discipline of management, we question ourselves about the effectiveness of managerial tools that managers of all types of organisations have at their disposal to face this crisis. We wonder if the tools available before the crisis have evolved or have been implemented while leading with the crisis in a simultaneous manner.

Hence, following the theoretical tradition of business ethics (see Solomon, 1998; Waddock & McIntosh, 2009), we reflect about the consequences of measures of some managerial behaviours during the COVID-19 crisis. To us, some of the daily crucial experiences during these transformations at work were the lack of transparency towards employees (disclosure of critical information regarding employees' concerns). Ever since the principles of governance have been introduced broadly in managerial practice, transparency is considered by some authors as a crucial aspect for workers (i.e. Aras & Crowther, 2009). To comply with ethical behaviour, the information disclosed by an organisation needs to be truthful and pertinent to stakeholders and governments. However, an organisation, a stakeholder or a manager could hide particular information arguing that it is not mandatory to disclose and still be transparent. Sometimes, the argument revolves around the manager showing only information considered compulsory in different society's instances; as such, any additional report is considered additional information for the stake of collaboration and not really a legal obligation.

What could be hidden? Anything going from informal conversations at work to internal norms and politics framing daily work. For instance, a manager could instruct junior officers to provide incentives for employees seeking a productivity increase, throughout, for instance, social recognition, or monetary stimulus. Sometimes, these practices, also known as external motivators in the academic field of organisation behaviour (see Morin, 2008), achieve an immediate response of productivity increase from employees. However, over time, as they do not represent an internal motivation (meaning or existential significance), they fail to work when they are applied repetitively among the same employees. Monetary gratification becomes relatively attractive for employees, as human beings who can reflect about their actions and consequences for their lives as a whole start to realise that in order to obtain financial compensations, or recognition, they are asked to accept work overload, which implies not only more physical and mental efforts but also giving up quality time spent before at home with family and friends.

In addition to the transformation of the family household living in the midst of telework comes the question of employees forced by circumstances, to learn how to operate new technologies, new software platforms, and also to continue to be as performant and productive as they were before the crisis. For this, many educational institutions offer online information to professors about teaching online. Nonetheless, there is a paradox, among many others; if all of a sudden, a professor who works with IT strictly for e-mail, or Word, how is he or she going to take a distance learning course? How is he or she going to be performant, all of a sudden, changing his or her pedagogical platforms almost immediately? There was no time for a profound conversion that would adapt to new pedagogical methods as telework was mandatory for the first 3 months; even the IT office was not available as the universities were closed. At the end, many professors with so little knowledge in pedagogy through IT were lost in translation, asking explanations via e-mail to the IT departments that formerly were always available offering personalised attention. Students had no choice but to interact with professors unable to offer a good communication. Moreover, almost immediately, faculties and academic councils inside the universities demanded to professors that these new courses developed with new pedagogical methods should be as performant and productive as they were former to the crisis. As such, workload increases because the normal activity of teaching now involves more than two tasks: the normal teaching, the transformation process plus the learning process. As a consequence, the level of stress increased as well as left mental health issues.

This dynamic was not exclusive for universities; it was also present in many businesses. Less people at work will result in a decrease in productivity, and as a solution, managers divide the workload of the absent employees to those who are present. As such, the employees present suffer now of work overload, most probably resulting in an increase of sick leave for mental fatigue in the near future. Thus, managers start stressing up as they are unable to answer to the organisation with their usual quotes of productivity, and in consequence, for some employees present at work, it derives into a breeding ground for violence, harassment and conflicts in the day-to-day operations. Thus far, our observations confirm what some authors (i.e. Feuvrier, 2014; Zaitseva & Chaudat, 2016) stated as sources of moral and psychological harassment at work.

During the telework mandatory periods, employees never imagined that their workload and family home space would change as much as it did. However, governments and organisations did not have to wait 2 years to try to alleviate the crumping or some of the unfairness in the treatment towards telework employees that we describe during the following pages. To this, for instance, the Canadian federal government, as well as the provincial Quebec government, gave teleworkers some tax credits for the years 2020 and 2021, in order to help them with some of the incurred costs of working at home (see Gouvernement of Canada, 2022b; Revenu Québec, 2022).

Evidence of these consequences was available during the first 2–3 months of the reshaped organisations.[3] Various evidences of the transformations were collected by employees and by unions, leading to an increasing level of demands. Thus, negotiations between directors, owners and unions took place, and in some

[3]For data about these evidences, see, for instance, *Université de Sherbrooke* (2022 –research conducted by Généreux et al.), Le Journal du Québec (2022) and INSPQ – Québec (2020).

cases, whenever accords were not attained, the justice system intervened to reach agreements up to this day.

Some countries and some organisations benefit from the privilege of these instances (unions, a robust justice system); nevertheless, that is not always the case. What happens then to employees who were not able to rely themselves on the assistance and support offered in these particular instances? In some developed countries, individuals could take their work demands directly to the justice system in their countries; however, that will take time and money.

When the abuse of employers became unbearable, these employees usually took sick days leave, or in some cases, the health system diagnosed those workers with burnout or mental health fatigue. With this, governmental programmes aid to pay, alongside with the organisations involved, for health insurance for the time established after medical consultation. For some of these employees, at the end of the sick leave, they go back to work, with a renewed energy and once again healthy mind and body. Nevertheless, for many of these employees, as they return to a workplace where nothing has changed in terms of managerial goals based exclusively in increasing productivity; hence the work climate and the organisational culture continue to be unchanged as it was before they left. They encounter the same work reality as when they left. At this point, on top of experiencing again the same work overload, new mental health problems arise as, for instance, depression or presenteeism, given the incapacity of organisations to at least alleviate working conditions, resulting in a spiral of constant emotional dissatisfaction affecting the private life of the employee (family, friends, among other aspects of life) as well as ineffective performance in the workplace. As such, our observations are consistent with what Duxbury and Higgins (2007) defined as the possibility of having negative interference of work in the private life.

And what is not transparent in the aforementioned example? In many countries, a social responsibility report is not mandatory, and whenever it is produced, it is the result of a managerial initiative. Even more, when produced, as it is mostly discretional, there is no format to follow. Every organisation may choose what to print in there, leaving important details behind, not showing a complete assessment of the real situation of the organisation. Hence, what you show and not show in a report you may purposely not mention the ways in which you have achieved productivity. However, reports mostly indicate improvements in the profitability of the project as well as performance and growth. We all know that in order to achieving higher performance levels, you need to increase productivity. However, workload increase on employees is not shown, regardless of the possibility to consult in the human resources archives of any organisation as they count absenteeism, financial costs of mental health leaves and indemnities. Other ways of knowing the cost of the employees' mental health are by the financial balances of insurance companies (which in many countries are open to public consultation by governmental mandate), in which it is possible to identify how much mental health has cost.

Repeatedly, examples of these kinds have been experienced by workers all around the world when telework was named as the magic solution in times of the pandemic. How and why? Let's refer some examples witnessed among the academia/university universe.

First, mental health issues at work appeared not only by means of workload increase, but they could also be triggered by new demands at work, by new ways of doing things. As mentioned by Saint-Leger and Beeler (2012), not feeling comfortable to do things differently many times obeys to a lack of some theoretical knowledge in a procedure; to our case, IT concepts, abilities and personal performance, not to mention lack of training. According to some authors in the field of psychology at work (e.g. Morin, 2008), organisations that facilitate training for employees through formal learning events and the development of abilities through practice and mentoring or coaching focussed in new working methods will benefit the employees as well as the organisation. By the same token, addressing intrinsic motivation implies that the employee needs to find a true meaning of what they are commanded to accomplish; as such, new theoretical and practical knowledge acquired by the individual (employee) need to be meaningful in order to render them useful for the remainder of the work contract. Contrary to financial bonus incentives (seen as extrinsic motivation), learning something meaningful makes part of the inner self of individuals and does not vanish plainly in the short term. To our case, based upon our observations, the meaning of learning new tasks comes also with the way in which this learning is commanded and implemented by means of the organisation. Sometimes, rejection comes not from the content of the new knowledge, but from the way in which it is imposed and how it facilitates the task.

As such, a growing discomfort among professors and students was evidenced during the telework transforming process, showing almost immediately that little training widely affected a teaching practice basically performed and dominated by face-to-face interaction where students and professors engage on a simulated IT synchronous interaction, as opposed to an asynchronous online interaction. Doing telework needs training. Teaching through IT needs two kinds of training: (1) In IT tools and (2) In IT pedagogical methods. Not every professor, not every student, not every university that changed its approach to distance education during the time of the pandemic had previously experienced on that matter, either in terms of knowledge and abilities to perform the task accordingly. When the change was declared 'temporarily' (there was no certainty of a time frame), some temporal adjustments were made for employees, i.e. professors, in terms of agreements of 'tolerance and flexibility' of the organisation regarding the performance of the course presentation. This could be the case of some fortunate professors who counted with a union that went to negotiate with the university administration. Unfortunately, that is not the case for many universities worldwide. With negotiations, and the managerial style of university directors, fast training for professors including tips of new pedagogical methods was delivered. As such, the model worked for some time, i.e. in some cases, 6 months, and in others up to 1 year. However, after 6 months, or a year, as the 'temporal' time frame agreement reached its end, tolerance and flexibility for professors' (employees) performance was terminated. In many cases, managers and directors considered they were generous enough in giving to employees (professors) 6 months for learning and to practice distance teaching. Therefore, distance courses will be evaluated upon the same criteria used for face-to-face courses. As such, managerial flexibility ended.

In some countries, or provinces, after 6 months, or even one-and-a-half years (in many cases, as the 1st and 2nd doses of the vaccine were available and some 60% of the population were already enlisted for their 2nd dose), governments demand universities to go to a 'hybrid format', in which some courses would be face-to-face, while others would be taught in a distance format. Therefore, who chooses which courses and ones in what format? What we have witnessed is that employees and middle managers (programme directors, deans, among others) handle a certain power act by applying their favouritism in assigning to each course the format they wanted. This is what Mintzberg (1982) call the coalition in power, and as in any political group, you, as employee, if you make part of the coalition, you get privileges, and if you do not make part of the coalition, you get whatever courses are left to assign.

In this dynamic, the abuse of power by those legally in power may generate various emotional reactions in different professors (as employees). For many employees, during the first 6 months, they felt alleviated by the fact of teaching from home while their kids had to take distance courses at primary schools and secondary levels. Almost everybody agreed to remain at home as scientific knowledge about the virus was little.

As time progressed, the consequences of telework, added to telelearning in kids, as well as the closure of many public and private amenities for diversion and leisure, compounding by the mounting worldwide evidence of increase in domestic violence, among other issues, led to growing intolerance among family members. For instance, research conducted by Généreux et al. at the University of Sherbrooke (Université de Sherbrooke, 2022) indicates that as a consequence of COVID-19 issues (e.g. isolation mandates, loss of jobs, telework, among others), violence against women committed by a partner increased in the province, and as such, for October 2021, 17.6% of women showed indices of violence/harassment (e.g. physical hurting, threats and insults).

It appeared as if many families did not know how to live 'enclosed' more than 2 weeks except during vacation time. For instance, early in the pandemic, the INSPQ – Québec (2020) reveals, as well as other government instances worldwide, this problem, arguing that not only women are victims of violence and harassment but also children, as they were obliged to witness their parents fighting (during periods of confinement mandates) as day-care centres were closed in many parts of the world during the first months of isolation. As mentioned before, home spaces were transformed to working stations and school stations; the comfort of homes was transformed into a multi-purposed space, creating discomfort and great pressure to accommodate to a place no longer feeling as home.

Furthermore, child psychologist and paediatricians witnessed that more children than even before were experiencing eating disorders and depression. In fact, the Quebec government acknowledged the issue (see *Gouvernement du*

Québec, 2021) and gave some guidelines and resources to parents through social programmes, as children were already experiencing anxiety and stress due to COVID-19. Hence, this government advocated, and in some cases took measures to boost for rapid reopening of face-to-face courses in primary schools, even before some businesses were allowed to do so. At the higher education level, directors wanted to open as well see (Gouvernement du Québec, 2021, 2022b).

As such, the 2-week intimate family living became 1 month, 2 months and then, in some provinces,[4] after 7 weeks of isolation, the government opened primaries schools with the choice for parents to send their kids to school or not. With this, accommodation and flexibility in the child evaluation of learning was stated by the government.

Thus, for many universities, professors and students, it became imperative to return to some face-to-face learning, as a means to perhaps escaping the pressure at home, or a way of performing a certain type of levelling while teaching a course, if a professor has been fortunate to be assigned a face-to-face course. Otherwise, teaching a distance course in the context of the hybrid model sanctioned by the government could entail in a bad evaluation of teaching, as not only the former evaluation criteria for face-to-face course was being applied but also new criteria regarding what is considering, from now on, a good quality of distance teaching. But it is precisely here where workload increase appears for professors in general, many times controlled by the aforementioned coalition in power. We all know that teaching, as any practice, needs practice, and experience, to become an art. In our first years as young professors, we learn, year after year, how to improve our abilities and consequently, in time, we perform better and better in our practice and we obtain better scores whenever our performance is evaluated. Hence, it is normal that changing our methods (i.e. IT tools and distance teaching) needs time for us to improve our performance. Nevertheless, directors and those among the coalition power only seek the performance indicator. This is not motivating, as it was evidenced by various professors (employees) in the education sector.[5]

Once again, some managers' lack of flexibility shows lack of human values/ qualities of tolerance, comprehension, empathy and support. And, if we talk about support, we talk undeniably about sustainability, most specifically, about its social component, as mental health and intrinsic motivation for the continuity of education in society is a moral duty (see Dewey, 1975) towards any population in any society.

Moreover, not only the lack of the aforementioned values/qualities is of concern but also the occurrence of psychological harassment[6] or moral

---

[4]As it was the case of Quebec (see some history at Gouvernement du Québec, 2022a).

[5]In fact, media present some data about this phenomenon in primary schools in Québec (i.e. Le journal du Québec, 2022).

[6]In Québec, the CNESST (*Comission des normes de l'équite de la santé et de la securité au travail*) acknowledge the psychological harassment in Quebec as a cause for distress at work (see CNESST – Québec, 2022).

intimidation (see Zaitseva & Chaudat, 2016) as we discuss it occurs from some among those inside the coalition in power, professors that do not belong in the circle of power. Intimidation and harassment have been documented and experienced by university professors while, for instance, they are being evaluated for promotions or merely evaluated in their teaching performances. For instance, a recent report of Statistics Canada (2021) containing pre-pandemic data (fall 2019) shows that at least 34% of women and 22% of men, professors at various post-secondary institutions in Canada, have declared they experienced at least one episode of harassment or violence at work (e.g. sexual and psychological harassment, verbal disrespect and threats, gender and racist bias, among others). This study also shows how these percentages are lower when compared to other professional workplaces (19% of women and 13% of men – referring by a previous Study conducted by Statistics Canada – 2016). The study also mentions that some of the harassment could have been transferred to distance learning (e.g. via e-mail, among others) as the country transitioned and came back various times between 2020 and 2022.

Nevertheless, as not every person is equal, for some professors and students, the return to face-to-face activities was not good, mostly for young students with babies at home or for some professors who felt very comfortable and knowledgeable with the IT tools and IT pedagogical methods. To other professors who live in one city and work in another, this new way of teleworking was fantastic. In either case, in some provinces, or countries, studies of the consequences for mental health and the need for socialisation among children, adolescents and young adult students indicate that education need to resume with the face-to-face model, not entirely 100%, but incrementally. In the interim, since the first closure from the pandemic (by March 2000), in some occasions, but very briefly, governments in various provinces,[7] countries, relied again in isolation policies, given the factor of some new very contagious variants of the viruses, among others.

Inside these changes are employees as a stakeholder able to participate, or not, in planning or defining the changes of their own work? Up to what extent is there imposition versus flexibility, or even freedom at work?

4. POWER, INFORMATION AND COALITION IN POWER

As presented before, in the transformation of universities it applies what Mintzberg (1982) indicated regarding how a dominant coalition in power in the organisation drives the way in which the organisation's decision are taken.

According to Mintzberg (1982), an individual does not need to belong to the formal hierarchy in order to obtain power or favours. The individual, at any hierarchical level, only need to belong to the informal political group in power. In this case, based on our ethnography and observations (Rouleau, 2013) of how telework transformed academia, we identify how different professors belonging

[7]For instance, in the case of Quebec, see some history of mandates at Gouvernement du Québec (2022a).

to the political coalition in power gain favours in terms of courses attributed to them, and mostly in terms of pedagogical modalities (in presence or distance learning) as well as in class schedules. For those who do not belong to the collation in power, courses are scarce and not necessarily fitted to the principle of 'family-working' conciliation, even though this social principle for societal progress has been thoroughly taught in our management programmes for more than two decades now. This incoherence between what we teach and what we practice in various of our administration faculties indicates an abuse of power. An example of the previous is a lack of transparency inside the daily organisation's dynamics.

At the same time, for those obtaining favours and privileges while belonging to the dominant coalition, work life is not necessarily full of freedom. The prices to pay come from the orders given from the leaders of the coalition with the purpose of calling favours later. Examples of these may include to evaluate other professor's researches as not scientifically valid, to punish or fire other professors who do not comply with the newly transformed courses 100% relying on IT pedagogical methods, or even more, to use power to put pressure among the institutional decision-makers to introduce some procedures that normalise and mandate ways of teaching that are more adequately measurable than when it was during the time of face-to-face interaction.

In addition, the coalition in power has the right to seek for experts in the IT department of organisations as they may have the answer to other ways of controlling employees. Yes, it is true that during the pandemic, telework helped greatly with health issues, but at the same time, once employees open their laptops at home to work and enter the remote office net, there is a register of each and every time they enter. There is a log register of how many times the employee entered and used any software application of their intranet. There are also ways for IT experts to calculate the time a remote employee was connected but not using the software of the intranet. In sum, with ITs, the control of employees' activities while at work became easier but also abusive. Previously, while working in the company premises of any organisation, it was understood that people in cubicles had the right to stand up, to go to the bathroom, to go for lunch, to have coffee breaks etc. There was here also an understanding that even someone seated in their cubicle, just staring at the computer keyboard, could be thinking, reflecting about the work, or the project, or even being creative or innovative. Nowadays, with the forced transformation of the space work, it is easier to over-control the time a telework person spends in front of the computer. By running algorithms, it is not difficult to calculate the productive time of a person in telework. Thus, the metaphor of the prison presented by Foucault (1975) in his radical humanism illustrate very well how over-technologised organisations, more than ever, may over-control the productivity of their workforce.

In order to confront this abuse at work, some governments start to legislate some laws to protect at least the schedule of family time for employees, as it is the case of the recent 'Written Policy on Disconnecting from Work' (see Ontario, 2022b) in the province of Ontario. Nonetheless, as it happens in a novel, employers fought back, and recently Ontario adopted another 'Written Policy on

Electronic Monitoring of Employees' (see Ontario, 2022c) in which the companies that use software of surveillance on telework employees may do so as long as they warn their employees of that act. Both written policies apply for companies of 25 employees and more. In contrast, as explained by some media,[8] this tactic did not work properly in the provinces of Quebec, Alberta and British Columbia because data disclosure is protected under privacy laws. In fact, in Québec there is the *Act Respecting the Protection of Personal Information in the Private Sector* (see Légis Québec, 2022a) and the *Act Respecting Access to Documents Held by Public Bodies and the Protection of Personal Information* (see Légis Québec, 2022b).

Are we doing better as societies, or are we just using some of the admirable advances of science and technology to enforce power, or even more, to establish a more modern form of slavery at work? To this, some authors had already stated that it is common to find no humanly and respectful practices at work (e.g. Aktouf, 1987; Chanlat, 2007; Cvenkel, 2021; Davila-Gomez & Crowther, 2012).

As Alvesson (2002) highlighted when talking about communication and power in organisations, the information that used to flow smoothly (supposedly destined to all employees) is now exclusive to the circle of power, transformed and re-scripted for the purpose of those in power.

In a more philosophical arena, these human behaviours can be experienced not only in university institutions but also in any kind of private or public organisation worldwide. We might assume that they occur less in democratic societies. However, that is not always the case. It is nevertheless more dangerous in those societies where the government who controls the information circulated to citizens because not only the information could be hidden, manipulated or transformed to justify governmental action, which in some cases, may result being immoral and inhuman to their own people and other societies. We enter as such into the arena of honesty and willingness of social progress, which can be seen as a top priority for any society's government, as well as in any public or private university institution. As expressed by Habermas (1971), communication gives us not only information but also a meaning to accept or to reject the orders of those in power. Thus, we argue that hidden information is also disinformation and creates doubt and discomfort. Not saying any is another form of lack of transparency. Being silent for those in power entails a human responsibility that is not achieved. While linking this concept with the idea of governance (either in the governmental society's statements, or a university institution), we identify that the components of transparency, responsibility and accountability are missing.

Why, an employee not belonging to the coalition in power would need to ask for strategic information about its organisation? It is supposed to already exist and to be shared beforehand to the stakeholders, to whom the employees are a vital part of it. Why, when employees not belonging to the coalition in power start to ask questions about the reshaping of their workstation and modalities of

---

[8]I.e., CBC News (2022).

teaching, they receive not clear answers, mostly evasive reactions, and in some cases, when employees become too persistent in their request, they could be even fired? Being fired and trying to demonstrate that it was the result of harassment coming from inside the organisation will cost money, time and energy. Yes, of course, many countries count with legislation against harassment at work; nevertheless, in many cases the investment to defend the cause comes from the individual (or in some countries, by law students in their last academic year who will not charge money – many cases with state financing that will be compensated only if the employee wins the legal battle). However, as we know by experiences in the past, defence attorneys for altruistic reasons, either for themselves, or for sympathy towards the victims, tend to accept causes of these kinds; at the end, despite leading a winning case with restitution of justice, there is always space for those in the coalition in power to regain control and continue with their mission.

In conclusion, are we slaves of the will of our managers (either administrators or owners)? If not, despite the fact that most societies worldwide advocate against slavery, where is the space for fairness and freedom of speech that includes trustworthy information, thus transparency, towards employees as stakeholders?

5. POWER AND FEAR – WHAT HOPE IS THERE FOR INTERNAL ORGANISATION'S FAIRNESS?

With power comes fear. Historically, many in power remain in power because of the fear of those below in the hierarchy. As described before, inside organisations, on occasions employees comply to some inconsistent or incoherent order, out of fear of being fired, or being radicalised, of not being able to escalate in the hierarchical pyramid or just out of fear for not belonging to the elite group of the coalition in power. To some extent, fears of these kinds are present when survival is at stake, in the case of societies where there are not enough means and welfare programmes to help families with no income, or even worse, when some societies worldwide would incarcerate those persons who step up and tell the truth altering the stability of the establishment.

Why do some of us submit to fear, while other show courage? Some educational scientist or psychologist could answer that inside every person, the different responses come as a result of an ongoing learning process that is cemented during infancy and later altered in adulthood mostly by drastic events. Piaget (1977a, 1977b) calls this the 'cognitive conflict' in which a person needs to accommodate its answers on a daily basis depending at the same time, in what the person knows already and what the person would incorporate as a new response. When new answers spontaneously arrive on top of past experiences, the conflict is resolved and the cognition process advances. However, these new answers are somehow anchored in what is taught as the truth by people in power. The problem relies in the fact that, since as parents and elementary teachers are our first sources of truth, these first lessons in life could be morally acceptable or not. What could happen if these sources are somehow untruthful, or partially truthful? Parents and teachers express ideas based in their set of beliefs, without knowing, in some cases, to what extent the contents they are teaching are morally, ethically or humanly acceptable.

In order to validate the nature thoughts, many parents and teachers had applied themselves a process of introspection. As explained by Kierkegaard (1813–1855), through introspection, in a spontaneous willing desire of becoming a better human being, a person could question the pertinence of knowledge, whereas another person has observed pleasure when this knowledge is applied towards others inflicting suffering. Why then, some people, after judging the good or the bad of knowledge, decide to continue believing (or make believe) in the bad way, while others decide to protest and change for good once for all? Hereby, Freud (1856–1939a, 1856–1939b) expressed that sometimes a person unconsciously 'accepts' suffering because this acceptance will protect the person against a more deeper uncomfortable suffering. For instance, an infant that cries or throws a tantrum in public and receives immediately a punishment (either physical or by means of prohibitions) could decide in future situations (i.e. adulthood) to accept physical, sexual or psychological abuse at work in order to avoid the suffering of being fired or being neglected to obtain a hierarchical promotion. As we already presented before, this internal acceptance of abuse can take many forms, coming from not making part of the coalition in power, to accept extra workload in order to increase productivity, to accept being over-controlled by IT gadgets, to accept the worst task at work etc.

Therefore, in order to contribute to a more humanly world, addressing the concerns of social elements of sustainable development, what could help to enlighten people at work to realise, or question, the morality of their tasks? What does the unforeseen crisis may teach us?

6. CONSEQUENCES OF HOME WORKING

Although much consideration of home working has been considered, it would be reasonable that some of the effects are only just starting to be noticed and the effects considered. For example, for many people working at home has been beneficial for being able to spend more time with the family and less time-commuting. It is important to realise however that a significant number of people live alone and home working has not been attractive because of the loss of the socialising aspect of working with other people. This is also noticeable among children whose development has been noticeably delayed because they were not able to socialise and play with other children. There are also a significant number of people who live in problematic relationships where home working has exacerbated the problems. One problem from lack of interaction with other which is becoming manifest is the number of people with psychological problems and a consequent rise in anti-social and petty crime behaviour.

For students – both at school and at university – the problem has been greater and the effects will be longer-lasting. Much of the learning process takes place through interaction – both with the teacher and with other students, and this may take place either during the class of later through discussion. With remote learning then this does not happen and the learning is therefore incomplete and less-internalised than during normal teaching. It is for this reason that thousands of university students in the United Kingdom are currently suing their universities and claiming that the education they paid for has not been properly delivered but was received at a lower quality. For all young people there, education has been damaged and this is likely to affect them and also society for the rest of their lives – or at least for a very long time.

In the workplace also there is a potential problem being stored up for the future. While people can work satisfactorily in many jobs, this is of course not possible for everyone. The question therefore arises as to whether this will cause social divisions between those who have teleworking jobs and those who do not. More significantly for those who undertake teleworking then they may be able to do their work very satisfactorily on a remote basis but only for standard work; unusual situations can be problematic and not dealt with satisfactorily. In a working environment people learn from their more experienced colleagues and from discussing issues with each other. When working is remote then this does not happen; this is the problem that call centres have with people working from a standard script. If people do not develop their skills in the workplace, then it is difficult to see how promotions will happen and will be given to the most experienced person – and the person best able to deal with others. The business itself will therefore suffer in the longer term.

In short, teleworking was introduced to solve a short-term problem but the longer-term issues were largely ignored. With the passage of time, these problems are becoming apparent and more significantly they are likely to be longer-lasting – the future sacrificed for the present!

7. CONCLUSION – HUMAN VALUES IN THE WORK PLACE

In the context of an unforeseen crisis (i.e. the COVID-19 pandemic) telework has social and psychological consequences not only affecting employees but also touching the lives of spouses and children, as well as teachers on all school levels, health employees and social workers, sectors that have been affected the most by this pandemic.

All along the previous points we have presented how in the case of telework, we as people could act in a more humanly or inhumanly way at work. Telework, as one of the tools that would hopefully to contain the widespread of a pandemic, while still producing work activity, has allowed us to realise various things. First, science and technology in their content are not bad; however, their use and the people controlling its implementation could generate positive or negative consequences especially in view of the mental health of employees. As such, telework as a generalised, mandatory norm could prevent a great part of the population to get physically sick; however, it has generated a constant growth of abuse of power at work as a consequence of privileges and over-control.

Second, any use of technologies opens the space for wrongdoing in favour of those in power, noting that this is not necessarily always the case.

Inside organisations, wrongdoing from those in power is not new; however, it is possible to identify frequent occurrences, thanks to the sharing of information, the same information that is basically controlled by those in the coalition in power.

Once again, in the discipline of management, we arrive to the point in which managerial behaviour depends on the inner beliefs and values of the individual in power, the manager. It is the manager who will decide to behave in a humane manner or not, to generate or not abuse of power, to promote or not the creation of a coalition in power, to share or not trustworthy information, to generate fear and dissension among their employees who are important stakeholders.

We then modulate this need for ethical questioning of managers' behaviours through the need for introspection, which may be developed somehow by tools such as teaching at the university level. It is our duty to prepare the next generation of leaders expecting to promote, in the years to come, more leaders able to questioning the fairness of actions inside and outside organisations, either in private or public spaces. It is not that we lack leaders of this kind. Quite the contrary, there are various courageous and humane leaders among us. We simply need more. We need more people in power that will avoid to inflict suffering towards others. We need to educate more and more future leaders in our educational institutions by means of contents that include teachings of humanism.

Some authors (i.e. Pauchant, 2002; Pava, 2007; Sen, 1998; Solomon, 1998, 1992) are already concerned by ethics and economy, or even, spirituality and management. They indicate the need for sympathy, compassion, empathy, listening, honesty, integrity, modesty, humility, as well as self-criticism and self-questioning. To us, this implies the need for ethical leadership in our actual and future managers, and not just the acclaimed, widely spread transformational leadership, because a manipulative leader might want to transform the beliefs of employees instilling ideas or attitudes, even if led by good reasons.

Taking a critical standpoint, as management professors, we have the educational moral duty (see Dewey, 1975) of covering thoroughly in our courses the aforementioned human values, as well as reflecting about the freedom and responsibilities towards others, that come with power. To reflect about the consequences of the wrongdoing of power over-control, control and manipulation of information, with the risk of indulging in favouritism at work and harassment. Consequences generated in the workplace will go from a decrease in productivity up to an increase of violence at work and cost of medical bills for mental health, as well as legal fees when extreme cases of harassment at work go to court.

Finally, based on our observations and analyses, telework and the consequent transformations for either workplace, families and social systems demonstrate that Organisation Theory needs to take into account the 'whole' of the individuals and not only the human part of the person as an isolated worker. Instead of addressing the family–work conciliation dilemma, some practicians claim the need for a family–work equilibrium. There is a need to update and theorise about the 'whole' of a person who is at the same time a citizen of a society, a member of a family (or one who asks for a private life) and an employee (with or without decision power). Equilibrium implies levelling (e.g. energies and results), whereas conciliation implies losing and winning. As humans, are we allowed to satisfaction and well-being, or just accommodation and acceptance of inequities?

REFERENCES

Aktouf, O. (1987). *Méthodologie des sciences sociales et approche qualitative des organisations – Une introduction à la démarche classique et une critique.* Presses de l'Université du Québec.

Alvesson, M. (2002). *Understanding organizational culture.* London: SAGE.

Aras, G., & Crowther, D. (2009). *Global perspectives on corporate governance and CRS.* Farnham: Gower.

CBC News. (2022). Is your boss tracking you while you work? Some Canadians are about to find out, N. Patel, October 11, 15, 2022. Retrieved from http://www.cbc.ca, consulted during the month of October 2022.

Chanlat, J. F. (2007). La logique de l'entreprise et la logique de la société: deux logiques inconciliables ? In D. J. P. Dupuis (Ed.), *Sociologie de l'entreprise* (2e éd., pp. 295–321). Montréal, QC: Gaëtan Morin.

CNESST – Québec. (2022). Le harcèlement psychologique ou sexuel au travail. Retrieved from http://www.cnesst.gouv.qc.ca, consulted during the month of October 2022.

Cvenkel, N. (2021). Employees' experiences of workplace violence: Raising awareness of workplace stress, well-being, leadership, and corporate social responsibility. In D. Crowther & F. Quoquab (Eds.), *CSR in an age of Isolationism* (pp. 69–92). Bingley: Emerald Publishing Limited.

Davila-Gomez, A. M., & Crowther, D. (2012). Caring, sharing and collective solidarity in management. In A. M. Davila-Gomez & D. Crowther (Eds.), *Human dignity and managerial responsibility* (pp. 41–72). Gower.

Dewey, J. (1975). *Moral principles in education,* Copyright 1909. Carbondale, IL: Southern Illinois University Press.

Feuvrier, M.-P. (2014). Bonheur et travail, oxymore ou piste de management stratégique de l'entreprise? *Revue Management et Avenir, 2*(68), 164–182.

Foucault, M. (1975). *Surveiller et punir: naissance de la prison.* Paris: Gallimard.

Gouvernement of Canada. (2022a). Coronavirus disease (COVID-19). Retrieved from http://canada.ca, consulted during the month of October 2022.

Gouvernement of Canada. (2022b). Home office expenses for employees. Retrieved from http://www.canada.ca, consulted during the month of October 2022.

Gouvernement du Québec. (2021). *My child is worried about the pandemic. What can I do to provide support?* Retrieved from http://quebec.ca, consulted during the month of October 2022.

Gouvernement du Québec. (2022a). Mesures prises par décrets et arrêtés ministériels en lien avec la pandémie de la COVID-19. Retrieved from http://www.quebec.ca, consulted during the month of October 2022.

Gouvernement du Québec. (2022b). Data on COVID-19 in Québec. Retrieved from http://www.quebec.ca, consulted during the month of October 2022.

Habermas, J. (1971). *Knowledge and human interest* (Trans J. J. Shapiro). Boston, MA: Beacon Press.

INSPQ – Québec – Institut nationale de Santé publique du Québec. (2020). Violence conjugale dans un context de pandémie. Retrieved from http://inspq.qc.ca, during the month of October 2022.

Kierkegaard, S. (1813–1855). *For self-examination and judge for yourselves! -1851.* London/Princeton, NJ: Oxford University Press/Princeton University Press [1974].

Le Journal du Québec. (2022). Contrecoup de la pandémie: la violence dans les écoles du Québec explose, D. Dion-Viens, September 30, 2022. Retrieved from http://www.journaldequebec.com, consulted during the month of October 2022.

Légis Québec. (2022a). Act respecting the protection of personal information in the private sector, updated 1 June 2022. Retrieved from http://www.legisquebec.gouv.qc.ca, consulted during the month of October 2022.

Légis Québec. (2022b). Act respecting access to documents held by public bodies and the protection of personal information, updated 1 June 2022. Retrieved from http://www.legisquebec.gouv.qc.ca, consulted during the month of October 2022.

Maxwell, J. A. (2013). *Qualitative research design: An interactive approach* (3rd ed.). Thousand Oaks, CA: SAGE Publications.

Ministère de la Santé et des Services sociaux – Québec, MSSS. (2022). Directives COVID-19 du ministère de la Santé et des Services sociaux. Retrieved from http://www.publications.msss.gouv.qc.ca, consulted during the month of October 2022.

Mintzberg, H. (1982). *Structure et dynamique des organisations*. Paris: Editions d'Organisations.

Morin, E. (2008). Sens du travail, santé mentale et engagement organisationnel. *Études et recherches (Institut de recherche Robert-Sauvé en santé et en sécurité du travail); R-543*. Montréal, QC: Institut de recherche Robert-Sauvé en santé et en sécurité du travail.

Ontario. (2022a). COVID-19. Retrieved from http://ontario.ca, consulted during the month of October 2022.

Ontario. (2022b). Written policy on disconnecting from work (February–July 2022). Retrieved from http://ontario.ca, consulted during the month of October 2022.

Ontario. (2022c). Written policy on electronic monitoring of employees (July 2022). Retrieved from http://ontario.ca, consulted during the month of October 2022.

Piaget, J. (1977a). *Mes idées*. Denoel, Gonthier, Coll. Médiations.

Piaget, J. (1977b). *El nacimiento de la inteligencia en el niño*. Ed, Grijalbo, 1994, Bogotá, trad. Delachaux et Niestlé, 1977.

Pauchant, T. C. (2002). Introduction: Ethical and spiritual management addresses the need for meaning in the workplace. In T. C. Pauchant (Ed.), *Ethics and spirituality at work: Hopes and pitfalls of the search for meaning in organizations*. Westport, CN/London: Quorum Books.

Pava, M. L. (2007). Spirituality in (and out) of the classroom: A pragmatic approach. *Journal of Business Ethics, 73*, 287–299.

Public Health Ontario. (2022). Ontario covid-19 data tool. Retrieved from http://publichealthontario.ca, consulted during the month of October 2022.

Revenu Québec. (2022). Dépenses relatives au télétravail engagées en raison de la crise liée à la covid-19. Retrieved from http://www.revenuquebec.ca, consulted during the month of October 2022.

Rouleau, L. (2013). L'ethnographie organisationnelle d'hier à Demain. *Revue internationale de psychosociologie et de gestion des comportements organisationnels*, 27–43. Supplément/2013 (HS).

Saint-Leger, G., & Beeler, B. (2012). Emergence d'une culture négociée dans le cadre des projets ERP. *Revue Management & Avenir, 3*(53), 54–71.

Sen, A. (1998). *On ethics and economics*. Oxford: Blackwell.

Solomon, R. (1992). *Ethics and excellence – Cooperation and integrity in business*. Oxford: Oxford University Press.

Solomon, R. (1998). The moral psychology of business: Care and compassion in the corporation. *Business Ethics Quarterly, 8*(3), 515–533.

Statistiques Canada. (2021). *Le harcèlement et la discrimination chez le corps professoral et les chercheurs des établissements postsecondaires du Canada*. D. Hango. Retrieved from http://www150.statcan.gc.ca, consulted during the month of Octobre 2022.

Université de Sherbrooke. (2022). Violence conjugale et covid-19: Un mélange explosive, recherche par M. Généreux et al. Retrieved from http://usherbrooke.ca, consulted during the month of October 2022.

Waddock, S., & McIntosh, M. (2009). Beyond corporate responsibility: Implications for management development. *Business & Society Review, 114*(3), 295–325.

Zaitseva, V., et Chaudat, P. (2016). Les determinants organisationnels du harcèlement moral: une analyse d'une revue actualisée de littérature. *Management & Avenir, 84*, 115–134.

BUILDING RESILIENCE FOR A FUTURE ORGANISATION

Elaine Conway and Parminder Johal

ABSTRACT

This chapter examines the key issues around organisational resilience – what it means for organisations, and the key elements they need to consider if they are looking to increase the ability of their operations to withstand challenges in their environment. Organisations have always had to adapt to changes in their environment, whether as a result of market-based, political, regulatory or technological developments. However, the pace of change and the number and frequency of external shocks, such as the global financial crisis, the COVID-19 epidemic, war and increasing nationalism, inflation, labour shortages, cyber-security threats and environmental crises have increased over recent years. Whilst some of these events could have been foreseen, in that they emerge relatively slowly, such as increasing nationalism, other crises, such as the COVID-19 pandemic could not have been readily anticipated, both for the speed at which it occurred, but the significant impact it had on people and organisations. Clearly, many of these events can have severe consequences not only for society but also for organisations, potentially threatening their survival. Hence organisations are increasingly recognising the need to be both more aware of potential threats or even opportunities by constantly monitoring their environment, but also creating contingency or mitigation plans to become more resilient to such change and shocks. By becoming more aware of changes in their environment and incorporating risk evaluations and mitigation plans into strategy and regular business planning cycles, organisations can become more adaptive and agile to respond more quickly and robustly to such events. Whilst it is not possible to fully mitigate all risks to the organisation, increased resilience can reduce the severity or longevity of negative impacts or support the organisation to seek opportunities from change.

Corporate Resilience
Developments in Corporate Governance and Responsibility, Volume 21, 53–72
Copyright © 2023 by Emerald Publishing Limited
All rights of reproduction in any form reserved
ISSN: 2043-0523/doi:10.1108/S2043-052320230000021003

This chapter introduces the concept of overall organisational resilience, and then discusses some more functional areas of resilience: operational, financial, technological, reputational and institutional. The chapter concludes with a consideration of the effects of building greater organisational resilience and what organisations should consider when evaluating where to start on such a journey.

Keywords: Organisational resilience; financial resilience; reputational resilience; institutional resilience; operational resilience; risk mitigation

1. INTRODUCTION: WHAT DOES ORGANISATIONAL RESILIENCE MEAN?

Interest in organisational resilience has risen considerably in the wake of global events such as the 2007–2008 financial crisis, the COVID-19 pandemic and the economic fallout from other world events, such as Brexit and the Ukraine war. Equally, more local events, such as natural disasters (flooding, fires etc.), can create substantial disruption to societies (Burnard & Bhamra, 2011). These events have caused (amongst other impacts) considerable economic challenges to organisations of all kinds, both profit-making and charitable. Whilst these dramatic and sudden events trigger concerns about how organisations can recover or survive, there are slower, less dramatic, but just as disrupting forces that continue to evolve the economic landscape, such as the rise in e-commerce, the Internet of Things (IoT), artificial intelligence and the use of technology to create new products and processes which require organisations to adapt to survive (Lelievre, Radtke, Rohr, & Westinner, 2016). Organisational resilience is therefore both the ability of an organisation to recover from the sudden challenges but also to adapt and address evolving uncertainty in their internal and external environments (Gibson & Tarrant, 2010). Essentially, organisational resilience is how organisations understand and treat risk, in particular shocks or non-routine or disruptive risks (Gibson & Tarrant, 2010), but also risk emanating from slower, but equally transformative changes.

Stemming from the Latin 'resiliens' and 'resiliere', resilience was originally regarded as the ability to 'recoil' or 'jump back' from an impact or stress (Klein et al., 2011; Paton & Johnston, 2017; Rogers, 2013). This sense of recoil or 'bouncing back' predominantly applied to raw materials' (such as wood or steel) elastic capability to survive stress testing without breaking or deforming, but then later took on the meaning to be able to survive a shock, but additionally to return to a 'steady state' following the shock (Klein et al., 2011; Rogers, 2013). The concept of resilience has since evolved from this engineering definition to a wider interpretation within the business continuity context and has led to a significant body of literature, standards and guidelines on how businesses can evaluate their risks and respond to them.

Resilience is intrinsically linked to risk monitoring and assessment. In order to build resilience, organisations need to build their risk monitoring and assessment capabilities. This requires organisations to regularly monitor their external environment for changes, whether that be from emerging technologies, changing competition, developing market requirements and expectations or broader economic and social changes. These are most readily encompassed within the traditional Political, Economic, Social, Technological, Legal and Environmental (PESTEL) (Perera, 2017) analysis which organisations may undertake as part of their annual budget cycle. However, in the modern, dynamic and fast-changing environment, this scanning of the environment should be continuously undertaken. Allied to this is an evaluation of the potential impacts of these changes on the organisation. This can be achieved by an assessment of the likelihood of the risk, the potential impact and potential mitigations the organisation could action to reduce the level of risk and the level of risk which the organisation is prepared to accept (appetite for risk) (Perera, 2017). This is a good starting point for developing organisational resilience, although it should always be accepted that not all risks can be anticipated, for example, the sheer speed and scale of the impact of COVID-19 globally was unprecedented and unforeseeable. However, many organisations found that they needed to develop contingency plans to address the pandemic which have subsequently been re-enacted following other crises, such as the cost-of-living crisis or where UK organisations are impacted by a skilled labour shortage following Brexit. These plans which can be enacted are the cornerstones of organisational resilience.

When considering organisational resilience for the first time, whilst the initial focus might be on identifying possible shocks or risks and seeking to mitigate them, it is important to note that these changes can also present significant opportunities to organisations (Lelievre et al., 2016). Indeed, it is the ability to respond and adapt to a new 'steady state' which is key in organisational resilience. For example, organisations can engage with new technologies to develop new products or processes and create new collaborations with partners, customers and suppliers. Smaller firms can work out ways in which they can compete with larger firms by embracing some of these new ways of working.

Undoubtedly, organisations that are resilient perform better than those who struggle to respond to environmental changes (Lelievre et al., 2016). Not only do they provide greater returns to investors compared to those less resilient, but they are quicker to recover from shocks than less resilient firms (Lelievre et al., 2016). Resilient firms tend to take more decisive action to control debt, improve efficiency and maintain relationships with key stakeholders than others, allowing them to make significant gains over time.

There are several different ways in which organisations can improve their resilience, including strengthening their 'hard' and 'soft' organisational capabilities. It is important to note that there is no single panacea to build organisational resilience: rather it is a careful consideration of the risks and profile of an individual organisation (Burnard & Bhamra, 2011; Gibson & Tarrant, 2010). Resilience can be improved by focussing on two components: productivity and flexibility. By maintaining rising productivity, organisations are able to protect profit margins and smooth out smaller fluctuations in the economy, allowing them to build resource to respond to larger shocks (Lelievre et al., 2016). Equally, flexibility is the ability to continue to be profitable in the face of varying supply and demand situations (Lelievre et al., 2016). This can entail being able to flex production and costs, including procurement, when demand rises or falls to take advantage of peaks and to reduce the impact of market troughs.

There are various models which can act as useful tools for organisations to consider their resilience. These include the 'principles model'.

The 'principles model' is based on six key principles that resilience is:

– An outcome
– Is not static
– Is not a single trait
– Is multidimensional
– Exists of a range of conditions
– Is grounded on good risk management (Gibson & Tarrant, 2010).

This approach, as other resilience models, suggests that organisations need to monitor their environment, consider their own multidimensional capabilities and have effective risk management strategies and responses which are triggered by the detection of a disruptive event or perceived change (Burnard & Bhamra, 2011). It is therefore essential that organisations have the ability to recognise threats and similar triggers, to feedback that information appropriately within the organisation such that mitigations or adjustments can be carried out proactively. This link between detection of triggers and activation of adjustments can be referred to as an organisation's adaptive capacity (Gunderson, 2000). This is supported by a constant monitoring of the environment and assessment of the nature and level of changing risks and opportunities, in order to consider appropriate mitigation measures. It should be acknowledged that not all risks can be identified as they may be unique and unforeseen (such as the COVID-19 pandemic). However, if mitigation plans are made flexibly, then the adaptive capacity of the organisation is then able to re-use those plans as the basis for mitigations for other unforeseeable events, should they occur (Wieland & Durach, 2021).

Adaptive capacity is one element to consider within organisational resilience. Not all organisations will wish to or be able to improve resilience across the organisation at the same time. Instead, they may want to focus on improving resilience in a particular part of their organisation, using business critical areas as the foundation to building wider organisational resilience. This chapter will now address some of most common functional facets of organisational resilience which form the foundations for gaining insights into performance improvement:

– Operational Resilience
– Financial Resilience
– Technological Resilience
– Reputational Resilience
– Institutional Resilience.

2. BUILDING FOUNDATIONS IN THE DIMENSIONS OF ORGANISATIONAL RESILIENCE

2.1 Operational Resilience

Operational resilience is the ability to 'plan and prepare for, absorb, respond to, and recover from disasters and adapt to new conditions' (NRC, 2012, p. 1) with a particular focus on the key operating assets and processes within an organisation. Operational resilience is necessary in any process-driven organisation, but it is particularly key in complex infrastructure projects, such as highways, dams, water and power generation sectors and other significant national infrastructure projects (Ganin et al., 2016; Ouyang & Wang, 2015). It is imperative to build in resilience to these key infrastructures in order to protect the population from natural disasters, epidemics and cybersecurity threats, but also to avoid the unquantifiable costs of injury and loss of life from such events (NRC, 2012). There are various approaches to support the building of operational resilience, across the physical, social and data management domains (Ganin et al., 2016).

A key step to building operational resilience is to assess the risks or threats posed to the operating system. These risks can emanate from the natural world, such as flood, fire, drought, volcanic eruptions, earthquakes, hurricanes/ tornadoes and the like. Organisations operating in geographic locations which are prone to environmental, or weather events need to build in a certain level of resilience to these 'known' threats. But equally risks to operations can stem from more deliberate acts, unknown or uncertain events, such as cyber-attacks, unauthorised access to key assets, engineering failures, sabotage etc. Not all events may be foreseeable, hence the aim should be on being able to react quickly to any event by focussing on the critical infrastructure functionality needed to continue operations by continuously monitoring environmental risks and their likely impact on this critical functionality.

Hence organisations need to plan for unknown events, absorb their impacts to the greatest extent possible, recover and predict and prepare for future events to adapt to the new environment (Essuman, Boso, & Annan, 2020; Ganin et al., 2016). Organisations need to be able to absorb stresses to their systems, and recover, predict and prepare for future events which could impact their operations, in order to adapt. Therefore, it is key to understand how organisations can absorb the disruptive event and how quickly they can recover. Ganin et al. (2016, p. 2) focus on identifying critical functionality: 'a metric of system performance set by the stakeholders, to derive an integrated measure of resilience'. They focus on assessing how a system or organisation needs to perform over time, and its robustness. This requires an assessment of the levels of desired resilience and robustness levels, and then trading off different elements of the operations model to achieve them, such as planning in redundancy of assets and allowing for backup supplies of key resources.

There is a variety of frameworks developed in the literature to help organisations to measure and improve their operational resilience. Bruneau et al. (2003) identified four dimensions of resilience from an operational standpoint:

– Technical
– Organisational
– Social
– Economic

Within these dimensions, they proposed measures of resilience to assess the capabilities of the organisation to cope with system failures and consequences:

– Robustness: the ability of the organisation's operations to withstand stresses without significant loss of functionality;
– Rapidity: the ability to address priorities and achieve objectives in a suitable time frame to minimise negative impact and future disruption;
– Resourcefulness: the ability to recognise problems, prioritise and mobilise resources to counter stresses to the system;
– Redundancy: the ability of elements within the organisation to be substituted.

To build an organisation's resilience, there will inevitably be trade-offs in efficiency, as a certain amount of slack or operational redundancy will be built in. Despite this, Essuman et al. (2020) found that increased organisational resilience (both the ability to absorb shocks and the ability to recover from those shocks) actually enhanced operational efficiency.

This consideration of organisational resilience can also extend to the supply chain in which an organisation operates. In this case, the considerations of risk and risk mitigation become more complicated due to the inherent levels of complexity in the chain as it may contain hundreds of organisations and links (Wieland & Durach, 2021) (this aspect of resilience is also considered later in this chapter). On the face of it, risk management in this kind of complex environment becomes untenable; however, the focus of operational resilience is on the characteristics of organisations to maintain an agreed level of functionality under crisis, rather than a tight focus only on risks. This focus on delivering this level of functionality within a supply chain helps participants to create innovative solutions which in a particularly severe crisis may not guarantee that level of functionality, but should at least allow the system to respond and recover more quickly than if the focus was purely on the management of the risks internal to just one organisation in the chain (Wieland & Durach, 2021). Anecdotally, many firms derived plans during the COVID-19 crisis to maintain a basic level of operations by redirecting staff to key areas of the business and have since used elements of these plans to maintain operations during other crises such as the Ukraine war (Katsos, 2022).

2.2 Financial Resilience

Despite the financial crisis in 2008, financial resilience is a term that has, perhaps, been given even more prominence over the last few years. The economic climate has been in a constant flux of change, with two profound disruptions, COVID-19 and Brexit. These events have touched almost all businesses and for most, the impact has been adverse. Brexit has called for 'SMEs to look at ways of improving profitability, working capital and cashflow, enabling their businesses to be more agile and flexible to respond positively to the changing economic landscape' (Beavis Morgan, 2017). Companies have needed to react promptly and those with more resilient business models, designed to be agile, such that their organisation can adapt quickly to recover and move forward out of a crisis zone, are the ones who are able to see the benefit of their investment and demonstrate strong financial resilience. In very simple terms, financial resilience in a business context refers to an organisation's ability to recover from a financial issue or crisis, which may or may not be of a temporary nature, in a planned manner, without having a knee-jerk reaction to the issue/crisis (Openwage, 2021).

To add a little more technical detail to the meaning of financial resilience, Knight and Kavanagh (2020) define financial resilience as an organisation's ability to 'withstand events that affect their capital structure, liquidity, revenue and assets'. Without this level of financial resilience, other aspects of resilience, such as operational and/or reputational resilience will become difficult to maintain. In addition to being capable of minimising the adverse effects of any unforeseen event (Linnenluecke, 2017), financial resilience also means that the organisation demonstrates its capability to predict and have in place necessary plans, should they need to respond to an unexpected crisis (Somers, 2009). The COVID-19 crisis brought to the fore how fragile global supply chains, health-care services, transport services, hospitality services and other services actually are.

Whilst COVID-19 has been the acid test for the financial resilience of many organisations over the last two years, it is important to remember that although this may have placed a spotlight on the topic of financial resilience, this is not the only phenomena to do so. Organisations need to be aware that advances in knowledge, the acceleration of climate change and the digitalisation of the global economy, which have been around prior to the pandemic, are also key players in fostering a business environment where conditions are always changing. Such an environment which is constantly evolving and that too with greater global connectivity creates complexity for organisations. It is this complexity of transactions, supply chains, competition, bargaining power, regulation, changes in consumer behaviour, expectations at society level, sanctions, natural disasters, civil wars and recession that will make organisations vulnerable and threaten their survival (Erol, Mansouri, & Sauser, 2009). It is this change and uncertainty at a very complex and global level that requires organisations to enrich financial resilience and recognise that it is engaged with the organisational decision-making process prior to, during and post any crises and shocks (McManus, Seville, Brunsdon, & Vargo, 2007).

Financial resilience cannot operate in isolation and if organisations are not financially resilient then this will impact their operational and reputation resilience. The COVID-19 crisis provides a very good example of how organisations across the globe, including the government have had to rely on and demonstrate their financial resilience. It has also prompted organisations to recognise the need to build or rebuild their businesses more resiliently; however, for some the question is how to do so (Reeves & Whitaker, 2020).

There are many approaches that organisations can take to move towards a position of financial resilience. In developing their financial strategies there needs to be consideration of financial resilience, for example, through greater scrutiny when evaluating capital investment decisions. The temptation to continue using the traditional net present value (NPV) approach may be high, but it may limit flexibility if not extended to reflect the market value of any cash flow adjustments should assumptions about future market conditions not hold true. The use of Real Option Theory (ROT) enables managers to be flexible and active, be able to change resource allocation decisions, rather than remain passive once an investment has been evaluated, resources are committed and decisions are made. However, this approach is not without its challenges, using ROT to complement NPV, rather than replace, may take many financial managers out of their comfort zone, as they will be required to make managerial judgements and not just focus on an approach which reduces costs to maximise profit (Simmons & Tinsley, 2011). It is noteworthy that this approach has received increasing attention as a tool for valuation in industries subject to volatile demand, as it offers the ability to value flexibility (Muharam & Tarrazon, 2017). As discussed earlier, being able to manage flexibility in one's complex business environment is key to financial resilience.

Other good practices to support organisations and their preparedness for uncertainties that lie ahead include a revisit to reassess and redefine the composition of their financial resilience framework (Knight & Kavanagh, 2020), one which may have been used to navigate their way through historic crisis periods. Knight and Kavanagh (2020) outline these good practices as follows:

- Reassessing capital structure, focussing more on generating alternative sources of capital to broaden capital sources and enable flexibility.
- Redefining liquidity policies and strategies, to enable early signs of any potential risk to the organisation's liquidity position.
- Better management of financial risk through strategies that minimise volatility, e.g. use of ROT.

By developing this flexibility into mitigation plans, and by continuously monitoring the external environment for risks and assessing their possible impact on the organisation and its financing, an organisation should be better able to react to and withstand even unforeseeable events.

In addition, it is worth noting any potential changes in regulations, around what information organisations of a certain status and size will need to supply to their stakeholders to offer reassurance of their financial resilience. A recent example of this is the requirement by the energy regulatory body, Office of Gas and Electricity Markets (OFGEM), which as of January 2022 requires energy suppliers to undergo financial stress testing to improve financial resilience in the energy sector. In cases where stress testing identifies weaknesses, OFGEM will work with the organisation to agree on an improvement plan (OFGEM, 2021). Another example is the proposal by Sir Donald Brydon that organisations need to provide a Resilience Statement in company annual reports, to provide more information and assurance about the resilience of a company (KPMG, 2020).

Whilst the current economic environment and the one that lies ahead may create challenges for organisations, whether they are a large global organisation, an SME or a charity, there is also opportunity. In particular, accounting practices and industry financial experts are in a position to lead the way to helping organisation to create stronger financial resilience.

2.3 Technological Resilience

Technological resilience is the ability to maintain operations where technology is critical to the delivery of the organisation's key business activities. This can involve the use of a range of technologies to ensure that the organisation can continue to operate and adapt following either a sudden or gradual change. Many organisations who rely on technology for their core functions carry out risk assessments of their technological systems, by ensuring that there are backups of key operational data, alternative server or cloud storage systems available and contingency plans in place for switching data access in case of disaster on their main site of operations. There are international standards to support organisations to build their technology resilience plans, such as ISO 22316 *Security and Resilience* (ISO, 2022b) and ISO 27000 *Information Technology* (ISO, 2022a).

Technological resilience can be considered to be at the nexus of risk management and resilience management, since it requires identification of key risks, a mitigation plan to address those unacceptable risks to maintain a defined minimum level of operations, whilst acknowledging that even the most basic of organisations rely on some form of technology to keep their operations running. Even at a rudimentary level, most firms depend on telecommunications and basic computer technology to run their operations, and of course most organisations rely on technology much more than this. Hence the term technology can encompass this rudimentary level but also extend to include the vast interconnected networks of organisations reliant on each other to operate, such as critical infrastructure industries, such as water and power, which themselves rely on computer technology to operate.

In simpler organisations, technology can be defined in a narrow sense, as the information systems of an organisation, and managed in accordance with standards such as ISO 27000 (ISO, 2022a). In this way, information is regarded as a key asset which needs adequate protection to prevent loss of data 'availability, confidentiality and integrity' (ISO, 2022a, sec. 4.1) to conduct efficient and effective business operations, enabling the organisation to meet its objectives and maintain its reputation and legal compliance. This can be achieved by identifying and assessing risks to the system, implementing and continuously evaluating appropriate controls to mitigate the most critical risks and monitoring both the controls for their effectiveness and continued appropriateness, and the ever-evolving environment in which the organisation operates.

However, technological resilience can also be interpreted more broadly, as the critical infrastructure network in which an organisation operates. The reliance of all members in the network on each other becomes both a strength (in terms of the ability of the network to adapt, learn and develop from each other), but also a potential weakness in that the failure of one part of the network may cause critical issues in some or all of the rest of the network. This is particularly true in critical infrastructure organisations such as power and water sectors, and hence these industries require much greater risk assessment and robustness incorporating into their operations to maintain a minimum level of function when disasters occur (Mottahedi, Sereshki, Ataei, Qarahasanlou, & Barabadi, 2021).

On a wider scale, Balland, Rigby, and Boschma (2015) studied the technological resilience of cities, evaluating why certain cities appeared to be more resilient than others to falls in economic performance following short-run shocks. They focused on three elements of resilience:

- Vulnerability (why some cities are more vulnerable than others)
- Intensity (why some cities suffer more in a crisis than others)
- Duration (why some cities recover more quickly from crises than others).

They found that technologically resilient cities had diverse and flexible knowledge bases, which caused them to avoid crises, reduce the impact of more severe crises and recover more quickly from such crises (Balland et al., 2015). These resilient cities re-invent themselves over time, moving away from obsolete sectors and institutional practices that can cause cities to stagnate. They do this by being engaged in regional knowledge networks which are well connected and open to knowledge created outside their own area, and being able to adopt and develop these new ideas (Crespo, Suire, & Vicente, 2014; Dahl Fitjar & Rodríguez-Pose, 2011).

Organisations can mirror this, by engaging in networks, such as their own supply chains, but also in trade associations, business groups and universities who can share new ideas and challenge their ways of working. This can improve the technological information exchanged between members of the network, enabling them to mitigate problems and innovate, particularly when networks are damaged during a crisis: the creation of inter-organisational trust is important, supporting the network when it is under pressure (Balland et al., 2015). This should be enabled by supportive institutions in the network, such as councils and business support organisations, who can encourage dynamic network structures between groups of organisations to leverage their cooperation and knowledge in a flexible way (MacKinnon & Driscoll Derickson, 2013). The resilience of these institutions is considered elsewhere in this chapter. Organisations in these networks promote knowledge production, recombining it to apply it to new situations (Davis, 2010), which can particularly be the case in supply chain networks, where one main player has the competence within the chain to influence the others (Rajesh, 2017). This network will act as a monitor of the environment and enable organisations to adjust to changes in technologies and demographics more effectively than organisations that do not engage in these networks (Balland et al., 2015).

In this sense, technological resilience can be perceived as organisational learning and organisational management having a growth mindset for their organisation. This means that organisations should remain open to new technologies to prevent them and their networks becoming static and entrenched and hence less able to endure shocks (Davis, 2010).

2.4 Reputational Resilience

An organisation's reputation is a key element in its identity and branding. Defined as 'a cognitive representation of a company's actions and results that crystallises the firm's ability to deliver valued outcomes to its stakeholders' (Fombrun, Gardberg, & Sever, 2000, p. 87), a company's reputation is critical to its success. Put simply, an organisation creates a good reputation if it consistently meets or exceeds stakeholder expectations, and a bad reputation if it fails to deliver to those expectations (Gaultier-Gaillard, Louisot, & Rayner, 2009). For good or bad, once a reputation is created and embedded, it becomes difficult to change: a good reputation is an enviable asset which can sustain a healthy business, while a poor reputation can destroy credibility and legitimacy in the marketplace and in financial markets (Coaffee & Rogers, 2008).

Indeed, much of the value of an organisation is its reputation: it is an inherent and intangible asset that the company and its management have the ability and credibility to deliver on their promises. Hence reputation is a strategic asset in its own right and needs to be managed appropriately (Coaffee & Rogers, 2008). Despite its intrinsic value, it is inherently difficult to place a quantifiable monetary value on reputation and similar intangible assets (Datta & Fuad, 2016), unless they are acquired as part of a takeover.

There are numerous benefits to creating and maintaining a good organisational reputation. These include the continuing trust and loyalty of customers, suppliers and employees, but also wider stakeholders such as investors and regulators (Gaultier-Gaillard et al., 2009; Kim & Choi, 2011). This can create significant competitive advantage which allows an organisation to differentiate itself from its competitors (Fombrun & van Riel, 2003). Hence there is a growing focus on the importance of maintaining a good reputation as part of mitigating key business risks, particularly in the light of real-time, always-on global communications and media scrutiny, which can capture and spotlight even the smallest negative incident in an organisation's operations globally (Coombs & Holladay, 2015; Gaultier-Gaillard et al., 2009).

There is also evidence of wider beneficial effects of maintaining a good organisational reputation. For example, it can act as a buffer or shield against crises to support organisational resilience. It can deflect possible damage from a crisis and also assist in repairing any damage done (Coombs & Holladay, 2002). So if an organisation has accumulated reputational 'capital' prior to a crisis, then there is evidence that it can maintain a positive image after the crisis, so reputation not only protects against some damage to the organisation, but it can also assist it to recover more quickly than an organisation which does not possess such positive reputational capital (Fombrun et al., 2000; Klein & Dawar, 2004). Jones,

Jones, and Little (2000) refer to this as a 'reservoir of goodwill' and describe reputation as 'the vessel in which goodwill accumulates'. This reservoir can be used as a source of exemplars to remind stakeholders of the responsible behaviours (such as charitable donations or community work) it has previously exhibited as a way of deflecting harm from crises (Kim, 2014), although some authors have found that this may send the wrong message that organisations have been engaging in these activities to the detriment of managing the business and averting crises (Kim, Kim, & Cameron, 2009). Nonetheless, customers may be reluctant to attach negative thoughts to a company with whom they have previously only had positive experiences and downplay any negativity (Eisingerich, Rubera, Seifert, & Bhardwaj, 2011). Conversely, Kim and Woo (2019) found that organisations with poor reputations prior to a crisis tend to experience a greater decline in reputation after a crisis, whether they were the cause of the crisis or the victim of a crisis from external causes.

Another beneficial effect good organisational reputation can have is the 'halo effect' (Klein & Dawar, 2004). This stems from the fact that reputation is multi-dimensional and the result of people's perceptions of different elements of an organisation. These elements may include: emotional appeal, products/ services, vision/leadership, workplace environment, financial performance and social responsibility (Fombrun et al., 2000; Fombrun & van Riel, 2003). The halo effect occurs when people's positive beliefs about the organisation in one element are projected onto another (Klein & Dawar, 2004), even if the person does not have personal experience of that particular aspect. So, they may, for example, look favourably on a firm's product quality, and extend that belief onto customer service, even though they may not have experienced the organisation's customer service. The opposite to this is the 'Velcro effect' (Coombs & Holladay, 2002), where a previous negative perception promulgates or 'snags' (hence the Velcro analogy) additional reputational damage when a crisis occurs. In other words, once a customer has a negative impression of an organisation, this impression becomes more entrenched under a crisis, whether justified or not.

Therefore, it is critical that an organisation's reputation is developed to be resilient in the face of various challenges which could severely undermine or destroy the fortunes of the organisation. There are numerous threats to an organisation's reputation, including actions its employees carry out themselves, such as fraud, but also external threats, such as cyber-security attacks and terrorism and the wider societal shocks such as the COVID-19 epidemic. Not all risks to the organisation's reputation can be identified as they may the result of unforeseeable events; however, often it is the reaction of an organisation to even unforeseeable events which can impact its reputation. For example, the initial reaction of BP management to shareholders and the public in the wake of the Deepwater Horizon oil spill was deemed inadequate and inappropriate, and it damaged the reputation of the company considerably (RiskLogic, 2010; Vaughan, 2022). Therefore, the organisation needs to have a pre-planned reactive strategy to invoke when faced with unexpected occurrences to prevent damage to their reputation.

So how can organisations build reputational resilience? A good reputation is usually built over several years, by demonstrating consistent adherence to stakeholder expectations. It can be most effective when organisations focus their actions and communications around a central message or theme (Fombrun, 2005), although some organisations have found that as reputation is multi-faceted, it requires effort on a number of different elements of the organisation (Fombrun & van Riel, 2003). This is often achieved as part of the organisation's corporate social responsibility (CSR) agenda, which can address key facets of contributions to social and environmental issues. Again, this is often most effective when part of a coherent corporate strategy, conducted over a long period of time, adding credibility to the organisation, even in times of crisis (Kim & Woo, 2019).

Hence the key to building reputational resilience is to:

– Derive a credible strategy and key theme(s) which resonate with organisational stakeholders
– Invest in activities to support this strategy and theme(s)
– Be consistent in approach
– Inform stakeholders of actions
– Maintain and monitor activities to ensure relevance.

Deriving the strategy will involve a process of identifying key areas of interest to the organisation, deciding on priorities and then setting objectives to achieve required outcomes. This can be part of CSR or wider governance activities (Coaffee & Rogers, 2008).

Equally important, once an organisation has built a good reputation, it should become part of the risk management processes of the organisation to protect it. This may mean adding reputational damage as a key risk on an organisational risk register and assessing potential events which could negatively or positively impact this reputation and/or brand. By evaluating the positive as well as the potential negative impacts, organisations may also find opportunities to enhance their reputation and build on their competitive advantage, all of which can improve their financial performance (Coaffee & Rogers, 2008).

2.5 Institutional Resilience

There is a consensus in the literature as to what is meant by resilience in the context of business. The overarching theme is that of an organisation's ability to recover, following a shock or crisis situation (Beavis Morgan, 2017; Gibson & Tarrant, 2010; Lelievre et al., 2016). Following this, as highlighted in the introduction to this chapter, resilience can be addressed in a more focussed manner, through the consideration of the different kinds of resilience and their contribution to recovery from a shock situation, for example financial, operational, technological and reputational resilience. However, it is important to also consider institutional resilience, which takes an overview of the business environment as a whole and how institutions within this environment work together as a social system to foster resilience.

Institutional resilience goes beyond individual institutions/organisations, and it addresses whole institutional systems and how they interact with people (UN, 2020). This form of resilience is still very much related to recovery from a shock/ crisis, but also to making long-term changes at the societal level. Therefore institutional resilience 'is the ability of a social system (society, community, organisation) to absorb and recover from external shocks, while positively adapting and transforming to address long-term changes and uncertainty' (Haider (2020) cited in Anderson and De Tollenaere (2020)). It is resilience at a much broader level. Although built on local knowledge, experience and sources, it impacts all organisations through the promotion of this knowledge to state and society level, and this can help develop social capital. The emphasis, therefore, is on trust, legitimacy and credibility, which in turn create sources of resilience (Barma, Huybens, & Vinuela, 2014). It follows, therefore, that the relations between state and society also prop up and contribute to institutional resilience (Aligicia & Tarko, 2014). The connection to social systems, e.g. health and education, is an important one, through investment in efficient and agile social systems, institutional resilience can be built to help to limit the economic and social impact of a shock/crisis (Strupat & Marschall, 2020).

In summary, the development of resilience at institutional level can help organisations in the business environment, in that, the more resilient and stable institutions can better support organisational resilience, whereas weaker ones will weaken organisational resilience. The importance of institutional development therefore as a way of building institutional resilience is crucial, particularly where business operations and transactions transcend across international borders and where the shock/crisis calls for rapid regulation, funding and/or process changes. Given the nature of recent events, such as COVID-19, the Ukraine war and the Sri Lankan economic crisis, which have resulted in shocks to the wider economy and therefore business environment, there will be an impact on society and institutional systems. If nations continue to experience multiple shocks, then there is a strong need to develop institutional resilience across sectors and into wider systems, rather than in silos (Haider, 2020). The recent and indeed current experience of COVID-19 has provided significant learning around practical approaches to developing institutional resilience, which are outlined by Anderson and De Tollenaere (2020):

- Identify and leverage organic resilience. This supports the idea of using existing sources of resilience which have developed through exposure to multiple shock/ crisis situations.
- Build on what already exists, replicating and scaling up what works. This practice is also focussing on identifying positive practice, replicating it and enhancing it for use in new shocks. The benefit of building on in-house practice is thought to be better than using practices from elsewhere.

- Adopt local social norms and values where feasible. This practice helps to provide solutions to collective problems.
- Take advantage of institutions' social capital. This practice lends itself to the concept of trust. Where the communities' trust is gained and relations are built through mediation of state and society, institutions become more resilient.

A useful illustration of the practices outlined above can be applied to the higher education system. This is a complex system, which according to Heylighen (2001) comprises small local interactions of various factors which can result in major changes at the higher institution level. COVID-19 has created both a challenge and a big learning opportunity for education systems, so that they can be prepared for potential future 'shocks' of whatever nature and move to a more resilient space. The 'shock'created by COVID-19 illustrates the vulnerability of education systems, as it is beyond their control, and therefore it has created the need to take steps to secure future resilience. Table 1 applies the practical approaches to developing institutional resilience (as outlined above) to the higher education system.

Table 1. Approaches to Developing Institutional Resilience in the Higher Education Sector.

Practical Approach	Application in Higher Education Systems
Identify and leverage organic resilience	Universities supported their existing endogenous capacity of their virtual learning platform. Continued to deliver their core function.
Build on what already exists, replicating and scaling up what works	Using existing pedagogy capacity and practice and then scaling this up to the use of remote learning technology, enhancing digital capability. To be then used as tools and practice to enhance teaching and learning in a post-pandemic era. But also to create stronger resilience to future 'shocks' where face-to-face teaching is under threat.
Adopt local social norms and values where feasible	Sustaining the value of education and lifelong learning.
Take advantage of institutions' social capital.	Continual provision of the service with the support of different stakeholder groups, e.g. guest speakers from local industry and practice.

The interplay of internal and external local forces to create institutional resilience is of course not limited to the above-suggested practices. However, through this process of using existing local sources, replicating what works through an enhancement process and above all through connectivity with the community, institutional resilience can strengthen resilience at the organisational level.

3. REFLECTIONS AND CONCLUSIONS ON RESILIENCE BUILDING

Organisational resilience has become increasingly important following the recent global shocks, and this chapter has discussed some key elements which can support organisations to consider how they might wish to build increased flexibility and the ability to withstand such shocks and more gradual change. Building resilience requires a certain amount of duplication of resources, to achieve the level of robustness which organisations require. However, this is clearly a trade-off, between the level of risk that an organisation is willing to accept and the level of performance they are keen to preserve when faced with the shock or change, versus the cost of achieving this level. It will clearly differ depending on the industry sector in which the organisation operates: key critical infrastructure organisations (such as power generation, water supply or health) will have different requirements to maintain key critical processes in contrast to a smaller private company. However, it should be acknowledged that all risks cannot be mitigated as it is impossible to foresee all potential shocks and their impacts within a feasible cost envelope (Mottahedi et al., 2021; Rød, Lange, Theocharidou, & Pursiainen, 2020). In that case, the focus should be on loss mitigation and the ability to recover functionality as quickly as possible.

Despite the advantages to improving business resilience, there are also some pitfalls to avoid. There are several principles, standards and benchmarks that support organisations to build their organisational resilience (such as ISO 31000 *Risk Management* (ISO, 2016), BS 65000 *Organisational Resilience* (BSI, 2022)). Whilst these are helpful to enable organisations to be aware of the need for resilience and to provide useful guidance as to how an organisation might improve it, strict adherence to such guidance may create a level of over-standardisation of approach. By applying standardised 'solutions' to organisations, it may introduce a level of bureaucracy and inflexibility to the organisation, which does not consider the individual characteristics and circumstances of the organisation itself. This rigidity of approach applied unthinkingly or unwittingly to an organisation can in fact reduce its flexibility and increase its vulnerability, and is the very antithesis of the flexibility and adaptability which resilience requires, creating a 'resilience trap' (Rogers, 2013).

Another downside to be aware of is that as organisations generally evolve into networks within their economic or geographical domain, their behaviours can become entrenched. Whilst these networks can be quite strong, they can also get themselves 'locked in', perpetuating certain ties and stifling variety and creativity (Balland et al., 2015). This can reduce network flexibility and hence resilience. Hence it is important to review networks that organisations participate in to ensure their continued relevance and growth, as part of a risk management strategy.

In conclusion, the recent global and local shocks (ranging from the global financial crisis, the COVID-19 pandemic and the Ukraine invasion to more local environmental disasters, such as bush fires and floods) have caused many organisations to take stock of their resilience to these and more gradual changes in their environment and society. When considering how to improve an organisation's resilience, it is important to ensure that the senior leadership of the organisation share the vision about what the organisation needs to achieve and to monitor the environment to track and pre-empt where possible, changes which may impact on that vision and objectives (ISO, 2022b). The management team must then assess possible challenges and risks in the context of achieving their objectives, but in terms of resilience building, this should be focussed on delivering an agreed level of operations or performance during crisis times. This is unlikely to be to the level of normal operations in most organisations (although critical infrastructure organisations such as power generation, water and health may well need to consider higher levels of operating capability in comparison with other organisations (Rød et al., 2020)). The level of operations expected and the complexity and flexibility of the operating environment in which the organisation operates will dictate the level of investment needed to maintain this level, but it is important to be able to respond quickly and effectively to change and to coordinate activities across the organisation and where appropriate, its supply chain.

Pre-planning and risk monitoring and management are key to building resilience plans which can be triggered where necessary. Whilst it is acknowledged that not all eventualities can be planned for within a reasonable cost (since a certain level of duplication is usually required), research has found that despite the apparent inefficiencies of resilience building, resilient companies tend to outperform less resilient companies, due to their management attitudes (constant awareness of their environment, risk monitoring and evaluation of potential organisational impacts, attitudes to learning and networking, for example) (Lelievre et al., 2016). They are not only more resilient to shocks but are quicker to recover from any shocks that do occur. Therefore, notwithstanding the effort and cost to increase organisational resilience, the benefits do appear to outweigh the disadvantages.

REFERENCES

Aligicia, P., & Tarko, V. (2014). Institutional resilience and economic systems: Lessons from Elinor Ostrom's work. *Comparative Economic Studies, 56*, 52–76.

Anderson, C., & De Tollenaere, M. (2020). Supporting institutional resilience. *Development Co-operation Report 2020: Learning from Crises, Building Resilience.* Development Cooperation Report.

Balland, P. A., Rigby, D., & Boschma, R. (2015). The technological resilience of US cities. *Cambridge Journal of Regions, Economy and Society, 8*(2), 167–184. doi:10.1093/cjres/rsv007

Barma, N., Huybens, E., & Vinuela, L. (2014). *Institutions taking root: Building state capacity in challenging contexts.* World Bank Group.

Beavis Morgan. (2017). SMEs plan to borrow £50 billion in 2017. *New frontiers of social policy* (1–33). Washington DC: World Bank Group. Retrieved from https://www.beavismorgan.com/smes-plan-to-borrow-50-billion-in-2017/

Bruneau, M., Chang, S. E., Eguchi, R. T., Lee, G. C., O'Rourke, T. D., Reinhorn, A. M., ... Von Winterfeldt, D. (2003). A framework to quantitatively assess and enhance the seismic resilience of communities. *Earthquake Spectra, 19*(4), 733–752. doi:10.1193/1.1623497

BSI. (2022). BS 65000. Organisational Resilience. Retrieved from https://www.bsigroup.com/en-GB/our-services/Organizational-Resilience/

Burnard, K., & Bhamra, R. (2011). Organisational resilience: Development of a conceptual framework for organisational responses. *International Journal of Production Research*, *49*(18), 5581–5599. doi:10.1080/00207543.2011.563827

Coaffee, J., & Rogers, P. (2008). Reputational risk and resiliency: Place-making. *Place Branding and Public Diplomacy*, *4*, 205–217. doi:10.1057/pb.2008.12

Coombs, W. T., & Holladay, S. J. (2002). Helping crisis managers protect reputational assets: Initial tests of the situational crisis communication theory. *Management Communication Quarterly*, *16*, 165–186.

Coombs, W. T., & Holladay, S. (2015). CSR as crisis risk: Expanding how we conceptualize the relationship. *Corporate Communications: An International Journal*, *20*(2), 144–162.

Crespo, J., Suire, R., & Vicente, J. (2014). Lock-in or lock-out? How structural properties of knowledge networks affect regional resilience. *Journal of Economic Geography*, *14*, 179–198.

Dahl Fitjar, R., & Rodríguez-Pose, A. (2011). When local interaction does not suffice; sources of firm innovation in urban Norway. *Environment and Planning*, *43*, 1248–1267.

Datta, S., & Fuad, S. M. (2016). Valuing intangible assets: A balance sheet approach for DS30 listed companies. *Australian Academy of Accounting and Finance Review*, *2*(2), 189–203.

Davis, L. S. (2010). Institutional flexibility and economic growth. *Journal of Comparative Economics*, *38*, 306–320.

Eisingerich, A. B., Rubera, G., Seifert, M., & Bhardwaj, G. (2011). Doing good and doing better despite negative information?: The role of corporate social responsibility in consumer resistance to negative information. *Journal of Service Research*, *14*(1), 60–75.

Erol, O., Mansouri, M., & Sauser, B. (2009). A framework for enterprise resilience using service oriented architecture approach. In *Proceedings of the 3rd Annual IEEE International Systems Conference*.

Essuman, D., Boso, N., & Annan, J. (2020). Operational resilience, disruption, and efficiency: Conceptual and empirical analyses. *International Journal of Production Economics*, *229*(April), 107762. doi:10.1016/j.ijpe.2020.107762

Fombrun, C. J. (2005). A world of reputation research, analysis and thinking — Building corporate reputation through CSR initiatives: Evolving standards. *Corporate Reputation Review*, *8*(1), 7–12. doi:10.1057/palgrave.crr.1540235

Fombrun, C. J., Gardberg, N. A., & Sever, J. M. (2000). The Reputation QuotientSM: A multi-stakeholder measure of corporate reputation. *Journal of Brand Management*, *7*, 241–255.

Fombrun, C. J., & van Riel, C. B. M. (2003). *Fame & fortune: How successful companies build winning reputations*. Upper Saddle River, NJ: Prentice Hall.

Ganin, A. A., Massaro, E., Gutfraind, A., Steen, N., Keisler, J. M., Kott, A., … Linkov, I. (2016). *Operational resilience: Concepts, design and analysis* (pp. 1–12). Nature Publishing Group. doi: 10.1038/srep19540

Gaultier-Gaillard, S., Louisot, J.-P., & Rayner, J. (2009). Managing reputational risk – From theory to practice. In J. Klewes & R. Wreschniok (Eds.), *Reputation capital*. Springer-Verlag. doi:10.1007/978-3-642-01630-1

Gibson, C., & Tarrant, M. (2010). A 'conceptual models' approach to organisational resilience. *The Australian Journal of Emergency Management*, *25*(2), 6–12.

Gunderson, L. H. (2000). Ecological resilience in theory and application. *Annual Review of Ecology and Systematics*, *31*(1), 425–439.

Haider, H. (2020). Mainstreaming institutional resilience and systems strengthening in donor policies and programming. Retrieved from https://reliefweb.int/report/world/mainstreaming-institutional-resilience-and-systems-strengthening-donor-policies

Heylighen, F. (2001). The science of self-organization and adaptivity. *Encyclopedia of Life Support Systems*, *5*, 253–280.

ISO. (2016). *ISO International Standards*. International Standards Organisation. Retrieved from https://www.iso.org/iso/home.html.

ISO. (2022a). *ISO/IEC 27000:2018*. Information Technology — Security Techniques. Retrieved from https://www.iso.org/standard/73906.html

ISO. (2022b). *ISO 22316:2017*. Security and Resilience. Retrieved from https://www.iso.org/standard/50053.html

Jones, G. H., Jones, B. H., & Little, P. (2000). Reputation as reservoir: Buffering against loss in times of economic crisis. *Corporate Reputation Review*, *3*, 21–29.

Katsos, J. E. (2022). Strategy, operations, and responsibility in crisis context: The Russian invasion of Ukraine. In *Corporate Responsibility Research Conference*. Queen's University Belfast.

Kim, S. (2014). What's worse in times of product-harm crisis? Negative corporate ability or negative CSR reputation? *Journal of Business Ethics*, *123*(1), 157–170.

Kim, Y. S., & Choi, Y. (2011). College students' perception of Philip Morris's tobacco-related smoking prevention and tobacco-unrelated social responsibility. *Journal of Public Relations Research*, *24*(2), 184–199.

Kim, J., Kim, H. J., & Cameron, G. T. (2009). Making nice may not matter: The interplay of crisis type, response type and crisis issue on perceived organizational responsibility. *Public Relations Review*, *35*(1), 86–88.

Kim, Y., & Woo, C. W. (2019). The buffering effects of CSR reputation in times of product-harm crisis. *24*(1), 21–43. doi:10.1108/CCIJ-02-2018-0024

Klein, J., & Dawar, N. (2004). Corporate social responsibility and consumers' attributions and brand evaluations in a product–harm crisis. *International of Research in Marketing*, *21*(3), 203–217.

Klein, R. J. T., Nicholls, R. J., & Thomalla, F. (2011). Resilience to natural hazards: How useful is this concept? *Global Environmental Change Part B: Environmental Hazards*. doi:10.1016/j.hazards.2004.02.001

Knight, A., & Kavanagh, A. (2020). *Financial resilience: Building and fostering trust*. Deloitte. Retrieved from https://www2.deloitte.com/uk/en/blog/risk-powers-performance/2020/financial-resilience-building-and-fostering-trust.html

KPMG. (2020). *Brydon's proposals for a new resilience statement*. KPMG London, UK. Retrieved from https://assets.kpmg.com/content/dam/kpmg/uk/pdf/2020/11/brydons-proposals-for-a-new-resilience-statement.pdf

Lelievre, D., Radtke, P., Rohr, M., & Westinner, R. (2016). *Building resilient operations* (Issue May). McKinsey & Company.

Linnenluecke, M. (2017). Resilience in business and management research: A review of influential publications and a research agenda. *International Journal of Management Reviews*, *19*(1), 430.

MacKinnon, D., & Driscoll Derickson, K. (2013). From resilience to resourcefulness: A critique of resilience policy and activism. *Progress in Human Geography*, *37*, 253–270.

McManus, S., Seville, E., Brunsdon, D., & Vargo, J. (2007). *Resilience management. A framework for assessing and improving the resilience of organizations*. Research report. Resilient Organisations, Christchurch, New Zealand. Retrieved from https://ir.canterbury.ac.nz/bitstream/handle/10092/2810/12606763_Resilience%20Management%20Research%20Report%20ResOrgs%202007-01.pdf?sequence=1&isAllowed=y

Mottahedi, A., Sereshki, F., Ataei, M., Qarahasanlou, A. N., & Barabadi, A. (2021). The resilience of critical infrastructure systems: A systematic literature review. *Energies*, *14*(6). doi:10.3390/en14061571

Muharam, F. M., & Tarrazon, M. A. (2017). Real option in capital budgeting for SMEs: Insight from steel company. In *IOP Conference Series: Materials Science and Engineering*.

NRC. (2012). *Disaster resilience: A national imperative*. National Research Council – The National Academies Press. doi:10.17226/13457

OFGEM. (2021). Raft of new measures to boost financial resilience in the energy sector. Retrieved from https://www.ofgem.gov.uk/publications/raft-new-measures-boost-financial-resilience-energy-sector

Openwage. (2021). What is financial resilience and why does it matter? Retrieved from https://openwage.com/what-is-financial-resilience-and-why-does-it-matter/

Ouyang, M., & Wang, Z. (2015). Resilience assessment of interdependent infrastructure systems: With a focus on joint restoration modeling and analysis. *Reliability Engineering & System Safety*, *141*, 74–82. doi:10.1016/j.ress.2015.03.011

Paton, D., & Johnston, D. (2017). In D. Paton & D. Johnston (Eds.), *Disaster resilience: An integrated approach* (2nd ed.). Springfield, IL: Charles C. Thomas Publisher Ltd.

Perera, R. (2017). *The PESTLE analysis* (2nd ed.). Avissawella: Nerdynaut.

Rajesh, R. (2017). Technological capabilities and supply chain resilience of firms: A relational analysis using Total Interpretive Structural Modeling. *Technological Forecasting and Social Change, 118*, 161–169. doi:10.1016/j.techfore.2017.02.017

Reeves, M., & Whitaker, K. (2020). A guide to building a more resilient business. *Harvard Business Review*. Retrieved from https://hbr.org/2020/07/a-guide-to-building-a-more-resilient-business

RiskLogic. (2010). 5 impacts of the BP oil crisis. Retrieved from https://www.risklogic.com.au/business-continuity/5-key-impacts-of-the-bp-oil-crisis/#:~:text=Reputational Impacts,especially the governm ent was inadequate

Rød, B., Lange, D., Theocharidou, M., & Pursiainen, C. (2020). From risk management to resilience management in critical infrastructure. *Journal of Management in Engineering, 36*(4), 1–13. doi: 10.1061/(asce)me.1943-5479.0000795

Rogers, P. (2013). The rigidity trap in global resilience: Neoliberalisation through principles, standards, and benchmarks. *Globalizations, 10*(3), 383–395. doi:10.1080/14747731.2013.787834

Simmons, G., & Tinsley, D. (2011). Financial elements of business resilience; A systematic approach to financial staying power. *Graziadio Business Review, 21*(14). Retrieved from https://gbr.pepperdine.edu/2011/06/financial-elements-of-business-resilience/

Somers, S. (2009). Measuring resilience potential: An adaptive strategy for organizational crisis planning. *Journal of Contingencies and Crisis Management, 17*(1), 12–23.

Strupat, C., & Marschall, P. (2020). Strengthening social systems. In *Development Co-operation Report 2020: Learning from Crises, Building Resilience*. OECD. Retrieved from https://www.oecd-ilibrary.org/sites/b44cf64b-en/index.html?itemId=/content/component/b44cf64b-en

UN. (2020). *Resilient institutions in times of crisis: Transparency, accountability and participation at the national level key to effective response to COVID-19*. United Nations Department of Economic and Social Affairs, Division for Sustainable Development.

Vaughan, A. (2022). Deepwater Horizon oil spill did no harm to BP's long-term share value. *New Scientist*. Retrieved from https://www.newscientist.com/article/2324039-deepwater-horizon-oil-spill-did-no-harm-to-bps-long-term-share-value/

Wieland, A., & Durach, C. F. (2021). Two perspectives on supply chain resilience. *Journal of Business Logistics, 42*(3), 315–322. doi:10.1111/jbl.12271

RETHINKING SUSTAINABLE DEVELOPMENT UNDER CLIMATE CHANGE IN NIGERIA: A STRATEGIC ANALYSIS

Lukman Raimi and Fatima Mayowa Lukman

ABSTRACT

Beyond the rhetoric of Nigeria's policymakers, there are multifaceted challenges threatening sustainable development (SD) in Nigeria under climate change (CC). To strengthen theory and practice, this chapter discusses SD under CC in Nigeria using SWOT analysis. The exploratory focus of this chapter made the qualitative research method, an interpretivist research paradigm, most appropriate. Data sourced from scholarly articles and other secondary resources were reviewed, integrated and synthesised using SWOT analysis. At the end of the SWOT analysis, four insights emerged. The strengths and opportunities of SD under CC include increased awareness and growing access to climate-friendly technologies, sustainable finance, climate-friendly agriculture, solar technologies and renewable energy solutions, among others. The weaknesses and threats include deforestation, unabated gas flaring, rising carbon emissions and exorbitant cost of climate-friendly technologies, among others. The chapter explicates the need for policymakers and regulatory agencies in Nigeria to consolidate the strengths, correct all weaknesses, harness opportunities and avert the looming threats of CC. The chapter contributes to the three themes of SD by affirming that CC comes with devastating consequences that evidently pose existential risks and threats to people, profits and the planet. Consequently, policymakers need to mobilise sufficient resources and capabilities for CC adaptation and mitigation to achieve SD in Nigeria.

Corporate Resilience
Developments in Corporate Governance and Responsibility, Volume 21, 73–91
Copyright © 2023 by Emerald Publishing Limited
All rights of reproduction in any form reserved
ISSN: 2043-0523/doi:10.1108/S2043-052320230000021004

LUKMAN RAIMI AND FATIMA MAYOWA LUKMAN

Keywords: Climate change; net zero emission; Nigeria; regulatory requirements; sustainable development; strategic analysis

1. INTRODUCTION

Globally, climate change (CC) is a catastrophic environmental challenge
affecting all countries in the North and South with different degrees of intensity,
risk and impact. The issue of CC and associated negative impacts are receiving
massive attention in academic, industry and policy circles in developed countries
(Hurrell & Sengupta, 2012; Schramek & Harmeling, 2001). In particular,
developed first-world countries with manufacturing companies, factories and
plants have realised the threats of CC; hence, they are working pragmatically to
adapt and mitigate the negative consequences of CC backlashes such as solid
wastes and carbon/gas emissions from factories and industrial plants on the
planet, people and profit (Raimi, Akoshile, & Adebambo, 2016). The G20
countries have made the impact of CC on sustainable development (SD) a
frontburner issue (Schramek & Harmeling, 2001), even though developed and
developing countries are unequally vulnerable to the scourge of CC, such as
diseases, security threats, environmental challenges and vulnerabilities (Brauch
et al., 2011; Eicke & Goldthau, 2021; Schramek & Harmeling, 2001).

To ensure sustained compliance by all stakeholders with international CC
adaptation and mitigation policies, environmentalists are mounting pressures on
countries, industries and people to reduce greenhouse gas (GHG) emissions and
other pollutants while at the same time advocating that manufacturing outlets
comply with enabling laws and regulatory requirements in their host countries
(Ortar, 2015; Raimi et al., 2016). Other environmental actions, protocols and
treaties formulated at international and national levels to mitigate CC backlashes
include forest and marine conservation measures (FMCMs), other effective
area-based conservation measures (OECMs), zero tolerance for gas flaring,
eco-vigilance in manufacturing and production, adoption of climate-friendly
production techniques, socially sustainable finance, responsible investment and
strict carbon emission compliance, reporting and disclosures. Despite all these
laudable policies, environmental abuses engendered by industrial plants and
manufacturing companies continued unabated, a situation that stifles international actions on CC (Agung et al., 2022; Raimi et al., 2016).

Pathetically, developing countries that are more prone to the negative effects
of CC have not done much to mitigate the associated existential risks and threats
because of other equally critical domestic challenges of bad governance, civil
wars, terrorism, food insecurity, endemic diseases, poverty scourge, poor living
standards, public finance problems and institutional corruption ravaging these
countries (Picciariello, Colenbrander, Bazaz, & Roy, 2021; Raimi et al., 2016).
The plight of poor countries is therefore pathetic; although they contribute less to
industrial externalities and GHG emissions, they bear the brunt, and they are
more vulnerable to threats and risks because they have less capacity to mitigate
the ravaging impacts of CC (Schramek & Harmeling, 2001). Across the world,
the unequal adverse impacts of CC have visibly manifested as ozone layer

depletion, extended fires, melting ice, continental global warming, shower of acid rain, heavy rainfall in some areas and poor rainfall in others, rise in sea level and other extreme climate-related events, which calls for coordinated actions at national, regional and international levels (Picciariello et al., 2021; Raimi et al., 2016).

Without proactive policy implementation on CC, especially limiting warming to 1.5° C and scaling up adaptation in commerce, agriculture and industry, the devastating CC impacts portend danger of poverty, heat-related mortality, food shortages, flooding, changes in the fertility of agricultural lands, reduction in fresh water supplies, growing number of respiratory diseases, pollution of water, air and land resources, inequality for developing countries, and inhibition of the progression towards the actualisation of a wide range of sustainable development goals (SDGs) (Berrang-Ford, Ford, & Paterson, 2011; Intergovernmental Panel on Climate Change, 2014; Mohammed, 2020; Schramek & Harmeling, 2001).

In Nigeria, CC is being aggravated through oil and gas resource exploration and production, which significantly contribute to global CO_2 emissions through gas flaring (Mohammed, 2020). Oil pollution is an endemic problem in fishing and farming communities in the Niger-Delta region, where water and land pollutants from oil and gas exploitation have destroyed the ecosystems and livelihoods. In 2020 alone, the central government reported 370 oil spills in oil-producing communities, which is equivalent to 106 oil tankers (NOSDRA, 2021; Watts & Zalik, 2020). Moreover, policymakers through the media and institutional reports have heightened discussions on the need to promote CC through responsible production, reduction of gas flaring by oil companies, pollution controls, respect for gender equality and human rights in all climate actions, reduction of carbon emissions in the manufacturing industry, adoption of renewable energy options, promotion of sustainable finance and investing (SFI), provision of new climate-friendly technologies, promotion of sustainable consumption by households, implementation of the 1.5°C limit, carbon emission reporting and control, adoption of climate-friendly agriculture and promotion of other sustainability practices in industry and society at large (Mohammed, 2020; Okoro, Adeleye, Okoye, & Maxwell, 2021; Soltanieh, Zohrabian, Gholipour, & Kalnay, 2016).

Beyond the policymakers' rhetoric and media reportages on CC, there are multifaceted issues on CC that threaten the progression towards SD in Nigeria. To bridge the gaps in this area of research, this chapter strengthens theory and practice by discussing the need to rethink SD under CC in Nigeria in terms of the strengths, weaknesses, opportunities and threats.

Apart from the introduction (Section 1) above, this chapter is structured into five sections. Section 2 discusses the chapter methods and approach. Section 3 focusses on the literature review, which covers important themes on climate change, green theory, SD and SDGs and regulatory frameworks on CC and the role of institutions in Nigeria. Section 4 presents the insights from the SWOT analysis carried out on the CC–SD nexus in Nigeria. Section 5 concludes by contextualising the insights through policy and theoretical implications and limitations, including further research directions.

2. METHODOLOGY

The exploratory nature of the study made a qualitative research method most effective for chapter development. A quantitative research method is an interpretivist research paradigm that provides deeper insight into the CC–SD nexus in Nigeria. The required information was sourced from scholarly articles, texts, policy documents and working papers on CC and SD. Data extracted from scholarly articles and other secondary resources were reviewed, integrated and synthesised using SWOT analysis. The use of SWOT analysis to review and synthesise insights from scholarly works has been widely reported in peer-reviewed literature. SWOT analysis is useful in qualitative research because it supports the in-depth analysis of organisations, industries and countries for situational analysis, strategic planning, and strategic positioning and action (Helms & Nixon, 2010). Several scholars have noted that SWOT analysis is beneficial research because it is helpful in reducing complex strategic situations and the quantity of information to a concise level for effective decision-making and remedial actions (Sutrisno, Kwon, Gunawan, Eldridge, & Lee, 2016; Yavuz & Baycan, 2013). Conceptually, the term SWOT analysis refers to a situation analysis technique used in management and related fields for a systematic evaluation of the strengths, weaknesses, opportunities and threats within an organisation, a plan, a project, a person or a business operation for the purpose developing necessary consolidation policies and mitigation policies (Gurl, 2017; Namugenyi, Nimmagadda, & Reiners, 2019). SWOT analysis is an impact measurement and quality management evaluation tool that systematically reveals the strengths, weaknesses, opportunities and threats, including how these weaknesses can be overcome and how threats can be sustainably approached through proper implementation of methodologies (Leiber, Stensaker, & Harvey, 2018; Leigh, 2009). For more clarity, the SWOT analysis follows a three-stage process explained further below.

i. *Stage 1: Data sourcing* – This stage sources numeric and nonnumeric secondary data on energy transition and SD under CC. For data sourcing, we previewed Google Scholar, JSTOR, Science Direct, EbscoHost and ProQuest for relevant articles. Over 120 articles were identified, but after preview for relevance and recency, 60 articles were selected through the purposive sampling technique.
ii. *Stage 2: Data development and conversion* – This stage compiles insightful information and secondary data on the energy transition and SD under climate change through a critical literature review, classification of emerging ideas and integration of the insights in readiness for analysis data and discussion.
iii. *Stage 3: Data analysis* – This focusses on the analysis of the extracted data to address the research problem. The numeric and nonnumeric data gathered from scholarly articles, texts and online climate change resources were appraised and analysed using a combination of SWOT analysis and content analysis to answer the four research questions that the study set out to

answer. This methodological approach is supported by (Leiber et al., 2018; Raimi, Olowo, & Shokunbi, 2021; Williams & Shepherd, 2017).

3. LITERATURE REVIEW

To embed this chapter within the body of extant knowledge on CC, SD and energy sustainability research, the author explores different dimensions of CC issues in the literature. Four types of literature were reviewed: conceptual, theoretical and empirical and policy-focussed studies.

3.1 Defining Climate Change and Impacts

CC is an important concept at the national, regional and international levels. A search of the Google search engine for climate change produced 1,990,000,000 results within 0.60 seconds (Google search, 2022) – an indication that it has become a buzzword. The United Nations (2021) defines CC as long-term shifts in atmospheric temperatures and weather patterns in a country or across countries attributed to natural causes (such as through variations in the solar cycle) or excessive human activities such as burning fossil fuels such as coal, oil and gas. Similarly, Warm Heart Worldwide (2022) describes CC as a significant, long-term change in the global climate with far-reaching distortions to the systematic connectedness of the climate system leading to rising temperature, shifts in global ocean currents, melting Antarctic ice, rising sea level, among others. Similarly, Zareian, Eslamian, Gohari, and Adamowski (2017) defined CC as a major long-term shift in the pattern of regional or global climate systems, which is attributed to unsustainable human activities (particularly at the household, commerce, agriculture and industry levels) that generate the accumulation of GHGs in the global atmosphere. However, the Intergovernmental Panel on Climate Change (2007) defines CC as any change in climate over time that is triggered by natural variability and the change attributed directly or indirectly to human activity (household, commercial, agricultural and industrial emitters) that significantly alters the composition of the global atmosphere apart from the influence of natural climate variability reported at different periods. From the foregoing definitions, the understanding of CC goes beyond the warmer temperature and accumulation of GHS; rather, it should be understood as a global disaster that affects the entire Earth system and connects every other living and nonliving thing. The visible spillover impacts of CC include worsening health issues, intense droughts that reduce the capacity to grow food, water scarcity, severe fires, rising sea levels leading to flooding in different countries and communities, melting polar ice, catastrophic storms and declining biodiversity across the globe (United Nations, 2022; Zareian et al., 2017).

3.2 Sustainable Development and Climate Change

The United Nations has long been promoting the agenda of SD. The current agenda of SDGs comprised 17 well-articulated goals, 169 carefully structured targets and 230 veritable indicators that aimed at eradicating endemic poverty and hunger, protecting the environment and fostering peace and inclusiveness in societies without exceptions (Bello-Bravo & Lutomia, 2020). After the adoption of the SDGs by several governments (Buse & Hawkes, 2015), discussions, summits and advocacy across the globe centred around sustainability issues, SD action plans, sustainable lifestyles, sustainable diets, and sustainable finance have become pervasive in sectors such as manufacturing/production, business, consumption, energy, architecture, finance and investment, tourism, banking and other financial services and education (Raimi, Olowo, & Shokunbi, 2021). For clarity, Table 1 summarises the 17 SDGs and pragmatic policies that member governments and development partners are expected to promote and execute within the terminal period of the agenda. The 17 well-articulated goals are critical and expedient to reinvent a better and more sustainable future for the Earth and the people in the face of daunting global challenges facing developed and developing countries (Yusuf & Raimi, 2021).

3.3 Green Policy and Climate Change

CC finds theoretical underpinning from green theory. Green has historically been associated with freshness, nature, health, growth, money, safety and sustainability (Ottman, 2017; Sanderson, 2011). Green as a philosophy was popularised by environmentalists and ecologists warning humans, groups and industrial societies to integrate green ideals and practices into production operations, consumption habits and manufacturing processes, a paradigm shift that would have sustainable positive impacts on the wellness of consumers and the environment in the long run (Abbey, 2012; Jermier, Forbes, Benn, & Orsato, 2006; Newman, 2011; Scheffer, 2013). The understanding of green extends to earth-based spirituality, and one of the proponents, Mikhail Gorbachev, said: 'Well, I believe in the cosmos. All of us are linked to the cosmos. Look at the sun. If there is no sun, then we cannot exist. So nature is my god. To me, nature is sacred. Trees are my temples, and forests are my cathedrals' (Taylor, 2001, p. 175).

The real economic risks and existential threats of CC to the global ecosystem necessitate the adoption of green policy, green infrastructure and green economic growth as adaptation interventions to guide human and industrial activities with a view to securing the future and averting the spill-over effects of CC (Scrieciu, Rezai, & Mechler, 2013; Sussams, Sheate, & Eales, 2015). The green philosophy encompasses green marketing, green lifestyle and green thinking, which are emerging adaptive perspectives that raise alarm on the detrimental side effects of unsustainable economic growth on the natural environment and the worsening of CC (Raimi et al., 2016; Singh & Pandey, 2012).

At the country level, developed and developing countries have come to appreciate that CC presents a mix of threats and opportunities to humanity (Garcia, Cabeza, Rahbek, & Araújo, 2014; Pearce-Higgins et al., 2017). Consequently, these countries are adopting green business models, green products, climate-friendly operations, sustainable consumption, responsible production and

Table 1. The 17 SDGs of the United Nations.

SN	Goal Description	Pragmatic Policies for SDGs Realisation
Goal 1	No poverty	Policymakers must pursue economic growth process that is inclusive enough to provide sustainable jobs and promote equality among the citizens.
Goal 2	Zero hunger	To attain zero hunger, the agriculture sector and related sectors must embrace smart agricultural practices that support sustainable development (SD), fight hunger and endemic poverty.
Goal 3	Good health and well-being	All countries that are signatories to SDGs must design and implement measures that would ensure healthy lives and promoting the well-being for all citizens.
Goal 4	Quality education	Investment in a quality education by all UN member nations is the most enduring approach to improving people's lives and SD.
Goal 5	Gender equality	Pursuance of gender equality by all UN member nations is expedient because SDG 5 is a fundamental human right, and a potent vehicle for building a peaceful, prosperous and sustainable world.
Goal 6	Clean water and sanitation	All responsive governments must make provision of clean water and sanitation key priorities for nation-building and SD.
Goal 7	Affordable and clean energy	To achieve the net zero target, all UN member nations must make affordable and clean energy a priority.
Goal 8	Decent work and economic growth	Decent work drives economic growth, and sustainable economic growth in return creates better conditions that allow people to have more quality jobs.
Goal 9	Industry, innovation and infrastructure	The 3IRs of industry, innovation and infrastructure are resilient strategies for building and promoting sustainable modern societies.
Goal 10	Reduced inequality	No meaningful development can take place in societies with endemic inequality. To reduce inequalities therefore, governments should pay attention institutional conditions that engender inequality and marginalisation.
Goal 11	Sustainable cities and communities	All governments must develop sustainable cities and communities because access to safe and affordable housing by the citizens accelerate SD.
Goal 12	Responsible production and consumption	The roles of industrial society and buying society are imperative for actualising the ideals of responsible production and consumption, respectively.
Goal 13	Climate action	All governments must design and implement climate change adaptation and mitigation measures to meet the UN net zero emission target.
Goal 14	Life below water	Water and its vast resources need careful management for an enduring and sustainable future for humans and other species.
Goal 15	Life on land	Sustainable conservation, utilisation and management of land resources and forests are enduring ways to combat desertification, halt and reverse land degradation, halt biodiversity loss and other threats to life on land.
Goal 16	Peace, justice and strong institutions	To forestall threats to peace and halt wars at national, regional and international levels, all UN member nations must build strong institutions to ensure peace, and provide access to justice for all citizens.
Goal 17	Partnerships for the goals	The realisation of the SDGs requires multilateral collaboration and global partnership among governments, international institutions and private sectors.

Source: United Nations (2018).

green policies as preventive and adaptation measures to mitigate the actual or
anticipated negative effects of CC on human systems and lifestyles while
exploiting beneficial opportunities in the various policy responses (Berrang-Ford
et al., 2011; Pearce-Higgins et al., 2017). Ultimately, CC adaptation through
green policy and philosophy intends to protect and enhance the natural environment through energy conservation, environmental disclosures, sustainable
utilisation of resources and reduction or elimination of toxic agents, pollution and
dangerous waste in agricultural, commercial and industrial activities (Singh &
Pandey, 2012; Stanny & Ely, 2008). Some positive green actions that promote CC
adaptation include renewable energy, green consumption, eco-vigilance policy,
carbon neutrality programmes, zero carbon targets, energy savings production
approaches, eco-efficiency measures, and waste recycling and upcycling production techniques (Harvey, Heidrich, & Cairns, 2014; Panait & Raimi, 2021; Park
& Lin, 2020). In the field of international relations, green theory articulates the
need for all global actors (individuals, groups, organisations, nations and international bodies) to be actively concerned with the environmental and economic
sustainability of their consumption and production activities in society
(Eckersley, 2010). This aligns with the ideals of SDG 7 (affordable and clean
energy), SDG 9 (industry, innovation and infrastructure), SDG 11 (sustainable
cities and communities), SDG 12 (responsible production and consumption) and
SDG 13 (climate action). Deliberate diffusion of the green perspective has infused
into people green orientations and sustainable lifestyle behaviours such as green
consumers, green bonds, green economy, green marketing, responsible investments, sustainable finance, green advocates, climate-oriented investments, smart
agriculture, sustainable supply value chain, among others (Grant, 2007; Panait &
Raimi, 2021; Szuster, 2008; Wagner, 2003).

   In pursuance of global green policy to manage climate change, the United
Nations developed the UN Global Compact. The seventh, eighth and ninth
principles in the Global Compact demand responsible actions from the industrial
society. The seventh principle made it mandatory for manufacturing companies
and industrial plants to adopt a precautionary measure on environmental management; the eighth principle requires corporations to promote greater environmental responsibility and the ninth principle obligates manufacturing companies
and industrial plants to deploy environmentally friendly technologies in their
production and operations (UN Global Compact, 2014, p. 6).

3.4 SWOT Analysis of Sustainable Development Under Climate Change in Nigeria

This section reviews SD under CC in Nigeria through SWOT analysis. In
particular, the SWOT analysis of eight CC issues was examined under SWOT
analysis. These include (i) commitment to Net Zero target; (ii) commitment to
sustainable energy for All initiative and SDG; (iii) renewable energy and clean
development mechanism; (iv) regulatory and institutional framework for CC; (v)
legal and regulatory regime for CC; (vi) key plans and strategies on CC; (vii)
innovation adoption and diffusion for CC and (viii) monitoring climate financing
and budgeting for CC.

3.5 Commitment to Net Zero Target

Nigeria, as a high gas flaring country, made a policy commitment to end flaring and CO_2 emissions by limiting warming to 1.5°C, as recommended by the international community. In the past, policymakers promised to end gas flaring between 1969 and 2016, but this past target was truncated by a number of socioeconomic and environmental challenges, such as civil war, frequent changes in governments, weak political will and inadequate technological and financial capabilities, through joint venture funding (Mohammed, 2020). Despite the weak policy environment of the past, Nigeria's current policies on CC are moving towards the actualisation of the 1.5°C threshold. This is an indication that the country's climate policies and action are progressing. The threat at present is that poor records on progression towards 1.5°C may prevent the country from meeting set targets on domestic full decarbonisation (Climate Action Tracker, 2022).

3.6 Commitment to Sustainable Energy for All Initiative and SDG

Nigeria, like all other responsive members of the United Nations, adopted the Sustainable Energy for All (SE4ALL) initiative, and the country is also a signatory SDG. The SE4ALL promotes universal access to clean, reliable, sustainable and affordable energy by 2030, including limiting the rising global temperature to below 2°C (Dioha & Emodi, 2018; Rogelj, McCollum, & Riahi, 2013). The SE4ALL initiative aligns with the SDGs that also obligate countries and people to be responsive and proactive with regard to climate action adaptation by developing clean and renewable energy options from low carbon energy sources to further the realisation of SDGs by 2030. Essentially, SDG 11 (sustainable cities and communities) promotes climate-friendly lifestyles and behaviours in cities and communities. SDG 12 (responsible production and consumption) suggests that the utilisation of earth's resources for production and consumption should be carried out in a manner that would not aggravate CC impacts. SDG 13 (climate action) underscores the need for nations to vigorously pursue all climate protocols, including limiting warming to 1.5°C (Raimi, Che, & Mutiu, 2021). It is therefore evident that there are encouraging signals on CC adaptation, mitigation behaviour and policy support in Nigeria.

3.7 Renewable Energy and Clean Development Mechanism

In the policy circle, Nigeria has embraced in principle the adoption of renewable and clean energy options to mitigate the ravages of CC, control GHGs and promote sustainable lifestyle choices among citizens (Haider, 2019). There presently a number of policy documents and legislation that support renewable energy and clean energy options, but functionally renewable energy projects are very few (Dioha & Emodi, 2018; Elum & Momodu, 2017). Emerging renewable energy options, including hydropower, solar energy and bioenergy, are expensive compared to fossil energy sources; hence, the level of development, adoption and diffusion of these low-carbon technologies are extremely low. Analysts have noted that there is a need for stakeholders in the energy sector to create sustainable innovative financing schemes to attract investors with capabilities to develop low-carbon technologies such as hydropower, solar energy and bioenergy fuels for use by consumers (Dioha & Emodi, 2018; Haider, 2019).

Related to the foregoing is the clean development mechanism (CDM) in Nigeria's oil and industry that was as a market-based emission reduction mechanism after the Kyoto Protocol. It provides new opportunities for nations to eliminate gas flaring by granting licences to oil and gas companies with clean technologies and environmental processes of oil exploration and exploitation. In 2005, the Nigerian government set up the Presidential Implementation Committee on the Clean Development Mechanism (PIC-CDM) to issue letters of approval for eligible CDM projects in Nigeria in conjunction with the Ministry of Environment. Regrettably, only five projects in the oil and gas industry have thus far been registered despite the high potential of CDM in the country (Climate Action Tracker, 2022).

3.8 Regulatory Agencies and Institutions for Climate Change

To implement national and international policies on CC adaptation and control in Nigeria, the federal government established key agencies with complementary roles and functions, namely, the National Council on Climate Change ('the Council'), Federal Ministry of Environment (FME), Department of Climate Change, Inter-Ministerial Committee on Climate Change (ICCC) and National Council on Environment. Unfortunately, the government ministries and regulatory agencies in charge of CC action are poorly coordinated; they have weak institutional capacities, as they depend on external consultants for most tasks, and worse, they still face capital and resource constraints. Consequently, CC policies, protocols and key strategies are ineffectively mainstreamed into policy plans and targets because of irregular meetings, and progress on decarbonisation pathways is difficult to measure (Climate Action Tracker, 2022). It is reassuring from the above discourse that there are adequate regulatory agencies and institutions for CC in Nigeria.

3.9 Legal and Regulatory Regime for Climate Change

According to Mohammed (2020), Department of Climate Change (2021a, 2021b), Climate Action Tracker (2022), PricewaterhouseCoopers Nigeria (2022), Nigeria has an adequate legal regime for implementing CC policies, as evident from the following laws and national legislations.

- *Petroleum Drilling and Production Act (PDPA), 1969:* This law obligates oil and gas companies to submit 5-year plans for the utilisation of natural oil after the commencement of oil exploration and operations.
- *Associated Gas Re-Injection Act (AGRA), 1979:* The ineffectiveness and poor compliance with the PDPA led to the promulgation of AGRA. The new legal instrument in support of CC compels oil and gas companies in Nigeria to

submit a plan of action for gas reinjection and viable use of gas resources being flared in oil fields.

- *Associated Gas Re-Injection (Amendment) Act 2004:* In 2004, it was amended as AGRA 1979. It was an enriched version of the previous legislation.
- *Flare Gas (Prevention of Waste and Pollution) Regulation, 2018:* The legislation is enacted to consciously reduce the environmental and social impacts of flaring of methane and natural gas in Nigeria.
- *Petroleum Industry Bill (PIB), 2021:* The new legislation seeks to reform the oil and gas sector, attract investment in the sector, ensure better transparency, develop infrastructure and comply with the Paris Agreement temperature limit and promote net zero emissions in 2050.
- *Flare Gas (Prevention of Waste and Pollution) Regulations, 2018:* This important law provides the legal foundation the Nigerian Gas Flare Commercialisation Programme. It also imposed a new payment regime for gas flaring on gas companies based on the polluter pays principle and mandated data reporting on producers.
- *National Building Energy Efficiency Code or BEEC, 2017:* The BEEC sets minimum national energy efficiency standards for new buildings in the country.
- *Nigeria's Climate Change Act, 2021:* The Act provides a detailed and sound legal framework for actualising the low GHG emissions target as well as mainstream CC actions into all relevant national plans, projects and programmes. To make the Act actionable, the Federal government established the National Council on Climate Change (NCCC) with the mandate to make policies and implement decisions on all matters relating to CC. The Council is also mandated to collaborate with the Federal Inland Revenue Service (FIRS) to develop a mechanism for carbon tax and emissions trading to serve as a sustainable funding source fund for climate change, including developing a proposal for the enactment of the Climate Change Fund (the Fund) Act in Nigeria.
- *International Protocols and Agreement:* Nigeria is a signatory to the United Nations Framework Convention on Climate Change (UNFCCC), the Kyoto Protocol and Paris Agreement, and the UN Climate Change Conference (COP26), among others.

It is obvious from the review of policy documents that Nigeria has adequate laws and environmental legislation for CC adaptation and mitigation.

3.10 Key Plans and Strategies on Climate Change in Nigeria

To ensure compliance with international protocols and treaties on CC as well the national policy on the reduction of carbon emissions, the following are some of the key plan strategies. The 2021 Energy Transition Plan provides the country with a clear roadmap to achieve its net zero target; 2050 Long-Term Vision (LTV) for Nigeria (2021) aims to pragmatically reduce the level of emissions in Nigeria by 50% by 2050 by ensuring all sectors adopt net zero emissions in their operations; Revised 2021 National Climate Change Policy (NCCP) and the

National Climate Change Programmes for Nigeria; the Medium Term National Development Plan (2021–2025) that prioritises the implementation of the Climate Change Act for developing decarbonisation pathways in the country; the National Action Plan on Gender and Climate Change for Nigeria (2020) that mainstreams gender inclusion and recognition in national CC initiatives, programmes and policies; the 2020 Economic Sustainability Plan (ESP); the Economic Recovery and Growth Plan (2017–2020) promotes sustainable economic development through multiple climate-related projects; the 2015 National Integrated Infrastructure Master Plan (NIIMP) is an action plan formulated to drive enduring infrastructure development and sustainable investment in climate-friendly projects in Nigeria for the period 2014–2043; and the 2012 National Climate Change Policy Response and Strategy provides guidance and policy direction on CC measures in the country through climate-related R&D, institutional capacity development, sensitisation and public awareness among others (Climate Action Tracker, 2022; Department of Climate Change, 2021a, 2021b).

3.11 Innovation Adoption and Diffusion for Climate Change

In line with international commitment, the country's vision by 2050 is to become a low-carbon circular economy committed to reducing the current level of emissions by 50%, cascading the net-zero emissions to all sectors of the economy in a gender-responsive manner. The above tall vision is to be driven by four types of innovation: social innovation, economic innovation, technological innovation and environmental innovation (Department of Climate Change, 2021a, 2021b). Social innovation entails the pursuance of social change by reinventing institutional factors that inhibit the goal of a low-carbon economy. Economic innovation entails diversifying the economy and adopting a new paradigm that balances economic growth and environmental sustainability by rejecting a trade-off of both goals. Technological innovation focuses on the adoption and utilisation of green devices and eco-friendly technologies, such as the usage of smart home devices, the Internet of Things (IoT), climate smart agriculture, energy smart and water-smart technologies, to mitigate CC and control carbon emissions. Environmental innovation seeks to change the way of doing things in a manner that promotes environmental integrity. It extends to the use of novelty in science, technology, manufacturing processes and agriculture in a way that enhances positive social and environmental outcomes while avoiding environmental risks and externalities (Department of Climate Change, 2021a, 2021b).

3.12 Monitoring Climate Financing and Budgeting for Climate Change

Nigeria is proactive with respect to CC mitigation by appropriating funds for CC and setting up Climate Public Expenditure and Institutional Review (CPEIR). In policy circles, CPEIR is an analytical framework that is utilised for identifying, reporting, monitoring, evaluating and accounting for all climate-related financial resources deployed into CC adaptation and mitigation measures (Department of

Climate Change, 2021a, 2021b). Unfortunately, the county has limited capacity and ability to track the utilisation of climate finance and other resources (Climate Action Tracker, 2022). Several scholars have noted that for a long time the issues of ineffective financial management, poor implementation of economic development policies and weak monitoring of development projects in agriculture, health, education and energy sectors have been weaknesses of the government and its agencies in Nigeria (Ajani & Igbokwe, 2014; Gungah, Emodi, & Dioha, 2019; Monday, 2015; Ogbuabor & Onwujekwe, 2019). The foregoing are worrisome issues that have made realisation of socioeconomic and environmental targets of policies, projects and programmes impossible in some instances and sluggish in other instances in the country.

3.13 SWOT Analysis Results/Findings

At the end of the SWOT analysis, four insights emerged, as summarised in Table 2. The strengths and opportunities of SD under CC include increased awareness and growing access to climate-friendly technologies, sustainable finance, climate-friendly agriculture, solar technologies and renewable energy solutions, among others. The weaknesses and threats include deforestation, bush burning, prolonged famine, recurring flooding, unabated gas flaring, rising carbon emissions and exorbitant cost of climate-friendly technologies.

3.14 Conclusion, Implications, Limitations and Future Research Directions

The chapter sets out to strengthen theory and practice by discussing SD under CC in Nigeria. Using the SWOT analysis, the chapter provided insightful revelations on (i) commitment to Net Zero target; (ii) commitment to sustainable energy for All initiative and SDG; (iii) renewable energy and clean development mechanism; (iv) regulatory and institutional framework for CC; (v) legal and regulatory regime for CC; (vi) key plans and strategies on CC; (vii) innovation adoption and diffusion for CC and (viii) monitoring climate financing and budgeting for CC. The strengths and opportunities of SD under CC include increased awareness and growing access to climate-friendly technologies, sustainable finance, climate-friendly agriculture, solar technologies and renewable energy solutions, among others. The weaknesses and threats include deforestation, bush burning, prolonged famine, recurring flooding, unabated gas flaring, rising carbon emissions and exorbitant cost of climate-friendly technologies. The carefully reported findings of this study obviously have far-reaching policy and theoretical implications for academics and policymakers in Nigeria and beyond that are discussed below.

4. NEED FOR A SYNERGISTIC APPROACH

Practically, the call on policymakers in Nigeria to mobilise sufficient resources and capabilities for CC adaptation and mitigation to achieve SD is entirely not within the control of the government because the country is an oil-dependent

Table 2. Summary of Findings From SWOT Analysis.

Strengths	*Weaknesses*
• Consent to 1.5° C Net Zero compliance • Steady low-carbon transition for oil and gas sector • Policy support for renewable and clean energy options • Adequate laws and climate change mitigation policies • Adequate regulatory agencies to enforce compliance • Emergence of sustainable lifestyle choices • Green consumerism • Gender inclusion in climate change action • Strong stakeholder consultations • Social innovation • Economic innovation, • Technological innovation • Environmental innovation • Key plans and strategies • Signatories to international protocols and treaty of climate change and SDGs	• Inability to meet deadlines to end oil spillages • Duplication of regulatory agencies on climate change • Poor coordination of regulatory agencies on climate change • High prices of low carbon technologies • Overlapping function of regulatory agencies • Weak laws and climate change legislations • Poor capabilities to implement climate change policies and targets • Poor ranking on Climate Change Vulnerability Index • Poor investment in climate change adaptation measures • Poor investment in climate change adaptation measures • Reliance on external climate change consultants • Poor record on tracking 1.5° C Net Zero compliance
Opportunities	*Threats*
Emergence of renewable energy products Biofuel energy stations Emergence of clean development mechanism (CDM) Conversion of escaping gas into income-yielding products Green Jobs for employment reduction Green companies for wealth creation Carbon Tax for sustainable funding of climate change adaptation and mitigation Electric recharge stations Innovative sustainable financing Investment in low carbon technologies Deployment of smart technologies in oil refining	Inability to achieve 1.5° C Net Zero mandate Extinction of freshwater due to unabated oil spillages Massive poisoning of the air dues to unabated gas flaring by industry Worsening temperature Rising ocean level in coastal communities Drought and Famine in Northern Nigeria Fast pace of desertification and deforestation Low investment in renewable energy options Impunity of oil companies in Nigeria Inability to meet domestic full decarbonisation Sabotage of climate action due to conflict among overlapping regulatory agencies

Source: Author's SWOT Analysis.

developing economy, where domestic prices respond to parallel exchange rate movement (Eregha, 2021). When viewed from the supply side of industry, the production of oil and gas for export is the mainstay of the Nigerian economy. Additionally, exports of oil and gas are also subject to demands from other countries when perceived from the demand side of the industry. For Nigeria to be able to reduce its carbon footprint sustainably by reducing the production of oil and gas, other countries buying these products would also need to agree to reduce their dependence on oil and gas resources. A number of empirical studies support these arguments. Using a dataset from 1981 to 2017, Onifade, Alagöz, Erdoğan, and Obademi (2020) affirmed that both Nigeria's oil and gas revenue and inflation exert significant diametric impacts on economic growth. Specifically, oil and gas revenue has a positive impact on economic growth, but inflation has a negative impact on economic growth. Therefore, if an attempt to reduce exports of oil and gas must be implemented successfully to reduce GHG emissions and achieve net zero target, it would require a synergistic approach and paradigm shift in the demand for oil and gas at the international level. Even if this move is achieved, it would have a catastrophic impact on the Nigerian economy. The ongoing Russian–Ukraine war that has threatened the European Union's energy security in gas supply lends credence to the foregoing argument, as war cut down the supply of oil to many European nations with other negative effects on global financial markets and investments, although it is a crisis between two countries (Adekoya, Oliyide, Yaya, & Al-Faryan, 2022). Therefore, Nigeria cannot unilaterally limit global warming to 1.5° C without a synergistic approach with all its oil trade partners at the level of international trade relations.

4.1 Policy and Theoretical Implications

A number of policy implications have emerged. First, the process of conducting a SWOT analysis on SD and CC will provide policy makers and regulator administrators with valuable resources for improving net zero targets.

Second, the mixed insights from the SWOT analysis explicate the need for policymakers and regulatory agencies in Nigeria to consolidate the strengths, correct all weaknesses, harness opportunities and avert the looming threats of SD under CC. Additionally, the study underscored the need for policymakers in charge of CC agencies and policies to consolidate the identified strengths and develop relevant technologies and policies for harnessing the humongous opportunities reported; work collaboratively with local and international stakeholders and agencies to manage the identified weaknesses and avert the looming threats.

Theoretically, the chapter contributes to the three themes of SD by affirming that CC comes with devastating consequences that evidently pose existential risks and threats to people, profits and the planet. Consequently, policymakers need to mobilise sufficient resources and capabilities to make a difference.

Despite the far-reaching theoretical and policy implications explicated above, the chapter has few limitations. First, the study used insights from 100 scholarly articles, texts and online resources to draw conclusions on SD in Nigeria under CC. Insights from 100 collections of academic resources may be inadequate and unrepresentative for making conclusions on CC in Nigeria. Second, the use of the purposive sampling technique in selecting the collection of academic resources may be a limitation because it is a nonrandom sampling seen as subjective. It was used in this study because the chapter requires academic resources that fit the context of Nigeria and are relevant to the CC phenomenon being investigated. Third, this study adopted an interpretivist paradigm that is viewed as subjective in the methodology literature. It is useful in this study because it provides a comprehensive scanning of eight thematic areas that are important in the country's CC adaptation and mitigation measures. Despite the enunciated limitations, this study is distinct and unique because it qualitatively opens the space for more rigorous empirical studies on the fundamental areas of strengths, weaknesses, opportunities and threats of climate change action in Nigeria in particular and Africa in general. Future research may consider using survey research to confirm and extend the frontier of the present qualitative insights and findings. Additionally, future research may consider adopting a mixed-methods design for extending the frontier or knowledge using the current study as a springboard.

REFERENCES

Abbey, H. N. (2012). The green archivist: A primer for adopting affordable, environmentally sustainable, and socially responsible archival management practices. Archival Issues, 91–115.

Adekoya, O. B., Oliyide, J. A., Yaya, O. S., & Al-Faryan, M. A. S. (2022). Does oil connect differently with prominent assets during war? Analysis of intraday data during the Russia-Ukraine saga. Resources Policy, 77, 102728.

Agung, M. F., Adhuri, D. S., Ferse, S. C., Sualia, I., Andradi-Brown, D. A., Campbell, S. J., … Ahmadia, G. N. (2022). Marine conservation beyond MPAs: Towards the recognition of other effective area-based conservation measures (OECMs) in Indonesia. Marine Policy, 137, 104939.

Ajani, E. N., & Igbokwe, E. M. (2014). A review of agricultural transformation agenda in Nigeria: The case of public and private sector participation. Research Journal of Agriculture and Environmental Management, 3(5), 238–245.

Bello-Bravo, J., & Lutomia, A. N. (2020). Supporting sustainability for a decent work and economic growth in Ghana. In W. Leal Filho et al. (Eds.), Decent work and economic growth. Encyclopedia of the UN Sustainable Development Goals (pp. 1–9). Springer Nature Switzerland. doi:10.1007/978-3-319-71058-7_120-1

Berrang-Ford, L., Ford, J. D., & Paterson, J. (2011). Are we adapting to climate change? Global Environmental Change, 21(1), 25–33.

Brauch, H. G., Spring, Ú. O., Mesjasz, C., Grin, J., Kameri-Mbote, P., Chourou, B., … Birkmann, J. (Eds.). (2011). Coping with global environmental change, disasters and security: Threats, challenges, vulnerabilities and risks (Vol. 5). Berlin, Heidelberg: Springer Science & Business Media.

Buse, K., & Hawkes, S. (2015). Health in the sustainable development goals: Ready for a paradigm shift? Globalisation and Health, 11(1), 1–8.

Climate Action Tracker. (2022). Climate Governance Assessment of the government's ability and readiness to transform Nigeria into a zero emissions society. Retrieved from https://climateactiontracker.org/documents/1014/2022_02_CAT_Governance_Report_Nigeria.pdf

Climate Change Act, 2021. Law of Federal Republic of Nigeria. Abuja. Retrieved from http://extwprlegs1.fao.org/docs/pdf/NIG208055.pdf

Department of Climate Change. (2021a). 2050 long-term vision for Nigeria (LTV-2050). Federal Ministry of Environment, Nigeria. Retrieved from https://unfccc.int/sites/default/files/resource/Nigeria_LTS1.pdf

Department of Climate Change. (2021b). National climate change policy for Nigeria (2021–2030). Retrieved from https://climatechange.gov.ng/wpcontent/uploads/2021/08/NCCP_NIGERIA_REVISED_2-JUNE-2021.pd

Dioha, M. O., & Emodi, N. V. (2018). Energy-climate dilemma in Nigeria: Options for the future. IAEE Energy Forum, 2, 29–32.

Eckersley, R. (2010). Green theory. Chapter 13. In T. Dunne, M. Kurki, & S. Smith (Eds.), International relations theories disciplines and diversity (2nd ed.). New York, NY: Oxford University Press.

Eicke, L., & Goldthau, A. (2021). Are we at risk of an uneven low-carbon transition? Assessing evidence from a mixed-method elite study. Environmental Science & Policy, 124, 370–379.

Elum, Z. A., & Momodu, A. S. (2017). Climate change mitigation and renewable energy for sustainable development in Nigeria: A discourse approach. Renewable and Sustainable Energy Reviews, 76, 72–80.

Eregha, P. (2021). Asymmetric response of cpi inflation to exchange rates in oil-dependent developing economy: The case of Nigeria. Economic Change and Restructuring, 1–18.

Garcia, R. A., Cabeza, M., Rahbek, C., & Araújo, M. B. (2014). Multiple dimensions of climate change and their implications for biodiversity. *Science, 344*(6183), 1247579.

Google search. (2022) Climate change. The author conducted a search on March 30, 2022.

Grant, J. (2007). *The green marketing manifesto.* Wiley & Son.

Gungah, A., Emodi, N. V., & Dioha, M. O. (2019). Improving Nigeria's renewable energy policy design: A case study approach. *Energy Policy, 130*, 89–100.

Gurl, E. (2017). SWOT analysis: A theoretical review. *The Journal of International Social Research, 10*, 994–1006. doi:10.17719/jisr.2017.1832

Haider, H. (2019). *Climate change in Nigeria: Impacts and responses.* K4D Independent consultant, Helpdesk Report. Retrieved from https://opendocs.ids.ac.uk/opendocs/handle/20.500.12413/14761

Harvey, J., Heidrich, O., & Cairns, K. (2014). Psychological factors to motivate sustainable behaviours. *Proceedings of the Institution of Civil Engineers-Urban Design and Planning, 167*(4), 165–174.

Helms, M. M., & Nixon, J. (2010). Exploring SWOT analysis – Where are we now? A review of academic research from the last decade. *Journal of Strategy and Management, 3*(3), 215–251. doi:10.1108/17554251011064837

Hurrell, A., & Sengupta, S. (2012). Emerging powers, North–South relations and global climate politics. *International Affairs, 88*(3), 463–484.

Intergovernmental Panel on Climate Change. (2007). Climate change 2007: The physical science basis. *Agenda, 6*(07), 333. Retrieved from https://www.slvwd.com/sites/g/files/vyhlif1176/f/uploads/item_10b_4.pdf

Intergovernmental Panel on Climate Change. (2014). *Climate change 2014 – Impacts, adaptation and vulnerability: Regional aspects.* New York, NY: Cambridge University Press.

Jermier, J. M., Forbes, L. C., Benn, S., & Orsato, R. J. (2006). *2.8 The new corporate environmentalism and green politics.* London: Sage Publications.

Leiber, T., Stensaker, B., & Harvey, L. C. (2018). Bridging theory and practice of impact evaluation of quality management in higher education institutions: A SWOT analysis. *European Journal of Higher Education, 8*(3), 351–365.

Leigh, D. (2009). SWOT analysis. In *Handbook of improving performance in the workplace* (*Vols. 1–3*, pp. 115–140). Wiley.

Mohammed, S. D. (2020). Clean development mechanism and carbon emissions in Nigeria. *Sustainability Accounting, Management and Policy Journal, 11*(3), 523–551. doi:10.1108/SAMPJ-05-2017-0041

Monday, J. U. (2015). Local content policy, human capital development and sustainable business performance in the Nigerian oil and gas industry. *Journal of Management and Sustainability, 5*(1), 75–83.

Namugenyi, C., Nimmagadda, S. L., & Reiners, T. (2019). Design of a SWOT analysis model and its evaluation in diverse digital business ecosystem contexts. *Procedia Computer Science, 159*, 1145–1154.

Newman, J. (Ed.). (2011). *Green ethics and philosophy: An A-to-Z guide.* Newbury Park, CA: Sage Publication Inc.

NOSDRA. (2021). Nigerian oil spill monitor. Retrieved from https://nosdra.oilspillmonitor.ng/

Ogbuabor, D. C., & Onwujekwe, O. E. (2019). Aligning public financial management system and free healthcare policies: Lessons from a free maternal and child healthcare programme in Nigeria. *Health Economics Review, 9*(1), 1–10.

Okoro, E. E., Adeleye, B. N., Okoye, L. U., & Maxwell, O. (2021). Gas flaring, ineffective utilisation of energy resource and associated economic impact in Nigeria: Evidence from ARDL and Bayer-Hanck cointegration techniques. *Energy Policy, 153*, 112260.

Onifade, S. T., Alagöz, M., Erdoğan, S., & Obademi, O. (2020). Inflation, oil revenue, and monetary policy mix in an oil-dependent economy: Empirical insights from the case of Nigeria. *International Journal of Business, Economics and Management, 7*(2), 96–109.

Ortar, L. (2015, December). Climate change and CSR: Can voluntarism pay? UNFCCC (COP 21) meeting in Paris.

Ottman, J. A. (2017). *The new rules of green marketing: Strategies, tools, and inspiration for sustainable branding.* London: Routledge.

Panait, M., & Raimi, L. (2021). Trends in sustainable behaviour of consumers in Eastern Europe and Sub-Saharan Africa: A critical discourse. In *Sustainable production and consumption systems* (pp. 41–58). Singapore: Springer.

Park, H. J., & Lin, L. M. (2020). Exploring attitude–behavior gap in sustainable consumption: Comparison of recycled and upcycled fashion products. *Journal of Business Research, 117,* 623–628.

Pearce-Higgins, J. W., Beale, C. M., Oliver, T. H., August, T. A., Carroll, M., Massimino, D., ... Crick, H. Q. (2017). A national-scale assessment of climate change impacts on species: Assessing the balance of risks and opportunities for multiple taxa. *Biological Conservation, 213,* 124–134.

Picciariello, A., Colenbrander, S., Bazaz, A., & Roy, R. (2021). *The costs of climate change in India. ODI Literature review.* London: ODI. Retrieved from https://www.developmentaid.org/api/frontend/cms/file/2021/06/cost-of-climate-change-in-india.pdf

PricewaterhouseCoopers Nigeria. (2022). Tax Bites: Nigeria's climate change Act – Things to know and prepare for. Retrieved from https://www.pwc.com/ng/en/assets/pdf/nigeria-climate-change-act%20.pdf

Raimi, L., Akoshile, O. K., & Adebambo, A. (2016). Corporate social responsibility and climate change. *Geography and You Magazine.* Retrieved from https://geographyandyou.com/corporate-social-responsibility-climate-change/

Raimi, L., Che, F. N., & Mutiu, R. M. (2021). Agricultural information systems (AGRIS) as a catalyst for sustainable development goals (SDGs) in Africa: A critical literature review. *Opportunities and Strategic Use of Agribusiness Information Systems,* 109–133.

Raimi, L., Olowo, R., & Shokunbi, M. (2021). A comparative discourse of sustainable finance options for agribusiness transformation in Nigeria and Brunei: Implications for entrepreneurship and enterprise development. *World Journal of Science, Technology and Sustainable Development.* doi:10.1108/WJSTSD-05-2021-0051

Rogelj, J., McCollum, D. L., & Riahi, K. (2013). The UN's' Sustainable Energy for All'initiative is compatible with a warming limit of 2 C. *Nature Climate Change, 3*(6), 545–551.

Sanderson, K. (2011). It is not easy being green: In the past two decades, the green-chemistry movement has helped industry become much cleaner. However, mindsets change slowly, and the revolution still has a long way to go. *Nature, 469*(7328), 18–21.

Scheffer, V. B. (2013). *The shaping of environmentalism in America.* Seattle: University of Washington Press.

Schramek, C., & Harmeling, S. (2001). *Climate change. Synthesis report.* Retrieved from https://careclimatechange.org/wp-content/uploads/2017/06/G20-REPORT-.pdf

Scrieciu, S., Rezai, A., & Mechler, R. (2013). On the economic foundations of green growth discourses: The case of climate change mitigation and macroeconomic dynamics in economic modelling. *Wiley Interdisciplinary Reviews: Energy & Environment, 2*(3), 251–268.

Singh, P. B., & Pandey, K. K. (2012). Green marketing: Policies and practices for sustainable development. *Integral Review, 5*(1), 22–30.

Soltanieh, M., Zohrabian, A., Gholipour, M. J., & Kalnay, E. (2016). A review of global gas flaring and venting and impact on the environment: Case study of Iran. *International Journal of Greenhouse Gas Control, 49,* 488–509.

Stanny, E., & Ely, K. (2008). Corporate environmental disclosures about the effects of climate change. *Corporate Social Responsibility and Environmental Management, 15*(6), 338–348.

Sussams, L. W., Sheate, W. R., & Eales, R. P. (2015). Green infrastructure as a climate change adaptation policy intervention: Muddying the waters or clearing a path to a more secure future? *Journal of Environmental Management, 147,* 184–193.

Sutrisno, A., Kwon, H. M., Gunawan, I., Eldridge, S., & Lee, T. R. (2016). Integrating SWOT analysis into the FMEA methodology to improve corrective action decision making. *International Journal of Productivity and Quality Management, 17*(1), 104–126.

Szuster, D. (2008). *Green marketing – A case study of British Airways. Dissertation on culture, communication and globalisation.* Aalborg University.

Taylor, B. (2001). Earth and nature-based spirituality (part I): From deep ecology to radical environmentalism. *Religion, 31*(2), 175–193.

UN Global Compact. (2014). *Corporate sustainability in the world economy.* New York, NY: UN Global Compact Office. Retrieved from http://www.unglobalcompact.org/docs/news_events/8. 1/GC_brochure_FINAL.pdf

United Nations. (2018). About the sustainable development goals. Retrieved from www.un.org/ sustainable-development/sustainable-development-goals/

United Nations. (2021). *What is climate change? The United Nations climate action.* Retrieved from https://www.un.org/en/climatechange/what-is-climate-change

United Nations. (2022). *IPCC | Climate Change 2022: Impacts, adaptation, vulnerability.* Retrieved from https://www.ipcc.ch/report/ar6/wg3/

Wagner, A. S. (2003). *Understanding green consumer behaviour: A qualitative cognitive approach.* London and New York, NY: Routledge.

Warm Heart Worldwide (2022). What is climate change? Retrieved from https://warmheartworldwide. org/climate-change/?gclid=Cj0KCQjw3IqSBhCoARIsAMBkTb1Jgoo9kXoVJ59Y0kTFs0M NWquSOxmsmAmoeO256Wlp2b-ty2ZS4c4aAos0EALw_wcB

Watts, M., & Zalik, A. (2020, January). Consistently unreliable: Oil spill data and transparency discourse. Retrieved from https://www.sciencedirect.com/science/article/pii/S221479 0X20301374

Williams, T. A., & Shepherd, D. A. (2017). Mixed method social network analysis: Combining inductive concept development, content analysis, and secondary data for quantitative analysis. *Organisational Research Methods, 20*(2), 268–298.

Yavuz, F., & Baycan, T. (2013). Use of SWOT and analytic hierarchy process integration as a participatory decision making tool in watershed management. *Procedia technology, 8,* 134–143.

Yusuf, T. O., & Raimi, L. (2021). How compatible are SDGs with divine principles? A critical literature review (CLR). In *Islamic wealth and the SDGs global strategies for socioeconomic impact.* Cham: Palgrave Macmillan. doi:10.1007/978-3-030-65313-2_1

Zareian, M. J., Eslamian, S., Gohari, A., & Adamowski, J. F. (2017). The effect of climate change on watershed water balance. In *Mathematical advances towards sustainable environmental systems* (pp. 215–238). Cham: Springer.

SOCIO-CULTURAL AND RELIGIOUS DRIVERS OF CORPORATE SOCIAL RESPONSIBILITY (CSR) IN INDIA

Amit Kumar Srivastava, Shailja Dixit and AkanshaAbhi Srivastava

ABSTRACT

India is a country of socio-cultural diversity. Every society and culture existing in India is full of values, ethics and morality regarding good deeds. The exhaustive survey of corporate social responsibility (CSR) literatures from Indian philosophical perspectives observes many studies based on the socio-cultural and religious aspects. It has been observed all these philosophical views and concepts covering socio-cultural and religious backgrounds have received attention in the field of CSR. It is observed that almost all views have been fully explored in the context of CSR. Therefore this chapter tries to detect the drivers of CSR with all these philosophies prevalent in the culture of Indian society. This study utilises the hermeneutics, a qualitative research methodology which involves an in-depth study, critical analysis, thoughtful understanding and explanatory interpretation of the concepts of CSR originated from diversified Indian society and culture. In a nutshell, from these viewpoints and philosophies of different cultures, CSR is seen from an inside-out perspective.

Keywords: Social CSR driver; cultural CSR driver; religious CSR driver; dharma and karma; Zakat; Daashant; business ethics

LIST OF ABBREVIATIONS

AED—Currency Code of United Arab Emirates *Dirham*
RSD—Currency Code of *Dinars*

Corporate Resilience
Developments in Corporate Governance and Responsibility, Volume 21, 93–105
Copyright © 2023 by Emerald Publishing Limited
All rights of reproduction in any form reserved
ISSN: 2043-0523/doi:10.1108/S2043-052320230000021005

1. INTRODUCTION

Many researchers have provided insights about the reasons why companies have to engage in corporate social responsibility (CSR) activities. Mostly, work is centred on either functionalist approaches that provide premeditated reasons of the companies to keep in CSR (Chaudhri & Wang, 2007) and other vital approaches that probe the companies' concealed motives to involve in CSR activities (Cloud, 2007). In spite of the importance of an interpretive approach CSR has been characterised by severely challenging tensions and contradictions (May, Cheney, & Roper, 2007). The understanding of interpretive research in CSR is lacking to create easier understanding among the people (Ihlen, Bartlett, & May, 2011). This chapter highlights an interpretive approach with its capacity to reveal critical understanding by researching more into the norms and beliefs of corporate, societal groups and policymakers involved in framing the policies of CSR.

The definition of CSR, therefore, is still being debated, and there is no consensus among academicians or practitioners. CSR practices are entrenched within explicit socio-cultural boundaries which need to be studied (Mohan, 2001). In this context we can realise the significance of the concept of two different cultures of Japan and China like Kyosei and Confucianism, respectively, for creating the understanding of the drivers of CSR in the cross-cultural diversity of Japan and China, respectively (Wokutch & Shepard, 1999). However initially emerging economies were slightly acknowledged with CSR. So this study in an Indian context has some significant reasons. First, the continuous commercial history of India has been characterised by profound customs of social responsibility since the Vedic periods (Sundar, 2000). Further, the good deeds in the form of dharma have been derived from Indian culture which has faith in giving. Hence commercial communities with an Indian mindset are very close towards the newly devised so-called CSR (Mitra, 2007). With the passage of time Indian companies have been creating their new benchmarks in this era of globalisation. An Indian business tycoon Ratan Tata is a well-known figure for his social and philanthropic work in India and abroad (Srivastava, Negi, Mishra, & Pandey, 2012). The above-said facts are significant to explore the major drivers of CSR in India. The understanding of key drivers is very significant to know the status of CSR in India. With the critical evaluation of material aspects like practices and processes the study of CSR also emphasises the discursive fundamentals such as the written edifice of CSR. The key values of professionals that drive their engagement with the social responsibilities are also important in this regard. In the light of this positive development, CSR has attracted discussions from academic and practitioner viewpoints. It also demands some inputs from the socio-cultural and religious groups with high preference for ethics and values. As a result, modern organisations and individuals working in them are becoming more ethically conscious and religious with regards to their business actions and inactions.

The argument of this chapter is that socio-cultural and religious values could be better drivers for strengthening CSR, where implementations of regulations have been unsuccessful. There are a number of theoretical and empirical studies on the religious perspective of CSR from different angles of Indian socio-cultural and religious backgrounds. All the angles of CSR in these backgrounds have been discussed on the basis of methodological hermeneutics. Methodological Hermeneutics is a systematic process of studying, understanding critically and making meaning from the whole text and statements being interpreted or its parts and taking cognizance of the fact that they are interdependent and treated in interpretative enquiry and critical research (Kinsella, 2006; Schwandt, 2001).

2. OBJECTIVE OF THE STUDY

The major objective of this study is twofold:

- To explore the culturally grounded approach of CSR to critically examine the different cultures, religions and societies existing in India as the major driver of CSR.
- The next objective of this study is to evaluate the plausibility of cultures, religions and societies in strengthening CSR by observing the perception of people from the different socio-cultural and religious backgrounds regarding the drivers of CSR.

In completing these tasks, this chapter adopts an exploratory research approach which entails reviewing the different sources like journal articles on socio-cultural aspects of CSR. The whole process also covers the review of perception of the people from the different social and cultural backgrounds. This unique way of extracting and collecting data from the different sources has been made possible by using methodological hermeneutics.

3. METHODOLOGY USED: (IN ENSURING THE UNDERSTANDING OF KEY DRIVERS OF CSR IN INDIA)

The understanding of key drivers is very significant to know the status of CSR in India. With the critical evaluation of material aspects (practices and processes), the study of CSR also emphasises the discursive fundamentals such as the written edifice of CSR. The ways in which the professionals in the corporate, manufacturing and other sectors deceptively shape the understandings of key values that drive their engagement with the social responsibilities are also important in this regard.

So, for completing the twofold objective of the chapter this study will undergo an exhaustive literature review of the available related studies and a focus group interview specially with the top level corporate managers/policymakers and the different other expert groups directly or indirectly involved in the formulation, discussion and decision of the CSR policies in the companies. Involvement of focus group should be an appropriate way to know the different drivers of CSR

(Lee, 2010). So, on the basis of critical analysis of statements of the people selected in a focus group for the completion of the study, the whole chapter aims to generate socio-cultural and religious understanding of the key drivers of CSR in India which will help the researchers from cross-cultural regions to involve in comprehensive analysis of specific socio-cultural variables that might influence the drivers of CSR in their country also.

3.1 Feasibility of Methodology Used in the Selection of Respondents in Focus Group

This study is based on the recorded and semi-structured interviews of Indian businessmen, personal interviews of top level managers, policymakers and the other expert groups practicing on social and governance parameters. So, convenient and purposive random sampling seems to be suitable for completing the study.

Apart from the exhaustive review of literature this study has been completed with the critical analysis of recorded and semi-structured interviews and speeches of Indian business tycoons, top level managers, and policymakers and members of expert groups from different social, cultural and religious backgrounds. This combination of respondents in the focus group has also been given the impression to be suitable because it ensures the perceptions of the people from diverse industries, including telecommunication, manufacturing, education, social and media. Along with the social, cultural and religious backgrounds, the suitability of participants was also judged by considering the criterion of their roles and responsibilities in their organisations and had been correlated with the objectives of the chapter, i.e. evaluation of culturally grounded approach and the drivers of CSRs in India.

It was found that all the respondents selected in the focus group were directly or indirectly involved in the policies of CSR by holding the positions of chairman, directors, top level managers, educationists, psychologists and media. Most importantly, the participants from the corporate sector are not only heads of their companies but also leaders in national industry associations and chambers of commerce who actively shape corporate discourse on CSR in India.

The recorded interviews and speeches were taken from YouTube and their duration ranged between 30 and 40 minutes and the semi-structured interviews ranged from 10 to 15 minutes. The whole procedure of data collection was based on the research question and sensitising concepts of ethics, golden rules of life, principle of dharma – karma and the principle of sharing the earnings in charity.

For accomplishing the study, content analysis of available literature has been carried out and a semi-structured interview was followed by the main question: 'What are the key drivers for your company to engage in CSR?' Further, the questions were asked with the requests to exemplify all those drivers with full explanation.

4. MODELLING FOR THE STUDY

The whole study has been done by drafting a model which combines the different studies which provide a strong springboard for this chapter. Initially on the first level, this study has recommended the Epstein model of 2002 which has examined the linkage of society, culture and religion with business. On the second level this study has utilised the Angelidis Ibrahim (2004) model, which has explored the impact of an individual's religiosity and culture on corporate social responsiveness orientation. The third level of this study is based on the work of (Brammer, Williams, & Zinkin, 2007), which has been taken to investigate the perceptions and attitudes of people from different social, cultural and religious backgrounds towards CSR (Fig. 1).

Epstein study, (2002)   Angelidis & Ibrahim Study, (2004)   Brammer, Williams & Zinkin Study, (2007)

Fig. 1. Model of the Study. *Source:* Author.

5. LITERATURE REVIEW

CSR in India has historically had both socio-cultural and religious affiliations. Life principles such as Seva which translates to service have been a core tenet of Hinduism, which is followed by over a population of 600 million people in India. Other Indian religions like Islam, Christianity, Sikhism and Buddhism also share the same path of humanity.

Philosophers from different socio-cultural and religious backgrounds have proposed the drivers of CSR from different ethical, moral and strategic perspectives which dominate the discussion. The moral perspective highlights that companies engage in CSR practices because it is 'the right thing to do' and they are or ought to be motivated by intrinsic factors such as ethical values and moral leadership (Dhanesh, 2015). On the contrary, the strategic perspective suggests that companies engage in the practices of social responsibility because of extrinsic factors like society, market and government pressures, and there is a reason also that this type of responsible behaviour for society will generate benefits of increased employee commitment and customer loyalty etc. (McWilliams & Siegel, 2011).

The book of Atkinson and Field, for instance, highlights ethical perspectives by providing detailed antecedences of the Christian ethics and their relevancies to the secular world. Many studies discussed that business is part of God's work in the world. Delbecq in 1999 observed Christian principles provide an insight in shaping the leadership style in the managers who embrace the faith (Allen & Williams, 2020).

Gambling and Karim in 1991 discussed the business and accounting ethics of Islam. Zakat from the theological viewpoint is a compulsory alms or tithe payable annually by rich Muslims (individuals and corporations) at the rate of 2.5% of net incomes/wealth (often called zakatable amount), which is fixed as equivalent of 20 RSD worth of gold or 200 AED worth of silver (Raimi, Patel, Adelopo, & Ajewole, 2013).

Just like the Zakat in the Muslim community there is a system in Sikhian community in the form of daashaant (Haque, 2016). Many philosophers observed that, the poetic composition of Guru Nanak Dev depicts man as a dynamic personality who should be a personification of spiritual and social virtues. He should have his interests with humanity and his attitude towards life should be full of dynamism, optimism and welfare of other beings. In short, Sikhism expounds the ideals of a cultured person who lives holistically with inner awareness of the Lord and with the purpose of serving the nation selflessly.

Buddhism upholds ethics and high moral values in business relationship, a concept called 'Sila' (Ethical conduct). Sila means the totality of human conduct that helps to purify the mind cultivates the correct relationship with other sentient beings and reduces the negative causal impact of deeds (Mossley & Smith, 2010, p. 6).

5.1 Socio-Cultural and Religious Roots of CSR in India

The exhaustive literature review provides the different findings from the CSR perspectives prevailing in India from traditional to the globalised modern period. Various studies observed that strategic perspective of CSR, arguing that Indian companies are engaged in CSR only for the sake of reputation, financial and relational benefits (Mehra, 2006; Mitra, 2007; Sagar & Singla, 2004; Sharma, 2011; Sood & Arora, 2006). However, some studies have examined that Indian firms are engaged in CSR only due to moral values and commitment of top management (Arevalo & Aravind, 2011; Lee, 2010). Then Arora and Puranik (2004) and Gautam and Singh (2010) argued on the philanthropic dimension of CSR, and a more recent study of Coopers in 2013 found a drastic shift in CSR and it is turning into a new shape in India which is more strategic in nature (Pricewaterhouse Coopers, P.W.C., 2013). The Christianity ethics or social views like public service, paternalism and selfless service have been shaped by the historical realities in the scriptures. For instance, John Howard Yoder is credited with the religious statement that our responsibility is to be faithful, not successful in worldly pursuits. An organised Zakat system therefore is designed to empower and create social justice in Muslim societies and non-Muslim societies (Jawad, 2009). Researchers have explained that Zakat represents one of the key social institutions that could be used to build social justice, fairness, equity and enduring peace in Muslim societies. Similar to Islam's Zakat, Sikhs followed what they called daashaant (Haque, 2016). Besides, CSR was observed as true in two Jewish ethics, namely: benevolence and free will. Benevolence consists of positive traits like caring for others, forgiveness and giving to the poor, while free will is a belief that humans have the liberty and freedom to embrace benevolence (Lee, 2009).

5.2 Interpretation of First Objective (Through Literature Review)

The insights of CSR in India can be drawn from the mythological perspective of the different socio-cultural and religious texts. Dharma/righteous duty and Karma/costs and benefits of actions have been observed in the Hindu mythology. In a case study in Indian context, Pio (2005), applied these principles and confirmed their significance in examining CSR critically; this study appreciated the Indian notion of dharma because it has been broadly discussed in the context of CSR (Das, 2009). Pio in 2005 explained dharma as the proper behaviour, right conduct and right endeavour. It is the right way to maintain order and balance in the universe. As long as every element in the cosmos, the sun, rain, animals, plants and humans act according to their dharma, the order and balance is maintained (p. 68). By critically examining an Indian epic *Mahabharata*, Das in 2009, has explained the notion of dharma. By following CSR, companies are showing their behaviour of 'being good', but he identified the multiple meanings of dharma which are equating it with law and rituals. The outcome of this study is that it employed the notion of dharma as 'righteous duty' (Pio, 2005, p. 68) and hence this definition seems to be most compatible with the concept of CSR. In other words, different literatures on CSR in India have exposed the various perspectives like ethical, strategic etc. for exploring the key drivers of CSR in India. Studies based on Indian mythological perspective like dharma and karma may be underdeveloped but seem to be more promising.

On the theological foundation for CSR and conventional business practices in Islam, Cone in 2003 explained that the Quran has endless list of provisions, ethical values and rules of conduct on socio-economic matters. The socio-economic dealings of Muslims as individuals and a corporate group are hinged strictly on four principles of Islam, viz Tawheed means unity, Al'adl wal ihsan means equilibrium, Ikhtiar means free will and Fardh means social responsibility, which are mutually reinforcing (Cone, 2003).

The goal of the public service philosophy as taught by Christianity is centred on the spirit of selfless service and concerns for the prosperity of the society. It was the church's philosophy that inspired ethical consciousness and personal sense of responsibility, which was later adopted and taken the form of christened social responsibility (Chita & Mwale, 2017).

Judaism accords importance to Tzedakah, which connotes charity and act of giving to the poor, an obligation that cannot be forsaken, even if those giving charity are themselves in need (Tracey, 2011). By combining these philosophies, it has been observed that it is the ethical, moral and strategic perspective which suggests that businesses are motivated by an intricate interaction of both intrinsic and extrinsic factors (Child & Tsai, 2005).

So, on the basis of an exhaustive review of literature this, part of the study suggests that there is a very high impact of socio-cultural and religious factors on the attitude and behaviour of people in India. It also indicates the thought that root of CSR exist in socio-cultural and religious factors is correct. The drivers of social responsibility grounded in the socio-cultural and religious factors working with ethical and moralistic notion right from the early days of industrialisation which is becoming increasingly strategic in this arena of globalisation.

6. INTERPRETATION OF SECOND OBJECTIVE (THROUGH THE STUDY OF FOCUS GROUP PERCEPTION)

For the purpose of evaluating the plausibility of cultures, religions and societies in strengthening CSR, the perception of people has been observed from the different socio-cultural and religious backgrounds with the help of focus group study. Methodological Hermeneutics was used for finalising and giving shape to the interpretation from the available information and secondary data set. Besides this, this part of the study has also completed the critical analysis of recorded speeches and in-depth interviews of the people selected in the focus group. This study has ensured that the people selected in the focus group are engaged in doing, promoting or fighting for CSR activities like running schools, orphanage houses, handling child labour issues, clean drinking water issues, sanitation, women empowerment, creating livelihood programmes and compassion for the family of patriots etc. What motivates these people from different part of industries and society to come forward and involve in these types of social activities? After critical analysis of the responses of every member of the focus group this study has analysed that the socio-cultural and religious lessons have a major role in creating a drive of good deeds in them in the form of moral perspective followed by an economic perspective in this era of materialisation.

6.1 Moral Perspective of CSR

The sentiment in the statements of focus group has shown the moralistic urge as the predominant driver of CSR, as the visionary chairman from the Hindu community running a famous Trust in Bareilly U.P. stated, 'In a world where crores of people are poor ... can we sit idle and say that I don't have an opinion? I will nothing?' We should be reciprocative. The director, CSR of an Agro Oil company in Bareilly following Hinduism, disclosed the vision of his company that it wants to do something tangible, which will become an example of morality in the future... in the form of something which is sustainable and which would really have a deep impact on the community. The young director of an Institute of Medical Sciences Bareilly from the Hindu community also believes in morality and says… 'Whatever wealth we earn, part of it ought to go back to the underprivileged so that we have a more equitable society'.

This study analysed that they also emphasised on the human psychology that we have a vicious circle of desires to accumulate prosperity, but with this we have to express our urge to balance social disparities. Some of them have highlighted that the manufacturing companies have larger impacts on immediate human and natural environments, compared to service-sector firms. One of the Sikh member in the focus group; who is the CEO & social worker of a famous foundation said that we should remember the teachings of Guru Granth Sahib – 'the presence of morality in human being is important because it is the only factor which makes us different from animals'. She said that 'We cannot imagine our life in some kind of island of prosperity'. The, Trustee & CEO of a famous foundation in India a member from Muslim community inveterate this views by remembering the Islamic mythology that 'We cannot be islands of prosperity if people around us are poor. So there has to be an assortment of people and we have to be involved in give and take in the society'.

One interviewee by a famous reporter of the Times of India has drawn attention to the slums of Mumbai to underscore her point that companies with their huge wealth existed in between large swathes of poverty. With the great and kind moral gesture of responsibility towards the unprivileged, her voice echoed with overtones of Kantian ethics focussing on, 'our actions are morally right only when they originate from a sense of duty' (L'etang, 1994).

6.2 Economic Perspective of CSR

In the other dimension of CSR this study found that the companies are motivated towards the social responsibility due to economic perspective; this is the second, but almost equally important factor of motivation for companies to engage in CSR. The people from the selected group perceived the benefits of CSR on corporate longevity, creation of goodwill in society and their strong relationships with employees.

People from every sector in the study agreed that our socially responsible behaviour is significant in the long-term success and continuity of the companies. A member following Hinduism and the General Manager, Marketing of a telecom company of U.P. East, said, 'by doing corporate social responsibility, we ensure the sustainability of both the people and corporate in economic terms. All of our efforts are ensuring our long-term endeavours for the organisation'. Towards the end he said, 'I strongly accept that if we expect our company to be profitable and successful over long periods of time, then it will only be possible when we try to maintain peace and economic sustainability of people in society'. By recalling the life principles from the Bible a member from the Christian community and CEO of a Marine Services Pvt. Ltd said that 'Giving is more blessed than receiving….we should create future business goodwill for the economic profit and repeat business by giving stakeholders good value for their resources' further emphasising on 'living a full life… to constantly improve the standards of every aspect of life of our society'. The people from all the selected sectors agreed that being socially responsible will help us create goodwill and increase our economic profit by strengthening our relationship with local communities and employees.

7. CONCLUSION

The significant insights of ethics, values from society, culture and religion which motivates people from the corporate and non-corporate world to actively involve in the CSR has been explored in the present study with the help of a literature review. It has been observed under the study that moral and economic imperatives have a major role just like a driver to perform CSR in India. This belief was supported by the second phase of findings of this study which highlight the arousal of moral imperative in us is based on an intrinsic sense of responsibility while an economic imperative is based on the pressure of extrinsic factors like competition, economic profit, economic sustainability of company and society etc. The dynamic interplay between the moralistic and economic imperatives as drivers of CSR was explained by the other members of focus group with the help of ancient Indian concepts of dharma and karma. The available literature of (Das, 2010) explains the notion of dharma as based on the sense of duty and responsibility that resonates with the ethics of Western Kantian philosophy. So, dharma is naturally present in an individual's character and 'Being good' not only depends on consequences but also on motives. Lord Krishna in the *Mahabharata* said, 'One should not act for the sake of the fruits of dharma. He should act because he must' (*Mahabharata*, III.32.2-4, as cited in Das, 2009, p. 65). The CSR perspective full of duty and responsibility resonates with the argument of L'etang (1994), that a Kantian sense of ethics must drive corporations' CSR. This perspective was present in the words of an Indian psychologist and rector in the university, 'Why do we believe [that we need to help in social development]? We believe. I mean there's no [other reason].... You can't have reasons beyond that'. She also expressed her great feelings about the dharma that practice of dharma leads to good karma because good acts produce good consequences, and dharma yields good fruits for the individual as well as society. Both the individual and society seem to be benefited in India through dharma, and it appears compatible with the idea behind the second main driver of CSR in the form of economic imperative that focusses on mutual benefit for every stakeholder.

By exploring the concept of dharma, Das (2009) has highlighted its significance comparing the notion of dharma with the notion of virtue and ethics. This point was supported by a famous academician of the capital of Uttar Pradesh, India, that dharma gives disciplines to the pursuit of desires and provides balance to human lives and it connects the virtue and ethics with character for fulfiling the purpose of human life. He said that dharma can be grounded in self-interest without being amoral and the notion of reciprocal altruism, wherein good behaviour is reciprocated.

So, by creating a culturally grounded understanding of the key drivers of CSR in India, the findings of this study also supplement the knowledge on drivers of CSR on global level in a unique way. This study concludes that companies are generally driven by these imperatives, but some complex webs of factors are also there which cover these imperatives.

7.1 Limitations and Future Research

Although India is the country which possesses enormous names of big and famous business tycoons and top level managers running their companies, with huge profit and they all are also playing an important role in meeting the objectives of CSR, but this study was limited to some people in the sampling frame. This study covers the limited outside expert suggestions and feelings about the CSR. Therefore, in the future research some more famous personalities should also be covered which could be helpful in exploring other new dimensions and drivers of CSR in India. Government of India has enacted the Companies Act 2013 under which Schedule 7 provides the regulation for CSR which was not covered under this study, but it could have an enormous impact on the practices and policies of CSR of Indian corporates. So, this will become a new area for the future research to evaluate the government's mandates and regulations as a key driver of CSR in India. With these limitations, the present study has contributed to providing a richer, culturally grounded understanding of the key drivers of CSR in India.

REFERENCES

Allen, S., & Williams, P. (2020). Teaching management, spirituality, and religion: André Delbecq as a pioneer. *Journal of Management, Spirituality & Religion, 17*(1), 37–44.

Angelidis, J., & Ibrahim, N. (2004). An exploratory study of the impact of degree of religiousness upon an individual's corporate social responsiveness orientation. *Journal of Business Ethics, 51*(2), 119–128.

Arevalo, J. A., & Aravind, D. (2011). Corporate social responsibility practices in India: Approach, drivers, and barriers. *Corporate Governance: The International Journal of Business in Society, 11*(4), 399–414.

Arora, B., & Puranik, R. (2004). A review of corporate social responsibility in India. *Development, 47*(3), 93–100.

Brammer, S., Williams, G., & Zinkin, J. (2007). Religion and attitudes to corporate social responsibility in a large cross-country sample. *Journal of Business Ethics, 71*(3), 229–243.

Chaudhri, V., & Wang, J. (2007). Communicating corporate social responsibility on the internet: A case study of the top 100 information technology companies in India. *Management Communication Quarterly, 21*(2), 232–247.

Child, J., & Tsai, T. (2005). The dynamic between firms' environmental strategies and institutional constraints in emerging economies: Evidence from China and Taiwan. *Journal of Management Studies, 42*(1), 95–125.

Chita, J., & Mwale, N. (2017). The Church's Social Responsibility in Zambia: The Catholic Response to the 2016 prejudiced attacks on 'others'. *Alternation Journal*, (19), 132–156.

Cloud, D. L. (2007). Corporate social responsibility as oxymoron. The debate over corporate social responsibility 219.

Cone, M. H. (2003). Corporate citizenship: The role of commercial organisations in an Islamic society. *The Journal of Corporate Citizenship*, (9), 49–66.

Das, G. (2009). *Difficulty of being good*. Haryana: Penguin UK.

Das, G. (2010). *The difficulty of being good: On the subtle art of dharma*. New York: Oxford University Press (Originally Published: New Delhi: Allen Lane).

Dhanesh, G. S. (2015). Why corporate social responsibility? An analysis of drivers of CSR in India. *Management Communication Quarterly, 29*(1), 114–129.

Gambling, T., & Karim, R. (1991). *Business and accounting ethics in Islam*. London: Mansell.

Gautam, R., & Singh, A. (2010). Corporate social responsibility practices in India: A study of top 500 companies. *Global Business and Management Research: An International Journal, 2*(1), 41–56.

Haque, M. N. (2016). Insight into History of CSR practice in India with special reference to communication. *Amity Journal of Media & Communications Studies (AJMCS), 5*(3), 232.

Ihlen, O., Bartlett, J., & May, S. (Eds.). (2011). *The handbook of communication and corporate social responsibility*. Hoboken, NJ: John Wiley & Sons.

Jawad, R. (2009). *Social welfare and religion in the Middle East: A Lebanese perspective*. Bristol: Policy Press.

Kinsella, E. A. (2006, May). Hermeneutics and critical hermeneutics: Exploring possibilities within the art of interpretation. *Forum Qualitative Sozialforschung/Forum: Qualitative Social Research, 7*(3).

L'etang, J. (1994). Public relations and corporate social responsibility: Some issues arising. *Journal of Business Ethics, 13*(2), 111–123.

Lee, M. E. (2009). Galilean Journey revisited: Mestizaje, anti-Judaism, and the dynamics of exclusion. *Theological Studies, 70*(2), 377–400.

Lee, S. (2010). *Corporate social responsibility in India*. A Case Study for the Oxford-Achilles Working Group on Corporate Social Responsibility (pp. 3–4).

May, S. K., Cheney, G., & Roper, J. (Eds.). (2007). *The debate over corporate social responsibility*. New York, NY: Oxford University Press.

McWilliams, A., & Siegel, D. S. (2011). Creating and capturing value: Strategic corporate social responsibility, resource-based theory, and sustainable competitive advantage. *Journal of Management, 37*(5), 1480–1495.

Mehra, M. (2006). Corporate social responsibility in emerging economies. *The Journal of Corporate Citizenship*, (24), 20–22.

Mitra, M. (2007). *It's only business!: India's corporate social responsiveness in a globalized world*. New York, NY: Oxford University Press.

Mohan, A. (2001). Corporate citizenship: Perspectives from India. *The Journal of Corporate Citizenship*, (2), 107–117.

Mossley, D., & Smith, S. (2010). *Faith guides for higher education: A guide to Buddhism*. Leeds: Subject Centre for Philosophical and Religious Studies.

Pio, E. (2005). Eastern karma: Perspectives on corporate citizenship. *The Journal of Corporate Citizenship*, (19), 65–78.

Pricewaterhouse Coopers, P.W.C. (2013). *Handbook on corporate social responsibility in India*. Confederation of Indian Industry.

Raimi, L., Patel, A., Adelopo, I., & Ajewole, T. (2013). Full Length Research Paper Tackling Poverty Crisis in the Muslim Majority Nations (MMNs): The Faith-Based Model (FBM) as an Alternative Policy Option. Retrieved from https://www.researchgate.net/publication/269520156_Tackling_Poverty_Crisis_in_the_Muslim_Majority_Nations_MMNs_The_Faith-Based_Model_FBM_as_an_Alternative_Policy_Option; https://www.academia.edu/27391996/Corporate_social_responsibility_Waqf_system_and_Zakat_system_as_faith_based_model_for_poverty_reduction

Sagar, P., & Singla, A. (2004). Trust and corporate social responsibility: Lessons from India. *Journal of Communication Management, 8*(3), 282–290.

Schwandt, T. A. (2001). *Dictionary of qualitative research*. Thousand Oaks, CA: Sage.

Sharma, S. (2011). Corporate social responsibility in India. *Indian Journal of Industrial Relations, 46*(4), 637–649.

Sood, A., & Arora, B. (2006). *The political economy of corporate responsibility in India*. Geneva: UNRISD.

Srivastava, A. K., Negi, G., Mishra, V., & Pandey, S. (2012). Corporate social responsibility: A case study of TATA group. *IOSR Journal of Business and Management, 3*(5), 17–27.

Sundar, P. (2000). *Beyond business*. New Delhi; Thousand Oaks; London: Sage Publication.

Tracey, R. R. (2011). Tzedakah: Charity. Retrieved from http://www.jewfaq.org/tzedakah.htm

Wokutch, R. E., & Shepard, J. M. (1999). The maturing of the Japanese economy: Corporate social responsibility implications. *Business Ethics Quarterly, 9*(3), 527–540.

PART 2

CORPORATE RESILIENCE

A PARADIGM FOR EXAMINING THE INTERPLAY OF ENVIRONMENTAL INVESTMENT, ENVIRONMENTAL DISCLOSURE AND FIRM PERFORMANCE IN CHINA

Ruopiao Zhang and Carlos Noronha

ABSTRACT

Drawing upon resource-based view (RBV) and attribution theoretical lenses, this chapter provides a paradigm for examining the interplay among environmental investment towards green innovation, environmental disclosure as well as firm performance using the structural equation modelling (SEM) methodology. This chapter demonstrate a growing environmental awareness among stakeholders of the relevance of environmental performance to share value. It is also suggested that the mediating power of environmental disclosure between environmental investment and firm value as well as incremental goodwill is crucial. The findings of this chapter provide critical implications for several stakeholders that if environmental performance is hypothesised to affect the firm's value, companies may take proactive measures to avert potential environmental-related violations. Besides, investors may trade based on the evidence as to how firm value and its goodwill from acquisition will be affected by news of its environmental performance.

Keywords: Resource-based view; attribution theory; environmental investment; environmental disclosure; firm performance; Corporate social responsibility (CSR)

Corporate Resilience
Developments in Corporate Governance and Responsibility, Volume 21, 109–128
Copyright © 2023 by Emerald Publishing Limited
All rights of reproduction in any form reserved
ISSN: 2043-0523/doi:10.1108/S2043-052320230000021006

1. INTRODUCTION

China's accession to the World Trade Organization (WTO) at the end of 2001, which was described by Ciuriak (2002, p. 59) as a landmark event bringing one of the world's major trading economies fully into the rule-based system, has enabled the country to achieve tremendous economic gains. During these 20 years, China's trade has increased nine fold, exports have increased 870% and imports 740%: completely outstripping the 180% overall global trade increase for the same period (Kawate, 2021). However, the low-cost manufacturing and less stringent environmental regulations have resulted in serious pollution (Duanmu, Bu, & Pittman, 2018). China's carbon dioxide emissions have grown at their fastest pace in more than a decade, increasing 15% year-on-year in the first quarter of 2021 (Wang & Feng, 2021).

In recent years, the Chinese government has been actively encouraging and supporting enterprises to invest in green practices such as energy conservation and emission reduction (Dietzenbacher, Pei, & Yang, 2012; Yao, Zhang, & Guo, 2020). Companies are implementing business programmes and policies which emphasise investments in advanced environmental technology to differentiate themselves from competitors. This can be a way of exhibiting corporate social responsibility (CSR), which some authors refer to as 'investment with values' (Mallett & Michelson, 2010).

'Green' topics have been a major motivation for industrial practitioners and academics recently (Melay, O'Dwyer, Kraus, & Gast, 2017; Vallaster, Kraus, Lindahl, & Nielsen, 2019; Zhang, Wang, Tan , 2015). Researchers have gradually switched their focus from a general deliberation to specific constructs such as green human resource practices (Singh, Del Giudice, Chierici, & Graziano, 2020), green supply chain competition (Wu & Kung, 2020), green bonds (Tolliver, Keeley, & Managi, 2020) as well as investment in green innovation (Singh, Dureja et al., 2020).

For several decades, academics have evaluated certain attributes of corporations using CSR (Ali et al., 2020). Investment in green innovation is regarded to be a strong determinant of firm performance (Yadav, Han, & Rho, 2016). Agustia, Sawarjuwono, and Dianawati (2019) and Li, Liao, and Albitar (2020) have shown that environmental investment is critical to achieving long-term success. Assessing the impact of environmental investment is essential in the sustainable development of both businesses and the community as a whole. From the efficiency or instrumental viewpoint, companies may participate in substantial social and environmental initiatives in order to safeguard shareholders' interests and improve their financial performance (Aguilera, Rupp, Williams, & Ganapathi, 2007; Tang, Walsh, Lerner, Fitza, & Li, 2018).

On the other hand, Kraus et al. (2020) have pointed out that there is still room to explore the connection between CSR and environmental performance. Several empirical studies have analysed the impact of a company's environmental reporting on its value and have found equivocal (both positive and negative) associations between them (Loh, Thomas, & Wang, 2017; Schadewitz & Niskala, 2010). Thus, the literature reveals that the association between environmental performance and corporate performance is not yet conclusive (Connelly & Limpaphayom, 2004; Galbreath & Shum, 2012).

Furthermore, companies have long associated increased voluntary reporting with additional benefits such as an enhanced corporate image and an increased trading volume (Hamrouni, Miloudi, & Benkraiem, 2015). From the perspective of discretionary disclosure theory (Verrecchia, 1983), enhanced voluntary disclosure by corporations boosts their stock liquidity by lowering transaction costs and raising the demand for shares. Furthermore, companies expect that increased transparency will reduce uncertainty about future cash flows, making equities less risky by providing more reliable information (Cheng, Courtenay, & Krishnamurti, 2006; Dye, 1985; Jiang, Habib, & Hu, 2011).

There is also evidence that businesses are concerned about misrepresentation and do not want to publish potentially discreditable environmental data (Solomon & Lewis, 2002). As a result, corporate officers need to be convinced that increased corporate environmental disclosure has benefits which might outweigh the costs in order to achieve greater transparency. Enhanced corporate environmental disclosure can add value to a company by lowering its cost of capital, increasing cash flows, or both. However, due to the disparate criteria which have been employed to measure the constructs of environmental disclosure, the current empirical evidence is equivocal and difficult to generalise (Hassan, 2018; Hassan & Romilly, 2018). Consequently, this chapter intends to address these limitations in the literature by examining the interactive relationship between environmental investment and firm performance as well as the mediating role of environmental disclosure in China.

This study adopts two measurements of firm performance, namely, firm value and incremental goodwill. The former is measured by Tobin's Q while the latter is defined as the surplus that can be attributed to favourable shareholder perceptions of the company's environmental positioning. Structural equation modelling (SEM) is used to investigate the interrelationships between the variables of interest for a sample of A share-listed companies in China from 2008 to 2020 with a sample size of 30,048 firm years. According to Baron and Kenny (1986, p. 1177), SEM offers the advantage of explicitly testing all relevant paths, rather than excluding any as does Analysis of Variance. Furthermore, the structural equation model incorporates complexities such as measurement errors, correlated measurement errors and even feedbacks (Barrett, 2007; Kelloway, 1995).

The findings of this study provide critical implications for several stakeholders. If environmental performance (environmental investment and environmental disclosure) is hypothesised to affect the firm's value, companies may take proactive measures to avert potential environmental violations. Investors may trade based on the evidence as to how that firm value and its goodwill from acquisition will be affected by news of its environmental performance.

The rest of this chapter is organised as follows. In Section 2, a thorough literature review discusses the mechanisms of how environmental performance impacts firm value in which the meditating role of green innovation is presented. Sections 3 and 4 present the data and methodology as well as the research findings. Lastly, Section 5 consists of a discussion and conclusions.

2. LITERATURE REVIEW

2.1 Environmental Investment and Firm Performance

Research has shown that there are two behavioural manifestations of environmental investment by companies. One is based on the view that environmental investment is a passive behaviour whereby companies simply meet government environmental regulations (Liao, 2018; Tang et al., 2018). Another is based on the view that environmental investment is a proactive behaviour, which helps companies establish a good social reputation (Tang et al., 2018), reduces the cost of environmental protection and improves their profitability and competitive advantage. Therefore, environmental investment can be a combination of both passive and active behaviours. On the one hand, purchasing environmental protection equipment and investing in green research and development are very expensive and the benefits to the company are uncertain, which increases the risk for environmental investment. On the other hand, this kind of investment is conducive to suppressing industrial waste emissions, controlling environmental pollution and establishing a green corporate image (Pipatprapa, Huang, & Huang, 2017; Woo, Chung, Chun, Han, & Lee, 2014).

Environmental investment puts resources into green technology and renewable resource development which aim to reduce energy consumption, improve the efficiency of resource utilisation and achieve pollution control (Xie, Huo, Qi, & Zhu, 2015). However, there is a paradox in balancing the financial savings from energy efficiency against the increased business costs to control pollution (Hart & Ahuja, 1996). This is because environmental investments take resources away from the normal operations of the company, resulting in disruptions to existing production and sales, therefore undermining financial performance (Weng, Chen, & Chen, 2015). According to the resource-based view (RBV) (Barney, 1991), environmental policies and green innovation are critical in determining long-term performance (Hart, 1995; Rusinko, 2005). Companies focussing on environmental issues will respond promptly to address environmental challenges by investing more in ecological innovation and reflect a responsible stance to their stakeholders (Park, Mezias, & Song, 2004). These businesses will try to prevent or eliminate business operations that have greater negative environmental impacts (Lin & Wu, 2014; Richard, 2000). Thus, companies which are eager to make green investments may have a greater competitive advantage in the market than others. They will have more related technologies and information, thus making green investment an important driving force for their sustainable development which will ultimately improve financial performance. Therefore, the following hypothesis is formulated.

H1: Environmental investment positively influences firm value.

While 'green economics' aims at a broad definition of sustainability, incremental goodwill is defined as a surplus that can be attributed to favourable shareholder perceptions of the company's superior positioning. This goodwill may actually stem from implicit liabilities for compensation and the likelihood of future stringent environmental enforcement necessitating significant investments by competitors, which in turn brings in healthy competition leading to boosted corporate reputation and enhanced operational efficiency (Kwon & Lee, 2019). Various studies have shown that CSR is an influential component in both business decision-making and consumer-purchasing decisions because it epitomises the company's image, and therefore goodwill, among customers (Alsayegh, Abdul Rahman, & Homayoun, 2020; Singh, Dureja et al., 2020). Managerial decisions to invest in pollution-reducing technologies, according to Friedman (1970), can be a goal to maximise profits by earning public adulation, receiving media attention and using it to entrench their market position by generating external goodwill and support. Similarly, Kriström and Lundgren (2003) observe that output prices and profits for Swedish pulp plants positively correlate to changes in corporate goodwill. Yet scant attention so far has been paid to whether environmental investment in green innovation serves as an effective signal of superior environmental performance to promote corporate goodwill. Therefore, the following hypothesis is formulated.

H2: Environmental investment positively influences incremental corporate goodwill.

2.2 Environmental Disclosure and Firm Performance

As environmental awareness grows and environmental action is taken at various levels, including by governments, non-governmental organisations (NGOs), international non-governmental organisations (INGOs) and the United Nations (Dasgupta, Laplante, & Mamingi, 2001), businesses are joining the global effort by adopting environmentally friendly management policies (Coglianese, 1999). Strategies are implemented to mitigate harm and help create a healthy environment, depending on the type of industry and the environmental challenges faced.

Attribution theory suggests that those who follow current affairs perceive events and link them to their thinking and behaviours (Martinko & Mackey, 2019). The theory studies perceived causalities and repercussions (Kelley & Michela, 1980). Attribution theory has been applied in a variety of scenarios to better understand stakeholder reactions to corporate activities. For example, Tom and Lucey (1997) used attribution theory to analyse the relationship between customer satisfaction and delays in supermarket queues. Sjovall and Talk (2004) examined the cognitive processes that drive attributions and describe how this theory might be applied to the building of company performance evaluation based on corporate actions. The theory has also been utilised in post-crisis management and reputational effect research (Chen et al., 2020; Flanagan & O'Shaughnessy, 2005; Laufer & Coombs, 2006; Zhou & Ki, 2018).

Poor environmental disclosure may attract attention and harm a corporate reputation, which further jeopardises the value of the company. This growing social awareness has led to a call for companies to take responsibility for the environment in which they operate (Martin & Moser, 2016). Other stakeholders, such as the government, as well as international and other associated organisations, demand that companies participate in environmental stewardship by imposing rules and regulations. The impact of environmental disclosure on business value is likewise controversial. According to Deswanto and Siregar

(2018), there is no direct relationship between environmental disclosure and corporate financial performance. On the other hand, according to studies conducted by Clarkson et al. (2008), Donald (2009), Iatridis (2013), Qiu et al. (2016), and Rinsman and Prasetyo (2020), more extensive environmental disclosures lead to higher corporate value. Thus, the current study hopes to shed light on whether environmental disclosure affects corporate value by formulating the following hypothesis.

H3: Environmental disclosure positively influences firm value.

Superior environmental disclosure attracts resources to the organisation, such as more competent staff and wider market prospects (Barnett & Salomon, 2006). Furthermore, proactive environmental measures require less tangible skills (e.g. cross-disciplinary activities and problem-solving) and related efforts generate more valuable resources and can serve as the basis for a competitive advantage (Hart, 1995; Russo & Fouts, 1997). Prior studies also imply that brand loyalty is determined by ethical strategies, CSR and environmental performance. As a result, companies enjoy more goodwill (Devalle & Rizzato, 2012; Mazzi, André, Dionysiou, & Tsalavoutas, 2017). Furthermore, greater environmental disclosure may lead to good publicity, improved reputation, goodwill and staff loyalty, as well as increased efficiency and competitive advantages, all of which affect a company's earnings. Therefore, the following hypothesis is formulated.

H4: Environmental disclosure positively influences incremental corporate goodwill.

2.3 Mediating Effect of Environmental Disclosure

Environmental disclosure fosters trust among a diverse set of stakeholders. Multi-stakeholder pressures are likely to influence management's decisions whether to release environmental information. Facing environmental pressures, investments in new technologies for environmental management and protection will become a valuable resource for companies to gain competitive advantage. Saunila, Ukko, and Rantala (2018) argue that the more attention is paid to economic, institutional and social sustainability, the better environmental performance companies will achieve through green innovation. The influence of green investment on corporate performance is not isolated, but is mediated by the environmental pressures exerted by various stakeholders. Timely and comprehensive environmental disclosure assures that concerns from various stakeholders such as the government, investors, competitors, community residents and consumers are accounted for (Rantala, Ukko, Saunila, & Havukainen, 2018; Ukko, Nasiri, Saunila, & Rantala, 2019).

Prior research has indicated that the relationship between environmental innovation and corporate performance is associated with the quantity of environmental information reported by the company Aerts & Cormier, 2009; (Brown & Deegan, 1998; Cormier, Ledoux, & Magnan, 2011). Environmental disclosure indicates that stakeholders are aware of a company's environmental challenges and, as a result, they will demand complete transparency (Cormier, Aerts, Ledoux, & Magnan, 2009). It is suggested that environmental disclosure promotes legitimacy and rationalises investments towards green innovation. Furthermore, the signalling effect of environmental investment is also augmented through environmental disclosure. This implies that environmental disclosure can help to mediate the impact of environmental investment on a company's value. In view of the above arguments, the following hypotheses are formulated.

H5: Environmental disclosure mediates the relationship between environmental investment and firm value.

H6: Environmental disclosure mediates the relationship between environmental investment and incremental corporate goodwill.

3. DATA AND METHODOLOGY

This study investigates the interplay of environmental investment, environmental disclosure and firm performance using a sample of A share-listed firms in China from 2008 to 2020. The sample size is 30,048 firm years. Table 1 presents the sample distribution. Panel A shows that the number of sampled companies with environmental disclosure has been increasing yearly. Panel B shows the industry distribution based on the 2012 China Securities Regulatory Commission (CSRC) classification. Over 50% of the companies are from the manufacturing sector (Industry C). In China, this sector involves as many as 42 major subsectors and industries covering almost every aspect of life, including agricultural and foodstuffs processing, food manufacturing, textiles, leather, entertainment products, furniture manufacturing, pharmaceuticals, metal products, automobiles and so on. Industry C is further classified into four subcategories according to the first digits of the subcategories under their industry codes.

This study adopts the environmental disclosure metrics of the China Stock Market & Accounting Research Database (CSMAR) to evaluate the environmental disclosure performance of all firm years. Table 2 presents the evaluation metrics of environmental disclosure. The total score for the environmental disclosure evaluation framework is 32.

The data for environmental investment and incremental goodwill are manually collected and calculated. This chapter uses Mueller and Supina's (2002) definition of goodwill, which is defined as the unexplained residual in a publicly listed firm's market valuation after subtracting prior investments in advertising, research, capital assets and other tangible assets. Specifically, the regression residuals of the goodwill expectation model are used as proxy variables for incremental goodwill. There are various indicators predicting the normal goodwill, including: (1) characteristics of mergers and acquisitions (the method of payment, whether it is a related acquisition or a tender offer, the shareholding of management, equity incentives and whether the executives have a tendency to be overconfident); (2) industry goodwill level (the average value of goodwill of other companies in the industry year) and (3) company characteristics (the size of the acquiring company, the size of the acquired company, profitability, growth, management shareholding ratio, degree of separation of powers). Industry and year dummy variables are used to analyse the level of company goodwill and the

Table 1. Sample Distribution.

Panel A: Yearly Distribution			
Year	Frequency	%	Cumulative %
2008	1,263	4.2	4.20
2009	1,340	4.46	8.66
2010	1,470	4.89	13.55
2011	1,888	6.28	19.84
2012	2,190	7.29	27.13
2013	2,227	7.41	34.54
2014	2,150	7.16	41.69
2015	2,273	7.56	49.26
2016	2,544	8.47	57.72
2017	2,751	9.16	66.88
2018	3,206	10.67	77.55
2019	3,283	10.93	88.48
2020	3,463	11.52	100
Total	30,048	100	
Panel B: Industry Distribution[a]			
Industry	Frequency	%	Cumulative %
A	440	1.16	1.46
B	707	2.35	3.82
C1	2,058	6.85	10.67
C2	5,717	19.03	29.69
C3	11,088	36.9	66.59
C4	582	1.94	68.53
D	996	3.31	71.85
E	761	2.53	74.38
F	1,603	5.33	79.71
G	911	3.03	82.74
H	115	0.38	83.13
I	1,886	6.28	89.4
K	1,394	4.64	94.04
L	382	1.27	95.31
M	261	0.87	96.18
N	340	1.13	97.31
O	28	0.09	97.41
P	23	0.08	97.48
Q	59	0.2	97.68
R	346	1.15	98.83
S	351	1.17	100
Total	30,048	100	

[a]*Notes*: Panel B shows the distribution of firms sampled across industries based on the 2012 'Guidance on the industry category of listed companies' issued by the China Securities Regulatory Commission (CSRC), where A = agriculture; B = mining; C = manufacturing; D = electricity, gas, and water; E = building and construction; F = wholesale and retail trade;

G = transportation and logistics; H = accommodation and catering industry; I = information technology; J = financial industry; K = real estate; L = leasing and commerce services; M = scientific research and technical services; N = public facilities management; O = residential service industry; P = education; Q = health care; R = culture and entertainment industry; S = other. Of these, manufacturing is the pillar industry of the Chinese economy with the largest number of firms.

residuals obtained from the regression are used as a proxy for incremental corporate goodwill.

Environmental innovation, often known as green innovation, is defined as a new or improved technique, practice, system or manufacturing process that helps to lessen the impact of environmental degradation (Rennings & Rammer, 2011). New technology (hardware or software) related to products or manufacturing processes that will eventually lead to energy efficiency, pollution reduction, waste recycling, green product design and corporate environmental management are all classified as green innovation (Chen, 2008). The amount of environmental investment towards green innovation is manually collected by downloading annual reports, social responsibility reports, sustainability reports and environmental reports of Shanghai Stock Exchange and Shenzhen Stock Exchange-listed companies published by Juchao Information. By scanning in the annual reports for the related keywords in the notes to the financial statements, it is possible to obtain the environmental investment amounts for green innovation under the accounts of construction-in-progress, other payables, research and development expenses etc. Environmental investment includes environmental protection facilities and equipment, environmental protection technology improvement, improvement of waste water facilities, waste gas facilities, dust removal and management facilities, waste residue facilities, heavy metal treatment technology, noise treatment and environmental protection research and development etc.

4. RESULTS

This study uses structural equation modelling (SEM) to test the hypotheses posed. Fig. 1 illustrates the research framework represented by the structural equation model. The dotted lines represent the mediating effects of environmental disclosure in *H5* and *H6*. SEM provides the researcher with the ability to deal with a large quantity of data, increasing the degrees of freedom for any statistical tests and lower collinearity among the explanatory variables, hence boosting the efficiency of estimates. It also mitigates the severity of some econometric issues such as omitted variable biases (Golob, 2003).

This study also includes other control variables that may impact firm value and incremental goodwill. The respective data are obtained from the CSMAR database. The definitions and descriptive statistics of the major variables are presented in Table 3 and Table 4, respectively.

The findings of the test for direct effect are shown in Panel A in Table 5, whereas the results of the test for indirect effect are in Panel B of the same table.

Table 2. Evaluation Metrics of Environmental Disclosure.

Theme	Topics	Score Description
Environmental Management		
	Environmental Protection Concept	Disclosure of the companies' environmental protection concept, environmental policy, environmental management organisation structure, circular economy development model, green development etc. Assign a value of 1 to the above disclosure, otherwise 0.
	Environmental Protection Goal	Disclosure of the companies' achievement of past environmental protection goals and future environmental protection goals. Assign a value of 1 to the above disclosure, otherwise 0.
	Environmental Protection Management System	Disclosure of a series of management systems such as relevant environmental management systems, regulations and responsibilities formulated by companies. Assign a value of 1 to the above disclosure, otherwise 0.
	Environmental Protection Education and Training	Disclosure of the environmental protection education and training that companies have participated in. Assign a value of 1 to the above disclosure, otherwise 0.
	Environmental Protection Special Action	Disclosure of special environmental protection activities, environmental protection and other social welfare activities that companies have participated in. Assign a value of 1 to the above disclosure, otherwise 0.
	Environmental Event Emergency Mechanism	Disclosure of the companies' establishment of emergency mechanism for major events related to environment, emergency measures taken and treatment of pollutants etc. Assign a value of 1 to the above disclosure, otherwise 0.
	Environmental Protection Honour or Reward	Disclosure of the companies' honours or rewards in environmental protection. Assign a value of 1 to the above disclosure, otherwise 0.
	Three Simultaneities System	Disclosure of the companies' implementation of 'three simultaneities' system. Assign a value of 1 to the above disclosure, otherwise 0.
Environmental Liabilities		
	Waste Water Discharge	0 = No Description; 1 = Qualitative Description; 2 = Quantitative Description (Currency/Numerical Description)
	Chemical Oxygen Demand (COD)	0 = No Description; 1 = Qualitative Description; 2 = Quantitative Description (Currency/Numerical Description) (COD)
	SO_2 Emission	0 = No Description; 1 = Qualitative Description; 2 = Quantitative Description (Currency/Numerical Description)
	CO_2 Emission	0 = No Description; 1 = Qualitative Description; 2 = Quantitative Description (Currency/Numerical Description) (Main Components of Greenhouse Gas)
	Soot and Dust Emission	0 = No Description; 1 = Qualitative Description; 2 = Quantitative Description (Currency/Numerical Description)
	Industrial Solid Waste Production	0 = No Description; 1 = Qualitative Description; 2 = Quantitative Description (Currency/Numerical Description)

Table 2. *(Continued)*

Theme	Topics	Score Description
Environmental Performance and Management		
	Waste Gas Emission Reduction and Management	0 = No Description; 1 = Qualitative Description; 2 = Quantitative Description (Currency/Numerical Description)
	Waste Water Discharge Reduction and Management	0 = No Description; 1 = Qualitative Description; 2 = Quantitative Description (Currency/Numerical Description)
	Soot and Dust Control	0 = No Description; 1 = Qualitative Description; 2 = Quantitative Description (Currency/Numerical Description)
	Solid Waste Utilisation and Disposal	0 = No Description; 1 = Qualitative Description; 2 = Quantitative Description (Currency/Numerical Description)
	Control of Noise, Light Pollution, Radiation etc.	0 = No Description; 1 = Qualitative Description; 2 = Quantitative Description (Currency/Numerical Description)
	Implementation of Cleaner Production	0 = No Description; 1 = Qualitative Description; 2 = Quantitative Description

The results in Panel A of Table 5 show that *H1* (EI→Firm Value) and *H2* (ED→Firm Value) are supported ($\beta = 0.026$; $t = 2.83$, $p < 0.01$) and ($\beta = 0.030$; $t = 2.51$, $p < 0.05$), respectively. In other words, environmental investment and environmental disclosure influence firm value in a positive manner. Similarly, *H3* (EI→Incremental Goodwill) and *H4* (ED→Incremental Goodwill) are supported ($\beta = 0.027$; $t = 2.65$ $p < 0.01$); ($\beta = 0.004$; $t = 6.66$, $p < 0.01$) respectively. These findings suggest that environmental investment and environmental disclosure

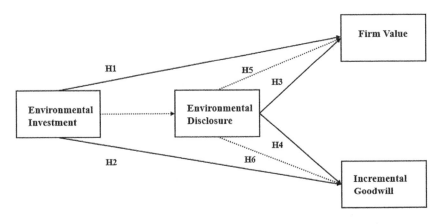

Fig. 1. The Research Framework.

Table 3. Definitions of Variables.

Variable	Definition
Major Variables of Interest in the SEM	
Environmental Investment	Natural logarithm of one plus environmental investment amount manually collected from annual reports, CSR reports and environmental reports.
Environmental Disclosure	Natural logarithm of one plus environmental disclosure score evaluated using the CSMAR environmental disclosure database.
Firm Value	Tobin's Q (market value/total assets).
Incremental Goodwill	Regression residuals of the goodwill expectation model
Control Variables	
ROA	Return on assets: (total profits + financial expenses)/total assets
BM	Market to book ratio: total number of shares multiplied by the closing price per share in the year, divided by the book value at the end of the fiscal year.
Size	Natural logarithm of the market value of equity (MV)
Lev	Total liabilities at the end of the year divided by total assets at the end of the year
FirmAge	Ln(current year - year of company establishment + 1)
ListAge	Ln(current year - year of listed + 1)
ATO	Operating income/average total assets
Growth	Operating income for the year/Operating income for the previous year - 1
Board	Natural logarithm of 1 plus the number of board members
Indep	Number of independent directors divided by the number of directors
Dual	Chairman and general manager are the same as 1, otherwise 0
SOE	State-controlled enterprises as 1, others are 0

positively and significantly affect corporate incremental goodwill. Therefore, *H1*, *H2*, *H3* and *H4* are all supported.

The mediating roles of environmental disclosure between firm value and incremental goodwill are presented in Panel B of Table 5. *H5* (EI→ED→Firm Value) and *H6* (EI→ED→Incremental Goodwill) are supported with ($\beta = 0.009$; $t = 8.36$ $p < 0.01$) and ($\beta = 0.003$; $t = 8.46$, $p < 0.01$), respectively. The results demonstrate that environmental disclosure significantly mediates the influence of environmental investment on firm value and environmental investment on incremental goodwill. The goodness-of-fit for the entire model is within the acceptable range ($\chi 2/df = 1.259$, $p = 0.308$; GFI = 0.932).

5. DISCUSSION AND CONCLUSION

Since the beginning of market-oriented reforms in 1978, the rapid economic growth in China has been causing serious environmental deterioration (Child & Tsai, 2005; Managi & Kaneko, 2009). This is demonstrated by the fact that an increasing number of environmental violations are being made public (Meng, Zeng, Shi, Qi, & Zhang, 2014). As the world's largest transitional economy with

Table 4. Descriptive Statistics.

Variable	Observations	Mean	SD	Min.	Max.
Major Variables of Interest in SEM					
Environmental Investment	30,048	3.966681	7.035507	0	27.06361
Environmental Disclosure	30,048	0.8066901	1.033811	0	3.496508
Firm Value	30,048	2.248018	4.319971	0.152768	393.0135
Incremental goodwill	30,048	8.50E-06	0.062013	−0.19225	0.465506
Control Variables					
ROA	30,048	0.0371645	0.199452	−14.586	20.78764
BM	30,048	1.056186	1.529723	0.002865	143.8035
Size	30,048	22.08748	1.336527	15.41772	28.54266
Lev	30,048	0.4654411	1.339686	−0.1947	178.3455
FirmAge	30,048	2.830907	0.366783	0.693147	4.143135
ListAge	30,048	2.157969	0.786291	0	3.433987
ATO	30,048	0.6608117	0.560152	−0.04786	12.37286
Growth	30,048	5.583826	781.5129	−1.30916	134607.1
Board	29,982	2.136428	0.200726	1.098612	2.995732
Indep	29,982	0.3738212	0.055069	0.090909	0.8
Dual	30,048	0.2613818	0.439395	0	1
SOE	30,022	0.3691293	0.482577	0	1

frequent and serious environmental mishaps and a steady degradation in the quality of the environment, China's people have become increasingly concerned about corporate environmental performance (Meng, Zeng, Tam, & Xu, 2013).

Table 5. Results of Direct and Indirect Impacts.

Relationships	Standardised Direct Effect	Standard Error	*t*-value	Sig. Level	Hypothesis Testing
Panel A: Test for Direct Impact					
EI→Firm Value	0.026	0.034	2.83	$p < 0.01$	*H1* accepted
ED→Firm Value	0.030	0.012	2.51	$p < 0.05$	*H2* accepted
EI→Incremental Goodwill	0.027	0.001	2.65	$p < 0.01$	*H3* accepted
ED→Incremental Goodwill	0.004	0.002	6.66	$p < 0.01$	*H4* accepted
Panel B: Test for Indirect Impact					
EI→ED→Firm Value	0.009	0.003	8.36	$p < 0.01$	*H5* accepted
EI→ED→Incremental Goodwill	0.003	0.000	8.46	$p < 0.01$	*H6* accepted

Therefore, companies have also been making greater efforts to develop green practices and environmental conservation (Qiu et al., 2016).

Previous literature has provided exploratory discussions on green investment and environmental performance, respectively, but more empirical studies to examine the impact of green investment on firm performance are necessary. In addition, there is still no solid conclusion in the literature about the mediating role of environmental disclosure as an example of the effect of environmental investment on corporate performance. This could be largely due to discrepancies in the measurement constructs used in prior research. For example, Deswanto and Siregar (2018) found that environmental disclosures did not mediate the effect of corporate financial performance on firm market value nor do they mediate the impact of environmental performance on firm market value. Nevertheless, they pointed out that the sampled companies only covered those which were given a Green Industry Award in Indonesia. Also, their study included only five industries in the country and therefore the ability to draw general conclusions from the work may be limited. The current study attempts to remedy some of these shortcomings.

Drawing upon RBV and attribution theoretical lenses, this study provides a paradigm for examining the interplay among environmental investment towards green innovation, environmental disclosure as well as firm performance using the SEM methodology. Specifically, environmental investment and environmental disclosure influence firm value and incremental goodwill in a positive and significant manner. In addition, environmental disclosure mediates the impact of environmental investment on firm performance in a positive and significant way.

In terms of the RBV, this study will probably draw attention to the long-neglected relation between company goodwill and company resources (Kristandl & Bontis, 2007). It has been generally accepted that the difference between the market value and the book value of the company represents the intellectual capital, and therefore the goodwill. However, the inadequacy of this definition of goodwill has also been identified (e.g. Wade & Hulland, 2004). It is rather unusual to point out that corporate social disclosure can also act as a valuable resource under the RBV, especially as an intangible competitive advantage. Institutional theory mainly sees corporate social disclosure as an instrument or a means to achieve legitimacy. If we reverse our perspective using the RBV, corporate social disclosure becomes goodwill which in turn eventually adds to firm value. This leads to an interesting further investigation of corporate social disclosure as intellectual capital and the value of the disclosure itself (the value of the depth and fullness of the disclosure).

Attribution theory was used in this study to support the proposed and tested relationships between environmental investment, environmental disclosure and firm value as well as incremental goodwill. As advocated above (using RBV analysis), a firm's corporate social disclosure is a valuable intangible asset which can help to build corporate reputation. Additionally, attribution by stakeholders can further augment total firm value and goodwill. On the other hand, if corporate social disclosure is poorly conducted or is not sufficiently informative, stakeholders' attribution can have a negative multiplier effect causing deterioration in firm value and goodwill. It is suggested that further research be conducted in this direction to include stakeholders' attributions as a result of their perceptions in the model in order to investigate the augmentative or deteriorative effect.

The findings of the current study offer important theoretical and practical implications for corporate environmental management strategies. First, there is now a growing environmental awareness among stakeholders of the relevance of environmental performance to share value (see, e.g. the social contribution value per share (SCVPS) advocated by Zhang et al. (2021a, 2021b)). It is also demonstrated that the mediating power of environmental disclosure between environmental investment and firm value as well as incremental goodwill is crucial. Those who follow corporate news are becoming more and more sophisticated in their demand for information and they are concerned about companies' environmental and social impacts. For the purpose of displaying a company's fulfilment of its environmental duties, the publication of an environmental report not only provides a marketing advantage but also creates an intangible asset which can increase firm value as discussed above. Furthermore, such reports can also help identify strengths and weaknesses (by comparison with international standards and competitors or benchmark companies) and the means by which the long-term sustainability of both company goodwill and the environment can be preserved.

This study also points out the importance of environmental investment towards green innovation. Technology has increased market competition considerably, but environmental investment in green innovation techniques can also offer a significant competitive advantage for companies. As a result, it is suggested that they deploy resources for environmental investment activities in order to perform better and more sustainably. Osazuwa and Che-Ahmad (2016) also found a positive association between eco-efficiency and firm value and encouraged the use of new processes to adapt to eco-efficient environments. Finally, stakeholders with strong environmental awareness may choose companies with good environmental performance as a result of green innovation techniques. This can lead to customer loyalty and an enhanced corporate image and reputation. For example, Barboza (2019) extensively discussed endogenous consumers' preferences about green CSR which can offset other external damage. This study has provided both theoretical and practical implications. Disclosure of environmental information holds companies accountable for their environmental stewardship, which can consequentially influence company performance and corporate image. Companies and researchers can take a step forward to consider how other attributes of companies mediate the influence of corporate environmental performance in view of various externalities and challenges in different emerging economies.

REFERENCES

Aerts, W., & Cormier, D. (2009). Media legitimacy and corporate environmental communication. *Accounting, Organizations and Society*, *34*(1), 1–27.

Aguilera, R. V., Rupp, D. E., Williams, C. A., & Ganapathi, J. (2007). Putting the S back in corporate social responsibility: A multilevel theory of social change in organizations. *Academy of Management Review, 32*(3), 836–863.

Agustia, D., Sawarjuwono, T., & Dianawati, W. (2019). The mediating effect of environmental management accounting on green innovation-firm value relationship. *International Journal of Energy Economics and Policy, 9*(2), 299–306.

Ali, H. Y., Asrar-ul-Haq, M., Amin, S., Noor, S., Haris-ul-Mahasbi, M., & Aslam, M. K. (2020). Corporate social responsibility and employee performance: The mediating role of employee engagement in the manufacturing sector of Pakistan. *Corporate Social Responsibility and Environmental Management, 27*(6), 2908–2919.

Alsayegh, M. F., Abdul Rahman, R., & Homayoun, S. (2020). Corporate economic, environmental, and social sustainability performance transformation through ESG disclosure. *Sustainability, 12*(9), 3910.

Barboza, G. (2019). Endogenous consumers' preferences as drivers of green corporate social responsibility. *Social Responsibility Journal, 15*(4), 424–450.

Barnett, M. L., & Salomon, R. M. (2006). Beyond dichotomy: The curvilinear relationship between social responsibility and financial performance. *Strategic Management Journal, 27*(11), 1101–1122.

Barney, J. (1991). Firm resources and sustained competitive advantage. *Journal of Management, 17*(1), 99–120.

Baron, R. M., & Kenny, D. A. (1986). The moderator–mediator variable distinction in social psychological research: Conceptual, strategic, and statistical considerations. *Journal of Personality and Social Psychology, 51*(6), 1173.

Barrett, P. (2007). Structural equation modelling: Adjudging model fit. *Personality and Individual Differences, 42*(5), 815–824.

Brown, N., & Deegan, C. (1998). The public disclosure of environmental performance information—A dual test of media agenda setting theory and legitimacy theory. *Accounting and Business Research, 29*(1), 21–41.

Chen, Y. S. (2008). The driver of green innovation and green image – Green core competence. *Journal of Business Ethics, 81*(3), 531–543.

Cheng, E. C., Courtenay, S. M., & Krishnamurti, C. (2006). The impact of increased voluntary disclosure on market information asymmetry, informed and uninformed trading. *Journal of Contemporary Accounting and Economics, 2*(1), 33–72.

Chen, W. C., Hsieh, K. M., Lin, C. S., Lee, C. C., Yu, C., Lin, Y. C., & Hong, J. C. (2020). Relationships between sales ethics, corporate social responsibility, trust, attitude, and loyalty in the real estate brokerage industry. *Social Behavior and Personality: An International Journal, 48*(3), 1–9.

Child, J., & Tsai, T. (2005). The dynamic between firms' environmental strategies and institutional constraints in emerging economies: Evidence from China and Taiwan. *Journal of Management Studies, 42*(1), 95–125.

Ciuriak, D. (2002). China after the WTO. *American Journal of Chinese Studies, 9*(1), 59–93.

Clarkson, P. M., Li, Y., Richardson, G. D., & Vasvari, F. P. (2008). Revisiting the relation between environmental performance and environmental disclosure: An empirical analysis. *Accounting, Organizations and Society, 33*(4–5), 303–327.

Coglianese, C. (1999). The limits of consensus: The environmental protection system in transition: Toward a more desirable future. *Environment: Science and Policy for Sustainable Development, 41*(3), 28–33.

Connelly, J. T., & Limpaphayom, P. (2004). Environmental reporting and firm performance: Evidence from Thailand. *Journal of Corporate Citizenship, 13*, 137–149.

Cormier, D., Aerts, W., Ledoux, M. J., & Magnan, M. (2009). Attributes of social and human capital disclosure and information asymmetry between managers and investors. *Canadian Journal of Administrative Sciences, 26*(1), 71–88.

Cormier, D., Ledoux, M. J., & Magnan, M. (2011). The informational contribution of social and environmental disclosures for investors. *Management Decision, 49*(8), 1276–1304.

Dasgupta, S., Laplante, B., & Mamingi, N. (2001). Pollution and capital markets in developing countries. *Journal of Environmental Economics and Management, 42*(3), 310–335.

Deswanto, R. B., & Siregar, S. V. (2018). The associations between environmental disclosures with financial performance, environmental performance, and firm value. *Social Responsibility Journal, 14*(1), 180–193.

Devalle, A., & Rizzato, F. (2012). The quality of mandatory disclosure: The impairment of goodwill. An empirical analysis of European listed companies. *Procedia Economics and Finance, 2*, 101–108.

Dietzenbacher, E., Pei, J., & Yang, C. (2012). Trade, production fragmentation, and China's carbon dioxide emissions. *Journal of Environmental Economics and Management, 64*(1), 88–101.

Donald, S. S. (2009). Green management matters only if it yields more green: An economic/strategic perspective. *Academy of Management Perspectives, 23*(3), 5–16.

Duanmu, J. L., Bu, M., & Pittman, R. (2018). Does market competition dampen environmental performance? Evidence from China. *Strategic Management Journal, 39*(11), 3006–3030.

Dye, R. A. (1985). Disclosure of nonproprietary information. *Journal of Accounting Research*, 123–145.

Flanagan, D. J., & O'Shaughnessy, K. C. (2005). The effect of layoffs on firm reputation. *Journal of Management, 31*(3), 445–463.

Friedman, M. (1970). A theoretical framework for monetary analysis. *Journal of Political Economy, 78*(2), 193–238.

Galbreath, J., & Shum, P. (2012). Do customer satisfaction and reputation mediate the CSR–FP link? Evidence from Australia. *Australian Journal of Management, 37*(2), 211–229.

Golob, T. F. (2003). Structural equation modeling for travel behavior research. *Transportation Research Part B: Methodological, 37*(1), 1–25.

Hamrouni, A., Miloudi, A., & Benkraiem, R. (2015). How does corporate voluntary disclosure affect asymmetric information and adverse selection? *Corporate Ownership & Control*, 419.

Hart, S. L. (1995). A natural-resource-based view of the firm. *Academy of Management Review, 20*(4), 986–1014.

Hart, S. L., & Ahuja, G. (1996). Does it pay to be green? An empirical examination of the relationship between emission reduction and firm performance. *Business Strategy and the Environment, 5*(1), 30–37.

Hassan, O. A. (2018). The impact of voluntary environmental disclosure on firm value: Does organizational visibility play a mediation role? *Business Strategy and the Environment, 27*(8), 1569–1582.

Hassan, O. A., & Romilly, P. (2018). Relations between corporate economic performance, environmental disclosure and greenhouse gas emissions: New insights. *Business Strategy and the Environment, 27*(7), 893–909.

Iatridis, G. E. (2013). Environmental disclosure quality: Evidence on environmental performance, corporate governance and value relevance. *Emerging Markets Review, 14*, 55–75.

Jiang, H., Habib, A., & Hu, B. (2011). Ownership concentration, voluntary disclosures and information asymmetry in New Zealand. *The British Accounting Review, 43*(1), 39–53.

Kawate, I. (2021, November 7). China's trade with world surges ninefold after 20 years in WTO. *Nikkei Asia*. Retrieved from https://asia.nikkei.com/Economy/China-s-trade-with-world-surges-ninefold-after-20-years-in-WTO

Kelley, H. H., & Michela, J. L. (1980). Attribution theory and research. *Annual Review of Psychology, 31*(1), 457–501.

Kelloway, E. K. (1995). Structural equation modelling in perspective. *Journal of Organizational Behavior, 16*(3), 215–224.

Kraus, S., Rehman, S. U., & García, F. J. S. (2020). Corporate social responsibility and environmental performance: The mediating role of environmental strategy and green innovation. *Technological Forecasting and Social Change, 160*, 120262.

Kristandl, G., & Bontis, N. (2007). Constructing a definition of intangibles using the resource-based view of the firm. *Management Decision, 45*(9), 1510–1524.

Kriström, B., & Lundgren, T. (2003). Abatement investments and green goodwill. *Applied Economics, 35*(18), 1915–1921.

Kwon, H. B., & Lee, J. (2019). Exploring the differential impact of environmental sustainability, operational efficiency, and corporate reputation on market valuation in high-tech-oriented firms. *International Journal of Production Economics*, *211*, 1–14.

Laufer, D., & Coombs, W. T. (2006). How should a company respond to a product harm crisis? The role of corporate reputation and consumer-based cues. *Business Horizons*, *49*(5), 379–385.

Liao, Z. (2018). Social capital and firms' environmental innovations: The moderating role of environmental scanning. *Business Strategy and the Environment*, *27*(8), 1493–1501.

Li, Z., Liao, G., & Albitar, K. (2020). Does corporate environmental responsibility engagement affect firm value? The mediating role of corporate innovation. *Business Strategy and the Environment*, *29*(3), 1045–1055.

Lin, Y., & Wu, L. Y. (2014). Exploring the role of dynamic capabilities in firm performance under the resource-based view framework. *Journal of Business Research*, *67*(3), 407–413.

Loh, L., Thomas, T., & Wang, Y. (2017). Sustainability reporting and firm value: Evidence from Singapore-listed companies. *Sustainability*, *9*(11), 2112.

Mallett, J. E., & Michelson, S. (2010). Green investing: Is it different from socially responsible investing? *International Journal of Business*, *15*(4), 395.

Managi, S., & Kaneko, S. (2009). Environmental performance and returns to pollution abatement in China. *Ecological Economics*, *68*(6), 1643–1651.

Martinko, M. J., & Mackey, J. D. (2019). Attribution theory: An introduction to the special issue. *Journal of Organizational Behavior*, *40*(5), 523–527.

Martin, P. R., & Moser, D. V. (2016). Managers' green investment disclosures and investors' reaction. *Journal of Accounting and Economics*, *61*(1), 239–254.

Mazzi, F., André, P., Dionysiou, D., & Tsalavoutas, I. (2017). Compliance with goodwill-related mandatory disclosure requirements and the cost of equity capital. *Accounting and Business Research*, *47*(3), 268–312.

Melay, I., O'Dwyer, M., Kraus, S., & Gast, J. (2017). Green entrepreneurship in SMEs: A configuration approach. *International Journal of Entrepreneurial Venturing*, *9*(1), 1–17.

Meng, X. H., Zeng, S. X., Shi, J. J., Qi, G. Y., & Zhang, Z. B. (2014). The relationship between corporate environmental performance and environmental disclosure: An empirical study in China. *Journal of Environmental Management*, *145*, 357–367.

Meng, X. H., Zeng, S. X., Tam, C. M., & Xu, X. D. (2013). Whether top executives' turnover influences environmental responsibility: From the perspective of environmental information disclosure. *Journal of Business Ethics*, *114*(2), 341–353.

Mueller, D. C., & Supina, D. (2002). Goodwill capital. *Small Business Economics*, *19*(3), 233–253.

Osazuwa, N. P., & Che-Ahmad, A. (2016). The moderating effect of profitability and leverage on the relationship between eco-efficiency and firm value in publicly-traded Malaysian firms. *Social Responsibility Journal*, *12*(2), 295–306.

Park, N. K., Mezias, J. M., & Song, J. (2004). A resource-based view of strategic alliances and firm value in the electronic marketplace. *Journal of Management*, *30*(1), 7–27.

Pipatprapa, A., Huang, H. H., & Huang, C. H. (2017). The role of quality management & innovativeness on green performance. *Corporate Social Responsibility and Environmental Management*, *24*(3), 249–260.

Qiu, Y., Shaukat, A., & Tharyan, R. (2016). Environmental and social disclosures: Link with corporate financial performance. *The British Accounting Review*, *48*(1), 102–116.

Rantala, T., Ukko, J., Saunila, M., & Havukainen, J. (2018). The effect of sustainability in the adoption of technological, service, and business model innovations. *Journal of Cleaner Production*, *172*, 46–55.

Rennings, K., & Rammer, C. (2011). The impact of regulation-driven environmental innovation on innovation success and firm performance. *Industry and Innovation*, *18*(03), 255–283.

Richard, O. C. (2000). Racial diversity, business strategy, and firm performance: A resource-based view. *Academy of Management Journal*, *43*(2), 164–177.

Rinsman, T. C. S., & Prasetyo, A. B. (2020). The effects of financial and environmental performances on firm value with environmental disclosure as an intervening variable. *Jurnal Dinamika Akuntansi*, *12*(2), 90–99.

Rusinko, C. A. (2005). Using quality management as a bridge to environmental sustainability in organizations. *SAM Advanced Management Journal, 70*(4), 54.

Russo, M. V., & Fouts, P. A. (1997). A resource-based perspective on corporate environmental performance and profitability. *Academy of Management Journal, 40*(3), 534–559.

Saunila, M., Ukko, J., & Rantala, T. (2018). Sustainability as a driver of green innovation investment and exploitation. *Journal of Cleaner Production, 179*, 631–641.

Schadewitz, H., & Niskala, M. (2010). Communication via responsibility reporting and its effect on firm value in Finland. *Corporate Social Responsibility and Environmental Management, 17*(2), 96–106.

Singh, S. K., Del Giudice, M., Chierici, R., & Graziano, D. (2020). Green innovation and environmental performance: The role of green transformational leadership and green human resource management. *Technological Forecasting and Social Change, 150*, 119762.

Singh, R., Dureja, J. S., Dogra, M., Gupta, M. K., Jamil, M., & Mia, M. (2020). Evaluating the sustainability pillars of energy and environment considering carbon emissions under machining ofTi-3Al-2.5 V. *Sustainable Energy Technologies and Assessments, 42*, 100806.

Sjovall, A. M., & Talk, A. C. (2004). From actions to impressions: Cognitive attribution theory and the formation of corporate reputation. *Corporate Reputation Review, 7*(3), 269–281.

Solomon, A., & Lewis, L. (2002). Incentives and disincentives for corporate environmental disclosure. *Business Strategy and the Environment, 11*(3), 154–169.

Tang, M., Walsh, G., Lerner, D., Fitza, M. A., & Li, Q. (2018). Green innovation, managerial concern and firm performance: An empirical study. *Business Strategy and the Environment, 27*(1), 39–51.

Tolliver, C., Keeley, A. R., & Managi, S. (2020). Drivers of green bond market growth: The importance of Nationally Determined Contributions to the Paris Agreement and implications for sustainability. *Journal of Cleaner Production, 244*, 118643.

Tom, G., & Lucey, S. (1997). A field study investigating the effect of waiting time on customer satisfaction. *The Journal of Psychology, 131*(6), 655–660.

Ukko, J., Nasiri, M., Saunila, M., & Rantala, T. (2019). Sustainability strategy as a moderator in the relationship between digital business strategy and financial performance. *Journal of Cleaner Production, 236*, 117626.

Vallaster, C., Kraus, S., Lindahl, J. M. M., & Nielsen, A. (2019). Ethics and entrepreneurship: A bibliometric study and literature review. *Journal of Business Research, 99*, 226–237.

Verrecchia, R. E. (1983). Discretionary disclosure. *Journal of Accounting and Economics, 5*, 179–194.

Wade, M., & Hulland, J. (2004). The resource-based view and information system research: Review, extensions and suggestion for future research. *MIS Quarterly, 28*(1), 102–124.

Wang, M., & Feng, C. (2021). The consequences of industrial restructuring, regional balanced development, and market-oriented reform for China's carbon dioxide emissions: A multi-tier meta-frontier DEA-based decomposition analysis. *Technological Forecasting and Social Change, 164*, 120507.

Weng, H. H. R., Chen, J. S., & Chen, P. C. (2015). Effects of green innovation on environmental and corporate performance: A stakeholder perspective. *Sustainability, 7*(5), 4997–5026.

Woo, C., Chung, Y., Chun, D., Han, S., & Lee, D. (2014). Impact of green innovation on labor productivity and its determinants: An analysis of the Korean manufacturing industry. *Business Strategy and the Environment, 23*(8), 567–576.

Wu, T., & Kung, C. C. (2020). Carbon emissions, technology upgradation and financing risk of the green supply chain competition. *Technological Forecasting and Social Change, 152*, 119884.

Xie, X., Huo, J., Qi, G., & Zhu, K. X. (2015). Green process innovation and financial performance in emerging economies: Moderating effects of absorptive capacity and green subsidies. *IEEE Transactions on Engineering Management, 63*(1), 101–112.

Yadav, P. L., Han, S. H., & Rho, J. J. (2016). Impact of environmental performance on firm value for sustainable investment: Evidence from large US firms. *Business Strategy and the Environment, 25*(6), 402–420.

Yao, X., Zhang, X., & Guo, Z. (2020). The tug of war between local government and enterprises in reducing China's carbon dioxide emissions intensity. *Science of the Total Environment, 710*, 136140.

Zhang, R., Chu, T., Noronha, C., & Guan, J. (2021b). Corporate value creation, stock price syn-
    chronicity and firm value in China. *Journal of Accounting in Emerging Economies*. doi:10.1108/
    JAEE-06-2021-0212
Zhang, R., Noronha, C., & Guan, J. (2021a). The social value generation perspective of corporate
    performance measurement. *Social Responsibility Journal, 17*(5), 613–630.
Zhang, Y. J., Wang, A. D., & Tan, W. (2015). The impact of China's carbon allowance allocation rules
    on the product prices and emission reduction behaviors of ETS-covered enterprises. *Energy
    Policy, 86*, 176–185.
Zhou, Z., & Ki, E. J. (2018). Does severity matter? An investigation of crisis severity from defensive
    attribution theory perspective. *Public Relations Review, 44*(4), 610–618.

CHOICE OF LAW AND JURISDICTION UNCERTAINTIES IN E-CONTRACT'S COMMERCIAL GOVERNANCE: A RECOMMENDATION FOR MAURITIUS

Ambareen Beebeejaun and Rajendra Parsad Gunputh

ABSTRACT

E-commerce is gaining popularity across the globe and Mauritian businesses are also increasingly making use of online platforms to engage in cross-border electronic transactions. However, there are several implications arising from online trading which need to be addressed, among which one is the validity of e-contracts. This research will therefore emphasise on two main components of e-contracts: choice of law and the applicable jurisdiction. While Mauritian laws were amended to give effect to digital signatures and e-agreements, there is no extensive or substantive domestic legal provision on choice of law and jurisdiction. Hence, the purpose of this study is to advocate for a greater clarity on the legal framework governing the applicable law and jurisdiction governing a conflict situation in e-contracts, with the view of increasing trust in international e-commerce and to bring in consistency with international commercial relations. This study will be carried out in the Mauritian context by adopting the black letter approach which will analyse the relevant rules and regulations concerning e-contract formation and validity. Additionally, a comparative analysis will be conducted on the legal framework relating to the applicable law and jurisdiction in e-contracts for selected countries: the European Union and the United States. These countries have been chosen for

Corporate Resilience
Developments in Corporate Governance and Responsibility, Volume 21, 129–149
ISSN: 2043-0523/doi:10.1108/S2043-052320230000021007

the comparison due to their high involvement in e-commerce and their advanced as well as comprehensive rules on e-commerce.

Keywords: Electronic commerce; electronic contracts; Rome I Regulation; Brussels Regulation; choice of law; jurisdiction

1. INTRODUCTION

In today's digitalised era, people's way of doing business has changed drastically. Moreover, coupled with sanitary and lockdown measures prompted by COVID-19, the world has experienced an unprecedented and unforeseen massive shift from traditional commerce to electronic commerce (e-commerce) (UNCTAD, 2021a). As businesses and consumers went digital, on one hand, this new trend has helped mitigate the economic downturn caused by the pandemic, but on the other hand, various legal issues have emerged and the relevant stakeholders began to experience several issues in the e-commerce arena. It is therefore imperative to recognise these challenges and take the appropriate steps to support businesses, customers and the government as people continue to embrace new methods of transacting and working.

In a recent report published by UNCTAD in 2021 on COVID-19 and e-commerce, the findings demonstrate that consumers in emerging economies are more numerous in numbers to have made the shift to online shopping during the pandemic (UNCTAD, 2021b). For instance, an African e-commerce platform has noted an increase of 50% in transactions during the first 6 months of 2020 and China's online share of retail sales rose from 19.4% to 24.6% between August 2019 and August 2020 (World Bank, 2020). However, there are some countries notably the least developed ones who have not been able to take advantage of digital platforms for online shopping due to the persistent barriers to capitalise on the appropriate infrastructure to induce e-commerce transactions such as lack of broadband facilities, poor digital literacy skills among the population, over-reliance on cash or lack of government's attention to the e-commerce industry. Nevertheless, the UNCTAD has forecasted that the e-commerce uptake is likely to be sustained even post recovery from the COVID-19 pandemic (UNCTAD, 2021b). Also, given consumer's enthusiasm to trade online, governments across the globe have started to respond to challenges or obstacles encountered to better harness the potential of e-commerce. For example, Senegal has established a sensitisation campaign for its population emphasising on the benefits of e-commerce while Indonesia has launched a capacity building programme to expedite digitalisation among micro, small and medium enterprises (WTO, 2020).

In the context of Mauritius which is an island located in the Indian Ocean, it was common practice prior to COVID-19 for Mauritians to do 'online window shopping' rather than purchasing the product in the traditional manner that is, having physical contact with the seller. However, 2 months of total confinements in each of the years 2020 and 2021 have changed the manner in which Mauritians do business. Basically, numerous enterprises such as MedActiv, Winners,

PriceGuru, Ayvavia or MyChauffeur among others have gone online to display their goods or services ranging from the sale of basic stuff like food, clothing, medicines to the provision of services like gardening, babysitting or house-keeping. Consequently, with the view of facilitating the establishment of e-commerce platforms, Mauritius has upgraded to fibre-broadband with speeds between 10MB and 30MB (International Trade Administration, 2022). Coupled with an enhanced connectivity, Mauritian banks do have sophisticated online payment systems and platforms which have also encouraged both businesses and consumers to resort to e-commerce during the COVID-19 crisis. This statement is evidenced by the official statistics from the Bank of Mauritius (2021) which found that there was a 66% rise in the transaction value of internet banking transfers during the period starting from April 2020 up to April 2021. Nevertheless, building online platforms and relying on the banking system do not solely guarantee the sustainability of the e-commerce sector. If the government will want digital trading to thrive and be more efficient in the future, a long-term strategy needs to be devised since e-transacting encompasses more than money transfers. As Jetsan (2020) has rightly mentioned, there are numerous implications arising from online shopping which needs to be thoroughly examined for the purpose of addressing the associated issues.

Alongside the necessary infrastructure and technical know-how, there is a dire need to establish an appropriate legal and regulatory framework for digital transactions since e-commerce presupposes the existence of money transfers, digital signatures, the conclusion of electronic contracts (e-contracts) as well as the exchange of confidential information. Essentially, e-contracts are 'structured in electronic form and are born out of the need for speed, convenience and efficiency' (Subaashini & Shaji, 2018). In fact, there exist some common similarities between e-contracts traditional (paper based) contracts. That is, there is an offer of products on an online platform which sets the qualities, prices and terms of the goods and then, prospective buyers can access the same platform in order to consider their options and they may even enter into negotiation over prices, terms and conditions (in some instances). If customers are agreeable, then they may place orders and make the payment as appropriate. As such, this method of trade is relatively simpler and less time consuming since there is no need for delayed couriers and additional travelling costs. There was contention amongst legislatures to pass on the relevant rules to give formal recognition to this new method of transacting, but now various countries have adopted laws to recognise electronic contracts (e-contracts). E-contracts are the underlying foundations of e-commerce and therefore, sufficient attention must be paid towards the formation of valid e-contracts before finalising and going ahead with transactions.

One among the most pertinent issues underlying e-contracts is the applicable law and jurisdiction. Since e-contracts have a foreign factor, the laws of several countries may all be related to the contract or dispute, but the determination of the appropriate applicable law and jurisdiction in the absence of this specific mention in the relevant e-contracts becomes complicated (Wang, 2011). For instance, if a Mauritian citizen enters into an online contract by clicking on the relevant icon and an agreement is established with a supplier in India while the server is in South Africa, the issue is where the contract has been formed and which court will have the competency to hear any dispute between the parties. While it is advisable to identify the proper law and jurisdiction based on party autonomy (Balaban, 2018), there is still the presence of risk due to unequal bargain power of the parties. This is because law practitioners that draft e-contracts for e-businesses have the tendency of designing the terms in favour of their clients which thereafter implies that customers are often left unaware of the meaning and consequences of such clauses like choice of law and jurisdiction. Moreover, in the majority of e-contracts, customers are not given the possibility to negotiate the terms prior to acceptance and it has also been noted that e-businesses are often inclined towards choosing the law which offers the least protection to consumers (Wang, 2011).

As such, the purpose of this study is to advocate for a greater clarity on the legal framework governing the applicable law and jurisdiction governing a conflict situation in e-contracts, with the view of increasing trust in international e-commerce and to bring in consistency with international commercial relations. This study will be carried in the Mauritian context by adopting the black letter approach which will analyse the relevant rules and regulations concerning e-contract formation. Additionally, a comparative analysis will be conducted on the legal framework relating to the applicable law and jurisdiction in e-contracts for some selected countries and these are the EU and the United States. These countries have been chosen for the comparison due to their high involvement in e-commerce and their advanced as well as comprehensive rules on e-commerce.

At present, this study will be amongst the first academic writings in the field of private international law concerning Mauritius and the determination of applicable law and jurisdiction in the context of e-contracts in the country. The outcomes of this research may be of interest to the authorities concerned in the pursuit of encouraging the conduct of electronic transactions across the globe. Whilst the first part of this research has introduced the subject matter of the research, the objectives and methods, Part 2 will elaborate on some essential and common characteristics and types of e-contracts. Part 3 will discuss the Mauritian legal and regulatory framework on contracts in general with a particular focus on e-contracts in international transactions whilst Part 4 will critically assess the relevance of choice of law clause in e-contracts and the laws of the EU and the United States on this subject will be considered. Part 5 will focus on the applicable jurisdiction clause in e-commerce and will examine the laws of the EU and the United States on the topic. Thereafter, Part 6 will compare Mauritian laws against the laws of the EU and the United States on choice of law and applicable jurisdiction in e-contracts and will make some recommendations in the Mauritian context. The final Part 7 will conclude the research.

2. THE SCOPE OF E-CONTRACTS

Basically, the Cooperative Research Centre for Construction Innovation of Australia (2008) had issued a publication highlighting the need to establish guidelines and policies for e-contracting in the construction industry in Australia. This publication provided for an all-encompassing set of factors that recognise the existence of e-contracting and these are summarised below:

– one party approaches another person by using electronic means of communication for negotiation purposes,
– once negotiation is completed, the parties proceed to sign the contract digitally and then, execution, administration and management of the contract is carried out under the contractual terms that were agreed initially. In this process, electronic communication remains the sole method of liaison, and
– on completion of the underlying transaction of the contract, records and communication messages are stored electronically.

From the above features, it is apposite to mention some essential features of e-contracts which are the exemption for having to meet physically, no requirement for handwritten signatures, no limitation regarding physical borders since transactions can be made across various jurisdictions. Additionally, there are several ways in which information technology can be used to conduct e-contracting but the most ideal method will depend on the needs of the business, the size of the organisation, the ease of contracting by the customer, the timeframe for executing the obligations under the contract among others.

According to Triparthy and Mishra (2017), e-contract formation can either be asynchronous or synchronous which means that the former refers to contract formation by using email while the latter entails an online collaboration. While e-contracting formation using email seems to be quite straightforward, there are some embedded challenges regarding the identity of the parties involved and the integrity of documents. This issue will be apparent if anyone party loses its email and password credentials and hackers get possession of these information which may in turn modify the underlying rules and conditions of offer and acceptance. Moreover, the absence of digital signatures in this form of e-contracting may decrease the evidentiary nature of records that may be presented in courts. There is also the issue of monitoring in executing the obligations of the e-contract since the document is not stored in a comprehensive manner which can be easily retrievable by third parties.

The alternative way to asynchronous e-contract formation is to complete the e-contracting process by online collaboration through either a shared platform or one which is set up by the parties (Krishna, Karlapalem, & Dani, 2005). In this context, e-contracting uses a collaboration system which takes the form of an online database whereby all the relevant information are stored and are easily accessible to all parties involved and also, it allows the conduct of online meeting, instant chat or video conferencing. While this online system of e-contracting may be tailor made to the specific requirements of the business concerned, there is somehow some security and costs issues that may be encountered. For instance, some of these online platforms do not use safe internet protocols which in turn comprise the privacy of the data being transferred amongst parties. Additionally, there are some high investment costs involved in developing its own web-based collaboration system and to ensure its ongoing operation and monitoring, a feature which may not be attractive for the small and medium enterprises who just started trading online.

Apart from asynchronous and synchronous e-contracting, Boykin (2005) states that the most common types of e-contracts are click-wrap, sign-in wrap and browse-wrap agreements. In simple terms, click-wrap also known as click-accept is an online agreement where users accept the terms and conditions by clicking on the 'I agree' button. In this case, signature replaces a simple click gesture and upon acceptance, the details of the consenting party are saved by the web server providing this function. In fact, a click-wrap agreement is used for the purpose of forming the contract only and where no formal method of administration or monitoring of obligations are required (Cooperative Research Centre for Construction Innovation of Australia, 2008). These are used by B2C businesses and are considered to be a legally binding method to enter into a contract with another B2B as well (Johansson, 2015). Sign-in wrap and browse-wrap agreements, on the other hand, are online contracts which do not require any clicking from users but are automatically deemed to be entered into by simply using a website or a software, respectively. That is, upon using a particular website or licence, there is a statement or a hyperlink often located at the bottom of the screen, which mentions that the person consents to the terms and conditions by using the website or software as the case may be. According to a recent report published by Ironclad (2022), click-wrap agreements had a 70% enforceability success rate in courts as compared to 64% for sign-in-wrap and 14% for browse-wrap agreements. The enforceability issues for each form of e-contracting will be discussed at a later stage in this research.

3. CONTRACT LAW OF MAURITIUS

It is noteworthy to highlight that the majority of rules governing contract in Mauritius are inspired from the laws of France since Mauritius was once under the reign of the French government. Consequently, the provisions concerning contract law are governed by the Code Civil of Mauritius (CCM), most precisely from Articles 1101 to 1383.

3.1 General Contract Formation

In principle, the rules of a traditional contract formation also apply to e-contracts. A general definition of contract is provided by Article 1101 of CCM which refers to a convention where one or more persons have an obligation towards another or more persons, to give, to execute or not to execute. In addition, Article 1108 of the CCM provides the four essential characteristics which need to be met to validly constitute a contract, and these are detailed hereunder:

(1) Acceptance: That is, the offer needs to be accepted and acceptance is evidenced by the signature of the offeree on the contract as the Supreme Court of Mauritius rules in the case of Colonial Government of Mauritius v. Mauritius Estates and Assets Company Limited. In fact, an offer is revocable at any time until the acceptance is made. Concerning e-contracts, modes of formation can be e-mail, web site forms and online agreements. Offers and acceptances can be exchanged entirely by e-mail or can be combined with paper documents, faxes or telephonic discussions. The seller can offer goods or services, for instance air tickets or software through his website. The customer places an order by completing and transmitting the order form provided on the website. The goods may be physically delivered later for example clothing or be immediately delivered electronically for instance, e-tickets.

(2) Competency to contract: The competency of capable persons authorised to contract under Mauritian laws is detailed by Article 1123 of the CCM which stipulates that any person is entitled to enter into contracts unless prohibited by the law. Essentially, the latter category of persons refers to minors and persons of unsound mind. In the context of e-contracts, it becomes difficult to ascertain the identity of the person behind the screen who is entering into electronic agreements. Nevertheless, in order to form a valid contract, the law states that all the parties must be legally competent to enter into the agreement.

(3) Lawful consideration: Any contract to be enforceable by law must have lawful consideration, which implies that both parties must give and receive something in return. Therefore, concerning online trading, if an auction site facilitates a contract between two parties where one person provides a pornographic movie as consideration for purchasing an mp3 player, then such a contract is deemed to be void.

(4) The presence of a lawful object or a legal purpose if an object is not involved under the contractual arrangement. A valid contract presupposes a lawful object which may take up the form of an existing subject matter or one which is yet to follow but its description has to be fully described in the contract in terms of nature, quality and quantity as the Supreme Court of Mauritius mentioned in *Jean-Louis v. Jenkins*. Thus, a contract for selling narcotic drugs or pornography online is void.

In addition to the above formal conditions to constitute a valid contract, it is apposite to note that an executed contract has to be registered with the Registrar General of Mauritius in order to be validly produced as evidence in a court of law and the registration is also equivalent to an act of rendering the contract public. However, it is not mandatory to register all types of contracts unless some particular agreements are compulsorily required by law to be registered under the Registration and Duties Act of Mauritius 1804 such as a fixed and floating charge agreement.

3.2 Legal Provisions on E-contracting

Apart from the specificities of each country's domestic laws on contract formation, at the international level, the United Nations Commission on International Trade Law (UNCITRAL) has issued several legislative models which may be adopted by countries across the globe in order to enable and facilitate the use of electronic means to engage in commercial activities (UNCITRAL, 2022). One among its laudable initiative is the establishment of the UNCITRAL Model Law on E-Commerce in 1996 which provides guiding principles on equality of treatment between paper-based and electronic data, the legal recognition of e-transactions and processes which are all based on the philosophies of non-discrimination, functional equivalence and technology neutrality (UNCITRAL, 2022). A related companion to this model law is the UNCITRAL Model Law on Electronic Signatures (2005) and these two aforementioned model legislative texts have been transposed into the domestic laws of various countries one among which is Mauritius through the enactment of the Electronic Transactions Act 2000 (*ETA*) and through some amendments made to the CCM.

Primarily, the preamble of the ETA mentions that this Act purports to provide for an appropriate legal framework to serve as the foundation to facilitate electronic transactions and communications by regulating electronic records and electronic signatures. In brief, the ETA is comprised of eight sections which set out rules on legal recognition of digital records and electronic signatures, liability of network service providers, e-contracts, effects of and obligations relating to digital signatures, regulation and authorisation of certification authorities. Explicit for the purpose of this research, Part IV of the ETA governs e-contracts and Section 10 underlies the principle of non-discrimination by providing that no contract shall be denied legal effect, validity or enforceability solely on the ground that an electronic record was used in its formation. An electronic record is defined as a message which was created, generated, sent, communicated, received or stored by electronic means (Section 2 of the ETA). Moreover, Section 12(2) of the ETA provides for the necessity to apply a particular security procedure to determine the identity of the person who has used the electronic signature or an electronic record. In this respect, Section 12(3) of the ETA provides for further guidance to ascertain if an electronic record has indeed been emanated from the intended originator by stipulating that the addressee needs to apply a procedure previously agreed to by the originator for that purpose.

Also, the ETA has emphasised the importance of acknowledging receipt of an electronic record by the addressee by virtue of its Section 13(1). If no such acknowledgement is received, then the electronic record shall be treated as it had never been sent (Section 13(3) of ETA). A final provision governing e-contracts under the ETA is the time and place of sending and receipt of an electronic data as provided by Section 14. Accordingly, an electronic record is deemed to be sent when it enters an information processing system outside the control of the originator (Section 14(1) of the ETA) and the time of receipt is the particular time when the electronic record enters the information processing system which has been designated between the originator and the addressee for that purpose.

However, if no information processing system has been agreed upon, then the time of receipt occurs when the electronic record is retrieved by the addressee on any information processing system that the addressee usually uses. On the other hand, the place of sending the electronic record is the place of business of the originator and the place of receipt is the addressee's place of business and if the latter is a body corporate, it will be the place of incorporation or registration.

Apart from the ETA, it is apposite to highlight that the CCM has been amended in the year 2000 by providing the admissibility of digital signatures and e-contracts as permissible evidence to be used in a court of law subject to fulfilling the corresponding formality requirements of the ETA, under the provision of Article 1316-1. Moreover, the CCM has also recognised in its Article 1317 the validity of public instruments or documents that have been drawn up electronically but subject to the related provisions of the ETA. Yet, despite these various endeavours undertaken by the Mauritian authorities to formally recognise e-transactions, some major issues pertaining to e-contracts are still left unattended, one among which is the applicable choice of law and jurisdiction which have not been clarified under Mauritian laws as of date.

3.3 Court's Jurisdiction in Mauritius

Essentially, there is a strong connection between contract law and the laws of civil procedure in Mauritius. Hence, according to Section 5 of the District and Intermediate Court (Civil Jurisdiction) Act 1888 of Mauritius, the forum having competence to hear the matter in dispute is the relevant court of the district where the defendant resides or carries on his business. However, if the subject matter of the suit concerns an immovable property, then the applicable jurisdiction is the district court where this property is located.

It is apposite to note that there are various courts in Mauritius ranging from district court, intermediate court, industrial court, bail and remand court and the supreme court being the highest court of the country. In determining the competency of each court, it is imperative to ascertain the amount of the relevant claims and regarding civil matters, district courts have the jurisdiction to hear cases that do not exceed MUR 250,000 (USD 5,717) while the intermediate court are entitled to hear cases of up to MUR 2,000,000 (USD 45,738). Any legal suit above MUR 2,000,000 (USD 45,738) is heard at the level of the supreme court.

In international transactions as well as for cross-border e-commerce activities, the laws of Mauritius do not explicitly mention the application of this principle for jurisdiction. Nonetheless, by extenso, it follows that the applicable jurisdiction remains the court where the defendant resides or conducts his business activities in any type of private international transactions.

4. CHOICE OF LAW IN E-CONTRACTS

4.1 The Relevance of Applicable Law

Primarily, choice of law clauses is imperative in commerce since they form the underlying principles that govern the duties and obligations of each party to an e-contract. Hence, the protection of consumers will be governed and limited to that particular law which will have to be abided by all the parties concerned. The issue is that e-businesses who have a better understanding of the law or are able to avail of the services of legal experts, are more likely to choose the law of a country that offers the most favourable treatment to them and that comprises less bureaucracy for them without considering the low protection afforded to consumers (Balaban, 2018). The problem is further accentuated in the case of click-wrap, sign-in wrap and browse-wrap agreements because customers do not have the option of negotiating the terms thereof since they are put in the situation of "accept or leave" at the outset itself. Nevertheless, Mauritian laws are silent as to the protection afforded to consumers in the event that the choice of law clauses are used in an abusive manner by e-businesses.

4.2 Implied Choice of Law in the EU

If an e-contract does not mention the choice of law, it is usual practice for English courts and European courts to ascertain the applicable law through an implied choice of law by referring to the jurisdiction clause or assessing which country has the closest connection to the contract (Spindler & Borner, 2013). In this respect, Article 4 of Rome I Regulation 2008 (*Rome I Regulation*) provides some guiding principles such as in the case of a contract for:

(a) sale of goods or services, the applicable law is the habitual residence of the seller or service provider as the case may be,
(b) selling or renting an immovable property, the governing law is the law of the country where the property is located,
(c) a franchise or distribution, the proper law is that of the country where the franchisee or the distributor has his respective habitual residence.

This legal provision in fact relies on the principle of demonstrable choice of law that can be inferred by courts of law. Additionally, there are some other features that can justify the demonstrable choice of law such as the use of standard forms of e-contracts for a particular legal system, the nationality and language used by parties or even the currency of payment (Balaban, 2018). Accordingly, an implied choice can only be challenged and rejected if there are sufficient evidences to prove that a valid choice was made by the parties in the e-contract itself by expressing their autonomy.

4.3 Legal Provision on Choice of Law in the EU

Unlike Mauritius where the law is silent on the choice of law principle, the EU is able to rely to the Rome I Regulation for issues concerning e-contracts. In fact, this Regulation applies only to those e-contracts that were entered into after 17 December 2009 and is comprised of provisions governing freedom of choice, applicable law, contracts of carriage, consumer contracts, insurance contracts, overriding mandatory provision, employment contracts, consent and material validity, formal validity, incapacity, voluntary assignment, burden of proof, liability, public policy among others.

Basically, Rome I Regulation adopts a protective approach by affording special treatment to customers who are regarded as the weaker party as per Recital 23 of this Regulation which mentions that for 'contracts concluded with parties regarded as being weaker, those parties should be protected by conflict-of-law rules that are more favourable to their interests than the general rules'. In fact, Article 6 of Rome I Regulation affords protection to natural persons who contracts (consumers) with 'another person acting in the exercise of his trade or profession (the professional)' concerning the applicable law for this particular contract (Article 6(1)). In particular, this section stipulates that the e-contract shall be governed by the law of the country where the consumer has his habitual residence, which is defined as the principal place of business of that person and shall be determined at the time of conclusion of the agreement. The same Article 6 then recognises the party's autonomy by providing in its sub-section 2 that the parties may choose any country's law provided that this choice is made expressly and is clearly demonstrated by the terms of the contract or the circumstance of the case.

Nevertheless, despite the prevalence of party's autonomy for the expressed choice of law, most countries reserve the right to use their overriding mandatory rules and public policy principle to protect their political, economic and social rights that risk to be violated by the application of the laws of another country and this leeway is provided by Article 9(1) of Rome I Regulation (Chen, 2022). However, in the majority of cases, it is less probable that a simple e-commercial transaction and any dispute arising therefrom will affect the public interest and policy of any particular country. Yet, there is one particular case which is worth mentioning in which the court applied the overriding principle over an agreed choice of law. The case concerns Amazon (2016) which had a company incorporated in Luxembourg and had concluded e-contracts with customers from Austria. The governing law of this agreement was that of Luxembourg and it was mentioned in the e-contract that Amazon has the right to use the personal information of customers which they supplied during the normal course of trade. A consumer protection body then asked for an injunction to stop Amazon make use of such abusive terms and the court ruled that where the interests of consumers are affected due to unfair contractual terms, the applicable law shall be that of the country of the consumers, and in this case, the proper law was Austrian law.

In essence, the establishment of this Rome I Regulation demonstrates the willingness of the EU to harmonise private international rules on traditional contracts and e-contracts among its members. The adoption of the same governing law principle across countries may reduce and eliminate uncertainties when transacting online which in turn help in foster greater e-commerce activities at the international level.

4.4 Legal Provision on Choice of Law in the United States

In the United States, upon the reading and interpretation of the Second Restatement on the law of contracts (1981), courts are more inclined to give recognition to parties' autonomy in upholding choice of law clauses in e-contracts with consumers (Section 187). Essentially, choice of law clauses are considered to be valid unless public policy is at stake or if it can be proven that the e-contract was entered into with bad faith (Section 197 of Second Restatement). Additionally, huge emphasis is placed on the question of unconscionability by US courts in determining if the consumer was aware of the terms and conditions of the e-transactions and their implications. Basically, if the unconsciousness of the customer is proven, then the e-contract is declared void but this unconscionability principle applies only for the choice of law clause. In its determination, US courts usually consider the fairness that the clause purports to offer to the consumer and if this chosen law deprives the customer some of its protective rights that he would have enjoyed under the law of the country with the closest connection, then the public policy element may be invoked to give effect to US laws as the applicable law in the relevant matter under dispute in the e-contract (Section 198 of the Second Restatement).

However, for a particular choice of law to be invalidated, both procedural and substantial unconscionability have to be identified (Balaban, 2018). Thus, two areas of concern are to be considered, firstly, whether the customer is conscious of the existence of a choice of law clause and secondly, if the same customer was aware of the terms and conditions or implications of this clause. For instance, in Specht v. Netscape, in a browse-wrap agreement, consumers had to download free software at the click of a button and court ruled that a reasonable prudent internet user would not have known or learnt of the existence of the licence terms before downloading the software since the defendants did not give reasonable notice of these terms. Consequently, court stated that clicking a download button does not merely indicate acceptance to the licence terms and conditions and no contractual relationship existed at the outset. Regarding click and accept licence terms, court ruled in the case of Williams v. America Online Inc that the choice of law clause could not be enforced since the customer was not aware of the terms of service of the e-contract. In this case, users were asked to upgrade a version of the software and once installation was done, they were then given the opportunity to accept the choice of law clause and other terms of the agreement. The damage to their computer systems occurred before they had the chance to read the agreement and thus, the court found that they could not be bound by the e-contractual terms to remedy precontractual damages. In the context of substantial conscionability, in *Pollstar v. Gigmania*, the court held the choice of law clause as being valid even if the parties entered into the agreement without looking at the terms and conditions of the contract. The issue in this case concerned the downloading and sharing of a recent news by one webpage from another although downloading implied the existence of a licence agreement. The plaintiff filed a case for misappropriation under contract law and unfair competition under copyright's act. Court held that since the notice of the licence agreement was provided after the download, the browse-wrap contract was regarded as valid and enforceable.

Nevertheless, despite the huge importance given to parties' autonomy by US courts, Section 199 of the Second Restatement on contract law mentions that the choice of applicable law needs to underlie a reasonable ground so as to ensure protection against bad faith. In meeting this reasonability test, it is firstly imperative to prove a substantial relationship and secondly, some other grounds may be considered. Section 114 of the Second Restatement further sheds light on the principle of substantiality to the effect that the chosen law is usually that of the country where either the obligation is carried out or the place of execution of contract or the location that involves some personal connection with the parties concerned. In some other instances, another country's law may be selected if it can be justified for instance on the ground that the foreign country has an advanced system of e-commerce legislative framework than the existing laws of the parties' respective countries of origin.

5. APPLICABLE JURISDICTION IN E-CONTRACTS

5.1 The Relevance of Applicable Jurisdiction

In simple terms, jurisdiction simply refers to the forum or court which has the capacity to hear disputes arising from contracts. In fact, Whytock (2022) noted that e-businesses chose the jurisdiction that is closest to them in proximity for convenience purposes in e-contracts whilst disregarding the consumer's opinion or personal circumstances. Accordingly, it becomes difficult for the latter to seek justice for any breaches of e-contractual terms since customers will have to travel to a foreign court thus forcing them to incur travelling expenditure to be physically present at the selected court. As such, for fairness' sake, it is vital to establish some formal guidelines on the jurisdiction clause in e-contracts specially in the light of international nature of e-transactions. Unfortunately, Mauritian laws are silent on the determination on jurisdiction but this is not the case for the EU and the United States.

5.2 Legal Provisions on Applicable Jurisdiction in the EU

In essence, jurisdictional issues are dealt in the EU in accordance with the Brussels Regulation (2012), mainly by its Section 4 comprised of Articles 17 to 19. The primary objective of the Brussels Regulation is to afford protection to consumers by allowing them to start a legal claim at their place of habitual residence (Article 18(1) of the Brussels Regulation) although several exceptions exist to this rule. In particular, these exceptions imply that the choice of jurisdiction selected by the e-business may be enforced if this clause offers additional protective mechanisms to consumers. However, this additional protection is considered in the light of a real existence of a consumer contract rather than the consideration of a commercial understanding. That is, customers must be able to rely on the protective perception designed in the legislations of the selected court which regard customers as the weaker parties.

Section 4 of the Brussels Regulation refers explicitly to the terms 'jurisdiction over consumer contracts'. Nevertheless, there is no universally accepted definition of the term 'consumer' but the European Court of Justice had in the case of Cape

Snc v. Idealservice Srl defined consumers by referring to the Brussels Regulation, as being natural persons who enters into a commercial agreement for the purposes outside trade or commercial activity that he practices. The case has also classified consumers as being the weaker party from an economic perspective and one that is less informed about juridical matters. Given this interpretation, one can question the scope of the term 'consumer' as it entails extensive protection, but Alavi and Khamichonak (2015) are of the opinion that a strict interpretation must be given to this terminology. This is because Section 4 of the Brussels Regulation is a departure from the general private international law principle that a defendant must be sued in the jurisdiction of his domicile, but the existence of an e-consumer contract according to Section 4 implies that the applicable jurisdiction in the case of disputes will be the place of the consumer or one offering a more favourable treatment to the same consumer. Accordingly, Section 4 will not apply to a purchaser who buys a product in an online transaction for any purpose apart from his personal needs especially if the latter is said to conduct a business or an e-business as court stated in Francesco Benincasa v. Dentalkit. Hence, Section 4 of the Brussels Regulation applies only to B2C transaction and not to B2B ones.

Yet despite emphasis by the Brussels Regulation which gives effect to consumer's place of domicile as the applicable jurisdiction, the Brussels Regulation does recognise the concept of parties' autonomy by allowing the business and customer to decide on a particular jurisdiction in case of disputes but this chosen court will have the duty to assess whether the selection is substantially valid. For this purpose, Article 25(1) of the Brussels Regulation may be invoked which states that a jurisdiction clause will only be valid if it is concluded in writing and Article 25(2) enables electronic means of communication to be considered as a written form. Additionally, the European Court of Justice has confirmed in the case of Estasis Salotti di Colzani Aimo e Gianmario Colzani *s.n.c. v Rüwa Polstereimaschinen GmbH* that a jurisdiction clause will be valid if the consumer has been given sufficient and apparent notice about its existence. As such, in online transactions, if the customer is not directed to the specific jurisdiction paragraph which forms part of the terms and conditions of the e-contract, the agreement will not be a valid one. One way of drawing the customer's attention to this clause is to oblige the latter to read all the terms and conditions by scrolling down till the end of the webpage before enabling the 'accept' function. This technique intends to provide assurance to e-businesses that customers will read the terms and conditions of the e-contract and thus, the jurisdiction clause meets the formal condition criteria.

5.3 Legal Provisions on Applicable Jurisdiction in the United States

Due to the fact that the United States has large online platforms across which innumerable B2C transactions take place, there is more risk of disputes arising (Trivedi, 2021). Nonetheless, specific rules concerning jurisdiction clauses are not provided for by the majority of states forming part of the United States. Hence, the concept of parties' autonomy prevails and as a matter of common practice,

US courts will look for genuineness of the intention of parties involved. In the context of e-contracts, it is expected that a clear and proper communication on the jurisdiction clause be provided to the consumer by the business and the same customer be afforded with a real opportunity to read and interpret correctly this clause before giving consent. However, these two conditions appear to be challenging in the field of e-commerce especially for click-wrap and browse-wrap contracts. In click-wrap agreements, the terms and conditions of the e-contract as well as the jurisdiction clause are presented on the website or online platform and consumers have to click on 'agree' or 'accept' button. One apparent enforceability issue with this method of e-contracting is the lack of signature which is replaced by a simple gesture of clicking agree or accept button. Hence, US courts rely on the consciousness of the customer in understanding the existence of a jurisdiction clause. One example is the case of Comb v. PayPal Inc, where the court held invalid an arbitration clause included in a click-wrap agreement by PayPal on the ground that the consumers were not aware that the average value of a claim under local courts was much smaller than the arbitration expenditure. Moreover, in another case of *Scarcella v. America Online Inc*, the court invalidated the jurisdiction clause in a membership agreement because America Online gave its customers the option of avoiding to read the e-contract in its complete form before signing the agree button. Consumers on their side were indeed comfortable with this arrangement since the e-agreement terms comprised of lengthy pages with small-font characters and they were able to simply skip the reading of these clauses. However, the court regarded this as a deceptive practice which would put the consumer in a disadvantaged position.

Similarly, regarding browse-wrap agreements whereby no express clicking is required to give consent to the terms of service of the e-contract which are often accessible through a hyperlink, US courts have pertinently considered whether customers have been given sufficient notice of these conditions for enforceability purposes. In this regard, the case of *Pollstar v. Gigmania* indicates that courts will invalidate an e-contract if the e-business does not provide sufficiently clear notice to customers on the relevant terms and conditions. In the case, the e-contract hyperlink was written in grey colour on grey paper and no highlighting or underlining of the hyperlink was made to direct customer's attention. Hence, this omission on behalf of the defendant was regarded as an insufficient notice to consumers.

6. COMPARATIVE STUDY AND RECOMMENDATIONS
6.1 Choice of Law
According to Article 1108 of the Mauritian Civil Code, any agreement is valid if it meets the underlying conditions of acceptance, competency, lawful consideration and a lawful object or purpose. It is commonly accepted by Mauritian courts that acceptance is made by the traditional paper-based signature but the law was amended previously to give effect to digital signatures further to the enactment of the ETA and some amendments made to the Civil Code. Basically,

digital acceptance may be verified by the procedures set out in the ETA and are admissible for evidential purposes in a court of law. Thus, from a reading of the ETA and the Civil Code, it can be inferred that Mauritian courts will uphold the validity of an e-contract if digital signatures are involved and are established as well as processed in accordance with the ETA although this matter has never been disputed in the courts of Mauritius as of date.

Nevertheless, the law is silent on the validity and enforceability procedures involved in click-wrap, sign-in wrap and browse-wrap agreements where consumers do not have or have the limited option of negotiation. Accordingly, there is the fear that Mauritian customers' rights are prejudiced by e-businesses who have the wide choice of drafting the e-agreement especially regarding the choice of law and jurisdiction clauses according to their wishes and convenience. In contrast, the EU has in place the Rome I Regulation to provide directives on the determination of choice of law and jurisdiction with the view of protecting consumers. In a nutshell, the choice of law is the law of the jurisdiction of the customer who is regarded as the weaker party unless if the parties have for some justifiable reasons, chosen another applicable law. Even in the latter case, Rome I Regulation further protects consumers by providing that such alternate choice will not deprive the customers from the legal protection afforded by the laws of their habitual residence.

Similarly, the US has clear guidelines taken from case laws and the Second Restatement on contract law in determining the validity of the choice of law clause. In essence, the customer needs to be aware of the existence of this clause and also, he must understand the implications of this applicable law. The case laws referenced earlier in this research evidences the strict application of the procedural and substantial rules concerning conscionability of consumers before enforcing the choice of law provision in an e-contract. Moreover, the Second Restatement on contract law provides some additional protection to customers by requiring the parties to give reasonable grounds when choosing another foreign country's legislation as the applicable law.

Due to the mushrooming of e-commerce business providers in Mauritius, it is imperative to advocate for some clarity regarding the choice of law in e-contracts especially in the light of click-wrap, sign-in wrap and browse-wrap agreements. While the enforceability of choice of law in e-agreements has never been disputed in Mauritian courts, it does not mean that issues will not crop up regarding this aspect in the future. Without proper guidance, parties will be engaged in costly and time-consuming procedures for resolving disputes and accordingly, to avoid these inconveniences, it will be wise for the Mauritian authorities to adopt a pro-active approach by establishing guidelines concerning the applicable law in e-commerce transactions whilst having regard to consumers' protection and rights. However, in Mauritius, the Consumer Affairs Unit is not eligible by the consumer protection laws of Mauritius to issue official and binding guidelines since its role is limited only to educating the public on consumer's rights, handling of complaints, conducting surveys, ensuring compliance and processing applications for registration of warehouses (Ministry of Commerce and Consumer Protection, 2022). The only method to provide clarity on the applicable law is to set standards in legislative text and for this purpose, this research suggests a mixture of both EU and US approaches on the subject. In particular, it is proposed that a consumer protection regulation on e-contract be specifically drafted to inter alia shed light on competency, object, purpose, consideration, choice of law, jurisdiction in an e-agreement in an e-commerce transaction. This regulation needs to restrict the applicable law to that of the country of habitual residence of the customer similar to the Rome I Regulation in order to avoid any abuse from e-businesses but simultaneously, the law needs to give effect to party's autonomy. In other words, an exception needs to be provided in order to allow parties to choose the law of any other foreign country but subject to meeting some conditions. Firstly, this selection needs to be reasonable that is there shall be a connection with the chosen law with the transaction or parties concerned, secondly, customers need to be aware of the existence and implications of this applicable law similar to the provisions of the US Second Restatement. Moreover, the law needs to expressly mention that irrespective of the selected law, the customer is still afforded legal protection under the laws of his habitual residence. Through this new customer regulation, it is believed that the civil society will be more at ease to enter into e-transactions and this will indeed flourish the e-commerce sector in Mauritius whilst at the same time, facilitating dispute resolution processes.

6.2 Applicable Jurisdiction

Generally, the principles of private international law suggest that the competent court to hear the matter in dispute is the court of the domicile of the defendant. Nevertheless, the concept of parties' autonomy enables them to choose their own forum to hear disputes and it was noted that e-businesses select the court which is closest to them in proximity even if this may prejudice the rights of consumers. This is because due to the cross-border nature of e-transactions, consumers will have to travel abroad and incur costs to start legal proceedings in a foreign country to seek remedies for breaches under the respective e-contract. To avoid such abuses, it is imperative to establish clear guidelines on the applicable jurisdiction clause in e-agreements and in the absence of specific legal provision on this subject in Mauritius, the approaches adopted by the EU and United States are considered to suggest some recommendations for the Mauritius legal landscape.

With the view of protecting customers, the EU follows the Brussels Regulation in determining the applicable jurisdiction when drafting e-contracts. Basically, this regulation provides that the competent court is the one where the consumer is domiciled in an e-commerce transaction but it was noted that European Court of Justice interprets the term 'consumer' quite strictly and hence the jurisdiction provision of the Brussels Regulation applies only to B2C e-transactions and not B2B online activities. On the other side, the same Brussels Regulation give recognition to parties' autonomy by enable the latter to select any other forum for dispute resolution provided that two conditions are met. The first condition refers to the formal condition of writing the jurisdiction clause which also includes an electronic form of communication and the second one requires the provision of a sufficiently clear notice of this clause to the customer by the e-business before accepting the terms of service of the e-contract. The existence of this second condition is very much relevant for click-wrap and browse-wrap agreements since customers have the limited choice of amending their respective terms. Likewise, a quite similar approach is adopted by US courts in considering the validity of a jurisdiction clause in an e-agreement. While US laws are silent on the determination of the applicable jurisdiction in an e-commerce transaction, a reading of US case laws suggests that courts rely on the consciousness of the customer in understanding the existence of a jurisdiction clause. That is, firstly it has to be ascertained whether the customer has been provided due notice of the existence of the jurisdiction clause and secondly, whether the latter has been given the opportunity to interpret such a clause before consenting to the e-contract's terms and conditions.

One cannot deny the importance of the jurisdiction clause since it is the forum where the aggrieved party will go to at the first instance for the purpose of seeking relief for any damage suffered from breaches of contract. While the Mauritian government is endeavouring various initiatives to foster an environment conducive to e-commerce, one must not undermine the relevance of official rules on the applicable jurisdiction in international transactions. To bring clarity on this subject and in the absence of precision in Mauritian laws or Mauritian court's ruling on the determination of applicable jurisdiction in e-commerce transaction, this research advocates for the domestication of the relevant part of the Brussels Regulation on applicable jurisdiction. It was noted initially that the principles of the Brussels Regulation are also acted upon by US courts despite the fact that US laws are silent on the applicable jurisdiction determination in cross-border transactions. Hence, as suggested for the choice of law clause earlier in this section, it is recommended for the Mauritian authorities to enact another set of consumer protection regulation on applicable jurisdiction in cross-border affairs to firstly depart from the general private international law principle to require the applicable jurisdiction to be set at the place of domicile of the customer. Secondly, being a democratic country, this domestic regulation must also give effect to parties' autonomy by allowing parties to select another forum as the applicable jurisdiction but subject to fulfiling two requirements. The first one concerns the obligation of the e-business to give reasonable notice of this clause to the customer and the second condition requires that the consumer be afforded with the opportunity to read and interpret such a clause before assenting to the e-contracts. With this new enactment, undeniably, uncertainties regarding the relevant forum to start a legal suit will diminish and Mauritian courts also will have a clear set of guidelines for determining competency to hear disputes.

7. CONCLUSION

E-commerce is gaining popularity across the globe and Mauritian businesses are also increasingly making use of online platforms to engage in cross-border electronic transactions. However, there are several implications arising from online trading which need to be addressed, one among which is the validity of e-contracts. This research has therefore emphasised on two main components of e-contracts: choice of law and the applicable jurisdiction. While Mauritian laws have been amended to give effect to digital signatures and e-agreements, there is no extensive or substantive provision on choice of law and jurisdiction. Thus, the laws of the EU and the United States have been considered in order to assess their respective legal framework on each topic and it has been seen that the EU Rome I Regulation, the EU Brussels Regulation, the US Second Restatement on contract law and case laws precedents from the EU and United States each do provide detailed guidelines on choice of law and jurisdiction with a particular focus of protecting customers who are regarded as the weaker party in e-commerce transactions. Consequently, in order to depart from the private international law principle, this research recommends that the Mauritian authorities enact a separate consumer protection regulation by requiring the applicable law to be the laws of the domicile of the customer and the jurisdiction to be the court of the domicile of the customer as well. However, a leeway has to be provided under this regulation by giving recognition to parties' autonomy which will allow them to select any other applicable law or jurisdiction but subject to meeting certain conditions as mentioned in the recommendation section of this research. Through these legal clarities, there will be a win-win situation for both parties to an e-commerce transaction since on one hand, customers will be convinced that their rights are being protected and they will be more comfortable to enter into e-commerce transactions. On the other hand, e-businesses will save time and money in settlement of disputes if they follow the appropriate safeguards established by the law. Ultimately, the e-commerce industry of Mauritius will indeed thrive in a sustainable manner.

REFERENCES

Alavi, H., & Khamichonak, T. (2015). A step forward in the harmonisation of European Jurisdiction: Regulation Brussels I Recast. *Baltic Journal of Law & Politics*, *8*(2), 159–181. doi:10.1515/bjlp-2015-0023. Accessed on June 1, 2022.

Balaban, T. (2018). *Choice of law and jurisdiction in e-commerce contracts with focus on B2C agreements*. Unpublished Masters Thesis. Central European University.

Bank of Mauritius. (2021). *Financial Stability Report December 2021*. Retrieved from https://www.bom.mu/sites/default/files/bank_of_mauritius_financial_stability_report_-_december_2021_0_0.pdf. Accessed on May 17, 2021.

Boykin, D. (2005). Survey of e-contracting cases: Browsewrap, clickwrap and modified clickwrap agreement. *The Business Lawyer*, *68*(1), 257–262. Retrieved from https://www.jstor.org/stable/23527090. Accessed on May 22, 2022.

Cape Snc v. Idealservice Srl [2001] ECR I-09049, C-541/99.

Chen, Z. (2022). Jurisdiction and choice of law rules over electronic consumer contracts. *Maastricht Journal of European and Comparative Law*, *1*(1), 1–23. doi:10.1177/1023263X221090352. Accessed on May 26, 2022.

Colonial Government of Mauritius v. Mauritius Estates and Assets Company Limited [1900] MR 19.

Comb v. PayPal Inc. [2002] 218 F.Supp.2d 1165 N.D.

Cooperative Research Centre for Construction Innovation of Australia. (2008). *e-contracting – Security and Legal Issues*. St Leonards: Icon.Net Pty Ltd.

EC Regulation on the law applicable to contractual obligations. (2008). *Official Journal of the European Union No. 593/2008*. Retrieved from https://eur-lex.europa.eu/legal-content/EN/TXT/PDF/?uri=CELEX:32008R0593&from=EN. Accessed on May 26, 2022.

Estasis Salotti di Colzani Aimo e Gianmario Colzani s.n.c. v Rüwa Polstereimaschinen GmbH [1976] ECR 1831, C-24/76.

EU Regulation on jurisdiction and the recognition and enforcement of judgments in civil and commercial matters. (2012). No. 1215/2012, OJ L 351, 1-32. Retrieved from https://eur-lex.europa.eu/legal-content/EN/ALL/?uri=celex%3A32012R1215. Accessed on June 1, 2022.

Francesco Benincasa v. Dentalkit [1997] ECR I-3797, C-269/95.

International Trade Administration. (2022). Mauritius commercial guide – E-Commerce. Retrieved from https://www.trade.gov/country-commercial-guides/mauritius-ecommerce. Accessed on May 17, 2022.

Ironclad. (2022). *Clickwrap litigation trends*. Retrieved from https://ironcladapp.com/lp/clickwrap-litigation-trends-report/. Accessed on May 22, 2022.

Jean-Louis v. Jenkins. 1907 MR 71.

Jetsan, D. (2020). Digital transformation can be a powerful driver for business outcomes. Retrieved from https://www.iblgroup.com/diya-nababsing-jetshan-digital-transformation-can-be-powerful-driver-business-outcomes. Accessed on May 17, 2021.

Johansson, A. (2015). *The enforceability of clickwrap agreements* (pp. 1–74). UMEA University. Retrieved from https://www.diva-portal.org/smash/get/diva2:807840/FULLTEXT01.pdf. Accessed on May 22, 2022.

Krishna, R., Karlapalem, K., & Dani, A. (2005). From contracts to e-contracts: Modeling and enactment. *Information Technology and Management*, 6, 363–387. doi:10.1007/s10799-005-3901-z. Accessed on May 17, 2022.

Ministry of Commerce and Consumer Protection. (2022). Consumer affairs unit. Retrieved from https://commerce.govmu.org/Pages/Departments/CAU.aspx. Accessed on June 6, 2022.

Pollstar v. Gigmania Ltd [2000] 170 F Supp 2d 974.

Scarcella v. America Online Inc [2005] 4 Misc. 3d 1024 N. Y. 2d 348.

Specht v. Netscape. [2002] 306 F. 3d 17 2d Cir.

Spindler, G., & Borner, F. (2013). E-Commerce Law in Europe and the USA. *Science and Business Media*, 1(1), 240–260.

Subaashini, S., & Shaji, M. (2018). Legal issues arising in e-contracts in India: An analysis. *International Journal of Pure and Applied Mathematics*, 120(5), 4601–4618.

Triparthy, B., & Mishra, J. (2017). A generalized framework for e-contract. *International Journal of Service Science, Management, Engineering, and Technology*, 8(4), 1–18. doi:10.4018/IJSSMET.2017100101. Accessed on May 17, 2022.

Trivedi, V. (2021). E-commerce fraud to surpass $20B in 2021. Retrieved from https://www.paymentsdive.com/news/e-commerce-fraud-to-hit-20-billion-2021-an-18-jump-from-prior-year/599312/. Accessed on June 3, 2022.

UNCITRAL. (2022). Electronic commerce. Retrieved from https://uncitral.un.org/en/texts/ecommerce. Accessed on May 24, 2022.

UNCTAD. (2021a). How Covid-19 triggered the digital and e-commerce turning point. Retrieved from https://unctad.org/news/how-covid-19-triggered-digital-and-e-commerce-turning-point. Accessed on May 12, 2022.

UNCTAD. (2021b). *Covid-19 and E-commerce: A global review*. Report published by UNCTAD, UNCTAD/DTL/STICT/2020/13. Retrieved from https://unctad.org/system/files/official-document/dtlstict2020d13_en_0.pdf. Accessed on May 12, 2022.

Verein für Konsumenteninformation [2016] C-191/15, EU:C:2016:612.

Wang, F. (2011). Choice of law in electronic contracting. In *Internet jurisdiction and choice of law – Legal practices in the EU, US and China* (pp. 93–99). Cambridge: Cambridge University Press.

Whytock, C. (2022). Transnational litigation in US Courts: A theoretical and empirical reassessment. *Journal of Empirical Legal Studies*, 19(1), 4–59. doi:10.1111/jels.12306. Accessed on June 1, 2022.

Williams v. America Online Inc. [2001] WL 135825 Mass. Super.

World Bank. (2020). *The potential impact of COVID-19 on GDP and trade: A preliminary assessment.* Washington, DC: World Bank. Retrieved from http://documents1.worldbank.org/curated/en/295991586526445673/pdf/ThePotential-Impact-of-COVID-19-on-GDP-and-Trade-A-Preliminary-Assessment.pdf. Accessed on May 12, 2022.

WTO. (2020). *Helping SMEs navigate the Covid-19 crisis.* Retrieved from https://www.wto.org/english/tratop_e/covid19_e/msmes_report_e.pdf. Accessed on September 9, 2021.

WHAT SHAPES INTERNET FINANCIAL REPORTING IN AFRICA? EXPLORING FIRM V COUNTRY FACTORS

Dineshwar Ramdhony, Oren Mooneeapen and Ajmal Bakerally

ABSTRACT

This study investigates the effect of corporate governance mechanisms and country-level factors on the extent of Internet Financial Reporting (IFR). We used a sample of 106 listed firms from five African countries. A financial reporting disclosure index was used to compute the aggregate IFR scores, which are made up of two components: content and presentation. Our results indicate that IFR relates to board size, firm size, country-level governance, economic development and index return. These results evidence the predominance of country-level factors over firm-specific factors in explaining the extent of IFR in Africa. It also shows that corporate governance mechanisms via board practices are insufficient to explain IFR in Africa. By further extending our analysis into the two components of IFR, we find that factors affecting the content and presentation dimensions are different. This study is among the first to investigate the extent of IFR in several African countries and adds to the existing evidence that has mainly focussed on firm-specific factors.

Keywords: IFR; Internet reporting; board practices; content analysis; corporate governance; country governance

Corporate Resilience
Developments in Corporate Governance and Responsibility, Volume 21, 151–172
Copyright © 2023 by Emerald Publishing Limited
All rights of reproduction in any form reserved
ISSN: 2043-0523/doi:10.1108/S2043-052320230000021008

LIST OF ABBREVIATIONS

IFR—Internet Financial Reporting
IPR—Internet Penetration Rate
IAS—International Accounting Standards

1. INTRODUCTION

The Internet has revolutionised the world by turning it into a global village. Since the 2000s, firms have been slowly using the Internet to promote their products and image. The development of the Internet has reshaped the business world, with more and more firms making use of it in their business activities. Corporate reporting practices are also catching up. Firms are now adopting Internet financial reporting (IFR), that is, disseminating financial and non-financial information on their websites.

The Internet is a unique tool for disclosing information that encourages flexible forms of presentation and allows instant, broad and cheap communication to investors (Kelton & Yang, 2008). Numerous companies are adopting digital reporting because the Internet has become one of the tools used by investors to gather corporate information (Hindi & Rich, 2010). The Internet is a technology that has the power to transform external reporting significantly. It provides a flawless information delivery channel that targets a multitude of investors across the globe (Xiao, Jones, & Lymer, 2005). The benefits of adopting IFR compared to paper-based reporting are enormous.

The African region suffers from negative investor perception due to lack of transparency, weak corporate governance and failure to protect investors (Mangena & Tauringana, 2007). With digital reporting, firms can promote transparency by disclosing timely information on their websites. Developing internet infrastructure in Africa allows firms to adopt digital reporting. The chapter investigates the determinants of IFR in the African context. This is particularly important as African countries have pushed for improved corporate governance and enhanced external reporting to attract foreign investors (Mangena & Chamisa, 2008) and increase capital flow to their stock markets.

Research on IFR has been growing over the past two decades, but most studies have focussed on developed countries (Kelton & Yang, 2008). Research on IFR in developing countries started booming in the twenty-first century (Xiao, Yang, & Chow, 2004). However, there are strong grounds to believe that the findings of developed and developing countries cannot be extended to their African peers due to weak regulatory frameworks (Waweru, Mangena, & Riro, 2019).

African economies are among the fastest-growing in the world. Africa has recently witnessed massive development, often referred to as 'African opportunity'. In 2018, despite the global drop in foreign direct investment, the African continent recorded a 5% growth (UNCTAD, 2019). Yet, investors are still reluctant to invest in Africa. This is because corporate governance in Africa has endured heavy criticism. The mix between politics and business, whereby ownership is concentrated among the political elites, remains the weak link (Chigudu, 2018) for the African continent to attract more investment.

We intend to contribute to the literature in two ways. Research on corporate governance mechanisms and IFR in the African region is scarce and has been limited to cross-sectional studies (Agboola & Salawu, 2012; Manini, Abdillahi, & Hardy, 2014; Omran & Ramdhony, 2016). One of the rare non-country-specific studies on IFR in Africa was conducted by Waweru et al. (2019), but the sample was limited to only two countries. Our study extends prior IFR studies as it is the first to conduct a cross-country African IFR research by sampling five countries over two years. Extending the sample will help scholars to understand which corporate governance mechanisms (if any) are a common determinant of IFR. Our results are also relevant for African regulatory bodies aiming to improve governance mechanisms and financial reporting.

We argue that limiting our variables of interest to company-specific ones would give only a limited picture of the determinants of IFR. A firm's commitment to CSR issues, corporate disclosures and sustainability activities is heavily influenced by environmental regulations, institutional pressure, national governance systems and the economic development of the country in which the firm operates (Ortas, Álvarez, Jaussaud, & Garayar, 2015; Ziegler, Busch, & Hoffmann, 2011). Our research is, therefore, seminal for incorporating country-level factors as exogenous variables into the analysis of IFR. This innovative step allows the determination of whether country-level variables have a role in influencing IFR practices in Africa.

The rest of the chapter is organised as follows. Section 2 reviews the relevant literature, the theories underpinning IFR and develops the research hypotheses. The methodology used for this study is explained in Section 3. The results are presented and interpreted in Section 4. The penultimate section provides an in-depth discussion of these results. Finally, we provide conclusions to the study and explain the research implications and future research avenues.

2. LITERATURE REVIEW

2.1 Internet Financial Reporting

Many firms are embracing change by adopting the new trend of IFR as they are capitalising upon the opportunities and benefits provided by the Internet (Mustafa, Salaudeen, & Lasisi, 2018). Firms view the Internet as an alternative platform to disseminate financial and non-financial information to stakeholders. This alternative platform is a paperless-based reporting system and can be referred to as IFR (Puspitaningrum & Atmini, 2012). Momany and Al-Shorman (2006) pointed out that firms that adopt IFR tend to disclose their overall financial statements, including notes or a part of financial statements and important financial information such as a summary of financial statements. The Internet has become the most frequently used tool to gather financial and non-financial information about firms. Yet, like traditional paper-based reporting, IFR has both benefits and drawbacks.

The enhanced interactive interface is one of the benefits that IFR posits. According to FASB (2000), IFR can be explained through the content and presentation dimension. Disseminating financial and non-financial information on the web might lead to better understanding and comprehension of information among users. The Internet can present information in various file formats, such as PDF and HTML. Hodge and Pronk (2006) asserted that technologies that allow alternative formats for disseminating financial and non-financial information might support gathering information from investors, influence decision-making and enhance transparency. Users can access information that fulfils their needs as the sitemap and search engine tools enable them to navigate, search, filter, retrieve and download information easily (Wagenhofer, 2007).

In addition, disseminating financial and non-financial information through the web facilitates mass communication. With IFR, the firms can reach out to a bigger and broader audience, including local investors and foreigners (Ojah & Mokoaleli-Mokoteli, 2012). Foreign investors can translate the information into their local language quickly. Moreover, IFR enhances the timeliness of information disclosure (Ismail, 2012). Users are provided with updated and timely information, which firms release, thus reducing information asymmetry. Furthermore, it is cheaper for firms to disclose information online rather than producing paper-based reports. With just a few clicks, users can access this information anywhere, anytime.

2.2 Theoretical Framework

2.2.1 Agency Theory
Jensen and Meckling (1976) advocate that conflict of interest between managers and shareholders arises from the separation of ownership and control. Managers are more likely to act in their interest rather than work in the best interest of shareholders, thus leading to a divergence in the alignment of interest. Consequently, agency cost and monitoring cost increase. Voluntary disclosure helps to reduce these costs and promotes higher transparency. Watson, Shrives, and Marston (2002) added that managers need to improve disclosure to convince shareholders that they act in good faith because they are aware that their behaviour may be controlled through bonding and monitoring activities.

2.2.2 Stakeholder Theory
While the agency theory considers the relationship between agents and principals and aims to increase shareholder value, the stakeholder theory broadens the relationship by considering other stakeholders that can impact the activities carried out by the firms (Donaldson & Preston, 1995). Stakeholder theory attests that the firms should not solely be accountable to the shareholders but also need to consider other people's interests who contribute towards the firm's value. Firms have started to disclose corporate social responsibility elements in their annual reports to recognise other stakeholders' significance and accountability to society and the environment (Isukul & Chizea, 2017).

2.2.3 Impression Management

In financial reporting, impression management is ascribed to managerial efforts in strategically presenting information to project a positive image of corporate achievements (Godfrey, Mather, & Ramsay, 2003). The goal is to positively influence the users' perceptions of the reports about firm performance and prospects (Merkl-Davies et al., 2011). Besides alterations, management may discretionarily decide not to disclose information that may damage the firm's reputation. As an end purpose, impression management seeks to create a deceitful but self-serving view of corporate attitude (Leung & Snell, 2017). Aerts (2005) finds that specific contextual factors and management significantly influence managerial tendencies and concealed vested interests.

2.3 Hypothesis Development

2.3.1 Board Independence

The board of directors is considered the key internal corporate governance mechanism in a firm and plays an important role in monitoring the firm, thus reducing agency problems (Fama & Jensen, 1983). The executive directors are accountable for the day-to-day running of the business. In contrast, the non-executive directors, entrusted by shareholders, have the responsibility to act in the best interest of these shareholders (Akhtaruddin, Hossain, Hossain, & Yao, 2009). Al-Janadi, Rahman, and Omar (2013) contend that the board should include a higher percentage of non-executive directors to be more effective and efficient. Mustafa et al. (2018) added that firms with more non-executive directors are more likely to disseminate information online. Yet, there are mixed results regarding this variable. Yap, Saleh, and Abessi (2011) find a positive relationship between Board Independence and IFR, while Zadeh, Salehi, and Shabestari (2018) conclude that board independence tends to work against corporate disclosure despite popular belief. Razak and Zarei (2018) and Alfraih and Almutawa (2017) find that board independence does not significantly contribute to financial reporting. Based on the above, the following hypothesis is formulated:

H_1: There is a positive association between board independence and the extent of IFR

2.3.2 Board Size

Agency theory posits that a larger board size is synonymous with better monitoring, reducing the influence of a powerful CEO (Fauzi & Locke, 2012). On the other hand, studies such as Roberts, AbuGhazaleh, and Qasim (2012) claim that smaller boards are more effective as there is a better understanding and more coordination among members, improving performance. Al-Manaseer, Al-Hindawi, Al-Dahiyat, and Sartawi (2012) share a similar view that boards comprising many members result in coordination, communication and decision-making problems. However, from a stakeholder theory perspective, it can be contended that larger boards have a wide range of information as the members have wider experiences and matters are viewed from different perspectives (Adams, Almeida, & Ferreira, 2005). Monitoring capacities are enlarged with larger boards, thus enhancing disclosure of information. Mixed results have been found between board size and financial reporting. Akhtaruddin et al. (2009), Allegrini and Greco (2013), and Yassin (2017) came up with a positive finding, Djamhuri and Widya (2017) found a negative relationship, while Uyar, Kilic, and Bayyurt (2013) and Waweru et al. (2019) find no connection between these two variables. Based on the above, the following hypothesis is formulated:

H_2: There is a positive relationship between board size and the extent of IFR

2.3.3 Board Meeting

The issue of board meetings can be viewed from two perspectives. According to Vafeas (1999), holding too many meetings might hinder a firm's performance as these firms might incur high costs for preparing and processing information for the meetings. Conversely, Byrne (1996) contends that board meetings that are carried out more frequently are advantageous as the activities carried out by the firms are more supervised and reviewed by the board. Hence, more information will be disseminated to stakeholders to show that the interest of a variety of stakeholders are being considered. Djamhuri and Widya (2017) and Mustafa et al. (2018) report a positive relationship between the frequency of board meetings and IFR, while Yap et al. (2011) and Alhazaimeh, Palaniappan, and Almsafir (2014) exhibit no support for a significant relationship. Based on the above, the following hypothesis is formulated:

H_3: There is a positive relationship between board meeting frequency and the extent of IFR

2.3.4 Board Gender Diversity

Female directors bring some extra knowledge, skills and perspective since they play the role of mother and wife in society (Post & Byron, 2015). Adams and Ferreira (2009) observe that female directors have better attendance records at board meetings than male directors and are more likely to monitor activities. Female representation on the board often leads to a balanced board where any board member cannot dominate the decision-making process (Erhardt, Werbel, & Shrader, 2003). From a stakeholder theory perspective, female representation on the board promotes equity and fairness as different stakeholders are represented (Keasey, Thompson, Wright, 1997), thus showing that the firms consider other people's interests. Empirical evidence on the link between board gender diversity and IFR is scarce. Manini et al. (2014) and Mustafa et al. (2018) have found no relationship between board gender diversity and IFR. However, since board gender diversity can positively impact performance (Nguyen & Faff, 2007), the disclosures on such performance are likely to increase as well. The following hypothesis is thus formulated:

H_4: There is a positive relationship between board gender diversity and the extent of IFR

2.3.5 Board Expertise

Accounting practices are influenced by the national level of education or accounting professions (Doupnik & Salter, 1995). Wallace and Cooke (1990) advocate that there may be an increase in demand for corporate accountability if the national education level is improved. Directors with a background or degree in accounting and finance are beneficial as they have the necessary skills and knowledge to enhance financial reporting practices and ultimately promote transparency. Haniffa and Cooke (2002) admit that if a board comprises members having an academic background in accounting and finance, they will disclose more information to promote the management team's accountability and credibility and thus enrich the corporate image. Yap et al. (2011), Djamhuri and Widya (2017), and Mustafa et al. (2018) found a positive association between board expertise and IFR. Based on the above, the following hypothesis is formulated:

H_5: There is a positive relationship between board expertise and the extent of IFR

2.3.6 Firm Size

Firm Size is a significant predictor of IFR, and several studies (e.g. Mokhtar, 2017; Zadeh et al., 2018) have validated that a positive relationship exists between these two variables. This positive result can be explained through various arguments. According to the agency theory, larger firms face problems of conflict of interest more frequently, thus leading to increased agency costs. These larger firms may disclose more information to reduce such agency costs. Secondly, the public is more aware of larger firms' activities than smaller ones. Consequently, these larger firms need to enhance their image and reputation and thus disclose more information to the public (Alsaeed, 2006).

Similarly, it is believed that larger firms have the proficiency and resources to improve their financial reporting system and thus make greater use of IFR. A positive relationship has been found between firm size and IFR by Pervan (2006), Agboola and Salawu (2012), Dyczkowska (2014), and Yassin (2017), while Manini et al. (2014) and Sartawi, Hindawi, and Bsoul (2014) find no relationship between these two variables. Based on the above, the following hypothesis is formulated:

H_6: There is a positive relationship between firm size and the extent of IFR

2.3.7 Internet Penetration Rate (IPR)

Apart from company-level factors, changes in the institutional environment can also affect the extent of IFR. During the past few decades, the Internet has witnessed massive development and has spread worldwide, thus transforming it into a global village (Manjikian, 2010). Ariff, Bin-Ghanem, and Hashim (2018) added that the advancement of the Internet could meet stakeholders' demands since the Internet is considered an alternative medium to gather information for decision-making purposes. Xiao et al. (2004) asserted that the advent of the Internet has influenced accounting information practices. The internet penetration rate can be defined as the percentage of internet users in the total population of a given country. Debreceny, Gray, and Rahman (2002) added that firms operating in countries with higher IPR tend to adopt IFR for disseminating information. However, this variable has been considered in very few studies, and a positive relationship has only been found by Ojah and Mokoaleli-Mokoteli (2012) and Ariff et al. (2018). Based on the above, the following hypothesis is formulated:

H_7: There is a positive relationship between IPR and the extent of IFR

2.3.8 Country Governance

Country-level governance score is a summation of compliance with the legal framework, including security and the rule of law, and the effectiveness of enforcement mechanisms, among others. Empirical evidence is abundant on the influence of governance mechanisms on financial reporting (Christensen, Morsing, & Thyssen, 2015; Lattemann, Fetscherin, Alon, Li, & Schneider, 2009; Li, Fetscherin, Alon, Lattemann, & Yeh, 2010). A general belief exists that firms comply with the various market rules to be considered legitimate and not be the recipient of any kind of public scrutiny over their activities (Suchman, 1995). In their study, Li et al. (2010) distinguish between a rule-based society and a relation-based one, where the latter is slightly deficient in transparency and meritocracy. Such a culture within a country will bear a significant negative influence on its demand for reporting. Firms in countries with better governance are expected to use IFR to a greater extent to promote transparency, both in the private and public sectors, being a key element of good governance. Based on the above, the following is hypothesised:

H_8: There is a positive relationship between country governance and the extent of IFR

2.3.9 Level of Economic Development

IFR is gradually gaining momentum over conventional reporting mechanisms, and a key catalyst in the whole transitional process is a country's economic development level. A high-income developing country is characterised by proper internet infrastructure and a services-financed economy (Vilar & Simão, 2015). IFR is thus more likely to thrive in a country with high economic development. A country's economic development significantly influences firm financial reporting culture (Ioannou & Serafeim, 2012). Economic growth is also marked by high literacy rates, whereby the users of financial information must be kept informed about all firm level development so that informed decision-making can occur (Adhikari & Tondkar, 1992). Thus, a higher level of economic development can accelerate the dissemination process of financial reporting, making it easily accessible to the population by going paperless (Frost, Gordon, & Pownall, 2008). The variable has been used by Khlif and Souissi (2010) and Eddine, Abdullah, Hamid, and Hossain (2015) to prove similar linkages.

H_9: There is a positive relationship between Economic Development and the extent of IFR

2.3.10 Index Return and IFR

Index return is often seen as the dependent variable under scrutiny rather than an independent and key variable. Disclosure through annual reports or IFR was found to bear a unidirectional effect on index return (Kothari, Li, & Short, 2009). Index Return has two central characteristics. Firstly, it measures the financial openness of an economy and, thus, represents a country's macroeconomic health. Secondly, it is a key factor that shows the health of listed companies through market confidence. Per the impression management theory, disclosures can project an altered reality of the firms' affairs to reach optimum results reputation-wise. This opportunistic behaviour in view of tipping the scale is conceptualised as impression management (Michelon, Pilonato, & Ricceri, 2015). Hence, firms that perform poorly in the market might resort to IFR to improve their image vis-à-vis investors. Based on the above, the following is hypothesised:

H_{10}: There is a negative relationship between Index Return and the extent of IFR

3. RESEARCH METHODOLOGY

3.1 Sample

A total of 106 firms from Mauritius, Botswana, Ghana, Nigeria and Kenya have been considered. Financial reporting data were gathered from firms' websites. Corporate governance data were collected from their respective annual reports for the years 2017 and 2018, resulting in 212 observations.

3.2 Econometric Model

Our analysis consists of three models. Model 1 uses the aggregate IFR score as the dependent variable, while Models 2 and 3 use the Content score and Present score, respectively. The Hausman test was run to determine whether the random effect or fixed effect model is most appropriate. The results favour the use of a random effect model.

Model 1:

$$IFR = \alpha + \beta_1 BIND_{i,t} + \beta_2 BSIZE_{i,t} + \beta_3 BMEET_{i,t} + \beta_4 BEXP_{i,t} + \beta_5 BGENDER_{i,t} + \beta_6 FSIZE_{i,t} + \beta_7 IPR_{c,t} + \beta_8 IIAG_{c,t} + \beta_9 GDP_{c,t} + \beta_{10} INDEX_{c,t} + e$$

Model 2:

$$
\begin{aligned}
\text{Content} = {} & \alpha + \beta_1 \text{BIND}_{i,t} + \beta_2 \text{BSIZE}_{i,t} + \beta_3 \text{BMEET}_{i,t} + \beta_4 \text{BEXP}_{i,t} \\
& + \beta_5 \text{BGENDER}_{i,t} + \beta_6 \text{FSIZE}_{i,t} + \beta_7 \text{IPR}_{c,t} \\
& + \beta_8 \text{IIAG}_{c,t} + \beta_9 \text{GDP}_{c,t} + \beta_{10} \text{INDEX}_{c,t} + e
\end{aligned}
$$

Model 3:

$$
\begin{aligned}
\text{Present} = {} & \alpha + \beta_1 \text{BIND}_{i,t} + \beta_2 \text{BSIZE}_{i,t} + \beta_3 \text{BMEET}_{i,t} + \beta_4 \text{BEXP}_{i,t} \\
& + \beta_5 \text{BGENDER}_{i,t} + \beta_6 \text{FSIZE}_{i,t} + \beta_7 \text{IPR}_{c,t} \\
& + \beta_8 \text{IIAG}_{c,t} + \beta_9 \text{GDP}_{c,t} + \beta_{10} \text{INDEX}_{c,t} + e
\end{aligned}
$$

Where,

BIND represents the number of independent and non-executive directors expressed as a percentage of total directors.

BSIZE denotes the number of directors present on the board.

BMEET is a dichotomous variable that takes a value of 1 if the firm has a frequency of board meetings higher than average and 0 otherwise.

BEXP represents the number of directors qualified in accounting or business expressed as a percentage of total directors.

BGENDER represents the number of women sitting on the board as a percentage of total directors.

FSIZE is measured as the natural logarithm of the company's total assets.

IIAG refers to the overall governance score published by the Ibrahim Index of African Governance.

IPR is a dichotomous variable that takes a value of 1 if the firm belongs to a country where the internet penetration rate exceeds the average rate of the five countries sampled and 0 otherwise.

GDP captures the level of economic development through the GDP of the country.

INDEX is the annual stock market return of the exchange on which the firms are listed in different countries.

3.3 Dependent Variable

According to FASB (2000), financial reporting can be categorised into two main dimensions: content and presentation of information disclosed. Several studies point out that transparency can be enhanced through disclosure's content and presentation dimensions (Bin-Ghanem & Ariff, 2016; Kelton & Yang, 2008). The content dimension covers the information presented on the company's website, such as financial information. The presentation dimension relates to how information is presented, and the accessibility and usability of such information. The IFR index is based on the checklist in Table 1 and is similar to the one used by Omran and Ramdhony (2016).

This study makes use of an unweighted index to compute the IFR index. This method has been widely used to circumvent subjectivity (Agboola & Salawu, 2012). For each company, a dichotomous procedure is applied to compute the

Table 1. IFR Disclosure Checklist.

IFR Disclosure Index	
Content Items	Presentation Items
General Information	*Investor Relations and Related Conveniences*
1. Background or history of the organisation	1. Contact us
2. Services or products provided	2. E-mail
3. Market share of key products	3. Postal address
Current and Complete Set of Financial Information	4. Telephone number
4. Statement of Financial Position policies	5. Frequently asked questions
5. Statement of Comprehensive Income	6. Link to the stock exchange web sites
6. Statement of Changes in Equity	*Technology and User Support*
7. Statement of Cash Flows	7. One-click to get to investor relations or financial information
8. Notes to the accounts including accounting policies	8. Internal Search Engines
9. Annual Report	9. Table of content/sitemap
10. Quarterly Reports	10. Hyperlinks inside the annual report
11. Auditor's Report	11. PowerPoint or presentation of financial data
12. Share Prices	12. Use of frames and clear boundaries for annual reports
Past and Complete Set of Financial Information	13. Analysis tools and advanced features
13. Statement of Financial Position	*Material Processable Formats*
14. Statement of Comprehensive Income	14. Financial data in Excel
15. Statement of Changes in Equity	15. Financial data in Word
16. Statement of Cash Flows	16. Financial data in PDF format
17. Notes to the accounts including accounting	17. Graphics or diagrams
18. Annual Report	18. Financial data in HTML
19. Quarterly Reports	19. Video or audio files
20. Auditor's Report	
21. Share Prices	
Financial Indicators	
22. Usage of comparative figures	
23. Summary of financial data over a period of at least three years	
24. Disclosure of risk or risk management	
25. Earnings per share	
26. Other ratios	
27. Press releases	
28. Financial calendar	
29. Share price performance in relation to stock market index	
30. Auditor's signature	
31. Auditor's name printed	

IFR index; that is, a value of 1 is given if an item in the checklist is disclosed and a value of 0 is given otherwise. The actual score obtained by the company is then divided by the maximum possible score, which is 50.

$$\text{IFR Index} = \frac{\sum\text{Score obtained by company}}{\sum\text{Maximum possible score}}$$

A score for the content dimension was calculated by dividing the actual score of the company under the content dimension by the maximum possible score of 31. Similarly, the presentation score obtained by a company was found by dividing the actual score of the company under the presentation dimension by the maximum possible score of 19.

4. FINDINGS

The descriptive statistics of the variables are shown in Table 2. The mean IFR is 0.6663, inferring that, on average, firms disclose 66.63% of the 50 items included in the IFR Index. The maximum value is 0.90, while the minimum value is 0.27. On average, the sample companies' boards are composed of 10 directors, of which around 64% are independent. With a mean of 16% only, female representation on the board of directors in Africa is quite low. The percentage of directors having background knowledge in business is 47.63% on average. It can be seen that there is a large disparity between the governance of countries in the sample, with maximum and minimum IIAG scores of 81.4 and 47.9, respectively. Based on the standard deviation of 163.5051, it can be concluded that there is a lot of variance in the GDP of the countries under study as well. The minimum of

Table 2. Descriptive Statistics.

	Mean	Median	Maximum	Minimum	Std Dev
IFR	0.6663	0.6800	0.9000	0.2700	0.1236
CONSC	0.7557	0.7742	1.0000	0.2903	0.1615
PRESC	0.5489	0.5263	0.7895	0.2632	0.0933
BIND	0.6406	0.6363	0.9166	0.2500	0.1323
BSIZE	9.6226	9.0000	16.0000	4.0000	2.4239
BMEET	0.9622	1.0000	1.0000	0.0000	0.1914
BGEND	0.1621	0.1428	0.5000	0.0000	0.1258
BEXP	0.4762	0.4545	0.8750	0.1111	0.1644
FSIZE	9.7754	9.8870	12.4510	4.7002	1.2692
IPR	0.4433	0.0000	1.0000	0.0000	0.4991
IIAG	64.2970	65.0000	81.4000	47.9000	12.8810
GDP	143.6458	65.5560	398.1600	13.2590	163.5051
INDEX	6.4089	−2.4630	49.1270	−21.9490	23.5825

INDEX being −21.9490 infers that at least one of the country's stock exchanges had a negative return in one of the years under study.

Table 3 displays the correlation matrix for the independent variables. These variables are not highly correlated, as none of the reported correlation coefficients exceeds 0.50. As such, it can be concluded that our models have no multicollinearity issues.

Table 4 summarises the results of the regression analysis. BSIZE, FSIZE, IIAG and GDP are positively and significantly associated with the IFR score, while INDEX is negatively associated with the same. The adjusted R^2 of 0.2237

Table 3. Correlation Matrix.

	BIND	BSIZE	BMEET	BGEND	BEXP	FSIZE	IPR	IIAG	GDP	INDEX
BIND	1.000									
BSIZE	0.307	1.000								
BMEET	0.254	0.182	1.000							
BGEND	−0.022	−0.035	0.126	1.000						
BEXP	−0.033	−0.009	−0.073	−0.112	1.000					
FSIZE	−0.008	0.228	0.128	0.084	0.124	1.000				
IPR	0.093	0.091	−0.002	−0.108	0.105	−0.042	1.000			
IIAG	0.267	0.138	0.007	−0.171	0.148	−0.436	0.368	1.000		
GDP	−0.227	−0.041	0.052	0.049	−0.094	0.468	−0.155	−0.403	1.000	
INDEX	−0.066	0.094	0.135	−0.096	0.038	0.118	−0.387	−0.013	0.069	1.000

Table 4. Regression Results.

	Model 1 (IFR)	Model 2 (Content)	Model 3 (Present)
BIND	0.0277	0.0395	0.0022
BSIZE	0.1345*	0.1262**	0.1125*
BMEET	0.0142	−0.0098	0.0279
BGEND	−0.0465	−0.0022	−0.0190
BEXP	0.0015	0.0176	−0.0028
FSIZE	0.2403**	0.1703*	0.2317**
IPR	−0.0213	−0.0314	0.0108
IIAG	0.7990***	1.0064***	−0.0471
GDP	0.4436**	0.6495***	−0.1702
INDEX	−0.0681**	−0.0641**	−0.0333
Constant	−1.3937	−0.4803**	0.3516***
Observations	212	212	212
Adjusted R-Squared	0.2237	0.2392	0.1482
F-stat	5.736***	6.254***	1.596**
Durbin Watson Stat.	2.055	2.065	1.988

Significant (*** at 1% level or less, ** at 5% level or less and * at 10% level or less).

provides evidence that our model explains 22.37% of the variation in the IFR score, while the error term captures the remaining 77.63%. The Durbin–Watson statistic falls within the range of 1.5–2.5; in other words, the statistic is close to 2 and hence shows that autocorrelation is not present in the model.

The results also show the importance of running separate models for the content and presentation scores. It can be seen that while the significant results at the aggregate level with regards to BSIZE and FSIZE are consistent across both the content and presentation models, the significance of the country variables IIAG, GDP and INDEX relate to the content component rather than the present component since they are insignificant in the latter's model.

5. DISCUSSION

The hypotheses supported by the current study's results relate to board size, firm size, country governance, economic development and market index return. On the other hand, there is not enough evidence to support the hypotheses for board independence, board meeting, board gender diversity, board independence and internet penetration rate. The results for the supported hypotheses are discussed first, followed by the unsupported ones.

Board size has a significant and positive relationship with IFR at the 10% significance level. Therefore, we fail to reject the second hypothesis. This result infers that a larger board is more effective in Africa as the boards are made up of members possessing a wider range of experiences, skills, and expertise. Such a board might better understand the benefits of disseminating information on the Internet to assure investors that their firm operates soundly. This finding also aligns with the agency theory, which states that a larger board will reduce agency costs by increasing information dissemination. Such a positive association matches the results obtained by Akhtaruddin et al. (2009), Allegrini and Greco (2013), and Yassin (2017). Board size is positively related to both the separate components of content and presentation.

The sixth hypothesis asserts a positive relationship between firm size and IFR. The results show that firm size is positively and significantly related to IFR at the 5% significance level; hence, the hypothesis is not rejected. This implies that the larger the firm, the more it will have recourse to IFR. Larger firms have the resources and expertise required for IFR and would indulge in the latter to enhance their image and reputation. This finding confirms that the agency theory also applies in the African context. The theory advocates that larger firms tend to provide more information to reduce agency costs. This positive association is consistent across both the content and present models.

With its highly significant coefficient, the IIAG score is a factor that positively impacts IFR; hence, H_8 is not rejected. According to the IIAG Report (2018), there have been improvements in transparency and accountability in the last five years. This change is beginning to drive up the African average overall governance score. The report also points out that within the composition of the IIAG, transparency and accountability shows the strongest relationship with the governance scores. Our results align with such improvements in transparency as firms in countries with higher IIAG scores are found to use IFR more extensively as a channel to increase disclosure and improve transparency. African countries are thus on the right path to remedy their low sustainable economic opportunity that results from a lack of transparency and accountability (IIAG Report, 2018).

This result is consistent with only the content model, as IIAG is insignificant in the presentation mode. Countries with higher governance require firms to disclose more straightforward disclosures to minimise the sugarcoating of disclosures (Jaggi & Low, 2000). This way of priority reporting can explain the divergence in the presentation component results. The prime aim of financial reporting using any dissemination channel is to project the factual economic reality to support the decision-making of relevant stakeholders (Shahwan, 2008). Thus, country governance emphasises these key content aspects of reporting rather than secondary aspects such as presentation.

Economic development is evidenced to positively and significantly influence IFR. H_9 is thus not rejected. In our sample of African countries, a higher level of economic development contributes to higher disclosures, supported by previous studies (e.g. Vilar & Simão, 2015). This positive association between economic development and IFR can be due to several factors. An elevated economic growth rate signals that the reporting culture is well set up and effective (Brammer, Jackson, & Matten, 2012). Corruptive practices or governmental interference which act as a setback against IFR are also less prevalent in countries with higher economic development (Tang, Gallagher, & Bie, 2015). The insignificance of economic development in the presentation model can be explained by the lower level of economic development relative to other continents, which can prevent firms from providing better-presented information due to the associated reporting costs.

H_{10} asserts that Index Return bears a negative and significant effect on IFR. Based on the results obtained, H_{10} is not rejected. The rationale behind such a result is that stock market return trends of a particular exchange dictate the course of action related to disclosures (Meek & Gray, 1989). When the stock market in a country is performing poorly, increasing positive disclosures can be used to restore investor and market optimism, allowing companies to differentiate themselves from the otherwise poor overall exchange performance (Bochkay & Dimitrov, 2014). There is also an element of bias as firms disclose more content, as indicated by the separate content model, to ensure that their business activities are legitimate in the eyes of consumers, investors and other stakeholders. This somehow defeats the purpose of IFR or financial reporting (Mobus, 2005).

H_1 posits that there is a positive relationship between board independence and IFR. Based on the regression results, it can be seen that board independence is not significantly related to IFR. The first hypothesis is thus rejected. One explanation behind the insignificant relationship is that the directors are not fully independent. They might be closely related to executive directors or assume a rubber stamp role. This result is at odds with the agency theory, which suggests that more independent directors on a board strengthen their monitoring role.

Such an insignificant association is also found in previous studies such as Razak and Zarei (2018) and Alfraih and Almutawa (2017).

Board meetings refer to the number of meetings carried out by the board. H_3 asserts a positive relationship between board meeting frequency and IFR. However, the variable is insignificant, and thus the third hypothesis is rejected. This finding is supported by studies such as Yap et al. (2011) and Alhazaimeh et al. (2014). Another board characteristic that is found to be insignificant is board expertise. Hence, H_5, which posits a positive relationship between board expertise and IFR, is also rejected.

Board gender diversity was also hypothesised to impact IFR positively, but no significant association was found. One possible explanation may be the low emancipation of women in Africa. This is portrayed through the descriptive statistics that show that only 16.21% of the directors are female. The minimum of 0% for board gender diversity indicates that some firms do not have female directors (See Table 2). Once the underrepresentation of women on boards is remedied, a significant impact may be found. Legislative or voluntary initiatives have been implemented in many countries to promote women's presence on boards (Rao & Tilt, 2016). With proper education and guidance, the presence of women on African boards will most likely increase shortly. A similar result has been found by Manini et al. (2014), Sartawi et al. (2014), and Mustafa et al. (2018).

H_7 posits that there is a positive relationship between IPR and IFR. Since IPR is found to be insignificant, the seventh hypothesis is rejected. Chinn and Fairlie (2007) argue that first-world countries such as the United States avail from an IPR of 550 times that of third-world countries such as Ethiopia, where there is an average of 0.5 computers for use by a hundredth of the population. As such, this insignificance might be due to African nations still lacking the proper infrastructure for internet access and basic facilities such as internet banking, let alone information dissemination (Demirgüç-Kunt & Klapper, 2012). This is also supported by Waweru et al. (2019), who find that internet connectivity and financial inclusion in Africa are slow and expensive compared to other continents.

6. CONCLUSION

In recent years, the Internet has witnessed massive development in Africa, extending to the corporate world, with one of the latest breakthroughs being internet-based financial reporting. This study considers the impact of firm- and country-level factors on the level of IFR among five African countries. The findings show that board size, firm size, country governance and economic development are significantly and positively related to IFR. Index return is, however, proven to bear a significant and negative impact on IFR. However, no significant relationship is found between board independence, board experience, the frequency of board meetings, board gender diversity and IPR.

We therefore conclude that corporate governance mechanisms are insufficient to explain the extent of IFR in Africa. This is because, several countries suffer from a weak legal framework resulting in extremely concentrated proprietorship dominating the ownership structure with limited and minority shareholders (IFAC & CIPFA, 2014). Furthermore, it is also reported that political governance fraught with opaque economic and unaccountable practices leads to blurred lines between the private and public sectors, as well as poor governance (Chigudu, 2018). In some instances, board members are even party to malpractices, largely influenced by cronyism and favouritism, common in African countries (Mohieldin & Nasr, 2007).

By conducting a component analysis, we brought to light that the content of IFR is much more influenced by our independent variables, especially the macroeconomic ones. This places the presentation component on a secondary pedestal. Future presentation scores might be achieved by firms when sufficient content has been disclosed in accordance to the regulations of their jurisdiction and the board's discretion. Furthermore, as African investors become more sophisticated, the demand for better-presented disclosures will rise in the near future.

This study provides several practical implications. Firstly, it shows that a significant proportion of African firms have already turned to IFR to disseminate information, albeit to different degrees. It incentivises other firms to adopt or increase the extent of their IFR practices not to be left at a competitive disadvantage. With an IFR score as calculated in this study, firms in the same industry can compare their IFR scores to benchmark themselves.

The fact that only two firm-level variables were found to shape IFR as compared to three country-level variables significantly emphasises the lacuna of previous studies that focussed mainly on firm-level factors. This can be considered an important academic implication that urges future studies in the IFR field, or reporting field in general, to look at the broader picture and consider macro-level factors. Failing to do so would result in omitting elements that have a high significance in explaining IFR practices.

Legislative reforms targeting board gender diversity should also be implemented to increase the presence of women on African boards where females were found to be highly underrepresented. This prevents studies from providing a clear image of the potential impact of women on IFR. Firms may also consider increasing their board size as this variable was found to impact the extent of IFR positively. Improvements in IFR are important since they impact the perception of foreign investors on African stock exchanges (Waweru et al., 2019).

For African nations' transparency and accountability to improve, not only listed firms but all private firms should be incentivised to adopt and increase their extent of IFR to improve transparency. IFR is particularly relevant since it can act as a cheap and easily accessible alternative to hardcopy reports. When firms function more transparently, opportunities for corrupt behaviour and the grounds for outsiders to suspect corruption significantly decrease (Osborne, 2004). This would not only considerably increase the efficiency of firms but also improve investor confidence in African firms.

Investigating the association of corporate governance and IFR on five African countries at a time, rather than one at a time, is particularly important as countries, especially those on the same continent, are increasingly adopting similar reporting practices and it is important to look at the broader picture. For example, adoption of IAS by Kenya, South Africa, Tanzania and Zimbabwe is aimed at enhancing the quality of reporting (Waweru et al., 2019) and comparability across the countries. This broader approach hence provides an additional perspective to the IFR literature.

Additionally, the results should help policymakers and regulators build a framework for mandating IFR. Aligned with the vision of raising reporting and disclosure standards, this would help attract investors to local African projects due to proven responsibility and accountability. Higher regulations, particularly on markets that tend to perform poorly, could also prevent firms from increasing their disclosures to differentiate themselves from the market they operate in, as this may introduce bias that defeats the purpose of reporting (Mobus, 2005).

This study is not without limitations. The computation of IFR scores involves content analysis which has been effected manually and is subject to human error. We acknowledge that corporate governance practices are largely determined by the legal framework prevailing in every country although some board practices are becoming norms worldwide. We have included firm-specific factors and also country-level factors to this effect. Nevertheless, generalisation of the results must be done with care.

To have a more holistic view of IFR determinants, other corporate and macro-level variables that the current study has not considered can be investigated in future studies. Future research may explore audit committees' impact on IFR, which are viewed as an important mechanism in corporate governance, or even the ownership structure, such as managerial ownership and substantial ownership. In addition, the sample used can be extended to other African countries or even another continent to provide a comparative analysis.

7. CONFLICT OF INTEREST

Not Applicable

REFERENCES

Adams, R. B., Almeida, H., & Ferreira, D. (2005). Powerful CEOs and their impact on corporate performance. *The Review of Financial Studies*, *18*(4), 1403–1432.

Adams, R. B., & Ferreira, D. (2009). Women in the boardroom and their impact on governance and performance. *Journal of Financial Economics*, *94*(2), 291–309.

Adhikari, A., & Tondkar, R. H. (1992). Environmental factors influencing accounting disclosure requirements of global stock exchanges. *Journal of International Financial Management & Accounting*, *4*(2), 75–105.

Aerts, W. (2005). Picking up the pieces: Impression management in the retrospective attributional framing of accounting outcomes. *Accounting, Organisations and Society*, *30*(6), 493–517.

Agboola, A. A., & Salawu, M. K. (2012). The determinants of internet financial reporting: Empirical evidence from Nigeria. *Research Journal of Finance and Accounting*, *3*(11), 95–105.

Akhtaruddin, M., Hossain, M. A., Hossain, M., & Yao, L. (2009). Corporate governance and voluntary disclosure in corporate annual reports of Malaysian listed firms. *Journal of Applied Management Accounting Research, 7*(1), 1.

Al-Janadi, Y., Rahman, R. A., & Omar, N. H. (2013). Corporate governance mechanisms and voluntary disclosure in Saudi Arabia. *Research Journal of Finance and Accounting, 4*(4).

Al-Manaseer, M. F. A., Al-Hindawi, R. M., Al-Dahiyat, M. A., & Sartawi, I. I. (2012). The impact of corporate governance on the performance of Jordanian banks. *European Journal of Scientific Research, 67*(3), 349–359.

Alfraih, M. M., & Almutawa, A. M. (2017). Voluntary disclosure and corporate governance: Empirical evidence from Kuwait. *International Journal of Law and Management, 59*(2), 217–236.

Alhazaimeh, A., Palaniappan, R., & Almsafir, M. (2014). The impact of corporate governance and ownership structure on voluntary disclosure in annual reports among listed Jordanian companies. *Procedia-Social and Behavioral Sciences, 129*, 341–348.

Allegrini, M., & Greco, G. (2013). Corporate boards, audit committees and voluntary disclosure: Evidence from Italian listed companies. *Journal of Management & Governance, 17*(1), 187–216.

Alsaeed, K. (2006). The association between firm-specific characteristics and disclosure. *Managerial Auditing Journal, 21*(5), 476–496.

Ariff, A. M., Bin-Ghanem, H. O., & Hashim, H. A. (2018). Corporate ownership, internet penetration and Internet financial reporting: Evidence from the Gulf Cooperation Council countries. *Asian Journal of Business and Accounting, 11*(1), 185–227.

Bin-Ghanem, H., & Ariff, A. M. (2016). The effect of board of directors and audit committee effectiveness on internet financial reporting: Evidence from gulf co-operation council countries. *Journal of Accounting in Emerging Economies, 6*(4), 429–448.

Bochkay, K., & Dimitrov, V. (2014). Qualitative management disclosures and market sentiment. *Available at SSRN 2538812.*

Brammer, S., Jackson, G., & Matten, D. (2012). Corporate social responsibility and institutional theory: New perspectives on private governance. *Socio-Economic Review, 10*(1), 3–28.

Byrne, J. (1996). And you thought CEOs were overpaid. *Business Week, 26*, 34.

Chigudu, D. C. (2018). Corporate governance in Africa's public sector for sustainable development: The task ahead. *TDR: The Journal for Transdisciplinary Research in Southern Africa, 14*(1), 1–10.

Chinn, M. D., & Fairlie, R. W. (2007). The determinants of the global digital divide: A cross-country analysis of computer and internet penetration. *Oxford Economic Papers, 59*(1), 16–44.

Christensen, L. T., Morsing, M., & Thyssen, O. (2015). Discursive closure and discursive openings in sustainability. *Management Communication Quarterly, 29*(1), 135–144.

Debreceny, R., Gray, G. L., & Rahman, A. (2002). The determinants of Internet financial reporting. *Journal of Accounting and Public Policy, 21*(4–5), 371–394.

Demirgüç-Kunt, A., & Klapper, L. (2012). *Financial inclusion in Africa: An overview.* Policy Research Working Paper; No. 6088. World Bank. World Bank, Washington, DC.

Djamhuri, A., & Widya, Y. (2017). Corporate governance and internet financial reporting in Indonesia (an empirical study on Indonesian manufacturing companies). *The International Journal of Accounting and Business Society, 24*(2), 36–47.

Donaldson, T., & Preston, L. E. (1995). The stakeholder theory of the corporation: Concepts, evidence, and implications. *Academy of Management Review, 20*(1), 65–91.

Doupnik, T. S., & Salter, S. B. (1995). External environment, culture and accounting practice: A preliminary test of a general model of international accounting development. *International Journal of Accounting, 30*(3), 189–207.

Dyczkowska, J. (2014). Assessment of quality of internet financial disclosures using a scoring system. A case of polish stock issuers. *Accounting and Management Information Systems, 13*(1), 50–81.

Eddine, C. O. H., Abdullah, S. N., Hamid, F. A., & Hossain, D. M. (2015). The determinants of intellectual capital disclosure: A meta-analysis review. *Journal of Asia Business Studies, 9*(3), 232–250.

Erhardt, N. L., Werbel, J. D., & Shrader, C. B. (2003). Board of director diversity and firm financial performance. *Corporate Governance: An International Review, 11*(2), 102–111.

Fama, E. F., & Jensen, M. C. (1983). Separation of ownership and control. *The Journal of Law and Economics, 26*(2), 301–325.

FASB. (2000). *Business reporting research project: Electronic distribution of business information, financial accounting standards board.* Steering Committee Report Series.

Fauzi, F., & Locke, S. (2012). Do agency costs really matter? A non-linear approach to panel data. *Asian Journal of Finance & Accounting, 4*(1).

Frost, C. A., Gordon, E. A., & Pownall, G. (2008). Financial reporting and disclosure quality, and emerging market companies' access to capital in global markets. *Available at SSRN 802824.*

Godfrey, J., Mather, P., & Ramsay, A. (2003). Earnings and impression management in financial reports: The case of CEO changes. *Abacus, 39*(1), 95–123.

Haniffa, R. M., & Cooke, T. E. (2002). Culture, corporate governance and disclosure in Malaysian corporations. *Abacus, 38*(3), 317–349.

Hindi, N. M., & Rich, J. (2010). Financial reporting on the Internet: Evidence from the Fortune 100. *Management Accounting Quarterly, 11*(2), 11.

Hodge, F., & Pronk, M. (2006). The impact of expertise and investment familiarity on investors' use of online financial report information. *Journal of Accounting, Auditing and Finance, 21*(3), 267–292.

IFAC & CIPFA. (2014). *International framework: Good governance in the public sector.* New York, NY: International Federation for Accountants and Chartered Institute of Public Finance and Accountancy (CIPFA) CIPFA.

Ioannou, I., & Serafeim, G. (2012). What drives corporate social performance? The role of nation-level institutions. *Journal of International Business Studies, 43*(9), 834–864.

Ismail, N. A. (2012). Various aspects of internet financial reporting: Evidence from Malaysian Academician. *Journal of Global Business and Economics, 4*(1), 1–15.

Isukul, A. C., & Chizea, J. J. (2017). Corporate governance disclosure in developing countries: A comparative analysis in Nigerian and South African banks. *Sage Open, 7*(3).

Jaggi, B., & Low, P. Y. (2000). Impact of culture, market forces, and legal system on financial disclosures. *The International Journal of Accounting, 35*(4), 495–519.

Jensen, M. C., & Meckling, W. H. (1976). Theory of the firm: Managerial behavior, agency costs and ownership structure. *Journal of Financial Economics, 3*(4), 305–360.

Keasey, K., Thompson, S., & Wright, M. (Eds.). (1997). *Corporate governance: Economic and financial issues.* Oxford: OUP.

Kelton, A. S., & Yang, Y. W. (2008). The impact of corporate governance on Internet financial reporting. *Journal of Accounting and Public Policy, 27*(1), 62–87.

Khlif, H., & Souissi, M. (2010). The determinants of corporate disclosure: A meta-analysis. *International Journal of Accounting and Information Management, 18*(3), 198–219.

Kothari, S. P., Li, X., & Short, J. E. (2009). The effect of disclosures by management, analysts, and business press on cost of capital, return volatility, and analyst forecasts: A study using content analysis. *The Accounting Review, 84*(5), 1639–1670.

Lattemann, C., Fetscherin, M., Alon, I., Li, S., & Schneider, A. M. (2009). CSR communication intensity in Chinese and Indian multinational companies. *Corporate Governance: An International Review, 17*(4), 426–442.

Leung, T. C. H., & Snell, R. S. (2017). Attraction or distraction? Corporate social responsibility in Macao's gambling industry. *Journal of Business Ethics, 145*(3), 637–658.

Li, S., Fetscherin, M., Alon, I., Lattemann, C., & Yeh, K. (2010). Corporate social responsibility in emerging markets. *Management International Review, 50*(5), 635–654.

Mangena, M., & Chamisa, E. (2008). Corporate governance and incidences of listing suspension by the JSE Securities Exchange of South Africa: An empirical analysis. *The International Journal of Accounting, 43*(1), 28–44.

Mangena, M., & Tauringana, V. (2007). Disclosure, corporate governance and foreign share ownership on the Zimbabwe stock exchange. *Journal of International Financial Management & Accounting, 18*(2), 53–85.

Manini, M. M., Abdillahi, U. A., & Hardy, L. (2014). Corporate governance mechanisms and internet financial reporting in Kenya. *International Journal of Research in Management Sciences, 2*(4), 35–51.

Manjikian, M. M. (2010). From global village to virtual battlespace: The colonising of the Internet and the extension of realpolitik. *International Studies Quarterly*, *54*(2), 381–401.

Meek, G. K., & Gray, S. J. (1989). Globalisation of stock markets and foreign listing requirements: Voluntary disclosures by continental European companies listed on the London Stock Exchange. *Journal of International Business Studies*, *20*(2), 315–336.

Merkl-Davies, D. M., Brennan, N. M., & McLeay, S. J. (2011). Impression management and retrospective sense-making in corporate narratives. *Accounting, Auditing & Accountability Journal*, *24*(3), 315–344.

Michelon, G., Pilonato, S., & Ricceri, F. (2015). CSR reporting practices and the quality of disclosure: An empirical analysis. *Critical Perspectives on Accounting*, *33*, 59–78.

Mobus, J. L. (2005). Mandatory environmental disclosures in a legitimacy theory context. *Accounting, Auditing & Accountability Journal*, *18*(4), 492–517.

Mohieldin, M., & Nasr, S. (2007). On bank privatization: The case of Egypt. *The Quarterly Review of Economics and Finance*, *46*(5), 707–725.

Mokhtar, E. S. (2017). Internet financial reporting determinants: A meta-analytic review. *Journal of Financial Reporting & Accounting*, *15*(1), 116–154.

Momany, M. T., & Al-Shorman, S. A. D. (2006). Web-based voluntary financial reporting of Jordanian companies. *International Review of Business Research Papers*, *2*(2), 127–139.

Mustafa, M., Salaudeen, Y., & Lasisi, T. (2018). Corporate governance mechanism and internet financial reporting of listed companies in Nigeria. *Research Journal of Finance and Accounting*, *9*(14), 90–101.

Nguyen, H., & Faff, R. (2007). Impact of board size and board diversity on firm value: Australian evidence. *Corporate Ownership and Control*, *4*(2), 24–32.

Ojah, K., & Mokoaleli-Mokoteli, T. (2012). Internet financial reporting, infrastructures and corporate governance: An international analysis. *Review of development finance*, *2*(2), 69–83.

Omran, M. A., & Ramdhony, D. (2016). Determinants of internet financial reporting in African markets: The case of Mauritius. *The Journal of Developing Areas*, *50*(4), 1–18.

Ortas, E., Álvarez, I., Jaussaud, J., & Garayar, A. (2015). The impact of institutional and social context on corporate environmental, social and governance performance of companies committed to voluntary corporate social responsibility initiatives. *Journal of Cleaner Production*, *108*, 673–684.

Osborne, D. (2004). Transparency and accountability reconsidered. *Journal of Financial Crime*, *11*(3), 292–300.

Pervan, I. (2006). Voluntary financial reporting on the Internet: Analysis of the practice of stock-market listed Croatian and Slovene joint stock companies. *Financial Theory and Practice*, *30*(1), 1–27.

Post, C., & Byron, K. (2015). Women on boards and firm financial performance: A meta-analysis. *Academy of Management Journal*, *58*(5), 1546–1571.

Puspitaningrum, D., & Atmini, S. (2012). Corporate governance mechanism and the level of internet financial reporting: Evidence from Indonesian companies. *Procedia Economics and Finance*, *2*, 157–166.

Rao, K., & Tilt, C. (2016). Board composition and corporate social responsibility: The role of diversity, gender, strategy and decision making. *Journal of Business Ethics*, *138*(2), 327–347.

Razak, R. A., & Zarei, K. M. (2018). The influence of board characteristics and ownership structure on the extent of internet financial disclosure in Saudi Arabia. *Journal of Emerging Trends in Economics and Management Sciences*, *9*(2), 71–81.

Roberts, C., AbuGhazaleh, N., & Qasim, A. (2012). The determinants of web-based investor relations activities by companies operating in emerging economies: The case of Jordan. *Journal of Applied Business Reseach*.

Sartawi, I. I. M., Hindawi, R. M., & Bsoul, R. (2014). Board composition, firm characteristics, and voluntary disclosure: The case of Jordanian firms listed on the Amman stock exchange. *International Business Research*, *7*(6), 67.

Shahwan, Y. (2008). Qualitative characteristics of financial reporting: A historical perspective. *Journal of Applied Accounting Research*, *9*(3), 192–202.

Suchman, M. C. (1995). Managing legitimacy: Strategic and institutional approaches. *Academy of Management Review*, *20*(3), 571–610.

Tang, L., Gallagher, C. C., & Bie, B. (2015). Corporate social responsibility communication through corporate websites: A comparison of leading corporations in the United States and China. *International Journal of Business Communication*, *52*(2), 205–227.

UNCTAD. (2019). Foreign direct investment to Africa defies global slump, rises 11%. Retrieved from https://unctad.org/news/foreign-direct-investment-africa-defies-global-slump-rises-11. Accessed on April 29, 2023.

Uyar, A., Kilic, M., & Bayyurt, N. (2013). Association between firm characteristics and corporate voluntary disclosure: Evidence from Turkish listed companies. *Intangible Capital*, *9*(4), 1080–1112.

Vafeas, N. (1999). Board meeting frequency and firm performance. *Journal of financial economics*, *53*(1), 113–142.

Vilar, V. H., & Simão, J. (2015). CSR disclosure on the web: Major themes in the banking sector. *International Journal of Social Economics*, *42*(3), 296–318.

Wagenhofer, A. (2007). Economic consequences of internet financial reporting. In *New dimensions of business reporting and XBRL*. DUV. Retrieved from http://sci-hub.tw/10.1007/978-3-8350-9633-2_5

Wallace, R. S. O., & Cooke, T. E. (1990). The diagnosis and resolution of emerging issues in corporate disclosure practices. *Accounting and Business Research*, *20*(78), 143–151.

Watson, A., Shrives, P., & Marston, C. (2002). Voluntary disclosure of accounting ratios in the UK. *The British Accounting Review*, *34*(4), 289–313.

Waweru, N., Mangena, M., & Riro, G. (2019). Corporate governance and corporate internet reporting in sub-Saharan Africa: The case of Kenya and Tanzania. *Corporate Governance: The international journal of business in society*, *19*, 4.

Xiao, J. Z., Jones, M. J., & Lymer, A. (2005). A conceptual framework for investigating the impact of the Internet on corporate financial reporting. *International Journal of Digital Accounting Research*, *5*(10), 131–169.

Xiao, J. Z., Yang, H., & Chow, C. W. (2004). The determinants and characteristics of voluntary Internet-based disclosures by listed Chinese companies. *Journal of Accounting and Public Policy*, *23*(3), 191–225.

Yap, K. H., Saleh, Z., & Abessi, M. (2011). Internet financial reporting and corporate governance in Malaysia. *Australian Journal of Basic and Applied Sciences*, *5*(10), 1273–1289.

Yassin, M. M. (2017). The determinants of internet financial reporting in Jordan: Financial versus corporate governance. *International Journal of Business Information Systems*, *25*(4), 526–556.

Zadeh, F. N., Salehi, M., & Shabestari, H. (2018). The relationship between corporate governance mechanisms and internet financial reporting in Iran. *Corporate Governance: The International Journal of Business in Society*, *18*(6), 1021–1041.

Ziegler, A., Busch, T., & Hoffmann, V. H. (2011). Disclosed corporate responses to climate change and stock performance: An international empirical analysis. *Energy Economics*, *33*(6), 1283–1294.

EFFECTIVENESS OF THE LEAN SERVICE PRINCIPLE IN CONTROLLING THE CIVIL SERVICE WAGE BILL: A CASE STUDY OF THE GOVERNMENT OF ESWATINI

Sabelo G. Sifundza and Md. Humayun Kabir

ABSTRACT

The Government of Eswatini (GoE) civil service wage bill has continued to rise in recent years. The personnel budget is still the largest single recurrent expenditure item in the budget in Eswatini. To control the civil service wage bill, the GoE introduced Lean Service Principle through Management Services Division (MSD). The civil service wage bill continues to rise despite the implementation of the Lean Service Principle. So far, there are no tangible outcomes that indicate that the principles applied have been effective in the reduction of the wage bill. Thus, this research aims to examine the question of why the Lean Service Principle failed to effectively slow the rampant growth of the civil service wage bill in the Kingdom of Eswatini. This study used the quantitative research approach to collect data on amounts spent on wages, the percentage increase of the wage bill for the period 2010–2017, and the percentage increase in the number of civil servants as per the Establishment Registers, 2010–2017. The study investigated the wage bill push factors, the shortcomings of the Lean Service Principle, and the Just-In-Time (JIT) Technique in the management and reduction of the GoE civil service wage bill. The study found the MSD has been applying the wrong methodologies in wage bill control, which has been evident in the continued yearly increase of the wage bill. The study recommends that the MSD should consider the utilisation of Human Resources Forecasting and Planning Techniques instead of using the Lean Service Principle and the JIT technique. This study will enable the

Corporate Resilience
Developments in Corporate Governance and Responsibility, Volume 21, 173–200
Copyright © 2023 by Emerald Publishing Limited
All rights of reproduction in any form reserved
ISSN: 2043-0523/doi:10.1108/S2043-052320230000021009

Cabinet to make an appropriate decision on the mandate and future of the MSD, as there have been growing calls to disband the division due to the failure to reduce and/or control the wage bills as that is the core mandate of the division.

Keywords: Lean service principle; Just-In-Time Technique; personnel budget; wage bill push factor; Management Services Division; Eswatini government

1. INTRODUCTION

The Kingdom of Eswatini (previously called the Kingdom of Swaziland) is a small country located in Southern Africa. The Kingdom is living with many socio-economic challenges with a population of 1.2 million. For instance, a high HIV prevalence rate of 27% (between the age of 15 and 49) and more than one-third of its population have been living below the international poverty line, US$2.15 per day (World Bank, 2022).

There are a number of political and socio-economic policies that were adopted by many African countries (including Eswatini) that resulted in the need for the rapid expansion of the civil service as government machinery for the delivery of services. As such, there has been a steady increase in the civil service wage bill over the years and subsequently, the personnel cost to the Government of Eswatini (GoE) has increased exponentially due to the establishment of a large number of posts in the government sectors. The GoE established a Management Services Division (MSD) to review the training and localisation of the Eswatini civil service. In recent years the mandate of the division has been focussed on the ever-increasing wage bill. This has been an item that has been a concern not only for the government but also for international partners and money lenders. To this end, the MSD has been requested to apply the requisite tools and techniques to monitor, control and as far as possible reduce the wage bill. The MSD is an internal government consultancy on management and productivity issues, its main objective being to implement the Lean Service Principle and utilise Just-In-Time (JIT) techniques to reduce the size of the civil service in terms of head count. This was envisaged to enable ministries and departments to achieve more with fewer personnel who are highly trained, multitaskers and multi-skilled.

Madubula and Dawood (2011) highlight that there are a number of items that contribute to the wage bill annual increment. These constitute the annual cost of living adjustments coupled with promotion and job regrading, the increase in employee head-count (e.g. creation of posts) and the introduction of the occupation-specific dispensation (e.g. categorised recruitment and retention benefits). Also included are other contributory factors such as poor internal controls (e.g. poor management of the antiquated personnel salary system) and a lack of critical skills resulting in head-hunting, which is often expensive (e.g. doctors, engineers and pilots). There are also notable appointments made without proper planning and budgeting (e.g. politically influenced recruitment) and also poor organisational design (e.g. strategic plans not aligned with organograms).

Most notably in Eswatini, the huge wage bill is a result of the continued annual creation of positions (either for current departments) or the establishment of new departments/sections. Yet the country has over the years not been able to create any new sources of government revenue to fund not only capital projects but the wage bill itself. The Kingdom is mainly reliant on the Southern African Customs Union (SACU) receipts to fund 70% of its national budget. However, these receipts have been on a steady decline since the early part of the millennium. The remainder of the national budget is financed through national taxes and government loans. As noted the wage bill occupies 47% of the national budget (International Monetary Fund (IMF), 2015).

A number of studies on the impacts of the wage bill have been conducted by several researchers such as Okech and Lelegwe (2015), Poverty Reduction and Economic Management Unit (2010), and Madubula and Dawood (2011) for countries such as Kenya, Zimbabwe and the Republic of South Africa, respectively. However, none have been specific to Eswatini and most notably in a review of the institution set up as a gateway to the prevention of the exceptional increase in the wage bill. This study will contribute to the literature by investigating the causes of the continued increase in the wage bill.

1.1 Research Problem

The GoE civil service wage bill has continued to rise in recent years, out-pacing the growth of government revenue. The personnel budget is still the largest single recurrent expenditure item in the national budget. The underlying problem of high public sector personnel costs continues to be felt in the economy.

The wage bill has been increased by 22% since 2010 and is at 47% of the national budget. GoE (2016, p. 91) concedes that 'the size of the public sector in Eswatini is bloated when compared to other countries at the same stage of development'. It furthermore states that, over the years, there has been a steady increase in the number of government departments and ministries. There is general over-staffing in government ministries/departments. IMF (2015) postulates that in 2015 Eswatini's wage bill constituted over 14% of its GDP which was the highest within the Southern African Development Community (SADC).

The bulk of the annual budget is being channelled towards the payment of salaries at the expense of the pursuit of capital projects to improve the socio-economic welfare of the citizenry. GoE civil service wage bill continues to rise despite the implementation of the Lean Service Principle by MSD to contain the wage bill to a manageable level. So far, there are no tangible outcomes that indicate that the principles as applied have been effective in the reduction of the wage bill. Thus, this research aims to examine the question of why the Lean Service Principle failed to effectively slow the rampant growth of the civil service wage bill in Eswatini.

2. LITERATURE REVIEW

This section provides information on the Lean Service Principle and JIT technique. Selected data from Sub-Saharan Africa and the impact of the wage on Eswatini are also presented.

2.1 Lean Service Principle and JIT Technique

The application of the philosophy of Lean Service and JIT is transposed from the manufacturing sector and perfected by Toyota through its Toyota Production System (TPS) in the early 1950s. These philosophies have been pursued in an attempt to curb the ever-increasing civil sector, as Madubula and Dawood (2011, p. 15) rightly observe that 'the public sector wage bill has consistently constituted as the largest component of the government's recurrent expenditure. Reasons for this are varied: annual cost of living adjustments coupled with promotion and job regrading, poor internal controls in wage bill monitoring, appointments made without proper planning and budgeting, and poor organisational design (e.g., strategic plans not aligned with organogram)'.

Camel, Rosen, and Anderson (2000) and Duclos, Siha, and Lummus (1994) state that the JIT technique is designed to eliminate waste from the production/value system so as to create customer satisfaction. As JIT is customised for the manufacturing floor, it has been argued and observed that with the required adjustments JIT can be transferred onto the service sector, therefore, resulting in 'Lean Service'. Within the service sector, JIT is applicable in the rendering of service and therefore it has been noted to be an intangible item. To this end, Camel et al. (2000, p. 3) are of the view that 'JIT is more relevant in the service sector with regards to the process of delivering the service such that it adds value to the customer'.

Lauoie (2014, p. 2) in her clarification of the similarities of Lean Service as a paradigm and its usefulness to the service sector particularly the public service discerns that the most critical aspects of a successful Lean implementation are 'organisational readiness, leadership, management commitment, workforce engagement, and open communication'. The author also states that public organisations' rigid structure and top-down finance and policy-driven culture make them 'more inclined to use Lean to gain internal efficiency, rather than to increase end-user value' (2014, p. 2).

Applications of Lean Service in public settings only use specific tools of the methodology (which may translate to partial adoption of the Lean Service Principle), as a short-term targeted approach, rather than seeing it as a continuous improvement philosophy that focusses on long-term perfection of operational excellence. Nascimento and Francischini (2004, cited in Leite & Viena, 2013, p. 3) defined Lean Service as 'a standardisable system of service operations made up only by activities that generate value for customers, focussing on explicit tangibles and aiming to meet the customers' expectations for quality and price'. In addition to this view, Kanakana (2013, p. 9) is of the opinion that 'government cannot only rely on the number of civil servants in their payroll but must also strive for excellence'. In doing so, the author also advances the use of Lean as a tool kit for service sector effectiveness and efficiency. This is mainly because most governments are the single biggest employer, especially so in the African context and Sub-Saharan Africa in particular, where it has been noted that of the largest contributions to the GDP is from the public sector.

There are five principles of Lean Service:

- Value: What does the customer value? What value is created in the operational process?
- Value streams: Where is the value created for each product or service? What wasted steps can be eliminated?
- Flow: Create a continuous flow in the processes by introducing cross-functional thinking.
- Pull: Produce what is needed by the customer.
- Perfect: Employees should perform their tasks accurately the first time around.
                    (Camel et al., 2000; Kanakana, 2013; Lauoie, 2014).

Lean Service navigates through the improvement process using various tools, focussing on what customers value and what constitutes waste from their point of view. Radnor and Osborne (2013, cited in Lauoie, 2014, p. 8) stated 'value creation happens when value-adding activities are increased without raising the cost of the product or service, or when that cost can be reduced through waste elimination'. Worth noting again is that Lauoie (2014), Kanakana (2013) and Camel et al. (2000) establish that these principles as listed above, are channelled towards organisational cost reduction, increased competitiveness, redistribution of resources (but not necessarily redistribution from the wage bill to production) and a better understanding of customer value.

As a doctrine, JIT is a TQM tool that guarantees that systems are configured accurately to produce goods and services that meet customer satisfaction and do not deviate from the production systems calibrations. TQM stresses that quality is an organisational effort. It facilitates the solving of quality problems and also places great emphasis on teamwork. Using techniques such as brainstorming, discussion and quality control tools, teams work regularly to correct problems.

2.2 General Impact of the Wage Bill on Other Sub-Saharan African Countries

It has been noted that 'many government wage bills tend to siphon off much-needed financial resources for the delivery of core government services to the populace' (National Treasury, 2010; cited in Madubula & Dawood, 2011, p. 17). To demonstrate this further, Okech and Lelegwe (2015) noted that in Kenya, the maintenance of a huge wage bill as a component of recurrent expenditure, and domestic resources funding development is likely to be overcrowded. Available statistics show that the Kenyan government funding for development declined from a high of 7% of GDP in the 2011/12 financial year to 5% in the 2014/15 financial year. This decline was experienced despite the overall expenditure increment from 29% to 33% over the same period. Furthermore, in Kenya, there has been a steady increase in the share of revenue allocated to the payment of salaries and wages of civil servants, which is expected to have a negative impact on allocation towards development expenditures. For instance, the Kenyan wage bill was 47% in 2009/10; it increased to 48% and 55% in 2011/12, and 2012/13, respectively. These percentages are way above the internationally desirable level of 35% (Okech & Lelegwe, 2015).

Okech and Lelegwe (2015, p. 6) also advance that 'an enormous wage bill may contribute towards crowding out resources that could be used in other development priorities such as social and infrastructure development needed for long-term growth and development'. Economically this translates to large fiscal deficits with macroeconomic instability in terms of inflation which may lead to a wage-price spiral and exchange rate impact. Also, unsustainable public debt arising from high wage bills may lead to refinancing (from foreign lenders) and create sovereign risks. Furthermore, many African countries may have to borrow from international lenders which might place political reforms as a prerequisite to lending. A huge wage bill strains the government budget and denies the economy the much-needed resources for socio-economic development such as infrastructure and social services like health and education.

Poverty Reduction and Economic Management Unit (2010, p. 1) notes that in Zimbabwe, there is a relatively high share of the wage bill that is projected at 13% of GDP (which translates to 45% of total national revenue). This high share of the national budget is contended to be cutting into the budget allocation for non-wage operational expenditure in the social sector as well as critical capital expenditure.

To further give impetus to the negative effects of a huge wage bill, the Poverty Reduction and Economic Management Unit (2010) notes that in the context of Zimbabwe the high wage bill has cut into the budget for non-wage operational expenditure as well as capital expenditure. This has resulted in a high fiscal deficit, mainly as a determinant of the prevailing political discourse. This leads to an inflexible public expenditure pattern, thus the requirement for employment opportunity adjustment which is a short-term solution. 'It also has the propensity in the long-term to convert Zimbabwe into a welfare state as the populace will not be in a position to afford their livelihood, therefore the government must establish relevant social security programmes' (Economic Commission of Africa, 2010, p. 7).

2.3 Impact of the Wage Bill on the GoE

In relation to the GoE wage bill, the World Bank (2010, p. 1) concludes that 'the gaping fiscal deficit of about 15% of GDP in 2010/11, and the difficulty in securing the requisite financing has precipitated the need for a rapid intervention in curtailing the wage bill'. The irreversible reduction of the SACU revenue base is being addressed by earnest efforts to boost non-SACU revenue that will have an impact in the medium term, thus shifting the emphasis for expenditure restraint on an orderly roll-back of the wage bill.

There are clear indications from the preceding statement that GoE revenue generation is not sufficient for the ever-increasing wage bill. Such a scenario is peculiar and unsustainable and it is for this reason that GoE investments into other sectors of the economy have been disadvantaged and capital development projects stretched beyond their projected completion dates.

The Eswatini economy has been directly impacted by the increased wage bill as a result of the April 2016 implemented Salary Review as commissioned by the Government. However, there is an agreement between Government and Public Sector Associations to the effect that there shall be a salary review every five years and an annual Cost of Living Adjustment. Kariaki and Kannan (2017, p. 5) predicted that the 'implemented salary review of the 2016/17 budget mid-year results indicate the emergence of a fiscal crunch mainly due to a significant 25% decline in SACU revenues'. The budget provided for an expansion in government spending, particularly regarding capital outlays, in an attempt to boost real GDP growth. However, the major budget pressure emanated from the civil service wage bill, which is estimated to have increased significantly after the salary review implemented in July 2016 (and backdated to April 2016), which proposed pay rises ranging from 17% to 38% for the lowest paid cadres. In view of these circumstances, financing the deficit proved challenging. Most of the financing was covered by domestic borrowing. However, meeting such a large shortfall from the local financial system is complicated by the nascent domestic capital market and the relatively liquid domestic banking sector. As a result, the government has accumulated payment arrears that it plans to settle, one-on-one, with suppliers (Kariaki & Kannan, 2017).

It is from these statistics that one can fully grasp the impact of the huge wage bill, which is above the World Bank and IMF recommended 10% of GDP. It is, however, noted that this scenario is not peculiar to Eswatini but other African countries such as Zimbabwe, Kenya and Lesotho, with Eswatini having the highest in the SACU. The huge wage bill is the bases of this research study. Added impetus to the wage bill concern is given by the IMF as it notes in its 2015 assessment report on Eswatini, that the country needs rigorous fiscal discipline and debt management to ensure social development because the gains from the 2014/15 financial year reserves strengthening are not sustainable at the country's current recurrent expenditure (wage bill being the highest) rate (IMF, 2015).

To address the huge civil services, African governments have resolved more often than not to downsize their civil service. This has notably been under the disguise that the civil service is 'over extended' and 'boated', as a result of the colonial era that left many African countries underdeveloped. The governments that came into power after independence then established huge civil services. Eswatini under the auspices of the Public Sector Management Programme (PSMP) identified downsizing of the civil service as a strategy. To this end, the PSMP proposed the Enhanced Voluntary Early Retirement Scheme (EVERS) in 2006. This scheme was meant to motivate employees who had reached the age of 55 and had served the government for more than 10 years to exit and thus reducing its head count and wage bill. Markedly, EVERS was met with political resistance and to date never been implemented.

3. RESEARCH METHODOLOGY

Primary and secondary sources were used for data collection. From secondary sources, the study collected data on amounts spent on wages, the percentage increase of the wage bill for the period 2010–2017 and the percentage increase in the number of civil servants as per the Establishment Registers, 2010–2017. Monthly Wage Bill Trend Analysis Reports produced by the Ministry of Public Service (MoPS) for the period 2010–2017, the Eswatini Public Service Payroll and Skills Audit Report 2015, Annual Revenue Estimates Reports 2014–2017, Lean Service Principle and JIT Technique Studies were also analysed.

Trend analysis was used in the review of the Recurrent Wage Bill Expenditure Report and Annual Revenue Estimates Reports. Trend analysis enables researchers to determine patterns of increment or decline of a set of variables over an extended period of time. For this research, wage bill trends, revenue and capital expenditure spanning from 2010 to 2017 were used, as these are the most accurate data within the government database that were accessible. The data were retrieved from the Ministry of Finance (MoF) Revenue and Expenditure Report from the time period indicated and MoPS Recurrent Wage Bill Expenditure Report. It was believed that through the use of trend analysis future patterns of the civil service wage bill would be estimated based on past expenditures. The data have been presented in both graphical and linear pattern formats for ease of analysis.

The Swaziland Payroll and Skills Audit (SPRSA) Report 2015 was reviewed to identify MSD qualifications. This is a comprehensive document that was commissioned by the Government in 2014 and contains the payroll system data (established posts payments), skills and qualifications of more than 30,000 civil servants that were interviewed. It was commissioned after the GoS requested a Staff Monitoring Programme from the IMF, and the IMF was of the view that within the civil service there is a likelihood of the existence of 'ghost workers', of which would explain the huge wage bill. It is believed that these data are the most current as there has not been an updated version of the report. Above and beyond this report the officers will be cross-examined on their qualifications so as to provide a comprehensive understanding of their qualifications.

The population for this study was the 40 technical officers employed by the MSD and these 40 officers were the sample of the study. Primary data were collected through semi-structured questionnaires and interviews with the 40 officers. The questionnaires were distributed to all 40 officers. This was done so as to establish what the wage bill push factors are and whether the Lean Service Principle as applied was having a notable impact on the control of the wage bill, which provided qualitative information from the subject-matter specialist. The positions of the 40 officers that were interviewed within the MSD hierarchy ranged from Assistant Management Analyst (AMA), Management Analyst (MA), Senior Management Analyst (SMA), Deputy Director (DD) and Director. These officers are tasked with implementing the Lean Service techniques on wage bills so as to manage and control it. A population is a set of all elements of interest in a particular study. For this study, the population has been identified based on the mandate assigned to the respective departments and their role in the establishment of posts and budgetary support for the established posts in terms of wages.

4. RESULTS AND DISCUSSION

This section presents a picture of the state of the GoE civil service wage bill and the trend that has been observed over a seven-year period, the state of established positions and their vacancy rate, the application of the Lean Service Principle within the service sector and successful implementation. This was then transposed onto the context of Eswatini in line with the study area so as to respond to the objectives of this research.

4.1 Establishment Register 2010–2017 Data Analysis

Data collected from the Establishment Register 2010/11 and Establishment Register 2016/17, as depicted below, indicate that the Ministry of Education and Training (MoET) has the highest number of established posts. As of the 2016/17 financial year, they stood at 16,951 as compared to 14,772 during the 2010/11 financial year, which is an increase of 2,179 or 15%. This was associated with the development of the Free Primary Education (FPE) programme that was introduced by the government in 2010. This programme resulted in the establishment of more primary schools across the country.

The National Policy is clear on the government's intentions to offer basic Education for the first seven years but within the limits of 'available financial and other resource capacities'. The 'Free Primary Education Act' of 2010 compels parents to send their children to school for FPE schooling. Thus, a requirement of staffing complements to see this provision being a reality. Eswatini is like other countries in the Eastern and Southern African Region (ESAR) that are closely moving to implement the abolition of school fees at the primary level as one of the strategies to achieve the Millennium Development Goals (MDGs).

Additional positions and ultimately wage bill increases are expected, as a result of the Cabinet's pronouncement that Religious Education should form part of the core subject from grade 1 to form 5 with effect from January 2017. 'This also introduced a change in syllabus and a requirement for more curriculum designers in addition to the projected 1,370 additional teaching posts for the full roll-out of the Cabinet directive' (Sifundza, 2017, p. 3). The author further concluded that the Cabinet decision was not informed by a clear analysis of the resource requirements to facilitate the full implementation of the prescribed roll-out.

The data contained in the establishment registers reviewed are consistent in that they clearly indicate that the second largest groupings of civil servants are police personnel. There are currently 5,600 established posts vis-à-vis 4,528 in the 2010/11 financial year, which indicates an increment of 1,072 posts at a variance of 24%. However, this study could not establish the methodology and or police/ population ratio used for the increment over the time period under study.

Worth noting is that the health sector has the third highest number of established posts, 4,499 in 2016/17 as compared to the 2010/11 financial year, which is a 22% increment. This is one of the most crucial social services that any government must provide and sustain. As a result, several posts have been established in many clinics and hospitals in the country since 2010. Notably, the establishment and staffing of these additions was a political directive that was funded out of a Supplementary Budget, which resulted in the MoPS having no option but to facilitate the implementation of the Cabinet directive. This resulted in non-adherence to the principles of Lean Service, as per the dictates of the mandate of MSD.

Whilst Correctional Services Officers are the fourth highest with 2,565 in 2016/ 17, an increment of 46% from the 2010/11 financial year when they stood at 1,752 established posts. The research could not establish the warder/prisoner ratio that was used in the determination and projection of the posts as created.

All the first four sectors with the highest established posts are core functions of any government service delivery. There has not been a situation where a decrease in the number of established positions was observed by this study. This study also reveals that the ministries/departments that were identified by the PSMP Report as being possible candidates for outsourcing, privation and/or decentralisation, e.g. Ministry of Natural Resources and Energy (water management function, landscaping), Government Computer Services, MoPS (MSD) and Ministry of Commerce, Industry and Trade (MoCIT), to which such functions as the issuance of licences, Industrial Development and Industrial Estates Management, Handicraft Promotion can be outsourced.

The numbers of established positions per ministry are presented in Table 1 ranging from the largest ministries to the smallest. Furthermore, comparative data are presented based on the 2010/11 and 2016/17 financial years.

It should be noted that the establishment registers at the disposal of the study do not contain the established posts for the Army. However, the SPRSA Report 2015 indicates that there were 5,312 posts attached to the Army, inclusive of His Majesty's close protection unit as of February 2014 (MoPS, 2015). The report, however, does not include information on the yearly increment of established posts within the Army. The report additionally notes that in analysis, 9,822 (27% of the 37,027 expected civil servants, as of February 2014) members were not enumerated, of which 5,312 (54%) of these members were from the Ministry of Defence and State Security. This means that the members from the Ministry were accounted for on February 2014, although they were not verified to be occupying the number of established as indicted and at the authorised staffing levels (MoPS, 2015, p. 26).

The data contained in the establishment registers (as annually produced) do not specify the vacancy rate at any given time. However, the SPRSA Report 2015 reflects that as of February 2014, the core ministries with the highest number of established posts, i.e. MoET and Police, had a vacancy rate of 2,470 people against 381 posts. This is an indication of overstaffing, as each individual should

Table 1. Number of Established Posts per Ministry.

| Ministry/Department | No. of Posts 2016/17 and 2011/12 | | | |
	2016/17 Posts	2010/11 Posts	Varience	% Varience
Education	16,951	14,722	2,229	15.1%
Police	5,600	4,528	1,072	23.7%
Health	4,499	3,676	823	22.4%
Correctional Services	2,565	1,752	813	46.4%
Agriculture	2,472	2,595	−123	−4.7%
Public Works and Transport	2,050	1,544	506	32.8%
Housing and Urban Development	1,282	589	693	117.7%
Tinkhundla Administration	957	896	61	6.8%
Natural Resources and Energy	641	518	123	23.7%
Home Affairs	518	289	229	79.2%
ICT	490	453	37	8.2%
Finance	381	82	299	364.6%
Judiciary	288	280	8	2.9%
Commerce, Industry and Trade	268	273	−5	−1.8%
Economic Planning and Development	264	184	80	43.5%
Dep Prime Ministers Office	256	181	75	41.4%
Public Service	235	225	10	4.4%
Labour and Social Security	234	220	14	6.4%
Tourism and Enviromental Affairs	193	174	19	10.9%
Parliament	191	173	18	10.4%
Foreign Affairs	176	177	−1	−0.6%
Justice and Constitutional Affairs	171	155	16	10.3%
Audit	106	99	7	7.1%
Private and Cabinet	100	86	14	16.3%
Sport, Culture and Youth Affairs	73	75	−2	−2.7%
Statutory	65	29	36	124.1%
Anti-Corruption Commission	58	48	10	20.8%
Internal Audit	52	33	19	57. 6%
Elections and Boundaries Commission	24	33	9	−27.3%
Grand Totals	*41,160*	*34,089*	*7,071*	*20.756*

occupy a distinct post and post number. Therefore, this alludes to over-expenditure that is not captured in the establishment register, but payable under the Treasury Payroll System. In essence, the perceived savings from the vacancies were not realised due to the overstaffing under MoET. This is in line with the view of MoPs that there is 'a lack of adherence to the establishment register and an increase in employment costs' (MoPS, 2015, p. 39).

From the foregoing paragraphs, it is evident that the tools and techniques at the disposal of MSD, as per its mandate, were not utilised. Organisational studies were not conducted to inform the teacher posts as created and/or required, but there were clear political requirements as per the Constitution of Eswatini, 2005, and the education sector policies as promulgated by Cabinet through the approval of Parliament. 'Human Resource Planning (HRP) should have been engaged into as a means to get the right number of people with the right skills, experience and competencies in the right jobs at the right time and at the right cost', as suggested by Bulmash (2015, p. 1). However, it has been noted that this is not always possible with regard to political dispensation.

4.2 Annual Revenue and Expenditure Data Analysis

The GoE Financial Revenue and Expenditure Report 2014–2017 contain the government's expenditure and revenue collection for the year ended and the mid-term financial projections. It indicates sources of government revenue and government expenditure per ministry/department. The data from the above-captioned reports are shown in the following (Refer to Tables 2–4).

From Tables 2–4, it is evident that Eswatini is no exception to the conclusion that a high wage bill tends to crowd out capital expenditure. This, therefore, is a cause for concern on delivering social and infrastructure development. This picture becomes much clear when observed at a micro or monthly expenditure level. The wage bill as a recurrent budget far out-weighs other recurrent non-wage operational items and social expenditure. Also worth noting is that social expenditure has to compete with other government operational costs. This therefore greatly compromises the delivery of social services such as university bursaries, FPE, health care and social security items, e.g. elderly grants.

4.2.1 Eswatini Payroll and Skills Audit Data Report 2015 Analysis

The study reveals that 24 ministries/departments out of 34 had over-established responsibility centres. This means that 70% of the responsibility centres as of 28 February 2014 had more personnel than the total numbers prescribed in the

Table 2. GoE Revenue, Capital Expenditure and Wage Bill Distribution Data.

Government Revenue, Capital Expenditure and Wage Bill Distribution for the Financial Year 2014/2015 to 2016/2017						
Item	Revenue	Capital Expenditure	Wage Bill	Grand Totals	Capital Expenditure to Revenue	Wage Bill % to Revenue
2014/ 2015	13,952,966,000	3,610,421,000	4,804,480,777	8,414,901,777	26%	34%
2015/ 2016	14,122,910,000	3,725,278,000	5,319,826,765	9,045,104,765	26%	38%
2016/ 2017	13,538,082,000	5,296,092,000	6,505,357,592	11,801,449,592	39%	48%
Grand totals	41,613,958,000	12,631,791,000	16,629,665,134	29,261,456,134	30%	40%

Source: Ministry of Finance (2017).
Note: Amounts are shown in the local currency of Eswatini, i.e. Emalangeni.

Table 3. GoE Revenue, Capital Expenditure and Wage Bill Variance Data.

Government Revenue, Capital Expenditure and Wage Bill Distribution Variances for the Financial Year 2014/2015 to 2016/2017

Item	Revenue	Capital Expenditure	Wage Bill	Grand Totals	Capital Expenditure to Revenue	Wage Bill % to Revenue
2014/ 2015	–	–	–	–	0%	0%
2015/ 2016	169,944,000	114,857,000	515,345,988	630,202,988	68%	303%
2016/ 2017	(584,828,000)	1,570,814,000	1,185,530,827	2,756,344,827	−269%	−203%
Grand totals	**−414,884,000**	**1,685,671,000**	**1,700,876,815**	**3,386,547,815**	**−406%**	**−410%**

Source: Ministry of Finance (2017).
Note: Amounts are shown in the local currency of Eswatini, i.e. Emalangeni.

Table 4. GoE Revenue, Capital Expenditure and Wage Bill Percentage Variance Data.

Government Revenue, Capital Expenditure and Wage Bill Distribution % Variances for the Financial Year 2014/2015 to 2016/2017

Item	Revenue	Capital Expenditure	Wage Bill	Grand Totals
2014/2015	0%	0%	0%	0%
2015/2016	1%	3%	11%	14%
2016/2017	−4%	42%	22%	64%
Grand totals	**−3%**	**45%**	**33%**	**78%**

Source: Ministry of Finance (2017).
Note: Amounts are shown in the local currency of Eswatini, i.e. Emalangeni.

Establishment Register, 2014/15. A total of 131 responsibility centres had more personnel than stipulated in the Establishment Register, 2014/2015. Ministries of Health (MoH) and Ministry of Education and Training (MoET) had the most over-established responsibility centres.

According to the Establishment Register 2013/14, 5,155 officers were supposed to be occupying these posts, instead, 7,906 officers were occupying various posts as of 28 February 2014. This means that there was an excess establishment of 2,751 members. Ministries and Departments that were highly affected are Police (1,122), MoET (582), Correctional Services (339) and MoH (179) (MoPS, 2015).

4.2.2 Monthly GoE Wage Bill Report 2010–2017 Analysis

The MoPS in its awareness of the fact that the wage bill is an economic and service delivery performance issue, commissioned MSD to conduct a monthly wage bill analysis that is produced at the end of every quarter. Table 5 clearly indicates that the cost of government salaries has not gone down over the six-year period under review. Noteworthy is that during the period between 2010/11 and 2015/6 there was no salary review, as the government was going through financial challenges, yet the wage bill increased steadily. This has been attributed to two factors, namely the cost of living adjustment and the continued creation of posts.

During the financial years 2010/11 and 2011/12 there was no cost of living adjustments, therefore there were no wage bill increments. For the financial years 2012/13, 2013/14, 2014/15 and 2015/16 cost of living adjustments were 10%, 5%, 7%, and 7%, respectively. However, it was observed that the actual wage increments were higher to these adjustments owing to the addition of established posts within the civil service. It is, however, difficult to isolate the contribution of salaries paid to the Army from these data, as these data were collected from the amounts paid to all established posts by the Treasury Department.

During the 2016/17 financial year, the GoE implemented salary review adjustments as recommended by an independent consultant. The review had not been undertaken in over 10 years, yet the GoE has a standing agreement with Public Sector Associations to review the civil service salaries every five years. It is the implementation of this salary review that has significantly spiked salaries payable to civil servants. It is argued that during this period the government observed a zero growth personnel policy; however, it is noted that there were positions that were given special authority or sanctioned for creation, namely MoH, MoET, Police and Correctional Services.

A detailed month-to-month analysis for the time period understudy undoubtedly shows the cost increment of the wage bill (Refer to Table 5). Monthly salaries expenditure shows that government does not pay anything less than E 300,000 to its employees (Refer to Table 4). This is irrefutably a huge recurrent expenditure for a country of the size of Eswatini that is also reliant on ever-dwindling SACU receipts. It must further be pointed out that monthly capital expenditure is normally below the monthly government salaries. This should, without a doubt, be a cause for concern.

The month-to-month wage bill data for the financial years 2010/11–2016/17 have been summarised and presented in Table 5.

The above clearly shows the extent to which the wage bill is an issue. It must be noted that the additional posts as discussed were not informed by the application of the tools and techniques at the disposal of MSD, but were argued to have been politically motivated. Therefore, the impact of the lack of application of the Lean Service Principle on the wage bill has been confirmed by the statistics given by MoPS itself.

4.3 MSD Questionnaire Data Analysis

The response rate of the study was 90% (36 from 40 MSD officials). It is imperative to note that, during the data collection, 64% of the respondents indicated that they were not sure about the context of the questionnaire. As a result, they could not answer the questions which were based on the work that

Table 5. Month-to-Month Wage Bill Distribution Data.

Month	Month to Month Wage Bill Distribution for the Financial Year 2010/2011 to 2016/2017							
	2010/2011	2011/2012	2012/2013	2013/2014	2014/2015	2015/2016	2016/2017	Grand Totals
April	311,113,180	317,635,344	322,208,573	333,259,876	384,603,175	404,221,275	452,111,773	2,525,153,197
May	296,386,048	317,846,652	322,827,467	336,522,891	375,473,658	411,243,419	471,982,501	2,532,282,635
June	293,003,526	316,546,143	323,298,699	363,064,550	398,564,011	446,664,402	452,755,881	2,593,897,211
July	314,107,094	329,742,224	334,324,391	580,622,118	386,424,331	425,025,339	771,011,915	3,141,257,411
August	356,481,891	316,731,620	325,731,937	355,689,601	478,290,944	414,370,820	550,577,268	2,797,874,081
September	312,256,737	317,614,114	323,819,888	349,754,211	398,505,479	552,426,080	534,422,387	2,788,798,897
October	325,459,578	317,438,636	323,115,949	348,859,076	395,516,352	445,809,048	533,529,217	2,689,727,856
November	316,755,731	318,500,824	324,891,708	356,862,227	39,5,900,924	439,669,507	539,693,539	2,692,274,459
December	314,499,777	343,213,693	343,213,693	408,215,620	397,163,799	505,267,682	593,117,611	2,904,691,874
January	316,282,339	316,074,812	317,362,917	341,724,748	395,685,743	419,834,398	529,845,420	2,636,810,378
February	310,943,196	305,028,543	326,022,196	341,544,212	394,670,733	427,548,555	538,120,543	2,643,877,978
March	315,251,141	331,387,075	336,709,844	353,396,002	403,681,628	427,746,241	538,189,538	2,706,361,469
Grand totals	**3,782,540,239**	**3,847,759,680**	**3,923,527,263**	**4,469,515,131**	**4,804,480,777**	**5,319,826,765**	**6,505,357,592**	**32,653,007,447**

Source: Ministry of Public Service (2017a).
Note: Amounts are shown in the local currency of Eswatini, i.e. Emalangeni.

Table 6. Lean Service Principle Applicability to MSD Works.

	Yes	No	Not Sure
No. of respondents	10	–	3
Percentage	77	–	23

they performed. Although an explanation of the basic principles of Lean Service, the wage bill, the JIT technique, Human Resource Forecasting and Planning (HRFP) and the aim of the study were provided, the respondents could not respond. It was expected that only those within the rank of junior level could not have an in-depth understanding of the tools and techniques employed by MSD, mainly because this is an entry-level that is still at the learning curve. Nonetheless, it would be assumed that some form of in-house training, mentoring and/or orientation would have been done to familiarise these officers with the Division work methodology and tools.

The MSD is divided mainly into three sections, namely Consultancy, Research and Development (R&D), and Administrative Reforms. The Consultancy section is tasked with the provision of organisational development studies, while the R&D section is assigned to undertake research on the latest labour market remuneration and terms and conditions studies to inform government policy. The Administrative Reforms section initiates and administers civil service organisational reform programmes.

64% of respondents did not have the basic knowledge of the techniques applied in the monitoring and control of the wage bill as per the mandate of MSD. Therefore, 64% were not in a position to respond to the questionnaire. Worth noting is that of the 40 MSD officers only 13 officers possessed the Management Services Certificate (MSC) qualification and they were able to complete the questionnaire. The MSC pertains to training in Lean Service, Work Measurement, Time Study, Work Flow Analysis and Business Process Engineering. This qualification equips officers with practical skills in management services with regard to the identification of muda within a production process. It enables qualification holders to re-engineer business processes so as to reduce production costs and ensure customer satisfaction.

The study finds that there is an average of 8 years of work-related experience among MSD staff members. As such the relevant techniques to the achievement of the mandate of the Division should have been mastered and relevant training should have been afforded to the officers in building capacity, as this is a highly technical field.

Fig. 1 shows a summary of the contemporary body of knowledge for Management Services. The diagram identifies the main techniques and application areas used by the MSD in executing its portfolio mandate (Source: MoPS, 2017b).

Fig. 1. Summary of the Contemporary Body of Knowledge for MSD.

It is imperative to present the work methodology and outputs that MSD seeks to achieve. This knowledge gives added impetus to the relevance and need for training on the MSC. The diagram above clearly illustrates the tools utilised and how they are linked to the clientele in achieving the core mandate of the MSD.

The questionnaire that was distributed to the respondents is presented and analysed below based on the 13 respondents who were able to complete the questionnaire:

Question 1: Is the Lean Service Principle applicable to the works of MSD? Kindly elaborate on your response.

77% of respondents agreed that the Lean Service Principle, as defined on the questionnaire and based on their knowledge of the MSD, was applicable to the works commissioned by the Division (Refer to Table 6). It was interesting to note that when probed further the majority were not able to detail how the principle was actually applied. They merely related it to the end results of the mandate assigned to MSD. 23% of 13 respondents could not associate the theory with the mandate of the Division (Refer to Table 6).

Question 2: Is the JIT technique applicable to the works of MSD? Kindly elaborate on your response.

Although 85% of the respondents agreed that the JIT technique was applicable to works mandated by MSD, they could not, however, detail in a form of examples how they reached this conclusion. They did not fully grasp that the technique was applied to the production process in service delivery. The respondents were not aware that the technique enhances the reduction of inventory in the production process (Refer to Table 7).

Question 3: Have the above-mentioned principles as applied by MSD been effective in the containment of the wage bill? Kindly elaborate on your response.

The question required the respondents to provide details on how they arrived at the conclusion that the Lean Service Principle and the JIT technique were effective in the containment of the wage bill, these examples were not forthcoming. In fact, contradictions (from the 39%) in the success of these tools were noted, especially when it was pointed out to the respondents that established posts had never been reduced and/or remained stagnant over a ten-year period. 31% of the respondents only associated what the tools were designed to achieve with the assumption that the same would reduce staff numbers in any production line. They could not exactly pinpoint how these tools neither reduced staff numbers nor enabled present staff levels to perform better (Refer to Table 8).

Question 4: Are the Human Resources Forecasting and Planning (HRFP) techniques applied in your work methods in the determination of the required number of personnel to perform a function? Kindly elaborate on your response.

These HRFP techniques include amongst other tools; total turnover analysis, employee movement ratio trend analysis, skills audits, labour market trends, organisational placement models and succession planning to mention a few. A review of organisational development studies reports produced by MSD contradicted the 69% of the respondents that argued that these tools were used by MSD

Table 7. JIT Technique Applicability to MSD Works.

	Yes	No	Not Sure
No. of respondents	11	1	1
Percentage	85	8	8

Table 8. Application of Techniques by MSD.

	Yes	No	Mixed Results
No. of respondents	4	4	5
Percentage	31	31	39

(Refer to Table 9). In fact, human resource forecasting was understood by the respondents to merely mean concluding that a requested position was needed or not, based on the duties that are attached to the position. Studies conducted by MSD did not follow the human resource forecasting technique. The respondents themselves could not argue how exactly this technique was used.

31% of the respondents stated that the techniques were not used (Refer to Table 9). They were of the opinion that they could not associate it with the manner in which they conducted their organisational studies. The MSD organisational study reports reviewed agree with this conclusion. Worth noting is that only the determination of cleaners using work measurement tools was identified by only two respondents.

Question 5: In your opinion what are the major wage bill push factors?

At least 31% of the respondents were of the view that the Army was the major wage bill push factor. However, the SPRSA Report 2015 indicates that there were 5,312 posts attached to the Army inclusive of His Majesty's close protection unit as of February 2014 (MoPS, 2015). Also of interest was that 15% of the respondents are of the view that political interference was a major push factor. They believed that the work of the MSD was hindered by political directives. This study also notes that 31% of respondents are not aware of the wage bill push factors (Refer to Table 10). This indicates officers that do not seem to know what items of the wage bill must be targeted for review.

Question 6: There is a theoretical notion that a huge wage bill overcrowds capital expenditure in most developing countries; in your view is this true or false? Please elaborate on your response.

At least 54% of the respondents agree with this observation, which means that they recognise that the current GoE civil service wage bill is not sustainable and has antagonistic consequences for the development of the country, and the achievement of its service delivery agenda. The wage bill therefore cannot be

Table 9. Application of HRFP Techniques in MSD Work.

	Yes	No	Not Sure
No. of respondents	9	4	–
Percentage	69	31	–

Table 10. Major Wage Bill Push Factors.

	Not Sure	New Ministries/ Departments	Political Interference	Army	Redundant Posts	Allowances
No. of respondents	4	2	2	4	1	1
Percentage	31	15	15	31	8	8

allowed to outweigh the country's development agenda, under the pretext that governments must ensure employment, thus being the largest single employers in most Sub-Saharan Countries. It is, however, noted that there are those respondents (31%) that are not sure of the impact of the wage bill on other service deliverables, yet the wage bill is a major challenge of the country, and a major responsibility assigned to their division (Refer to Table 11).

Question 7: Data contained in the Establishment Registers dating from 2010 to 2016 indicate that there has been an annual average increase of 21% in the wage bill; in your view what is the main cause of this increase; is it the failure of the techniques employed by MSD or level of the developmental state of Eswatini? Please elaborate on your response.

The majority of the respondents (62%) argued that other factors contributed to the annual wage bill increment (Refer to Table 12). Chief amongst these was a political influence. However, the exact examples of the same were not given, but this alluded to political directives in the establishment of posts. Nevertheless, this could not be ascertained as such political directives were not documented.

Question 8: Political and administrative leadership is essential to any administrative and/or financial reforms; in your opinion has the same been forthcoming within your department? Please elaborate on your response.

It was interesting to observe that 39% of the respondents could neither agree nor disagree with the view that political and administrative support was given to MSD in its drive to reform the civil service (Refer to Table 13). This might to a large extent be confirmed by the failure of all wage bill reform initiatives, e.g. Alternative Service Delivery (ASD) and EVERS.

Table 11. Overcrowding of Capital Expenditure by Wage Bill.

	Yes	No	Not Sure
No. of respondents	7	2	4
Percentage	54	15	31

Table 12. Main Causes of the Wage Bill Increase.

	Failure of Techniques	Level of Development	Both	Not Sure	Other
No. of respondents	–	2	3	–	8
Percentage	–	15	23	–	62

Table 13. Forms of Support Given to MSD.

	Yes	No	Not Sure	Irrelevant
No. of respondents	2	6	5	–
Percentage	15	46	39	–

Table 14. Proportion of the Army Cost to the Wage Bill.

	Yes	No	Don't Know
No. of respondents	5	–	8
Percentage	39	–	62

Question 9: There is a notion within the civil service that the Army constitutes the largest proportion of the wage bill; is this statement factual?

Notably, the majority of the respondents' preferred to remain neutral on this matter, mainly because they contended that they did not have access to the actual Army personnel numbers (Refer to Table 14). Yet in response to question five, the majority cited the Army as the major wage bill push factor (Refer to Table 10).

Question 10: The Lean Service Principle was first recommended by the Public Sector Management Programme (PSMP) in 1999; Are you aware of this and/or do you have access to this report? *YES.........NO..........* if your answer is yes, what is your view of this recommendation considering the manner in which MSD performs its organisational development studies?

It is unfortunate to learn that the majority of the respondents were not aware of the core PSPM document that made a variety of recommendations that are now being pursued by MSD, e.g. revival of ASD, Performance Management System (PMS), Lean Service and Payroll and Skills Audits. Therefore, of those sampled (64%) that indicated they were not in a position to respond to the questionnaire were also not aware of the PSMP Report. This alludes to a management gap in the orientation of recruits into the division. It demonstrates a lack of a proper strategy in the planning and placement of new entrants into the division.

Question 11: There is a notion from Cabinet that MSD has not been successful in its mandate to contain the wage bill, what is your opinion on this statement? Kindly elaborate on your response.

Reasons given by the 77% of the respondents to maintain that the Cabinet was misguided in its conclusions on MSD, was that there was political interference in the undertaking of the mandate of MSD (Refer to Table 15). To this end, it was argued that unfounded and undocumented instructions on the creation of certain posts were made. These were mostly pointed to be rampant within the Armed

Table 15. Cabinet Perception of MSD.

	Notion Is Correct	Notion Is Misguided	Not Aware of the Notion	Partially True, but There Are Other Factors	No Opinion
No. of respondents	1	10	–	1	1
Percentage	8	77	–	8	8

Forces (i.e. Police, Correctional Services and the Army). However, further cross-examination into the question unearthed the desire to have MSD functional so as to ensure job security. The failure to manage the wage bill was not at all placed on the ineffectiveness of the tools at the disposal of MSD, even though many were not sure of how these tools were practically utilised.

4.4 Lean Service Principle, JIT Technique and PSMP Report Analysis

MSD conducts organisational reviews on systems and procedure audits to attain a 'Lean Civil Service' based on the PSMP that was initiated by GoE in 1995 and reviewed between 1999 and 2005. The programme identified a number of initiatives that would seek to curb the low service delivery rates by the civil service. Amongst these were that the civil service should be reconfigured to be more 'Lean and Efficient' and this was to be achieved through reduction and/or control of the posts/positions created for ministries/departments and the outsourcing of non-core government functions.

The PSMP was designed to raise the standards of service delivery and to realise greater efficiency and cost-effectiveness of the civil service. One of the objectives of PSMP is to 'improve the performance and productivity of the public service for efficient and effective delivery of services, through new or revised operating, technical and management systems and new or revised human resources management systems' (MoPS, 1999, p. 3).

In pursuit of the objectives as highlighted, Lean Service Principle was identified and is the guiding philosophy of the MSD based on the PSMP. Worth mentioning is that the PSMP project staff were absorbed by MSD to ensure the implementation of the PSMP objectives. To this end, Maleyeff (2007, p. 9) advocates that Lean Service can be defined as a 'management approach that seeks to maximize value to customers, both internal and external, while simultaneously removing wasteful activities and practices'. He also argues that Lean is not just an organisational development technique but a management principle that should be embraced to achieve efficiency and improved productivity.

There has not been a detailed appraisal of how well the Division has pursued and/or implemented the PSMP as a base for service delivery. The PSMP's usage as a mechanism to reconfigure the functionality of ministries and departments within the Lean Service Principle has also not been evaluated. However, as indicated in the previous section, 77% of the respondents were not aware of the PSMP Report (Refer to Table 16). They had no access to it nor were they oriented on its recommendations.

Table 16. Knowledge of PSMP Report.

	Yes	Aware but Have No Access	Not Aware of the Report
No. of respondents	2	1	10
Percentage	15	8	77

Public service reform becomes necessary when uncontrolled growth of the establishment combined with unsustainable levels of pay (often aggravated by a deterioration of the economy) force the wage bill to surpass its economic development. On the foundation of this statement, the GoE initiated the self-imposed Internal Structural Adjustment Programme (ISAP) through the implementation of the PSMP in 1999. It is this programme that observed the trend towards a ballooning civil service. The Lean Service Principle was born from this programme. It was promoted as a means by which the increase of the civil service would be curtailed. Chief amongst the methodologies that the PSMP recommended were retrenchments, early retirement programmes, freezing on recruitment, freezing of increases on pay scales and outsourcing. However, these recommendations do not fall within the tools advocated for by the Lean Service Principle.

The Lean Service Principle continues to be the cornerstone to the work methodology of MSD. The Honourable Minister for Public Service in his 2017/18 financial year budget request report noted that MSD shall continue to pursue Lean Service 'to control the size of the public service whilst ensuring a merito-rious quality service. The Ministry will additionally undertake work study and work reviews to determine the need for requested new positions' (MoPS, 2016, p. 1). However, as alluded to there is no direct linkage to the PSMP recom-mendations and the Lean Service tools that are utilised by MSD.

The forgoing is contrary to the spirit of the PSMP report, as it does not identify the items as indicated to be the means to the reduction of the wage bill. The respondents also did not identify the techniques as those that would result in retrenchments, early retirement programmes, freezing on recruitment, freezing of increases on pay scales and outsourcing.

Leite and Viena (2013, p. 15) argue that the most dominant human resource application of Lean Service is the 'empowerment' of employees and teams. This notion is in line with the principles of establishing an organisation that embraces the involvement of human resources in the value streaming of the production process. The PSMP report and the respondents did not identify the foregoing as items that can contribute to the reduction and/or control of the wage bill (Table 16).

The human resource component is also appreciated when reviewing the broad view of the organisation philosophy within the JIT technique. This view is of the notion that employees should not focus exclusively on their own tasks and/or duties, but must understand the processes within the entire spectrum of the organisation. This is suggested because each and every task or duty is linked to another in the production process, which must result in customer satisfaction, as all employees are responsible for satisfying customers. This is directly linked to the visibility of the production or service process. Once again it is witnessed that this technique as well is not purely and directly designed for the reduction of staff complements, as is the overreaching goal of MSD's application of these tech-niques. Furthermore, as noted the respondents did not identify the JIT techniques as explained to result in the reduction of the wage bill. In fact, 46% of the respondents identified downsizing as the methodology for wage bill reduction

Table 17. Best Wage Bill Reduction Techniques.

	Appropriate Skills Mix	Downsizing Options	Political and Administrative Support	Not Clear
No. of respondents	2	6	2	3
Percentage	15	46	15	23

(Refer to Question 12: Table 17). This methodology is not within the JIT technique application. It should be noted that the PSMP was the main doctrine that pushed for the Lean Service Principle, it was later evaluated and refocussed with objectives that were more streamlined.

Question 12: In your opinion what are the best methodologies that can be applied to contain the wage bill? Please elaborate on your response with examples.

Based on the literature on the Lean Service Principle and the JIT technique, the study notes that a more suitable methodology in personnel determination is HRFP. This includes a number of steps and processes that are postulated to result in more organisational structured human resource recruitment. This process entails a number of steps as highlighted by Bulmash (2015), the key to these is the establishment of a Human Resource Planning Team (HRPT), which in the context of GoE is the mandate given to MSD. It is this team that aligns the HRP with the organisational strategy. It is mandated to pursue the tools as assigned in the determination of personnel requirements. Firstly, the team must understand the Appropriate Planning Horizon, which is defined as a judgement about how far into the future predictions can be made, taking into consideration acceptable levels of operational, organisational and environmental uncertainties. Bulmash (2015) also postulates that this can be on a yearly base or within the mid-term.

5. CONCLUSION AND RECOMMENDATIONS

This research addressed the increase in the wage bill as a result of the failure of MSD in the implementation of the principles applied. The overall findings conclusively indicate that the civil service wage bill is an issue of concern. It has clearly shown that this item has outpaced the capital programme expansion and compromised development. There has been a clear indication that the lack of MSC qualification (64% of the officers do not possess the MSC) within the MSD has resulted in the failure to apply the requisite tools and techniques. There has not been a clear link between the provisions of the Lean Service Principle, the JIT techniques and the recommendations of the PSMP. The latter recommended retrenchments, early retirement programmes, freezing on recruitment, freezing of increases on pay scales and outsourcing as a means to the reduction of the wage bill. However, these methodologies do not form part of the provisions of the Lean

Service Principle and the JIT techniques. The usage of a lean and efficient civil service in the PSMP was not then correlated to specific tools that would result in the GoE civil service being lean and effective.

Regarding the Lean Service Principle and the JIT technique application, most of the respondents were not able to detail these tools' applicability to the reduction of the wage bill. 77% of the respondents (Refer to Table 15) did not know of the PSMP report that advocated for lean and effective civil service.

MoPS has not invested heavily in the capacity building of the MSD staff in Lean Service Principles and JIT technique, especially the 62% of officers that failed to respond to the study. The failure in the training of these techniques has resulted in these officers not being fully utilised. The wage bill has as a result continued to increase, and the political discourse has also made a huge contribution to the same.

It has been noted that there is a huge number of established posts that are manned by more employees than those that have been sanctioned. This is a major cause for concern as it is not clear how this was allowed to happen. This implies a failure by MSD to properly manage the establishment of posts. The major wage bill push factor has been the continued creation of posts mainly within the education sector and armed forces. Most notable is the political influence in the creation of many posts that were approved by the Cabinet without following due techniques and principles.

The study found that the MSD has been applying the wrong methodologies in wage bill control, which has been evident in the continued yearly increase of the wage bill. The major defect in the said tools and techniques is that they were not purely designed for wage bill control. They are designed for value creation in the delivery of goods or services to the end user. They are customer-centric techniques. The tools and techniques have failed, and this has also been a result of the lack of training on the said tools and techniques.

Based on the trend analysis employed in this research, it is evident that the wage bill is an issue and will continue to increase unless decisive action and techniques are employed. There has been a steady increase in the civil service head-count, even though the Cabinet has sanctioned establishment circulars that restrain the creation of additional posts, clearly, there is a major issue to be addressed with a great sense of urgency. The skills audit may assist the organisation to understand under which functions is it lacking and requires engaging in a capacity-building programme.

The expansion of the civil service was also viewed by many governments as a reaffirmation of their drive and devotion to service delivery and in many cases as a means for job creation, as much of those countries' private sectors had not been well developed. It is important to note that the GoE remains the major employer in Eswatini as the private sector does not have enough capacity for creating many jobs. On the other hand, since the GoE has a duty to the socio-economic development of the country and improves the standard of living in the country like any other government, the government can achieve its mission by approaching a mechanism such as establishing a vibrant entrepreneurial environment across the country through the 'income distribution of economic wealth'.

5.1 Recommendations

It is recommended that Lean Service Principle and the JIT technique should not be used to control and/or manage the wage bill. They should be used for process and systems improvement to create customer value. This is one of the main items that MSD has to achieve.

The study recommends that MSD employees that do not possess the MSC be afforded an opportunity to be trained in this qualification. This will enable the officers to understand the application of Lean Service and other relevant techniques to the individual ministries and departments. It is recommended that not only should the MSD staff be trained on the Lean Service Principle and the JIT technique but also be trained on the HRFP. This will enable a better appreciation of this technique and its tools. This will also broaden the officers' understanding and appreciation of the requirements of organisational processes and manpower planning.

However, if for example new positions have been created, it is then that the production process can be investigated to remove muda and streamline the activities to customer satisfaction. Value creation of any service must meet the strategic goals of the organisation as supported by the HRP. A continuous review of these activities must be undertaken so as to identify areas of adjustment and cost savings. Thus, it is recommended that HRFP be adopted as a more relevant technique to determine the number and calibre of required posts within the civil service. These techniques have been proven to be a more logical tool that has the potential to control the creation of posts as they purely deal with the relevance of a required function or duty in the attainment of an organisation's strategic direction. The personnel reduction programme such as Enhanced Voluntary Early Retirement (EVERS) can be reconsidered and revitalised so as to contribute to the reduction of the civil service head-count. The need for political support of these programmes cannot be over-emphasised. This is also on the strength that the majority of the respondents identified downsizing as the best option to reduce the civil service. However, this should be done with due consideration of all social-economic factors that may affect those identified under the downsizing programme.

5.2 Managerial Implication

From the findings of the study, the Cabinet of Eswatini will be in a position to make an appropriate decision on the mandate and future of the MSD, as there have been growing calls to disband the Division. This opinion has been fuelled by the failure of the MSD to reduce and/or control the wage bill. This study provided information on the shortcomings of the Lean Service Principle and JIT technique in the management and reduction of the GoE civil service wage bill. Furthermore, the study indicates the relevance of these principles in the context of the GoE civil service. As such, the findings of the study will enable the development of effective strategic pursuit by the management of the MoPS in realigning the most relevant aspects of the principles, tools and techniques as pursued by the mandate of the MSD.

This study will assist the MSD to identify if required, the relevant techniques for the determination and forecasting of required staff complement, progression planning and effective human resources planning. This will be done in cognisance of the prevailing government fiscal conditions and levels of customer satisfaction, essential to create customer value and value for taxes as paid by the citizenry.

REFERENCES

Bulmash. (2015). Human resources forecasting and supply. Retrieved from http://www.highered. mheducation.com/sites/dl/free/.../. Accessed on May 20, 2017.

Camel, C., Rosen, D., & Anderson, E. A. (2000). Just-In-Time is not just for manufacturing: A service perspective. Retrieved from http://www.cba.uh.edu/doctoral/scm/docs/fletcher-3.pdf. Accessed on January 19, 2017.

Duclos, L. K., Siha, S. M., & Lummus, R. R. (1994). JIT in service: A review of current practise and future direction. Retrieved from http://www.pdfs.sematicscholar.org/4c71/bb26304ofdca. Accessed on January 19, 2017.

Economic Commission of Africa. (2010). *Public Sector Management Reforms in Africa*. Addis Ababa: Economic Commission of Africa.

Government of Swaziland. (2016). *Strategy for sustainable development and inclusive growth. Government of Swaziland, Ministry of Economic Planning and Development*. Mbabane: Government Information Service.

IMF. (2015). *IMF country report no. 15/353: Kingdom of Swaziland; 2015 Article IV consultations-press release; staff report; and statement by the Executive Director of the Kingdom of Swaziland*. Retrieved from http://www.imf.org/external/pub/ft/scr/2015/cr15353. Accessed on January 10, 2017.

Kanakana, M. G. (2013). Lean service industry. Retrieved from http://www.conference.sun.ac.za/ index.php/saiic25/paper/viewfile. Accessed on June 27, 2017.

Kariaki, P., & Kannan, A. P. (2017). Swaziland 2017 Economic Outlook. Retrieved from http://www. africaeconomicoutlook.org/en/country-notes/Swaziland. Accessed on January 27, 2017.

Lauoie, R. (2014). Achieving operational excellence in the public sector: A lean journey? Retrieved from http://www.dtpr.lib.cothabascau.ca/action/download.php. Accessed on June 3, 2017.

Leite, H. D., & Viena, G. E. (2013). Lean philosophy and its applications in the service industry: Review of current knowledge. Retrieved from http://www.scielo.br/pdf/2015nahead/.../pdf. Accessed on January 12, 2017.

Madubula, N., & Dawood, G. (2011). Managing the provincial wage bill to contain fiscal stress and build a capable state. Retrieved from http://www.citeseerx.ist.psu.edu.viewdoc/download? doi=10.11.434andrep. Accessed on January 10, 2017.

Maleyeff, J. (2007). Improving service delivery in Government with Lean Six Sigma. Retrieved from http://www.doh.wa.gov/portals/1/documents/1000. Accessed on January 16, 2017.

Ministry of Finance. (2017). *Government of Swaziland financial revenue and expenditure report*. Government of Swaziland, Mbabane.

Ministry of Public Service. (1999). *Public Sector Management Programme*. Retrieved from http://www. gov.sz/images/stories/PublicService/PSMP_proj_docu_abrodged. Accessed on January 23, 2017.

Ministry of Public Service. (2015). *Swaziland payroll and skills audit report*. Government of Swaziland, Mbabane.

Ministry of Public Service. (2016). *Budget proposal: 2017/18 financial year*. Government of Swaziland, Mbabane.

Ministry of Public Service. (2017a). *Monthly wage bill analysis report*. Government of Swaziland, Mbabane.

Ministry of Public Service. (2017b). *Second quarter performance report*. Government of Swaziland, Mbabane.

Okech, T. C., & Lelegwe, S. L. (2015). Dissecting the Kenya wage bill dilemma: What is the missing link and which way to go? *International Journal of Economics, Commerce and Management*, *III*(12), 738–753.

Poverty Reduction and Economic Management Unit. (2010). *Zimbabwe: Public expenditure notes managing government wage bill for sustainable recovery*. Retrieved from http://www.documents.worldbank.org. Accessed on June 15, 2017.

Sifundza, S. G. (2017). Request for the creation of religious education teachers posts. Mbabane.

World Bank. (2022). Eswatini overview. Retrieved from https://www.worldbank.org/en/country/eswatini/overview. Accessed on November 5, 2022.

WorldBank. (2010). Achieving fiscal sustainability in Eswatini: Reestablishing control over the wage bill. Retrieved from http://www.documents.worldbank.org/curated/421471468340834194. Accessed on January 12, 2017.

TOWARDS SUSTAINABLE PROSPERITY FOR HOST COMMUNITIES: APPRAISAL OF THE NIGERIAN PETROLEUM INDUSTRY ACT 2021

Victor Ediagbonya and Comfort Tioluwani

ABSTRACT

There have been various concerns about the petroleum industry regulation in Nigeria, including issues regarding the protection of host communities. The host communities have hardly derived sustainable developmental value from petroleum resource exploration from their community. Instead, the exploration of petroleum and other mineral resources has caused some environmental, social and economic setback for these host communities. On 17 August 2021, the Petroleum Industry Act (PIA) 2021 was signed into law after over two decades of legislative stalemate. The PIA proposes a series of reforms purported to revolutionalise the petroleum industry. According to President Buhari, the Act will create a regulatory sphere that will ensure transparency and accountability across the oil and gas value chain (Ailemen, 2021). Chapter 3 of the Act deals with host communities' concerns. Its overall aim is to ensure host communities have access to sustainable prosperity. The notion of sustainable prosperity implies that the Act seeks to elevate host communities from the poverty baseline to a level of prosperity that satisfies the social, economic, environmental and intergenerational features. Therefore, this chapter examines the provisions of the Act, particularly Chapter 3, to determine its potential to achieve sustainable prosperity for host communities. The chapter shall also identify the weaknesses in the Act, which would otherwise limit its sustainable prosperity goal and how these challenges can be addressed.

Corporate Resilience
Developments in Corporate Governance and Responsibility, Volume 21, 201–218
Copyright © 2023 by Emerald Publishing Limited
All rights of reproduction in any form reserved
ISSN: 2043-0523/doi:10.1108/S2043-052320230000021010

Keywords: Petroleum exploration; stakeholders; host communities; mining; sustainable prosperity; Petroleum Industry Act

1. INTRODUCTION

For over 40 years, the mining industry, especially the oil and gas industry, has been the main source of revenue for the Nigerian economy. This has led to an increase in the income generated in the Nigerian economy; however, this is not without its consequence. Exploiting these resources has detrimental effects on the host communities where the explorations are carried out. There have been conflicts between communities, the government, host communities and corporations. Furthermore, the benefits from the industry have not been appropriately applied to the sustainable prosperity of the host communities who have suffered from the exploitation of petroleum and other mineral resources and the menace of the Nigerian state as a whole (Lugard, 2014). Ojakorotu and Okeke-Uzodike (2007) argued that host communities are violent towards oil companies because the activities of these corporations have led to high levels of damage to fishing areas and farmland within these communities. Thus, their source of livelihood is destroyed through the loss of productive farmland and marine resources.

More recently, there has been a growing distrust between the host communities and oil-producing companies. This has become rampant in most of the host communities in the Niger delta; therefore, if the extractive companies' activities are not adequately monitored, putting in place an effective corporate governance framework focussing on stakeholders' integration, the impacts of this distrust will be detrimental in the long run (Ojakorotu & Okeke-Uzodike, 2007). Therefore, it is argued that there is a need to protect the environment and monitor the extractive activities not just for the present generation but also for the future generation in order to have a sustainable future.

Sustainability refers to achieving goals without affecting the ability of future generations to achieve their own goals. The movement of sustainability has its foundation in social justice, conservationism, internationalism and other previous actions with strong histories (UN, 2021). Sustainability is a rounded approach that considers environmental, social and economic scopes, recognising that all must be taken into consideration together to achieve sustainable prosperity. In contrast, sustainable prosperity is a concept that demonstrates a broad, long-term vision for a community. It denotes a better and more comprehensive focus on positive change that aims at increasing the real community's wealth; thus, it refers to a healthier, happier and more prosperous future for the community (UN, 2021). Sustainable prosperity is essential in developing host communities, particularly regarding environmental protection and social and human development (Makpor & Leite, 2017). There have been various attempts by the Nigerian government to establish agencies and commissions and enact multiple regulations; however, these attempts have not yielded the desired result (Makpor & Leite, 2017). 16 August 2021 brought about a new dawn in the Nigerian petroleum industry as the President assented to the new Nigerian Petroleum Industry

Act (PIA) 2021; the Act included a plan to advance sustainable prosperity in host communities.

Thus, this chapter examines how oil exploration and exploitation in Nigeria have affected the host communities. The study will also evaluate the newly signed PIA to ascertain its level of protection for host communities and how the relevant aspect of the Act will achieve sustainable prosperity for host communities. The host communities are integral stakeholders for successful operations in the petroleum industry. This is why a chapter in Nigeria's PIA 2021 was dedicated to the development of the communities. Chapter 3 of the PIA deals with host communities' concerns. Its overall aim is to ensure those host communities have access to sustainable prosperity. The notion of sustainable prosperity implies that the Act seeks to elevate host communities from the baseline of poverty to a level of prosperity that satisfies the social, economic, environmental and intergenerational features. Some have suggested that Nigerian PIA 2021 creates a framework to support this development to foster sustainable prosperity and provides direct social and economic benefits to the host communities from petroleum activities. They further argued that the Act also encourages a cordial relationship between the oil corporations and host communities.

In light of the above, this chapter examines the provisions of the Nigerian PIA 2021, particularly Chapter 3, to determine its potential to achieve sustainable prosperity for host communities. This chapter will also identify the weaknesses in the Act, which would otherwise limit its sustainable prosperity goal and how these challenges can be adequately addressed.

2. CONCEPTUAL AND THEORETICAL FRAMEWORK

This study's theoretical framework is primarily based on stakeholder theory and sustainability. The aim is to investigate the relationships amongst study constructs, such as stakeholder rights and sustainability prosperity. It is argued that stakeholder theory deals with the satisfaction of stakeholder expectations by the corporation (Freidman, 1970).

Considering the increasing sustainability challenges, politicians, public interest groups, scholars and legal practitioners are paying more attention to the potentially negative environmental and social impacts of organisations' operations (Dyllick & Muff, 2016; Moldavanova & Goerdel, 2018). Thus, organisations are under increasing pressure to change how they conduct business and their internal procedures in order to support sustainable prosperity (Le Roux & Pretorius, 2016). However, sustainability scholars assert that those individual organisations do not know how to handle complex social and environmental sustainability issues alone but need to cooperate with their stakeholders to generate answers to sustainability challenges.

Using stakeholder theory in this chapter helps focus on only two parties: the organisation and the broad stakeholders. This perspective helps to efficiently analyse the relationship between the organisations, stakeholders and sustainable prosperity. To adequately address the issue of sustainable prosperity in host communities, it is essential to explore the stakeholder's theory, the concept of sustainability and its applicability in organisational sustainability.

2.1 Stakeholders' Theory

The stakeholder theory is a theory that rejects the shareholder perspective, which posits that directors only have the legal obligations to protect shareholders' interests because shareholders have a privileged place in an organisation as they bear the residual risks in the organisation (Freeman & Reed, 1983). According to Edward Freeman, who served as the foundation for this idea, shareholders are not the only ones in the organisation that bear the risk. Therefore, while pursuing profits, corporations must consider the interests of other interest groups (workers, clients, suppliers and creditors) without going against the moral values around which the corporation is built (Alfonso & Castrillón, 2021; Freeman, Harrison, & Zyglidopoulos, 2018).

Sternberg (1997) argued that the fundamental problem with the stakeholder theory is that the understanding can be stretched so that virtually everything, everywhere, can now be regarded as stakeholders. However, stakeholders will generally include taxpayers, local communities, management, employees, consumers, suppliers and creditors (Hill & Jones, 1992). Freeman's definition of stakeholders shows the important bi-directionality of stakeholders, defining stakeholders as: 'Any group or individual who can affect or [be] affected by the achievement of an organisation's objectives' (Freeman, 1984). Stakeholders can affect or be affected by the organisation's objective; it is also possible for some stakeholders to be on both sides, thus affecting and being affected by the organisation's objective (Freeman, 1984). In the view of the stakeholder theory, organisations cannot maximise the shareholder's interest at the expense of the other stakeholders, as this is not morally or economically efficient. Within the evolving research, the stakeholder theory has been conceptualised in three ways: the descriptive, instrumental and normative (Donaldson & Preston, 1995).

Although proponents of stakeholder theory argue that corporations consider the interest of all stakeholders, they do not stipulate how this should be addressed based on the varying interests of stakeholders. As a result, stakeholder theory has been criticised as unsuited with business operations and incapable of providing better corporate governance, business performance or business conduct (Donaldson & Preston, 1995). In this context, Michael Jensen (2001) suggests that the stakeholder theory can add to this a specification that the objective function of a firm is to maximise the overall long-term firm value and that all satisfaction is achieved when the overall long-term firm value is maximised. In this way, corporate executives may be better able to assess trade-offs between competing interest groups (Jensen, 2001).

2.2 Meaning of Sustainability

Sustainability, taken literally, refers to the ability to preserve an object, result or procedure across time (Basiago, 1999). However, within the development scholarship, most scholars and practitioners apply the concept to mean advancing and sustaining a strong economic, environmental and social system development (Milne & Gray, 2013). Sustainability is the practice of conducting business without causing harm to the environment, the community or society at large (Galpin, Whitttington, & Bell, 2015). In practical terms, increasing an organisation's long-term economic, social and environmental performance is what is meant by sustainability, corporate social responsibility, corporate social performance, turning green and the triple bottom line (Elkington & Rowlands, 1999). Firms today need systemic approaches to sustainability if they are to be competitive in the long term.

According to Stoddart et al. (2011), sustainability refers to the efficient and reasonable dispersal of resources intra-generationally and inter-generationally with the operation of socio-economic activities within the boundaries of a finite environment. On the other hand, Ben-Eli (2015) considers sustainability to be a dynamic balance in the interaction between the population and the carrying capacity of the environment such that the population increases to realise its full potential without creating irreversible adverse effects on the environment's carrying capacity on which it depends.

Hák, Janoušková, and Moldan (2016) argue that transforming society, the environment and the global economy into a sustainable one is one of the most challenging tasks facing people today because this has to be done in the context of planetary carrying capacity. The World Bank (2017) argues that this requires innovative approaches to managing reality. In furtherance of this argument, UNDESA (2017) argues that the ultimate goal of the concept of sustainability is essentially to ensure the appropriate alignment and balance between social, economic and environmental in terms of reproducibility. On the other hand, Mensah and Enu-Kwesi (2018) argued that the definition must also emphasise the concept of intergenerational justice, which is undoubtedly an important but difficult idea because the need of future generations is neither easily determined nor purposeful. Building on the above, contemporary theories of sustainability seek to prioritise and integrate social, environmental and economic models to address human challenges in a way that continuously benefits society (Farrukh, Chaudhry, & Batool, 2014).

2.3 Sustainable Development

When creating current development plans and practices, sustainable development can be understood as economic development which considers future generations' demands (Scopelliti et al., 2018). Government programmes make up a significant portion of the development process in developing and emerging markets; however, commercial groups play a far larger role in the process as these nations progress (Mensah, 2019). The phenomenon of sustainable development has gained recognition within the development discourse, having been linked to different definitions, meanings and explanations. Sustainable development is considered an approach to development that uses resources in a way that allows them (resources) to continue to exist for others (Mensah, 2019). Evers (2018) further aligns this concept with the principle of organising to achieve human development goals while maintaining the capacity of natural systems to provide natural resources and system services, ecology on which the economy and society depend.

2.4 Sustainable Prosperity

Prosperity does not only refer to wealth or economic growth, nor is it quantified by gross domestic product (GDP); it means developing the health of society, all-encompassing political structures, an assurance of human capital development and public freedom. It is also about the active involvement of the members of society in collaboratively structuring and producing their futures within the constraints of the planet's sustainability (Moore, 2015). People and economies should prosper, but they should do so in a way that allows them to withstand shocks, maintain a high quality of life and avoid exceeding planetary boundaries.

To achieve 'sustainable prosperity', there is a need for a new way of understanding and defining economic progress considering today's complex challenges, such as inequality, climate change, digitalisation, global health crises and conflict (EU, 2019). According to the development theory, there are three keys to prosperity: education, caring for common space and future-oriented thinking. The future-oriented thinking might signify the main key to prosperity (Nováçek, 2013).

To seriously consider long-term sustainable development, the problem of poverty cannot be completely avoided. Regarding the issue of income poverty, this depends on the standard of living of each society. A minimal income is required to meet the poverty threshold, such that it could provide, for example, food and shelter; the World Bank determined that a daily income of $1 (or $1.25 in today's dollars) per capita was the global cut-off for absolute (severe) poverty in 1990 (Nováçek, 2013). Not only is an agreement on the technique of sustaining and creating the resources necessary to live next to others at risk, but also some notion of how we wish to live with others. Focussing on values, living quality and what makes life valuable in unique situations differentiates prosperity from growth (Moore, 2015).

Sustainable prosperity is a concept that reflects the broader, longer-term vision of our community. It represents a higher and wider focus for positive change to foster true prosperity in our communities. In short, sustainable prosperity means a healthier, happier and more prosperous future. Sustainable prosperity depicts a consolidating and guiding vision that simultaneously targets gainful environmental and socio-cultural health. Sustainable prosperity includes efforts to maximise the value of place (environment) and identity (community) in local communities and foster healthy place-based economies. More specifically, the pursuit of sustainable prosperity better balances economic progress with environmental and public health concerns, social welfare, justice, happiness, community capacity, vitality and resilience (Padalino, 2011).

While the public sector needs to achieve long-term prosperity like in the United Kingdom, for example, the public sector bears major responsibility for health care, education and environmental protection, all of which are essential components of a thriving society (Moore, 2015). This is possible due to the presence of functioning institutions in the United Kingdom; so for a nation to be reformed to achieve sustainable prosperity, it requires an understanding of its existing institutions for mobilising labour and capital to grow and apply productive resources.

Sustainable prosperity is considered here, to cover the physical, mental, environmental, financial, educational and civic wellbeing of all individuals, families, communities and regions in a country. Furthermore, sustainable prosperity is one in which people everywhere have the ability to grow as human beings within environmental and resource limits. A prosperous country is concerned not only with its revenue and financial wealth but also with its citizens' health and wellbeing, access to good quality education and prospects for decent and rewarding work. Prosperity empowers fundamental human rights and freedoms. It must also grant the ability for people to participate significantly in common projects. Ultimately, a sustainable prosperous society must offer a credible and inclusive vision of social progress.

2.5 Stakeholders and Sustainability

The concept of stakeholder sustainability is closely related. Stakeholder theory is recognised as an overarching concept and part of the sustainability literature. With the evolvement of the concept of sustainability, stakeholders were increasingly considered as contributors to sustainable value creation, leading to a second shift focussing on value creation, not only for stakeholders. According to Marrewijk and Were (2003), corporate sustainability recognises organisations as part of a bigger framework whereby they cannot exist in isolation but only function through interaction with other parts of the framework. Accordingly, a number of scholars have argued that organisations should switch from purely managing stakeholders, which focusses on aligning stakeholder needs to reduce risks, to interaction-based approaches, in which organisations work with their stakeholders towards a common objective to achieve mutual benefits and collectively generate wealth.

Hörisch et al. highlight the role of educating stakeholders, establishing sustainability standards and creating stakeholder interactions based on a sustainability mindset and shared sustainability interest in order to overcome possible issues when applying stakeholder theory in sustainability management and strategies. As a result, more academics are recognising the need to move beyond the conventional logic of stakeholder impact and towards broader perspectives of stakeholder value creation, which include marginalised stakeholders and the environment as stakeholders.

Lock and Seele (2016) suggest putting sustainability at the centre of stakeholder conceptions and analysing how stakeholders may affect sustainability initiatives through their contributions. In a similar spirit, numerous academics emphasise the necessity of an overall issue-based approach that, when deciding with whom to contract, focusses not only on the organisation itself but also on a particular problem and the activities to deal with it. Furthermore, to develop a stakeholder business case for sustainability, Schaltegger, Hörisch, and Freeman (2019) emphasise involving all stakeholders who have an impact on or are impacted by the issue being resolved. In order to build products and services through stakeholder interaction, such a business case needs to establish stakeholder expectations towards a sustainability challenge.

3. HOST COMMUNITIES RIGHTS IN THE NIGERIAN OIL AND GAS COMMUNITIES

The Constitution of the Federal Republic of Nigeria (CFRN) 1999 (as amended) put Mines and Minerals, including oil fields, oil mining geological surveys and natural gas, under the exclusive legislative list; consequently, only the Federal Government has the ownership and control of minerals resources in Nigeria. Section 44 (3) of the CFRN 1999 (as amended) provide thus:

> Notwithstanding the foregoing provisions of this section, the entire property in and control of all minerals, mineral oils and natural gas in under or upon any land in Nigeria or in, under or upon the territorial waters and the Exclusive Economic Zone of Nigeria shall vest in the Government of the Federation and shall be managed in such manner as may be prescribed by the National Assembly.

The provision above forms the basis of ownership evident in several pieces of legislation, such as the Petroleum Act and the Nigerian Minerals and Mining Act 2007. For example, Section (1) (1) of the Petroleum Act provides that the entire ownership and control of all petroleum in, under or upon any lands to which this section applies shall be vested in the state; in the same vein, Section (1) (1) of the Nigerian Minerals and Mining Act, 2007 also vest control and ownership of all Mineral resources in the Federation government. In relation to the rights of host communities, Chapter 4 of the Nigerian Minerals and Mining Act, 2007 accorded host communities where mineral resources are found, and mining exploration is to carry out some rights, amongst other things; the Act provides that the communities have a right to winnings of materials such as salt, soda potash by host communities concerning areas covered by mining leases; prevention of mineral exploration in some areas; reserve of rights of titleholder or occupier of the land; imbursement of surface rents; evaluation of different compensations and payment; restoration of mined land; reclamation; Community Development Agreements; environmental obligations to include preparation and submission of environmental impact assessment and participation in the environmental protection and rehabilitation programme (Nwankwo, 2012; Olowokere & Abasilim, 2021).

3.1 Host Communities as Core Stakeholders in Oil and Gas Companies

According to Freeman 'a stakeholder in an organisation is any group or individual who can affect or is affected by the achievement of the organisation's objectives' (Freeman, 1984; Freeman et al., 2018). Different scholars have contributed to the literature on stakeholder discourse. This chapter adopts Clarkson's (1995) and Ostensson's (1997) specifications on stakeholders. Ostensson considers stakeholders in mining as individuals or group of persons, who has an interest, either economic, legal, political or ethical, in the result of a project or a process, and who has a stake in it (Ostensson). In the context of mining, stakeholder inclusion and the role they play is a dynamic process. Ostensson classified stakeholders into two parts, the primary (main) and secondary (peripheral) stakeholders. The primary stakeholders are those significantly affected by individual mining operations and whose objectives related to sustainable development relate primarily to those operations. This sets the case for the host communities (including the indigenous people and workers), the government and the mining companies themselves.

On the other hand, the secondary stakeholders are those who are by and large of a more extensive political, philosophical or social nature, such as Non-governmental Organisations (NGOs) and Intergovernmental Organisations (IGOs) (Ostensson, 1997). Investors, NGOs, workers for hire, shareholders, clients and insurers all fall under the secondary stakeholder because they have the ability to manipulate public opinion in favour of, or in contradiction to, the company's operations (Clarkson, 1995). This is evident, especially when issues emerge that draw their consideration, for example, project funding, environmental degradation to horticultural and traditional lands and water, corruption and lack of transparency, unjust income sharing, struggle and fundamental liberties infringement and so forth.

In the context of mining, this chapter also adopts Clarkson's (1995) and Ostensson's (1997) typology that categorises the government and host communities as their most significant stakeholders. Although this is a straightforward categorisation, they are contentious when mining communities differ in their expectations for mineral development. This turns out to be more delicate in situations where indigenous communities might be unrepresented and when there are gender orientation issues. The role of stakeholders also relies on local conditions and worldwide order or development; thus, Azapagic (2004) argued that identifying mining stakeholders is a pre-imperative for upgrading mining's commitment to development, even though working out the limits of rights and obligations had remained a challenge (Naibbi & Chindo, 2020).

3.2 Host Community and Their Rights Under the Petroleum Industry Act 2021

Under the recently signed PIA, it is stipulated that the purpose of the Act is to provide direct social and economic benefits from petroleum operations to members of the host communities, advance peaceful and harmonious co-existence between licensees and the host communities and finally create a structure to enhance the development of host communities (Section 234 (1) PIA 2021). The Act aims to provide social and economic benefits from petroleum activities. One of the innovations of the PIA 2021 is that it accords the host communities a right to be consulted before determining the membership of the board of trustees. So far as the memberships of the board of trustees must be persons of integrity with high professional standing; not only that but over and above all, the persons to be appointed must be members of the host community (Section 242 (2) PIA 2021). It is further argued that although the above provision is a novel addition which purports to recognise the rights of host communities generally, these are rights to which host communities are supposed to have been entitled but have been deprived of them for a long time.

3.3 Meaning and Types of Host Communities Within the Petroleum Industry Act

The PIA 2021 defines 'Host Community' as any community situated in or appurtenant to the area of operation of a licensee or lease (also known as the settlor), and any other community which the settlor identifies as a host community. Furthermore, for operators carrying out petroleum operations in shallow water and deep offshore, the host community will be the shoreline communities and any other community determined by the settlor. One would argue that the above definition is ambiguous because the coverage and range of host communities in Nigeria are not specified, making it difficult to determine which communities should be protected. The petroleum mining process involves different stages; there is the exploration and prospecting stage which is the identification of mineral deposits; there is also the discovery stage which includes the mine site design and planning; the next stage is the development stage, which is the longest stage of the process and the mine is prepared for production; the production stage, where the mine is finally ready for production and finally the reclamation stage which is the mine closure (Hughes, 2021).

From the preceding, it is clear that the mining process happens in different stages and different areas; therefore, it is essential to include all of these areas as the various processes occur in different parts or areas of the community. There are different types of host communities; this includes communities where the first stage, the exploration stage, takes place. The exploration stage is the most significant stage, and to open the mine, corporations must search for an economically adequate quantity of the mineral deposit which will make the exploitation worth it. The process includes surface mapping and sampling, tests, airborne and ground geophysical surveys and drilling, among others. However, in order to explore oil, there is a need to search through different areas within the community or communities. The stage alone cuts across different parts of the community and does not happen in a particular space; thus, in measuring or defining the host community, it is important to take into consideration the areas where all the stages of mining take place. The first stage of mining which is exploration might take place in a particular community and the discovery stage happens in another community, production stage might take place in another community, and this is because communities in Nigeria are close to each other and closely knitted, so it is crucial to have a clear definition of what host communities are and the specific acreage; it should not be restricted to only where the first stage of mining process takes place or generalised. The PIA further defines the host community as the community that the pipeline passes through (Section 235 PIA 2021). This definition excludes most stages within the mining process; for example, it outrightly excludes communities that do not produce oil. So communities where exploration or other stages of the mining process occur because the production stage does not take place there are excluded. The above definition is not misleading but is clearly unsustainable as it will further encourage corruption (Dagogo, 2021).

Given the above inadequacies in the PIA 2021 definition of the host community, exploring other definitions would no doubt help understand the scope and nature of the host community in the mining sector. The United Nations Framework Convention for Climate Change – Clean Development Mechanism, UNFCCC – CDM Projects as defined by European Union, EU Energy Security defines host communities as, 'communities that are 50-km radius within a project site' (Amaize, 2021). Therefore, in the interest of impacted host communities, it is important to adopt such a definition for clarity as it provides clear acreage on host communities.

4. ISSUES OF THE HOST COMMUNITIES DEVELOPMENT

The host community trust fund is a novel concept in Nigerian petroleum law primarily aimed at developing economic and social infrastructure in petroleum-producing communities. The PIA 2021 provides that there will be an establishment and financing of the host community trust. The settlor also known as the operator on behalf of a group of settlors must establish and be responsible for a trust, supervised by a board of trustees for the good of the host communities (Section 235 PIA 2021). The trust must be established with the Corporate Affairs Commission within 12 months of the Act's effective date or before the commencement of commercial operations for new licensees (Section 236 PIA 2021). The trust will establish a fund which will be funded by an annual contribution of three per cent of the actual yearly operating expenditure of the preceding financial year of upstream corporations. This fund can also be financed through gifts, grants, donations and interests accruing to the fund's reserve (Section 240 (2) PIA 2021).

4.1 Application of Host Communities Trust Funds

The board of trustees will every year allocate funds received in the following proportion: 75% is apportioned to the capital fund for capital developments, 20% is apportioned to the reserve fund to be invested for use where their settlor stops contributing to the settlor and 5% is apportioned for the administrative cost used for operating the trust (Section 244 PIA 2021). The funds of the trust will be exempted from taxation. Also, any payment made by the settlors to the fund will be deductible for tax purposes. In any year where an act of vandalism, sabotage or other civil unrest occurs that causes damage to petroleum and designated facilities or disrupts production activities within the host communities, the community will forfeit its entitlement to the extent of the cost of repairs. In the event that the settlors fail to incorporate a trust it will lead to revocation of licence or the lease (Section 257 PIA 2021). As a condition for the grant of a licence or lease and before the approval of the environmental management plan, the licensee or lessee is required to pay a prescribed financial contribution to an environmental remediation fund for the rehabilitation or management of negative environmental impacts of the petroleum operation. The financial contribution will take into consideration the dimensions of the operations and, therefore, the level of environmental risk. The major problem is the management of the fund; it is one to set up a trust fund, and it is another thing to put them to effective use. This financial responsibility on the part of the operators needs to be effectively monitored to ensure compliance, and the effective utilisation of the funds has to be monitored as well; however, the PIA 2021 failed to address this adequately.

4.2 Issues of Environmental Degradation

Another issue with host communities' development in Nigeria, particularly those within the oil-producing area, is that they experience environmental degradation ranging from pollution to oil spillages; as a result, the need to safeguard the environment cannot be exaggerated (Okongwu & Imoisi, 2020). Environmental pollution in Nigeria has severe implications for the public's health. The PIA 2021 provides environmental management by the Commission to foster environmental sustainability. By virtue of s.102 of the PIA 2021, a licensee or lessee who engages in upstream or midstream petroleum operations must submit an environmental management plan for approval to the Commission or Authority within a year or six months of the licence or lease's effective date or after it has been granted for the relevant project. Therefore, approval will generally be authorised if the applicant can mitigate and manage adverse environmental effects and the plan has been prepared to conform with the applicable Environmental Acts (s.102 (3) PIA, 2021).

It could be argued that though this is a laudable section as regards s.102 of the PIA 2021, it does not show a solid political commitment and thorough effort by the Nigerian government to reduce and eliminate environmental degradation that has besieged these oil-producing host communities in recent times (Okongwu & Imoisi, 2020). In fact, it is one thing for the PIA 2021, by virtue of s.102, to require those who carry out activities in the upstream and midstream to submit a management plan; however, the problem lies with the breaches that will occur, and they will enforce against those that fail to mitigate and effectively manage adverse environmental effects. In this regard, there is a need to strengthen the PIA 2021 and institutions that will effectively enforce the provisions.

Furthermore, the PIA 2021 also introduced the environmental management and annual control of gas flares. Section 102 (7) of the PIA 2021 provides an exception for gas flaring, which makes it legal after getting the minister's approval. Given that there are several instances of gas flaring and because it may now be allowed, things will get worse due to this failure. It is cliché that the nation does not enforce any of its laws about environmental damages or degradation. This is evident from the several breaches of these environmental laws around the country; in practical terms, it does not offer remedies to host communities other than deceit and abject poverty.

First, attaining environmental justice for host communities in the oil-producing areas in Nigeria affected by pollution entails more than just creating a rehabilitation fund under Section 235 of the PIA 2021, known as the 'host communities development trust'. Host communities have a fundamental right to a safe, healthy and positive environment. Conflicts over the environment are unavoidable, given the way oil exploration works. Regrettably, these oil-producing communities are the ones who suffer the most from the actions of multinational oil companies. One environmental issue, which is predominantly common in the Nigerian oil and gas industry, is frequently based on oil spills. The host communities in Nigeria's oil-producing areas suffer directly from these oil spills and other environmental issues. In Nigeria, the host communities in these oil-producing areas must contend with ongoing gas flaring because the PIA 2021 has normalised gas flaring as long as the minister's approval is sought. Gas flaring affecting the human habitat is a problem for host communities in these oil-producing areas in Nigeria (Adeola et al., 2022). Due to insufficient compensation for the adverse effects of oil exploration activities, host communities and oil companies in Nigeria continue to have disagreements (Hamilton, 2011).

However, it should be highlighted that environmental disputes frequently involve several parties and technical concerns, making them challenging to resolve. When you consider the significant environmental harm caused by oil exploration in the Nigerian oil-producing and mining region, the 3% allotted to the host communities by the PIA 2021 is insufficient. Sustainable local community development is advantageous to the extractive industry's profitability and ought to be a top priority in Nigeria's extraction of natural resources (Pedro et al., 2017).

4.3 Issues of Tribal Interrelation

Going by the numerous land-related conflicts in the oil-producing communities in the Niger Delta, there has undoubtedly been a shift in the character of the conflicts and an increase in the level of violence encompassing land ownership claims. This is especially true when such communal land has been discovered to contain oil or designated for oil exploration activities (Nwokolo, 2013). Imobighe (2004), using the Warri host communities as an example, claimed that as communities battle over land ownership, the violent trend, which is a recent phenomenon in the history of the Warri crisis, dates back to the early 1990s while the more recent unabating bloody conflict dates back to March 1997. As a result, such communities have suffered and continue to witness a period of communal violence due to disputes over control of oil-prospective land and seas in the Niger Delta (Imobighe, 2004).

Research has shown that several oil companies try to adopt the avoidance conflict handling mechanism. They do this by simply withdrawing and refusing to deal with the conflict; this, in turn, has enabled the communities to compete among themselves in different shapes and forms for control of such land and fishing water while the oil companies await the eventual winner from the conflict (Imobighe, 2004).

Okonta and Douglas (2003) characterised Shell's attempts to thwart collective demands from oil host communities by describing how 'Shell Police' are given 'service money' for gathering intelligence, buying information and making friends with residents of host communities in the oil spill areas. These villagers would then incite community disputes over conflicting compensation claims. Shell would then take advantage of this by alleging that it would not provide compensation because the communities were divided over who would receive what (Okonta & Douglas, 2003).

It is clear from the facts that each group makes every effort to show that they are legitimate owners and original landlords. They will stop at nothing to do this, even participating in a vigorous war for ownership and claims of such contested land. It is crucial to manage the interests of the competing host communities, especially before violent disputes over land ownership breaks out. Since 1960, the Nigerian government has formed about five unique agencies to promote regional development. These are the Federal Ministry of the Niger Delta, created in 2008, the Niger Delta Development Board, established under the 1960 Constitution by virtue of s. 159, there is also the Niger Delta River Basin Authority, inaugurated in 1976, as well as the Oil Minerals Producing Areas Development Commission (OMPADEC), constituted in 1992. There is also the Niger Delta Development Commission (NDDC), which replaced OMPADEC, established in 2000. Despite the various attempts to promote regional development within the oil-producing communities, no significant development has been drawn to the area. It is argued that these are steps in the wrong direction as it has opened up avenues for more communal clashes and tribal interrelation with the oil-producing host communities in the Niger Delta. The failures of previous interventions by the Niger Delta Development Commission (NDDC), Amnesty Programme, Ministry of Niger Delta Affairs and Niger Delta Basin and Rural Development Authority, among others, are due to a lack of stakeholders inclusion, particularly the Niger Delta people such as women in such interventions. It is argued that the aggravated environmental pollution caused by decades of oil exploration in the Niger Delta placed an extra burden on sustainable income and livelihood for families in the Niger Delta region, especially on women, who bear greater responsibility for caring for their families. These communal clashes can occur when these women tend to scavenge limited resources in order to fend for their families.

A review of the PIA 2021 shows no recourse to dealing with tribal and communal conflicts on oil-producing land and such a fundamental issue should have been taken very seriously. According to Cotula (2018), one of the most significant characteristics of sovereignty is the power of states to control activities on their soil. For long-term advantages to be sustained and gained from their natural resources, it is crucial to pursue economic development and sustainable environmental development (Cotula, 2018). Therefore, the PIA 2021 needs to provide a mechanism for dealing with tribal and communal conflicts for host communities in the oil-producing area of the Niger Delta.

5. CONCLUSION

Although the rationale behind the host community fund is based on advancing the overall socio-economic development of the oil-producing communities, the problem lies in the implementation of the Act. Indeed, similar obligations for remittances were utilised in the past under Oil Mineral Producing Areas Development Commission (OMPADEC) and Niger Delta Development Commission (NDDC) regimes (Ebeku, 2020). However, poor and/or corrupt implementation ravaged such exercises. Introducing the host community trust fund no doubt increases the administrative burden on the operators. This fund is a replica of the Niger Delta Development Commission (NDDC) fee, which is still in force. This is somewhat confusing and will become burdensome for the operators as it will also present an opportunity for settlors to pay the levy for the latter. Another curious and significant feature of the Petroleum Host Community Fund is the distinctive provision on the financiers: upstream petroleum-producing companies. There is an apparent absence of the midstream sectors, which involves refining, engineering and downstream sectors from the remittance obligation areas dominated by indigenous petroleum operators. The fact that International Oil Companies (IOCs) dominate the upstream sector seems to justify the premise that PIA 2021 is arguably targeted at international oil companies. It is submitted that the Nigerian PIA 2021 should have introduced a proportional remittance regime from both the midstream and downstream petroleum operations since their operations can similarly have harmful effects on the host communities similar to the upstream sector. Possibly at the very least, one per cent remittance regimes on midstream and downstream net profit would have sufficed to make things fair between the competing petroleum operators.

REFERENCES

Adeola, A. O., Akingboye, A. S., Ore, O. T., Oluwajana, O. A., Adewole, A. H., Olawade, D. B., & Ogunyele, A. C. (2022). Crude oil exploration in Africa: Socio-economic implications, environmental impacts, and mitigation strategies. *Environment Systems and Decisions, 42*, 26–50. doi:10.1007/s10669-021-09827-x

Ailemen, A. (2021, August 18). Buhari tells FEC that Nigeria lost $50b on delayed petroleum law. *Bussinessday Newspaper*. Retrieved from https://businessday.ng/news/article/buhari-tells-fec-that-nigeria-lost-50b-on-delayed-petroleum-law/

Alfonso, M., & Castrillón, G. (2021). The concept of corporate governance. *Visión de Futuro*, 173.

Amaize, E. (2021, July 28). Host com queries NASS on definition of host communities. *Nigerian Vanguard Newspaper*. Retrieved from https://www.vanguardngr.com/2021/07/hostcom-queries-nass-on-definition-of-host-communities/. Accessed on November 6, 2022.

Azapagic, A. (2004). Developing a framework for sustainable development indicators for the mining and minerals industry. *Journal of Cleaner Production, 12*, 639–662.

Basiago, A. D. (1999). Economic, social, and environmental sustainability in development theory and urban planning practice. *The Environmentalist*. Retrieved from https://www.amherst.edu/system/files/media/0972/fulltext.pdf. Accessed on October 20, 2022.

Ben-Eli, M. (2015). Sustainability: Definition and five core principles a new framework the sustainability laboratory New York. Retrieved from www.sustainabilitylabs

Clarkson, M. E. (1995). A stakeholder framework for analysing and evaluating corporate social performance. *Academy of Management Review, 20*, 92–108.

Cotula, L. (2018). Reconsidering sovereignty, ownership and consent in natural resource contracts: From concepts to practice. In M. Bungenberg, M. Krajewski, C. Tams, J. Terhechte, & A. Ziegler (Eds.), *European Yearbook of International Economic Law 2018* (Vol. 9). Cham: Springer. doi:10.1007/8165_2018_23

Dagogo, F. (2021, July 25). New definition of 'host community. Passed PIB, A Day-Break Robbery, *The Punch Newspaper*. Retrieved from https://punchng.com/new-definition-of-host-community-in-passed-pib-a-day-break-robbery-rivers-rep-dagogo/. Accessed on August 18, 2022.

Donaldson, T., & Preston, L. (1995). The stakeholder theory of the corporation: Concepts, evidence, and implications. *Academy of Management Review, 20*, 65–91.

Dyllick, T., & Muff, K. (2016). *Clarifying the meaning of sustainable business: Introducing a typology from business-as-usual to true business sustainability* (pp. 156). Thousand Oaks, CA: SAGE Publications.

Ebeku, K. (2020). Assessing the performance of the Niger Delta Development Commission (NDDC) 2001–2020: Another failed dream. *International Journal of Law and Society, 3*(3), 78–90. doi:10.11648/j.ijls.20200303.11

Elkington, J., & Rowlands, I. H. (1999). Cannibals with forks: The triple bottom line of 21st century business. *Alternatives Journal, 25*, 42–44.

European Commission. (2019). Sustainable growth for all: Choices for the future of social Europe. Retrieved from https://ec.europa.eu/social/main.jsp?catId=738&langId=en&pubId=8219#:~:text=%E2%80%9CSustainable%20growth%20for%20all%3A%20choices,to%20an%20environmentally%20sustainable%20economy

Evers, B. A. (2018). *Why adopt the sustainable development goals? The case of multinationals in the Colombian coffee and extractive sector*. Master Thesis. Erasmus University Rotterdam.

Farrukh, H., Chaudhry, M. N., & Batool, S. A. (2014). Assessment of key parameters in municipal solid waste management: A prerequisite for sustainability. *The International Journal of Sustainable Development and World Ecology, 21*(6), 519–525. doi:10.1080/13504509.2014.971452

Freeman, E. (1984). *Strategic management: A stakeholder approach*. Boston, MA: Pitman.

Freeman, R. E., Harrison, J. S., & Zyglidopoulos, S. C. (2018). *Stakeholder theory: Concepts and strategies*. Cambridge: Cambridge University Press.

Freeman, E., & Reed, D. (1983). Stockholders and stakeholders: A new perspective on corporate governance. *California Management Review, 25*, 88–90.

Freidman, M. (1970). The social responsibility of business is to increase profits. *New York Times Magazine*.

Galpin, T., Whitttington, J., & Bell, G. (2015). Is your sustainability strategy sustainable? Creating a culture of sustainability. *Corporate Governance, 15*, 1–3.

Hák, T., Janoušková, S., & Moldan, B. (2016). Sustainable development goals: A need for relevant indicators. *Ecological Indicators*, 565–573.

Hamilton, D. I. (2011, June). Oil and gas companies and community crises in the Niger Delta. *American Review of Political Economy*, 3–17.

Hill, C., & Jones, T. (1992). Stakeholder -agency theory. *Journal of Management Studies, 29*, 131. doi: 10.1016/S0959-6526(03)00075-1

Hughes, W. (2021). The stages of mining: 5 lifecycle processes explained. Retrieved from https://www.opens.co/articles/the-stages-of-mining

Imobighe, T. A. (2004). Conflict in Niger Delta: A unique case or a model for future conflicts in other oil-producing countries? In R. Traub-Merz (Ed.), *Oil Policy in the gulf of Guinea: Security and Conflict, Economic growth, social development*. Washington, DC: Fredrich Ebert Stiftin.

Jensen, M. (2001). Value maximisation, stakeholder theory, and the corporate objective function. *European Financial Management, 7*, 297–300.

Le Roux, C., & Pretorius, M. (2016). Conceptualising the limiting issues inhibiting sustainability embeddedness. *Sustainability, 8*, 364–366.

Lock, I., & Seele, P. (2016). The credibility of CSR (corporate social responsibility) reports in Europe. Evidence from a quantitative content analysis in 11 countries. *Journal of Cleaner Production, 122*, 186–200. doi:10.1016/j.jclepro.2016.02.060

Lugard, S. B. (2014). Stakeholder approach to corporate social responsibility: Recipe for sustainable peace in the Niger Delta Region? *Afe Babalola University: Journal of Sustainable Development Law and Policy, 4*(1), 154–173.

Makpor, M. E., & Leite, R. (2017). The Nigerian oil industry: Assessing community development and sustainability. *International Journal of Business and Management, 12,* 58–60.

Mensah, J. (2019). Sustainable development: Meaning, history, principles, pillars, and implications for human action: Literature review. *Cogent Social Sciences, 5,* 1–6.

Mensah, J., & Enu-Kwesi, F. (2018). Implications of environmental sanitation management for sustainable livelihoods in the catchment area of Benya Lagoon in Ghana. *Journal of Integrative Environmental Sciences, 16*(1), 23–43. doi:10.1080/1943815x.2018.1554591

Milne, M. J., & Gray, R. (2013). W(h)ither ecology? The triple bottom line, the global reporting initiative, and corporate sustainability reporting. *Journal of Business Ethics, 118*(1), 13–29.

Moldavanova, L., & Goerdel, H. T. (2018). Understanding the puzzle of organisational sustainability: Toward a conceptual framework of organisational social connectedness and sustainability. *Public Management Review, 20,* 55.

Moore, H. L. (2015). Global prosperity and sustainable development goals. *Journal of International Development, 27*(6), 801–804.

Naibbi, A. I., & Chindo, M. (2020). Mineral resource ex-tractive activities in Nigeria: Communities also matter! *Journal of Geoscience and Environment Protection, 8,* 212–214.

Novácek, P. (2013). Thinking oriented towards the future – Key to prosperity and sustainable development? *Foresight, 15*(5), 354–359.

Nwankwo, O. B. C. (2012). The challenges of political education in contemporary Nigeria: Re-thinking mission and re-planning strategies. *Education Research Journal, 2*(12), 392–399.

Nwokolo, N. N. (2013). The political economy of oil resource conflicts: A study of oil village communities in Nigeria. Retrieved from https://www.semanticscholar.org/paper/The-political-economy-of-oil-resource-conflicts%3A-A-Nwokolo/938750d664f4c5777774ce3dae2cabe0876687a2

Ojakorotu, V., & Okeke-Uzodike, U. (2007). Oil, arms proliferation and conflict in the Niger Delta of Nigeria. *African Journal on Conflict Resolution, 6,* 85–87.

Okongwu, C. J., & Imoisi, E. S. (2020). Enhancing environmental litigation: The key to sustainable environmental protection in Nigeria. *International Review of Law and Jurisprudence, 2,* 116.

Okonta, I., & Douglas, O. (2003). *Where vultures feast: Shell human rights and oil in the Niger Delta.* New York, NY: Crown Publisher.

Olowokere, E. N., & Abasilim, A. N. (2021). Rights of host communities to mineral resources for the empowerment of rural dwellers in Osun State Nigeria. *Journal of Sustainable Technology, 10,* 142–146.

Östensson, O. (1997). A brief background on social issues and mining. In *UNCTAD (United Nations Conference on Trade and Development),* Bandung, Indonesia, 14–15 October 1996. The Asian/Pacific Workshop on Managing the Social Impacts of Mining.

Padalino, T. (2011). What is sustainable prosperity? Pursuing Sustainable Prosperity. Retrieved from https://docs.google.com/viewer?a=v&pid=sites&srcid=ZGVmYXVsdGRvbWFpbnxwb3Npd2l2ZWNvbW11bml0eWNoYW5nZXxneDo0YzI5MDFiZTUwNzNjZWM1

Pedro, A., Ayuk, E. T., Bodouroglou, C., Milligan, B., Ekins, P., & Oberle, B. (2017). Towards a sustainable development licence to operate for the extractive sector. *Mineral Economics, 30,* 153–165. doi:10.1007/s13563-017-0108-9

Petroleum Industry Act (PIA). (2021). Retrieved from http://www.petroleumindustrybill.com/wp-content/uploads/2021/09/Official-Gazette-of-the-Petroleum-Industry-Act-2021.pdf

Schaltegger, S., Hörisch, J., & Freeman, R. E. (2019). Business cases for sustainability: A stakeholder theory perspective. *Organization & Environment, 32*(3), 191–212. doi:10.1177/1086026617722882

Scopelliti, M., Molinario, E., Bonaiuto, F., Bonnes, M., Cicero, L., De Dominicis, S., & Bonaiuto, M. (2018). What makes you a "hero" for nature? Socio-psychological profiling of leaders committed to nature and biodiversity protection across seven, EU countries. *Journal of Environmental Planning and Management, 61,* 970–993.

Sternberg, E. (1997). The defects of stakeholder theory. *Corporate Governance: An International Review, 5*(1), 3–10.

Stoddart, H., Schneeberger, K., Dodds, F., Shaw, A., Bottero, M., Cornforth, J., & White, R. (2011). A pocket guide to sustainable development governance (1st ed.). *Stakeholder Forum and Commonwealth Secretariat*. Retrieved from http://www.uncsd2012.org

UNDESA. (2017). *The Sustainable Development Goals Report*. Retrieved from https://desapublications.un.org/publications/sustainable-development-goals-report-2017

United Nations. (2021). *Development and international co-operation: Environment*. Report of the World Commission on Environment and Development: Our Common Future, Chapter 2: Towards Sustainable Development - A/42/427 Annex. Retrieved from http://www.un-documents.net/ocf-02.htm. Accessed on May 3, 2023.

Van Marrewijk, M., & Werre, M. (2003). Multiple levels of corporate sustainability. *Journal of Business Ethics, 44*, 107–119. doi:10.1023/A:1023383229086

REPORTING ON HUMAN RIGHTS BY LARGE CORPORATES: INTERPLAY BETWEEN COMPREHENSIVENESS AND NARRATIVE MANIPULATION

Leana Esterhuyse and Elda du Toit

ABSTRACT

Companies are often accused of using sustainability disclosures as public relations tools to manage financial and non-financial stakeholders' impressions. The purpose of our study was firstly to determine how comprehensive the human rights disclosures of a sample of large international companies were and secondly, whether different narrative styles are associated with levels of disclosure to manage readers' impressions about the company. We analysed the public human rights disclosures for 154 large, international companies obtained from the UN Guiding Principles Reporting website. On average, companies complied with only one-third of the UN Guiding Principles Reporting Framework criteria. Communication about policies has the highest compliance, whilst communication about determining which human rights aspects are salient to the company, remedies for transgressions and stakeholder engagement have the lowest disclosure. When we split the sample between high disclosure and low disclosure companies, we found that the readability of the human rights disclosures is exceptionally low and even more so for low disclosure companies. Low disclosure companies used words implying Satisfaction significantly more than high disclosure companies, which provides some support for suspecting that low disclosure companies practise impression management by only presenting a 'rosy picture', as well as obfuscation via low readability. We add to the literature on impression management by large corporations in their sustainability reporting, and specifically human rights disclosures, by revealing how the interplay of low disclosure, low readability and overuse of words signalling Satisfaction contributes to

Corporate Resilience
Developments in Corporate Governance and Responsibility, Volume 21, 219–242
ISSN: 2043-0523/doi:10.1108/S2043-052320230000021011

impression management, rather than sincere attempts at accountability to all stakeholders.

Keywords: Human rights; UN Guiding Principles on Business and Human Rights; UN Guiding Principles Reporting Framework; sustainability; impression management; accountability; narrative analysis

1. INTRODUCTION

Profit maximisation for the exclusive benefit of shareholders is no longer tolerated in the twenty-first century. Companies are now held accountable to a broader range of stakeholders, e.g., employees, customers, local communities, suppliers and environmental groups (Badia, Bracci, & Tallaki, 2020; De Villiers & Maroun, 2018b; Eccles & Saltzman, 2011; European Union, 2014; IIRC, 2013, 2021; OECD, 2011, 2015). Reporting requirements were first developed for the disclosure of financial information but now stretch much further. Various bodies, such as the Global Reporting Initiative (GRI), the United Nations (UN) Global Compact, the Organisation for Economic Co-operation and Development (OECD), the European Union (EU) and the International Integrated Reporting Council require the disclosure of non-financial information about factors that affect non-financial stakeholders of the company. The disclosure of non-financial information, e.g. about the environment, society and corporate governance (ESG)[1] has moved from trendy to necessary as financial and non-financial stakeholders demand better information (Böhling & Murguía, 2014; Camilleri, 2018, 2019; De Villiers, 2018; De Villiers, Low, & Samkin, 2014; De Villiers & Maroun, 2018a; Fonseca, 2010; Maubane, Prinsloo, & Van Rooyen, 2014). Apart from the rising demand for such non-financial information, the disclosure of non-financial aspects can also create a competitive advantage for preparers by attracting more customers and other interested parties (Cannon, Ling, Wang, & Watanabe, 2019). Sustainability reports also focus on the benefits a company brings to the larger society, e.g., employment opportunities and taxes paid to governments, contradicting the traditional profit maximisation dictum (Carroll & Shabana, 2010).

Corporate reporting on sustainability has become more widespread but it is still criticised for lack of value, as it requires significant resources without necessarily bringing about improved ESG performance (Shift and Mazars, 2017a). The various sustainability reporting guidelines are not (yet) compulsory in all regions of the world[2] and non-financial narrative reporting are in many cases not yet independently audited (Ackers, 2017; Hess, 2019; Ngwakwe &

---

[1]ESG and sustainability are used interchangeably.
[2]We note the recent release of draft sustainability disclosure standards by the International Sustainability Standards Board (ISSB) and the EFRAG Sustainability Reporting Board that will become compulsory at future dates in certain domains. These standards were not considered when the study was conducted.

Mtsweni, 2016). Management thus still has a lot of discretion in how they communicate to non-financial stakeholders about sustainability issues.

'Human rights' is one of the disclosure topics falling under the 'Social' category of ESG non-financial disclosures. Several recent academic studies investigated the scope of human rights disclosures by companies. Lauwo and Otusanya (2014), Cahaya and Hervina (2019), Krasodomska and Godawska (2020) and Wahab (2020) report low levels of disclosure and a lack of detail and substance. These studies focused on companies in developing economies and in single jurisdictions. The purpose of our study is firstly to answer these authors' calls for further research by evaluating the comprehensiveness of human rights disclosures of a sample of large, multinational companies headquartered worldwide and in a diversity of industries.

The second line of inquiry of our research into human rights disclosures focuses on the readability and narrative tone employed in these disclosures. The purpose of corporate reporting is to inform and persuade readers. Persuasion happens through the provision of objective information, but also via management's narrative choices deployed in the disclosures published that affect the readability and narrative tones of these disclosures. Both readability and tone can be used for impression management (IM) or obtaining/maintaining legitimacy by making the company's performance appear different from its actual performance (Diouf & Boiral, 2017) or to hide or obfuscate the truth (Hasan, 2018; Smeuninx, De Clerck, & Aerts, 2020). Sustainability disclosures often emphasise positive aspects while downplaying the negative (De Villiers & Maroun, 2018b; Diouf & Boiral, 2017; Emel, Makene, & Wangari, 2012). The second purpose of our study was thus to determine if there are associations between the comprehensiveness of human rights disclosures and the readability and narrative tones in those disclosures as a means to manage impressions.

Our study interrogated a database of human rights disclosures collected and curated by Shift Project Ltd and Mazars LLP and which is publicly available on the Reporting Framework Project website. Human rights disclosures were collected by staff from Shift Project Ltd and Mazars LLP from public sources for 154 large international companies and mapped in the database according to the disclosure requirements of the United Nations Guiding Principles (UNGP) Reporting Framework (Shift and Mazars, 2017b). We constructed a disclosure index based on the UNGP Reporting Framework as a measure of the comprehensiveness of human rights disclosures. Readability and narrative tone were analysed by two software programmes.

We find that on average, companies only complied with a third of the guidelines or criteria contained in the UNGP Reporting Framework (Shift and Mazars, 2017b). Companies focus on describing policies and procedures, but substance on implementation plans and remedies for transgression is scant. Human rights disclosures are difficult to read, especially for companies that fall into the low disclosure group. The narrative tone indicates the use of opportunistic use of language. Both readability and narrative tone were employed by companies in the low disclosure group to manage impressions or to obfuscate poor performance. Our main contribution lies in showing how narrative manipulation, intending to manage impressions, seems to be present in human rights disclosures of the sample companies, instead of clear, unbiased communication. If companies use specific narrative strategies or reduced readability in disclosures, it brings into question the reliability and informational value thereof and reduces the decision-making power of the information to the reader. When one examines the findings in terms of semiotics, the concepts that are signified to the reader by the signifiers (the words) are not grounded in reality, but specific words are used to form a favourable impression. Or the signifiers are so difficult to comprehend that the reader fails to 'receive' the concept that is signified, i.e., obfuscation. This research thus has value for all stakeholders with an interest in the activities of a company, as it illustrates whether the information contained in narrative human rights disclosures is balanced and understandable.

Section 2 reviews the prior literature and develops the research questions. In Section 3, we discuss our data and methodology. Section 4 presents the empirical results, and the discussion follows in Section 5. Section 6 concludes.

2. LITERATURE REVIEW

2.1 Theoretical Foundation

Companies are accountable to a wide variety of stakeholders (Eccles, Ioannou, & Serafeim, 2014; Hassan, 2019; IIRC, 2013, 2021; OECD, 2011, 2015), including investors, employees, customers, suppliers, the government, and a plethora of others. The interest of the stakeholders in the behaviour of the company goes beyond financial performance. Information on how companies protect and foster human rights in their dealings with employees, local communities, customers, and suppliers is important to these stakeholders. Stakeholder theory is thus the first theory on which this study is based (Freeman, 1984). Without stakeholders, a company cannot exist, and disclosure of sustainability information is supposedly aimed at all stakeholders (Badia et al., 2020) as it is the main (often only) source of dialogue between a company and its stakeholders (Zeng, 2017).

The publication of human rights information also extends to legitimacy theory (Dowling & Pfeffer, 1975; Suchman, 1995), as companies use such disclosures, as part of their broader ESG disclosures, to legitimise their actions for the benefit of stakeholder opinions (Badia et al., 2020; Böhling & Murguía, 2014; Camilleri, 2019; De Villiers et al., 2014; Maubane et al., 2014). In terms of human rights disclosures, stakeholders are not only interested in a company's actions and their direct impact on human rights but also in its indirect impact through relationships in the value chain (European Union, 2014; GRI, 2021; Shift and Mazars, 2017b). Reporting on policies alone is not sufficient; the actual implementation of processes to prevent human rights abuses is crucial and should form part of disclosures if the company wants to achieve legitimacy with its stakeholders.

Corporate reports could also be used for impression management (IM). IM theory is closely linked to legitimacy theory, as it is concerned with the manipulation of public perceptions to obtain or maintain legitimacy and support from stakeholders (Diouf & Boiral, 2017; Hess, 2019; Jones, Melis, Gaia, & Aresu,

2017; Stacchezzini, Melloni, & Lai, 2016; Zeng, 2017). IM strategies in the corporate reporting context can be used for either defensive or assertive purposes (Martins, Gomes, Oliveira, & Ribeiro, 2019; Tedeschi & Melburg, 1984).[3] IM defensive strategies include the deliberate hiding of under-performance through poor readability and rhetorical manipulation, or obfuscation (Diouf & Boiral, 2017; Hasan, 2018; Smeuninx et al., 2020) or writing disclosures in optimistic language to create the impression that all is well (Fonseca, 2010). IM assertive strategies aim to emphasise the positive through techniques such as overly positive word choices and repetition (Huang, Teoh, & Zhang, 2014; Kang, Park, & Han, 2018; Na, Lee, Choi, & Kim, 2020). Disclosures of human rights policies and practices can thus also be described using words that create favourable impressions.

To understand *how* word choice can affect readers' impressions, it is also important to briefly discuss a few seminal authors' works on communication theories. The Sapir–Whorf hypothesis (Lucy, 2001; Sapir, 1949; Whorf, 1956), also known as the linguistic relativity hypothesis, postulates that the particular language one speaks influences the way one thinks about reality. Corporate sustainability reports of large multination companies, including their human rights disclosures, are prepared in English. The reports would be written and/or quality controlled by persons with English as their first or home language. The words in the report would be relative to these authors' cultural experiences as English first-language speakers. The audience or readers of these disclosures are, however, situated anywhere in the world, and English is likely their second language. Hence, the meaning or perception created by the words might be different for the readers. Another theory of communication is called semiotics, or the study of signs. De Saussure (2011) proposed that each sign consists of a physical *signifier* (a symbol or word) and a *signified* (a concept). The other prominent influence in semiotics was Peirce (2003). Peirce categorised signs into three main types, namely an *icon*, which resembles its referent (e.g., picture of a campfire); an *index*, which is associated with its referent (e.g., smoke is a sign of fire); and a symbol, which is related to its referent only by convention (e.g., a $-sign for money). In the field of corporate reporting, the words in the reports are the signifiers and the meanings constructed by the readers are the signified. The signified for each reader will then be determined by their native language and other cultural contexts (Sapir–Whorf hypothesis). Hence, what the authors of a corporate report meant might not be perceived in the same way by every reader. Crowther (2018) applies the theory of semiotics to corporate reporting by describing the role players as participating in a movie. The company's officials are the authors of the script (the report), and the readers or stakeholders are the audiences. The author has no control over how the script is interpreted by the audience, nor who is in the audience. Hence, the author (company) should try to communicate in a language that is understandable by a diverse audience. In our

---

[3]For an excellent overview of defensive and assertive IM tactics explored in other studies see Martins et al. (2019).

paper, we argue that signifiers (certain words) in human rights disclosures are used to create signified concepts in the minds of readers that are beneficial to how the company's actions and policies are perceived (i.e., impression management). We do not consider how English second language speakers interpret the disclosures.

In the next section, we briefly describe the main domain-agnostic reporting frameworks that require companies to consider their impact on non-financial stakeholders and report on these impacts.

2.2 Global Stakeholder Reporting Frameworks

We start the discussion by considering who is deemed to be stakeholders of a company in addition to the shareholders and other funding providers (financial stakeholders). The Integrated Reporting Framework (IRF) (IIRC, 2013, p. 33) defines stakeholders as:

> Those groups or individuals that can reasonably be expected to be significantly affected by an organization's business activities, outputs or outcomes, or whose actions can reasonably be expected to significantly affect the ability of the organization to create value over time. Stakeholders may include providers of financial capital, employees, customers, suppliers, business partners, local communities, NGOs, environmental groups, legislators, regulators, and policy-makers.

This definition is echoed by the OECD Guidelines for Multinational Enterprises (OECD, 2011, p. 28) where it refers to 'a variety of users ranging from shareholders and the financial community to other constituencies such as workers, local communities, special interest groups, governments and society at large'. The G20/OECD Principles of Corporate Governance (OECD, 2015, p. 9) points out that 'The Principles recognise the interests of employees and other stakeholders and their important role in contributing to the long-term success and performance of the company'. The GRI 101: Foundation (GRI, 2016, p. 8) defines stakeholders as 'employees and other workers, shareholders, suppliers, vulnerable groups, local communities, and NGOs or other civil society organizations, among others'. In conclusion, since the early 2010s, various governance and reporting frameworks explicitly acknowledged that non-financial stakeholders should be considered as important stakeholders of the company.

Next, we consider whether non-financial stakeholders should be considered as the intended audience of sustainability reports and other communication that contain non-financial information. Paragraph 1.3 of the IRF (IIRC, 2013, p. 7) proposes that 'An integrated report benefits all stakeholders interested in an organization's ability to create value over time, including employees, customers, suppliers, business partners, local communities, legislators, regulators and policy-makers'. Paragraph 3.14 continues 'An integrated report enhances transparency and accountability, which are essential in building trust and resilience, by disclosing how key stakeholders' legitimate needs and interests are understood, considered and responded to through decisions, actions and performance, as well as ongoing communication' (IIRC, 2013, p. 18).

In Chapter III Disclosure of the OECD Guidelines for Multinational Enterprises (OECD, 2011, p. 27), paragraph 2 (g) stipulates disclosure of material information on 'issues regarding workers and other stakeholders'. Paragraph 3 (e) encourages additional communication of 'information on relationships with workers and other stakeholders' (OECD, 2011, p. 28). In Commentary paragraph 28, it is advised that 'enterprises should be transparent in their operations and responsive to the public's increasingly sophisticated demands for information (OECD, 2011, p. 28)'. In similar vein, Chapter V Disclosure and Transparency of the G20/OECD Principles of Corporate Governance (OECD, 2015, p. 38) in principle A 2 encourages companies 'to disclose policies and performance relating to business ethics, the environment and, where material to the company, social issues, human rights and other public policy commitments'. Principle B (OECD, 2015, p. 42) stipulates that 'Information should be prepared and disclosed in accordance with high quality standards of accounting and financial and non-financial reporting'. Lastly, GRI 101: Foundation (GRI, 2016, p. 8) stipulates that:

> When making decisions about the content of its report, the organization is to consider the reasonable expectations and interests of stakeholders. This includes those who are unable to articulate their views and whose concerns are presented by proxies (for example, NGOs acting on their collective behalf); and those with whom the organization cannot be in constant or obvious dialogue.

To summarise, we presented evidence of multiple governance and reporting frameworks that not only identifies non-financial stakeholders such as workers of the company or workers in its supply chain, as well as local communities, as legitimate stakeholders of a company but also require that companies report on policies and performance aspects that affect these non-financial stakeholders in their sustainability reports or via other communication channels.

Next, we discuss the specific framework we used to measure the comprehensiveness of human rights disclosures as a subset of sustainability disclosures.

2.3 UNGP Reporting Framework as Gold Standard for Reporting on Human Rights

Companies face multiple potential human rights matters, depending on the industry, location and other factors. Human rights violations the public is most familiar with include, amongst others, forced labour, child labour, unsafe working conditions and discrimination (Cahaya & Hervina, 2019; Hess, 2019; Lauwo & Otusanya, 2014; Wahab, 2020).[4] However, human rights violations are not limited to employees and include violations against the general populace, for example, the effect of pollution, the misuse of farmland or other natural resources

---

[4]Two examples of non-academic articles reporting on businesses that are not acting in the best interest of society are 'Fishing industry must do more to tackle human rights abuses – here's where to start' (Armstrong, 2020) and 'As cobalt demand booms, companies must do more to protect Congolese miners' (Baumann-Pauly & Cremer Iyi, 2020).

and the violation of people's privacy. Koch, Pesce, Fogelberg, and Steer (2016) argue that companies need to understand that they will be increasingly scrutinised by stakeholders for their impact on society, and that they must manage human rights issues for the entire value chain. Companies that fail to consider human rights in their activities face potential legal action and reputational risk (Elayan, Brown, Li, & Chen, 2019; United Nations, 2017).

Human rights concerns have been on the agenda since 1948 when the United Nations (UN) proclaimed the Universal Declaration of Human Rights. However, at that time only governments were responsible to uphold the principles of human rights protection. Since 2008, with the launch of the Protect, Respect, and Remedy Framework, the responsibility of companies in this drive to protect human rights has come to the fore (Ruggie, 2008). Companies' responsibility for human rights, in addition to that of state actors, was formalised with the release of the UN Guiding Principles (UNGP) on Business and Human Rights in 2011 (McPhail, Ferguson, & Adams, 2016; United Nations, 2011). Other sustainability reporting frameworks that address, amongst others, businesses' obligations concerning human rights practices and disclosures are the 10 principles and the 17 sustainable development goals (SDGs) from the United Nations Global Compact (United Nations, 2000, 2015), the standards of the Global Reporting Initiative (GRI, 2021) and ISO 26000 (International Standards Organization (ISO), 2010).

In 2015, Shift and Mazars (2017a) released the UN Guiding Principles (UNGP) Reporting Framework (updated in 2017) as a tool to assist companies with their reporting on human rights in their sphere of influence. The UNGP Reporting Framework is based on the UNGP on Business and Human Rights (United Nations, 2011). The UNGP Reporting Framework is grouped into three parts. Part A covers the Governance of Respect for Human Rights. Part B defines the Focus of Reporting and Part C guides the Management of Salient Human Rights Issues, supported by high-level questions and further guidance (150 criteria in total).

Sustainability reporting has increased significantly on a global scale (Arena, Liong, & Vourvachis, 2018; Cho, Michelon, & Patten, 2012), and progress has been made in attempts to understand the relevance of human rights disclosures in particular (GRI, 2021). Unfortunately, separate disclosure of ESG-related content (and thus human rights) is often criticised for being mere publicity tools (Boiral, 2013; Cho et al., 2012; Emel et al., 2012; Maas, Schaltegger, & Crutzen, 2016), to manage expectations as part of a legitimisation process (Arena et al., 2018; Badia et al., 2020; Cahaya & Hervina, 2019; Lauwo & Otusanya, 2014; Wahab, 2020), and thus failing to adequately describe progress in managing ESG matters (Martínez-Ferrero, Suárez-Fernández, & García-Sánchez, 2019). However, transparent disclosure of some topics can have a positive follow-through effect on a company's actual principles and operations, if managed effectively (Hess, 2019; McPhail & Adams, 2016; Wahab, 2020). However, Hess (2019) believes that many companies include human rights in non-financial disclosures just so that they can say they did, which results in imbalanced, incomplete and contradictory reports. Lauwo and Otusanya (2014) analysed human rights disclosures in Tanzania and found the disclosures to be vague and lacking in detail on how human rights issues are dealt with. They call for further research into the accountability of companies regarding human rights obligations. In their analysis of the human rights disclosures of 75 Indonesian companies, Cahaya and Hervina (2019) found low levels of disclosure, implying that these companies hide information related to child and forced labour. From a study of Polish companies, Krasodomska and Godawska (2020) concluded no relationship between the human rights practices that the companies declare and their human rights disclosures in terms of ISO 26000. In the human rights disclosures of palm oil companies in Malaysia, Wahab (2020) found a lack of detail and substance.

To conclude, these previous studies on human rights disclosures report low levels of disclosure, seemingly done for IM purposes and not for true transparency and accountability reasons. These studies focused on companies in developing economies and in single jurisdictions. The purpose of our study is firstly to answer these authors' calls for further research by evaluating the comprehensiveness of human rights disclosures of a sample of large, multinational companies.

Our first research question thus is:

How comprehensive are the human rights disclosures of the sample of large, multinational companies as measured against the UNGP Reporting Framework?

2.4 Qualitative Characteristics of Sustainability Disclosures

The purpose of corporate disclosures is to communicate companies' activities, but they can be written in a way that influences stakeholders' perceptions, i.e., IM, about corporate social responsibility issues by, for example, focusing on positive news and ignoring the negative. Koch et al. (2016) and Hess (2019) emphasise the importance of qualitative human rights disclosures and that qualitative information needs to be clear and free from bias. To prevent biased reporting from companies on sustainability issues, many frameworks provide reporting principles. The GRI standards require balance, comparability, accuracy, timeliness, clarity and reliability (Badia et al., 2020; Diouf & Boiral, 2017; Hassan, 2019). Unfortunately, the application of the GRI guidelines varies greatly and stakeholders opine that sustainability reports are prepared for IM and obfuscation purposes (Diouf & Boiral, 2017). We assume that these critiques also apply to reporting on human rights in terms of the GRI Standards. Along similar lines, the European Union (EU) Directive on the Disclosure of Non-Financial Information provides six principles, namely that disclosure should be material; fair, balanced and understandable; comprehensive but concise; strategic and forward-looking; stakeholder orientated; and consistent and coherent (Hess, 2019). However, Michelon, Pilonato, and Ricceri (2015) and Parsa, Roper, Muller-Camen, and Szigetvari (2018) found that the disclosure guidelines from the EU have not improved the quality of disclosure and that companies tend to simply increase the quantity of reporting in an attempt to obtain legitimacy and manage impressions. The UNGP Reporting Framework (Shift and Mazars, 2017b) has seven reporting principles. Principle F requires reporting entities to supply balanced examples from relevant geographies, i.e., disclosures 'should be balanced and broadly representative of the company's performance'. Principle G requires explanations of any omissions of important information. However, unless such disclosures are audited or independently verified, disclosure can potentially still be presented in a way that creates a good impression of a company (Arena et al., 2018; Emel et al., 2012; Merkl-Davies & Brennan, 2011).

Prior research indicates that stakeholders prefer short, focused and readable disclosures (Caglio, Melloni, & Perego, 2020; Lambert, Leuz, & Verrecchia, 2007; Zhou, Simnett, & Green, 2017). In the same way that obfuscation can be used to hide poor results (Smeuninx et al., 2020), it can also be used to hide the truth about the company's ESG impact by enhancing positive news and down-playing negative news (Jones et al., 2017; Stacchezzini et al., 2016). Companies can use poor readability to confuse the reader, while persuasive language (for example, overly optimistic language) can be used to subtly manipulate a reader's impression of the company. Corporate reports should be concise, apply a neutral tone and be written in plain language that enhances readability (Smeuninx et al., 2020; Stone & Lodhia, 2019). A low-quality report is recognised for being long, difficult to read and biased by using specific narrative tone(s) (Bonsall IV, Leone, Miller, & Rennekamp, 2017; Caglio et al., 2020; Huang et al., 2014; Loughran & McDonald, 2016). We were, thus, interested to find out what the readability and narrative tone differences are between companies that have greater compliance with the UNGP Reporting Framework versus those with less compliance. This could potentially point towards IM strategies to obfuscate or to be overly positive.

This leads us to our second research question:

Are there differences in the readability and dominant narrative tones between High Disclosure companies and Low Disclosure companies in the sample?

3. RESEARCH DESIGN

3.1 Sample and Disclosure Index

Our study made use of secondary data. To answer the first research question, we sourced the text of the human rights disclosures from the https://www.ungpreporting.org/ website that Shift and Mazars LLP co-developed. The *Database of Corporate Reporting* on the website was created and populated by a team of analysts that combed through their sample companys bodies of public disclosures and then captured and mapped individual human rights disclosures to the criteria in the UNGP Reporting Framework standard. Any human rights disclosures captured in the reporting database were publicly accessible from the sample companies' websites or other public sources. It excludes any documents, data or other material that was only available to the company's employees. We downloaded the most recent human rights disclosures available on the website on 23 August 2020. The

'Download all' function downloaded an excel file with the disclosures of 154 large multinational companies. It contained the most recent year's reporting for each company, which ranged from 2015 to 2019. A list of companies, industry, reporting year and continent where the headquarters are located is available in https://www.ungpreporting.org/database-analysis/explore-disclo sures/.

As described previously, the UNGP Reporting Framework (Shift and Mazars, 2017b) consists of three main parts, supported by high-level questions, sub-question and further guidance. We construct our disclosure score from the criteria listed in the downloaded excel file, which contained 150 criteria in total. The downloaded excel file contained separate sheets for each part of the reporting framework and its supporting high-level questions, i.e., 12 sheets. Within each sheet, each company had its column containing its human rights disclosures and an adjacent *Source* column that showed the public source where the Shift and Mazars assessors found the information. For Part C, Management of Salient Human Rights Issues, the six sheets had an added column listing *Salient Issues* if the company chose to disclose this. Within each sheet, some rows contained the text of the various disclosure criteria and beneath each criterium, each company's disclosures were contained in separate columns. If the criterium was addressed by more than one disclosure from different source documents, each disclosure was contained in a separate row. In order not to prejudice companies who made extensive disclosures in one source (i.e., their disclosure was captured in one row) vis-à-vis companies who made piecemeal disclosures in different sources (i.e., their disclosures were captured in multiple rows, one for each source), we used a dichotomous scoring system. If any number of disclosures were made for a criterium, it earned 1, otherwise, 0. We added all the scores and divided them by 150 (the maximum available marks) to obtain a total human rights disclosure score (THRDS) based on the UNGP Reporting Framework guidelines. Subgroups were similarly scored by dividing by the maximum available marks for that group.

3.2 Computerised Narrative Analysis Tools

To answer our second research question, we conducted computerised narrative analyses on the sample of human rights disclosures by 154 large, international companies. The use of software in textual analysis presents benefits such as inherent stability, comparability, coder reliability and the ease of processing large volumes of text (Al-Najjar & Abed, 2014; Laskin, 2018; Short, McKenny, & Reid, 2018). Various studies have investigated the readability of corporate disclosures (Bonsall IV et al., 2017; Bonsall & Miller, 2017; Du Toit, 2017; Hasan, 2018; Hemmings, Hodgkinson, & Williams, 2020; Loughran & McDonald, 2014, 2016; Smeuninx et al., 2020), while others investigated the tone of narrative disclosures (Arena, Bozzolan, & Michelon, 2015; Cho, Roberts, & Patten, 2010; Hassan, 2019; Laskin, 2018; Park, Byun, & Choi, 2020).

To measure the readability of the human rights disclosures, the study used Readability Studio 2019. We select the Flesch Reading Ease measure (Hasan,

2020; Smeuninx et al., 2020). The readability score is calculated as follows (Smeuninx et al., 2020, p. 56):

- 206.835 − 1.015 * average sentence length) − (84.6 * average syllables per word)

A higher Flesch Reading Ease score indicates better readability.

The narrative style of the disclosures was measured using Diction 7.1.3 and its associated built-in wordlists or dictionaries, similar to other sustainability and CSR studies (Arena et al., 2015; Cho et al., 2010; Hassan, 2019; Kim & Kim, 2017; Park et al., 2020). Hart (2000) developed Diction, which was improved by Hart and Carroll (2013). Diction measures the textual characteristics of a piece of text to determine if specific language strategies were applied. A Diction narrative analysis results in standardised scores based on the frequencies with which words from the various Diction dictionaries occur in the text. The individual dictionaries are added and subtracted in certain combinations to arrive at the five broader narrative strategies or tones, namely Certainty, Optimism, Activity, Realism and Commonality (Hart, 2000).[5]

The Readability Studio and Diction outputs for the human rights disclosures were captured and summarised in excel. The excel file with the readability, narrative tone and THRDS metrics was then imported into SPSS 26. We conducted Shapiro–Wilk tests to find whether our continuous variables were normally distributed. The THRDS and the three readability variables were normally distributed, as well as the Certainty narrative tone. After winsorising two outliers per variable of the other four tone variables, Commonality passed the normality threshold. Logarithmic transformations succeed to normalise the Activity tone variable, but not Optimism nor Realism. Tests involving these two variables were conducted on a non-parametric basis.

To answer our second research question, we then split the sample at the median for the THRDS variable into a high disclosure group (equal to and larger than the median) and a low disclosure group (less than the median count). We then conducted parametric and non-parametric tests to find whether there are significant differences between the two groups' readability and narrative styles.

4. RESULTS

4.1 Disclosure Comprehensiveness

Fig. 1 presents the frequency distribution for the 154 companies' THRDS as well as the descriptive statistics. We see that the mean for the THRDS is very low at 33.06% compliance (based on 150 criteria or guidelines from the UNGP Reporting Framework), and with a standard deviation of 11.13%. The minimum THRDS was six per cent, which is surprising for companies of this size. The

---

[5]See the appendix to Laskin (2018) for a full table with more details.

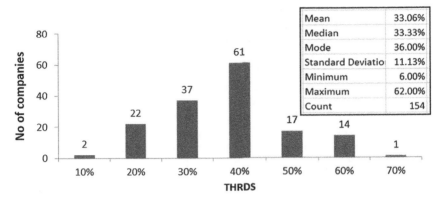

Fig. 1. Frequency Distribution of the Total Human Rights Disclosure Score (THRDS). *Source:* Authors' own analysis.

maximum THRDS was 62%. The median THRDS was 33.33% and the modus is in the band of 30–40% with a total of 61 companies. Tests confirmed that the data were normally distributed.

To better understand the criteria that companies struggle with or chose not to comply with, we present the compliance scores Part in Table 1. Not surprisingly, all the companies reported at least one salient area where human rights concern

Table 1. Disclosure Compliance Based on Guidelines From the UNGP Reporting Framework.

Criteria	Max	Average compliance
Part A – Governance	*43*	*40.47%*
Policy commitment	11	55.49%
Embedding respect for human rights	32	35.27%
Part B – Defining a focus	*18*	*16.67%*
Statement of salient issues	1	100.00%
Determination of salient issues	8	21.27%
Choice of focal geographies	4	4.87%
Additional severe impacts	5	2.47%
Part C – Management of salient human rights issues	*89*	*32.81%*
Specific policies	6	49.35%
Stakeholder engagement	19	30.93%
Assessing impacts	8	38.88%
Integrating findings and taking action	23	36.39%
Tracking performance	5	48.57%
Remediation	28	22.96%
Total	*150*	*33.06%*

Source: Authors' own analysis.

them. The second highest area of compliance was with respect to making policy commitments to address human rights issues (55.49%), followed by descriptions of specific policies regarding the management of human rights issues identified as salient to the business (49.35%) and then tracking performance to show impact from policy implementation (48.57%). The guidelines with the least disclosures centre on describing the impacts of other severe human rights issues that occurred in the period other than those salient issues identified (2.47%). This could be because there were no such issues, or legal advice cautioned management not to disclose it, or they chose not to disclose it due to negative publicity. Very few companies also disclosed a specific geographic area where they focus on human rights issues (4.87%).

4.2 Narrative Analysis of the Full Sample

Next, we discuss the univariate analysis of the narrative analysis for the full sample of 154 companies. From Table 2, we can see that the length of the disclosures varies from 820 to 27,573 words, resulting in a large standard deviation. The mean number of words for human rights disclosures per company is 9,359. Applying the general rule of thumb of 500 words per page (12-font, single-spaced, one-inch margins) means the human rights disclosures captured in the database cover on average about 19 pages per company.

The Flesch Reading Ease results in a score between 1 and 100, with lower values indicating poorer readability. The 'zero to 30' bracket refers to text that is *Very Difficult* to read, or for an individual holding at least a postgraduate degree (e.g., in the range of scientific material). The 24.37 average score for the Flesch Reading Ease measure means that the human rights disclosures tend to be *Very Difficult* to read.

As Diction standardises the measures, the five metrics for narrative tone can be compared directly to each other. From Table 2, we see that the most dominant narrative tone in our sample of large international companies is Certainty. Certainty relates to *[l]anguage indicating resoluteness, inflexibility, and completeness*

Table 2. Descriptive Statistics for Narrative Analysis (Full Sample).

$n = 154$	Mean	Std. Deviation	Minimum	Maximum
Readability				
Total words	9,358.29	6,189.52	820.00	27,573.00
Flesch Reading Ease	24.37	6.46	6.00	42.00
Narrative tones				
Certainty	50.26	2.68	42.05	58.27
Commonality	50.07	2.37	44.77	59.83
Activity	49.63	2.14	42.16	56.94
Optimism	49.47	3.21	32.01	56.69
Realism	48.92	4.61	35.01	57.05

Source: Authors' own analysis from Readability Studio and Diction output.

and a tendency to speak ex-cathedra. The high score for Certainty is founded on the high compliance with describing policies and procedures relating to human rights as these are determined by the company. In terms of IM, it also portrays a positive image of the company as a responsible corporate citizen that implements policies and procedures to manage human rights issues. Commonality follows with the next highest score. Commonality refers to *[l]anguage highlighting the agreed-upon values of a group and rejecting idiosyncratic modes of engagement.* This could be part of an IM strategy to secure legitimacy as the company is projecting that it has the same values as the community. It is also aligned with the theme of human rights in that they are using words that show cooperation and rapport, which is needed when addressing human rights. The tone with the lowest prominence in the human rights disclosures is Realism, which also had the highest standard deviation showing a wide range of applications of this style or tone. Realism is *[l]anguage describing tangible, immediate, recognizable matters that affect people's everyday lives'.* A low score for Realism in this sample could point to IM and obfuscation in that companies shy away from being specific and discussing sensitive issues in general or vague terms.

Optimism had the second-highest standard deviation. Realism and Optimism were the two metrics that did not follow a normal distribution, which is borne from their exceptionally low minimum scores compared to the other three tone metrics. Optimism was the second least visible tone in the texts. Optimism is *[l]anguage endorsing some person, group, or event or highlighting their positive entailments.* Activity was the third most used narrative tone, and it refers to *[l]anguage featuring movement, change, the implementation of ideas and the avoid-ance of inertia.* Companies could employ this tone to show that they are doing 'something' about human rights, but in this sample, they do not appear to be overstating their plans and actions for safeguarding human rights. Low compli-ance with guidelines to report on 'Integrating findings and taking action' as well as 'Remediation' supports the middle ranking for tones relating to Activity. We argue that this also supports IM as companies are good with talking about policies and processes, but less forthcoming about actual actions.

4.3 Analysis of Differences

For our second research question, we wanted to determine whether lower/higher compliance with human rights disclosure guidelines is associated with lower/higher readability and specific narrative tones. We split the sample at the median THRDS, resulting in a high disclosure group (80 companies) and a low disclosure group (74 companies). For the metrics with normal distributions, we ran independent sample *t*-tests to determine if there were significant differences between the two groups.

From Table 3 we can see that there are significant differences between the readability of disclosures by companies in the low disclosure group versus that of the high disclosure group. The low disclosure group's readability was significantly lower. Interestingly, when we look at the three metrics for the narrative tones that

Table 3. Differences in Means – Independent Samples t-test for Normally Distributed Variables.

	Disclosure Compliance Group	N	Mean	Std. Deviation	Std. Error Mean	t	Sig (2-Tailed)
Flesch Reading	Low disclosure	74	22.32	7.18	0.84	−3.958	0.000[a]
Ease	High disclosure	80	26.26	5.05	0.56		
	High disclosure	80	15.59	1.22	0.14		
Certainty	Low disclosure	74	50.58	2.83	0.33	1.426	0.156
	High disclosure	80	49.96	2.51	0.28		
Ln_Activity_win	Low disclosure	74	3.90	0.04	0.01	−0.532	0.596
	High disclosure	80	3.91	0.04	0.00		
Commonality_win	Low disclosure	74	50.37	2.28	0.27	1.741	0.084
	High disclosure	80	49.74	2.24	0.25		

Source: Authors' own analysis.
[a]Significant at the .000 level.

were normally distributed, none of them is significantly different between the two groups when applying the conventional five per cent significance cut-off.

Next, we conducted non-parametric tests on differences in mean ranks between the low disclosure group and the high disclosure group for the Optimism and Realism tone metrics (Table 4). We found that the low disclosure group scored significantly higher for Optimism than the high disclosure group, as their mean Optimism rank is much higher and statistically significant. When we ran the non-parametric Mann–Whitney U tests (untabulated) on the six subaltern dictionaries that constitute Optimism, we found that the biggest difference between the two groups lies in the Satisfaction score [$U = 2201.000, p = 0.006$]. The mean rank (mean) for the low disclosure group was 87.76 (2.2455) and that of the high disclosure group 68.01 (1.4966). Diction describes Satisfaction as *[t]erms associated with positive affective states (cheerful, passionate, happiness), with moments of undiminished joy (thanks, smile, welcome) and pleasurable diversion (excited, fun, lucky), or with moments of triumph (celebrating, pride, auspicious) ... words of nurturance: healing, encourage, secure, relieved.* Although not

Table 4. Differences in Mean Ranks – Mann-Whitney U tests for Tone Variables Not Normally Distributed.

	Disclosure Compliance Group	N	Mean Rank	Mean	Sum of Ranks	Mann-Whitney U	Asymp. Sig (2-Tailed)
Optimism	Low disclosure	74	87.08	50.16	6444.00	2251.000	0.010[a]
	High disclosure	80	68.64	48.82	5491.00		
Realism	Low disclosure	74	70.45	48.29	5213.00	2438.000	0.059
	High disclosure	80	84.03	49.50	6722.00		

Source: Authors' own analysis.
[a]Significant at .01 level.

statistically significant at conventional levels [$U = 2449.500$, $p = 0.065$], words signifying Inspiration are also used more by the low disclosure group. The mean rank (mean) for the low disclosure group was 84.40 (6.4601) and that of the high disclosure group 71.12 (4.7496). According to Diction, Inspiration is signified by *[a]bstract virtues deserving of universal respect. Most of the terms in this dictionary are nouns isolating desirable moral qualities (faith, honesty, self-sacrifice, virtue) as well as attractive personal qualities (courage, dedication, wisdom, mercy). Social and political ideals are also included: patriotism, success, education, justice.* Usage of the Praise, Blame, Hardship and Denial dictionaries show no significant differences between the two groups. Overall, the low disclosure companies managed impressions by describing the company as nurturing, caring and exhibiting high moral values.

For the Realism tone, the finding is the opposite, i.e., low disclosure companies had lower Realism tone words in their disclosure than the high disclosure companies, and the difference was not statistically significant at conventional levels of a five per cent cut-off (5.9%). This also supports IM strategies by low disclosure companies as they avoid using words that point to concrete actions and plans.

5. DISCUSSION

When considering the comprehensiveness of our sample's human rights disclosures, the mean human rights disclosure score (measured against the UNGP Reporting Framework) is 33.06%. Surprisingly, this indicates a low level of compliance with best practice guidelines by these 154 large companies located throughout the world. Our measure of comprehensiveness for human rights disclosures is marginally lower than the 36.74% reported for 75 Indonesian companies' human rights disclosures, as measured against the GRI guidelines (Cahaya & Hervina, 2019). Islam, Haque, and Roberts (2017) analysed the human rights disclosures of the top 50 Australian mineral companies against a disclosure checklist of 88 indicators. Companies in high-risk countries disclosed information in their annual reports against 25% of the indicators, whilst companies in low-risk countries only disclosed against 16% of the indicators. Parsa et al. (2018) reported on labour and human rights disclosures by 131 transnational companies using the GRI guidelines as well. No composite compliance metric is available as results are reported by indicator. They concluded that the companies failed to adhere to the guidelines. Wahab (2020) measured human rights disclosures of 16 Malaysian palm oil companies against a disclosures index consisting of 20 items and found poor disclosure of risks and the mitigation thereof. As only individual item disclosure frequencies were reported and no aggregate score, we cannot make direct comparisons to the findings of Wahab (2020). In answer to research question one, we conclude that it seems that companies, whether multinational or located in developing countries, are not very forthcoming in communicating how they secure human rights for their workers, communities and workers in the value chain. Companies focus on describing policies and procedures but are less willing to describe action plans and remedies where transgressions have taken place.

Hess (2019) argued that much of human rights disclosures are for the 'sake of disclosure and create reports that are unbalanced, incomprehensive, and inconsistent'. Hence, our second research question attempted to determine whether higher (lower) disclosure compliance is associated with improved (decreased) narrative quality of the disclosures. To answer the research question, we split our sample into companies that only complied with a low number of guidelines vis-à-vis those that complied with more guidelines. We report that low disclosure companies provide less readable human rights disclosures. For these companies, it supports the notion of IM tactics (an active strategy) through obfuscation of the few disclosures that are supplied. A slightly more benevolent interpretation could be that readability is low for low disclosure companies because they are still only considering their sophisticated institutional shareholders and funders as their only audience when they report minimally on human rights issues. What is encouraging, however, is that high disclosure companies, which strive to provide a fuller picture, i.e., disclose more in the different guidelines, also produce more readable reports. High disclosure companies seem to have better readability because they appear to be more sensitive to non-financial stakeholders as the intended audience of the human rights disclosures.

When it comes to the five narrative tones, only Optimism is significantly different between the two groups. We found that low disclosure companies are significantly more prone to use optimistic language. Specifically, the low disclosure companies used words signifying Satisfaction and Inspiration more. This might be a signal of assertive IM strategies, when low disclosure companies only provide selective disclosures, they use positive language to create the impression that is 'in control' of the human rights issues and that everything is rosy. They describe the company as nurturing, caring and exhibiting high moral values. For research question 2, we conclude that readability and narrative tone manipulation are present when large, international companies reported on how they managed human rights issues. Coupled overall with low compliance with disclosure standards for human rights, it points to these disclosures being mostly public relations exercises to manage impressions and to obtain or maintain legitimacy with stakeholders. The findings also support the theory of semiotics, i.e., the use of certain words (signifiers) to signal certain qualities (the signified) that supports assertive IM strategies.

6. CONCLUSION

Companies are increasingly required to report on how they manage human rights issues relating to their workers, nearby communities and in their supply chain. The first aim of our study was to determine the degree of compliance with human rights disclosure standards as advocated by the well-known UNGP Reporting Framework. We scored the human rights disclosures of 154 large international companies from multiple industries, located worldwide and covering the period from 2015 to 2019. The average disclosure compliance, based on the 150 criteria in the UNGP Reporting Framework (Shift and Mazars, 2017b), was only 33%. The low compliance level is surprising as it is not much different from compliance levels found in developing countries. The highest compliance was found regarding disclosures on human rights policies and procedures, whilst action plans and remedies received scant attention. The second aim of the study was to determine whether there are associations between compliance levels on the one hand and readability and narrative tone on the other. When we analysed the readability of low disclosure companies' human rights disclosures, we found them to be less readable and quite possibly attempts at obfuscation. However, for high disclosure companies, readability improved, pointing towards attempts at sincere accountability. When comparing the narrative tone between the two groups, we found no differences in the main narrative tones, except for Optimism. Further analysis pointed to low disclosure companies deploying a more Optimistic tone by increasing invoking concepts of Satisfaction and Inspiration, which points to the use of language as an IM tool. From a semiotic perspective, report authors seemed to use signifiers (words) that signified positive concepts (qualities) about the company being 'in control', whilst also being 'caring' and 'moral'.

Our main contribution is to the emergent stream of research on the 'S' in ESG reporting by focusing on human rights disclosures by companies. Prior research on human rights disclosures mostly focused on single-country studies in developing countries. We extend this research by evaluating the comprehensiveness of disclosures of a sample of large, international companies. The low levels of compliance point to the fact that even larger, better-resourced companies do not heed stakeholders' requests for better information on human rights issues. Our second contribution is to illuminate how low disclosure companies use low readability and Optimism as a narrative tone to manage impressions. As far as we can ascertain, ours is the first study to use computerised text analysis tools to study impression management in human rights disclosures specifically. We demonstrate how semiotics invoking positive concepts are used in managing impressions by corporate authors.

From a practical point of view, the publicly accessible https://www.ungpre porting.org website is a handy resource for other researchers and preparers of human rights disclosures. We also call on report preparers to be mindful of their word choices so that disclosures support accountability and IM and obfuscation are avoided. Corporate report authors can use the narrative analysis software, at minimal cost, to review their texts and correct overly biased reports. Report writers should be cognisant of the different cultural and language backgrounds of potential readers of the reports. Concomitantly, regulators should be aware of how companies use narrative styles which lead to biased and difficult-to-comprehend reports, which is counterproductive to the objective of being accountable. Despite multiple *voluntary* frameworks requiring that companies should consider the interest of non-financial stakeholders and report on that in a fair and unbiased manner, it seems that companies, even large ones, only comply notionally and uses narrative strategies to hide their poor performance. Regulators should consider requiring that sustainability disclosures for the largest corporate groups in the world should be compulsory as well as being assured. We note the current work of the ISSB and EFRAG in this regard.

Our study also has limitations. Our sample consisted of only 154 companies' disclosures. Even though this is larger than the samples used in many other human rights disclosure studies, it still limits robust statistical analysis. We encourage other researchers to expand the number of texts analysed by for example including more years' disclosures for each company. Panel data analyses could also indicate improvements over time (or not). Another avenue for investigation is exploring the impact of company characteristics, such as size, industry sector or location of headquarters on how IM manifests in human rights disclosures. Increasing mandatory standards of sustainability disclosure might improve future disclosures and reduce heterogeneity in disclosure quality. Future studies could also investigate how the companies are perceived by readers (audience) for whom English is not their first language.

CONFLICTS OF INTEREST

Both authors declare none.

REFERENCES

Ackers, B. (2017). The evolution of corporate social responsibility assurance – A longitudinal study. *Social and Environmental Accountability Journal, 37*(2), 97–117. doi:10.1080/0969160X.2017. 1294097

Al-Najjar, B., & Abed, S. (2014). The association between disclosure of forward-looking information and corporate governance mechanisms: Evidence from the UK before the financial crisis period. *Managerial Auditing Journal, 29*(7), 578–595. doi:10.1108/MAJ-01-2014-0986

Arena, C., Bozzolan, S., & Michelon, G. (2015). Environmental reporting: Transparency to stakeholders or stakeholder manipulation? An analysis of disclosure tone and the role of the board of directors. *Corporate Social Responsibility and Environmental Management, 22*(6), 346–361. doi: 10.1002/csr.1350

Arena, C., Liong, R., & Vourvachis, P. (2018). Carrot or stick: CSR disclosures by Southeast Asian companies. *Sustainability Accounting, Management and Policy Journal, 9*(4), 422–454. doi:10. 1108/SAMPJ-06-2016-0037

Armstrong, C. (2020). Fishing industry must do more to tackle human rights abuses – Here's where to start. *The Conversation.* Retrieved from https://theconversation.com/fishing-industry-must-do-more-to-tackle-human-rights-abuses-heres-where-to-start-149762. Accessed on November 23, 2020.

Badia, F., Bracci, E., & Tallaki, M. (2020). Quality and diffusion of social and sustainability reporting in Italian public utility companies. *Sustainability, 12*(11), 4525. doi:10.3390/su12114525

Baumann-Pauly, D., & Cremer Iyi, S. (2020). As cobalt demand booms, companies must do more to protect Congolese miners. *The Conversation.* Retrieved from https://theconversation.com/as-cobalt-demand-booms-companies-must-do-more-to-protect-congolese-miners-149486. Accessed on November 25, 2020.

Böhling, K., & Murguía, D. (2014). Sustainability reporting in the mining sector: Why institutional dynamics of reporting disappoint beliefs in its potentials for increased corporate accountability. Paper presented at the Conference on *Regulatory Governance between Global and Local ECPR Standing Group on Regulatory Governance,* Barcelona, Spain, 25–27 June 2014.

Boiral, O. (2013). Sustainability reports as simulacra? A counter-account of A and A+ GRI reports. *Accounting, Auditing & Accountability Journal, 26*(7), 1036–1071. doi:10.1108/AAAJ-04-2012-00998

Bonsall IV, S. B., Leone, A. J., Miller, B. P., & Rennekamp, K. (2017). A plain English measure of financial reporting readability. *Journal of Accounting and Economics, 63*(2–3), 329–357. doi:10.1016/j.jacceco.2017.03.002

Bonsall, S. B., & Miller, B. P. (2017). The impact of narrative disclosure readability on bond ratings and the cost of debt. *Review of Accounting Studies, 22*(2), 608–643. doi:10.1007/s11142-017-9388-0

Caglio, A., Melloni, G., & Perego, P. (2020). Informational content and assurance of textual disclosures: Evidence on integrated reporting. *European Accounting Review, 29*(1), 1–29. doi:10.1080/09638180.2019.1677486

Cahaya, F. R., & Hervina, R. (2019). Do human rights issues matter? An empirical analysis of Indonesian companies' reporting. *Social Responsibility Journal, 15*(2), 226–243. doi:10.1108/SRJ-10-2016-0171

Camilleri, M. A. (2018). The integrated reporting of financial, social and sustainability capitals: A critical review and appraisal. *International Journal of Sustainable Society, 9*(4), 311–326. doi:10.1504/IJSSOC.2017.090523

Camilleri, M. A. (2019). Theoretical insights on integrated reporting: Valuing the financial, social and sustainability disclosures. In S. Idowu & M. Del Baldo (Eds.), *Integrated reporting. CSR, sustainability, ethics & governance* (pp. 61–76). Cham: Springer.

Cannon, J. N., Ling, Z., Wang, Q., & Watanabe, O. V. (2019). 10-K disclosure of corporate social responsibility and firms' competitive advantages. *European Accounting Review, 1–29.* doi:10.1080/09638180.2019.1670223

Carroll, A. B., & Shabana, K. M. (2010). The business case for corporate social responsibility: A review of concepts, research and practice. *International Journal of Management Reviews, 12*(1), 85–105. doi:10.1111/j.1468-2370.2009.00275.x

Cho, C. H., Michelon, G., & Patten, D. M. (2012). Impression management in sustainability reports: An empirical investigation of the use of graphs. *Accounting and the Public Interest, 12*(1), 16–37. doi:10.2308/apin-10249

Cho, C. H., Roberts, R. W., & Patten, D. M. (2010). The language of US corporate environmental disclosure. *Accounting, Organizations and Society, 35*(4), 431–443. doi:10.1016/j.aos.2009.10.002

Crowther, D. (2018). *A social critique of corporate reporting: A semiotic analysis of corporate financial and environmental reporting.* Oxfordshire: Routledge.

De Saussure, F. (2011). *Course in general linguistics.* New York, NY: Columbia University Press.

De Villiers, C. (2018). Stakeholder requirements for sustainability reporting. In C. De Villiers & W. Maroun (Eds.), *Sustainability accounting and integrated reporting.* Abindon: Routledge.

De Villiers, C., Low, M., & Samkin, G. (2014). The institutionalisation of mining company sustainability disclosures. *Journal of Cleaner Production, 84*(1), 51–58. doi:10.1016/j.jclepro.2014.01.089

De Villiers, C., & Maroun, W. (2018a). The future of sustainability accounting and integrated reporting. In C. De Villiers & W. Maroun (Eds.), *Sustainability accounting and integrated reporting.* Abingdon: Routledge.

De Villiers, C., & Maroun, W. (2018b). Introduction to sustainability accounting and integrated reporting. In C. De Villiers & W. Maroun (Eds.), *Sustainability accounting and integrated reporting.* Abington: Routledge.

Diouf, D., & Boiral, O. (2017). The quality of sustainability reports and impression management: A stakeholder perspective. *Accounting, Auditing & Accountability Journal, 30*(3), 643–667. doi:10.1108/AAAJ-04-2015-2044

Dowling, J., & Pfeffer, J. (1975). Organizational legitimacy: Social values and organizational behavior. *Pacific Sociological Review, 18*(1), 122–136. doi:10.2307/1388226

Du Toit, E. (2017). The readability of integrated reports. *Meditari Accountancy Research, 25*(4), 629–653. doi:10.1108/MEDAR-07-2017-0165

Eccles, R., Ioannou, I., & Serafeim, G. (2014). The impact of corporate sustainability on organizational processes and performance. *Management Science*, *60*(11), 2835–2857. doi:10.1287/mnsc.2014.1984

Eccles, R., & Saltzman, D. (2011). Achieving sustainability through integrated reporting. *Stanford Social Innovation Review Summer*, *59*(2011), 56–61.

Elayan, F. A., Brown, K., Li, J., & Chen, Y. (2019). The market response to mandatory conflict mineral disclosures. *Journal of Business Ethics*, 1–30. doi:10.1007/s10551-019-04283-9

Emel, J., Makene, M. H., & Wangari, E. (2012). Problems with reporting and evaluating mining industry community development projects: A case study from Tanzania. *Sustainability*, *4*(2), 257–277. doi:0.3390/su4020257

European Union. (2014). Directive 2014/95/EU of the European Parliament and of the Council of 22 October 2014 amending directive 2013/34/EU as regards disclosure of non-financial and diversity information by certain large undertakings and groups. Retrieved from https://eur-lex.europa.eu/legal-content/EN/TXT/PDF/?uri=CELEX:32014L0095. Accessed on November 14, 2022.

Fonseca, A. (2010). How credible are mining corporations' sustainability reports? A critical analysis of external assurance under the requirements of the international council on mining and metals. *Corporate Social Responsibility and Environmental Management*, *17*(6), 355–370. doi:10.1002/csr.230

Freeman, R. (1984). *Strategic management: A stakeholder approach*. Boston, MA: Pitman.

GRI. (2016). *GRI 101: Foundation*. Retrieved from https://www.globalreporting.org/how-to-use-the-gri-standards/resource-center/. Accessed on July 31, 2021.

GRI. (2021). *Universal standards*. Retrieved from https://www.globalreporting.org/how-to-use-the-gri-standards/gri-standards-english-language/. Accessed on May 10, 2022.

Hart, R. (2000). *Diction 5.0: The text analysis program*. Thousand Oaks, CA: Sage.

Hart, R., & Carroll, C. (2013). *Diction 7: The text analyses program*. Austin, TX: Digitext.

Hasan, M. M. (2020). Readability of narrative disclosures in 10-K reports: Does managerial ability matter? *European Accounting Review*, *29*(1), 1–22. doi:10.1080/09638180.2018.1528169

Hassan, A. (2019). Verbal tones in sustainability assurance statements: An empirical exploration of explanatory factors. *Sustainability Accounting, Management and Policy Journal*, *10*(3), 427–450. doi:10.1108/SAMPJ-06-2017-0051

Hemmings, D., Hodgkinson, L., & Williams, G. (2020). It's OK to pay well, if you write well: The effects of remuneration disclosure readability. *Journal of Business Finance & Accounting*. doi:10.1111/jbfa.12431

Hess, D. (2019). The transparency trap: Non-financial disclosure and the responsibility of business to respect human rights. *American Business Law Journal*, *56*(1), 5–53. doi:10.1111/ablj.12134

Huang, X., Teoh, S. H., & Zhang, Y. (2014). Tone management. *The Accounting Review*, *89*(3), 1083–1113. doi:10.2308/accr-50684

IIRC. (2013). *The International Integrated Reporting Framework*. Retrieved from https://integratedreporting.org/resource/international-ir-framework/. Accessed on April 7, 2021.

IIRC. (2021). *The International Integrated Reporting Framework*. Retrieved from https://integratedreporting.org/resource/international-ir-framework/. Accessed on February 9, 2022.

International Standards Organization (ISO). (2010). *ISO 26000:2010 guidance on social responsibility*. Retrieved from https://www.iso.org/standard/42546.html. Accessed on December 7, 2020.

Islam, M. A., Haque, S., & Roberts, R. (2017). Human rights performance disclosure by companies with operations in high risk countries: Evidence from the Australian minerals sector. *Australian Accounting Review*, *27*(1), 34–51. doi:10.1111/auar.12108

Jones, M. J., Melis, A., Gaia, S., & Aresu, S. (2017). Impression management and retrospective sense-making in corporate annual reports: Banks' graphical reporting during the global financial crisis. *International Journal of Business Communication*, *57*(4), 1–23. doi:10.1177/2329488417712010

Kang, T., Park, D.-H., & Han, I. (2018). Beyond the numbers: The effect of 10-K tone on firms' performance predictions using text analytics. *Telematics and Informatics*, *35*(2), 370–381. doi:10.1016/j.tele.2017.12.014

Kim, D., & Kim, S. (2017). Sustainable supply chain based on news articles and sustainability reports: Text mining with Leximancer and DICTION. *Sustainability*, *9*(6), 1008. doi:10.3390/su9061008

Koch, I., Pesce, D., Fogelberg, T., & Steer, C. (2016). *Shining a light on human rights: Corporate human rights performance disclosure in the mining, energy and financial sectors*. Retrieved from https://media. business-humanrights.org/media/documents/files/documents/Shining_a_Light_on_Human_Rights_ 2016_report.pdf. Accessed on November 25, 2020.

Krasodomska, J., & Godawska, J. (2020). CSR in non-large public interest entities: Corporate talk vs. Actions. *Sustainability, 12*(21), 9075. doi:10.3390/su12219075

Lambert, R., Leuz, C., & Verrecchia, R. E. (2007). Accounting information, disclosure, and the cost of capital. *Journal of Accounting Research, 45*(2), 385–420. doi:10.1111/j.1475-679X.2007.00238.x

Laskin, A. V. (2018). The narrative strategies of winners and losers: Analyzing annual reports of publicly traded corporations. *International Journal of Business Communication, 55*(3), 338–356. doi:10.1177/2329488418780221

Lauwo, S., & Otusanya, O. J. (2014). Corporate accountability and human rights disclosures: A case study of Barrick Gold Mine in Tanzania. *Accounting Forum, 38*(2), 91–108. doi:10.1016/j. accfor.2013.06.002

Loughran, T., & McDonald, B. (2014). Measuring readability in financial disclosures. *The Journal of Finance, 69*(4), 1643–1671. doi:10.1111/jofi.12162

Loughran, T., & McDonald, B. (2016). Textual analysis in accounting and finance: A survey. *Journal of Accounting Research, 54*(4), 1187–1230. doi:10.1111/1475-679X.12123

Lucy, J. (2001). International encyclopedia of the social & behavioral sciences. *Linguistics: Sociolinguistics. Article Titles: S*, 13486–13490. doi:10.1016/b0-08-043076-7/03042-4

Maas, K., Schaltegger, S., & Crutzen, N. (2016). Integrating corporate sustainability assessment, management accounting, control, and reporting. *Journal of Cleaner Production, 136*(2016), 237-248. doi:10.1016/j.jclepro.2016.05.008

Martínez-Ferrero, J., Suárez-Fernández, O., & García-Sánchez, I. M. (2019). Obfuscation versus enhancement as corporate social responsibility disclosure strategies. *Corporate Social Responsibility and Environmental Management, 26*(2), 468–480. doi:10.1002/csr.1697

Martins, A., Gomes, D., Oliveira, L., & Ribeiro, J. L. (2019). Telling a success story through the president's letter. *Qualitative Research in Accounting and Management, 16*(3), 403–433. doi:10. 1108/QRAM-03-2018-0018

Maubane, P., Prinsloo, A., & Van Rooyen, N. (2014). Sustainability reporting patterns of companies listed on the Johannesburg securities exchange. *Public Relations Review, 40*(2), 153–160. doi:10. 1016/j.pubrev.2014.02.014

McPhail, K., & Adams, C. A. (2016). Corporate respect for human rights: Meaning, scope, and the shifting order of discourse. *Accounting, Auditing & Accountability Journal, 29*(4), 650–678. doi: 10.1108/AAAJ-09-2015-2241

McPhail, K., Ferguson, J., & Adams, C. A. (2016). Corporate respect for human rights: Meaning, scope, and the shifting order of discourse. *Accounting, Auditing & Accountability Journal*. doi: 10.1108/AAAJ-09-2015-2241

Merkl-Davies, D. M., & Brennan, N. M. (2011). A conceptual framework of impression management: New insights from psychology, sociology and critical perspectives. *Accounting and Business Research, 41*(5), 415–437. doi:10.1080/00014788.2011.574222

Michelon, G., Pilonato, S., & Ricceri, F. (2015). CSR reporting practices and the quality of disclosure: An empirical analysis. *Critical Perspectives on Accounting, 33*, 59–78. doi:10.1016/j.cpa.2014.10.003

Na, H. J., Lee, K. C., Choi, S. U., & Kim, S. T. (2020). Exploring CEO messages in sustainability management reports: Applying sentiment mining and sustainability balanced scorecard methods. *Sustainability, 12*(2), 590. doi:10.3390/su12020590

Ngwakwe, C. C., & Mtsweni, S. T. (2016). Extent of sustainability assurance in South African mining companies. *Journal of Accounting and Management, 6*(1), 59–74.

OECD. (2011). *OECD guidelines for multinational enterprises* (2011 Edition). Paris: OECD Publishing. doi:10.1787/9789264115415-en

OECD. (2015). *G20/OECD principles of corporate governance*. Paris: OECD Publishing. doi:10.1787/ 9789264236882-en

Park, K.-H., Byun, J., & Choi, P. M. S. (2020). Managerial overconfidence, corporate social responsibility activities, and financial constraints. *Sustainability, 12*(1), 61. doi:10.3390/ su12010061

Parsa, S., Roper, I., Muller-Camen, M., & Szigetvari, E. (2018). Have labour practices and human rights disclosures enhanced corporate accountability? The case of the GRI framework. *Accounting Forum, 42*(1), 47–64. doi:10.1016/j.accfor.2018.01.001

Peirce, C. (2003). Basic concepts of Peircean sign theory (1965). In M. Gottdiener, K. Boklund-Lagopoulou, & A. Lagopoulos (Eds.), *Semiotics* (Vol. 1). London: Sage.

Resolution adopted by the General Assembly on 25 September 2015: 70/1. (2015). Transforming our world: The 2030 Agenda for Sustainable Development, (2015).

Ruggie, J. (2008). *Protect, respect and remedy: A framework for business and human rights.* Retrieved from https://www.business-humanrights.org/en/latest-news/pdf-protect-respect-and-remedy-a-framework-for-business-and-human-rights/. Accessed on November 25, 2020.

Sapir, E. (1949). *The selected writings of Edward Sapir in language, culture, and personality.* Berkeley, CA: University California Press.

Shift and Mazars. (2017a). *Human rights reporting: Are companies telling investors what they need to know?* Retrieved from https://shiftproject.org/wp-content/uploads/2017/05/Shift_MaturityofHumanRightsReporting_May2017.pdf. Accessed on November 25, 2020.

Shift and Mazars. (2017b). *UN Guiding Principles Reporting Framework (with implementation guidance).* Retrieved from https://www.ungpreporting.org/wp-content/uploads/UNGPReporting Framework_withguidance2017.pdf. Accessed on December 10, 2020.

Short, J. C., McKenny, A. F., & Reid, S. W. (2018). More than words? Computer-aided text analysis in organizational behavior and psychology research. *Annual Review of Organizational Psychology and Organizational Behavior, 5,* 415–435. doi:10.1146/annurev-orgpsych032117-104622

Smeuninx, N., De Clerck, B., & Aerts, W. (2020). Measuring the readability of sustainability reports: A corpus-based analysis through standard formulae and NLP. *International Journal of Business Communication, 57*(1), 52–85. doi:10.1177/2329488416675456

Stacchezzini, R., Melloni, G., & Lai, A. (2016). Sustainability management and reporting: The role of integrated reporting for communicating corporate sustainability management. *Journal of Cleaner Production, 136*(1), 102–110. doi:10.1016/j.jclepro.2016.01.109

Stone, G. W., & Lodhia, S. (2019). Readability of integrated reports: An exploratory global study. *Accounting, Auditing & Accountability Journal, 32*(5), 1532–1557. doi:10.1108/AAAJ-10-2015-2275

Suchman, M. C. (1995). Managing legitimacy: Strategic and institutional approaches. *Academy of Management Review, 20*(3), 571–610. doi:10.5465/AMR.1995.950808033

Tedeschi, J. T., & Melburg, V. (1984). Impression management and influence in the organization. *Research in the Sociology of Organizations, 3*(31–58).

United Nations. (2000). The ten principles of the UN Global Compact. Retrieved from https://www.unglobalcompact.org/what-is-gc/mission/principles. Accessed on December 4, 2020.

United Nations. (2011). *Guiding principles on business and human rights.* Retrieved from https://www.ohchr.org/documents/publications/guidingprinciplesbusinesshr_en.pdf. Accessed on November 25, 2020.

United Nations. (2015). Transforming our world: the 2030 Agenda for Sustainable Development. (no. A/RES/10/1). United Nations. Retrieved from https://www.un.org/en/development/desa/population/migration/generalassembly/docs/globalcompact/A_RES_70_1_E.pdf. Accessed on September 22, 2022.

United Nations. (2017). *UN Guiding principles reporting framework investor statement.* Retrieved from https://www.ungpreporting.org/wp-content/uploads/2015/02/1_31_2017-UN-GUIDING-PRINCIPLES-REPORTING-FRAMEWORK-INVESTOR-STATEMENT.pdf. Accessed on November 25, 2020.

Wahab, A. (2020). The state of human rights disclosure among sustainably certified palm oil companies in Malaysia. *The International Journal of Human Rights, 24*(10), 1451–1474. doi:10.1080/13642987.2020.1716741

Whorf, B. (1956). *Language, thought, and reality: Selected writings of Benjamin Lee Whorf.* Cambridge, MA: MIT Press.

Zeng, X. (2017). *Human rights disclosure by global companies: An exploration.* Master of Business Dissertation. Auckland University of Technology: Auckland. Retrieved from https://openrepository.aut.ac.nz/handle/10292/10921. Accessed on June 27, 2022.

Zhou, S., Simnett, R., & Green, W. (2017). Does integrated reporting matter to the capital market? *Abacus, 53*(1), 94–132. doi:10.1111/abac.12104

Printed and bound by CPI Group (UK) Ltd, Croydon, CR0 4YY

06/09/2023

08109493-0001